IFIP Advances in Information and Communication Technology 321

IFIP – The International Federation for Information Processing

IFIP was founded in 1960 under the auspices of UNESCO, following the First World Computer Congress held in Paris the previous year. An umbrella organization for societies working in information processing, IFIP's aim is two-fold: to support information processing within its member countries and to encourage technology transfer to developing nations. As its mission statement clearly states,

> IFIP's mission is to be the leading, truly international, apolitical organization which encourages and assists in the development, exploitation and application of information technology for the benefit of all people.

IFIP is a non-profitmaking organization, run almost solely by 2500 volunteers. It operates through a number of technical committees, which organize events and publications. IFIP's events range from an international congress to local seminars, but the most important are:

- The IFIP World Computer Congress, held every second year;
- Open conferences;
- Working conferences.

The flagship event is the IFIP World Computer Congress, at which both invited and contributed papers are presented. Contributed papers are rigorously refereed and the rejection rate is high.

As with the Congress, participation in the open conferences is open to all and papers may be invited or submitted. Again, submitted papers are stringently refereed.

The working conferences are structured differently. They are usually run by a working group and attendance is small and by invitation only. Their purpose is to create an atmosphere conducive to innovation and development. Refereeing is less rigorous and papers are subjected to extensive group discussion.

Publications arising from IFIP events vary. The papers presented at the IFIP World Computer Congress and at open conferences are published as conference proceedings, while the results of the working conferences are often published as collections of selected and edited papers.

Any national society whose primary activity is in information may apply to become a full member of IFIP, although full membership is restricted to one society per country. Full members are entitled to vote at the annual General Assembly, National societies preferring a less committed involvement may apply for associate or corresponding membership. Associate members enjoy the same benefits as full members, but without voting rights. Corresponding members are not represented in IFIP bodies. Affiliated membership is open to non-national societies, and individual and honorary membership schemes are also offered.

Masakatsu Nishigaki   Audun Jøsang
Yuko Murayama   Stephen Marsh (Eds.)

Trust Management IV

4th IFIP WG 11.11 International Conference, IFIPTM 2010
Morioka, Japan, June 16-18, 2010
Proceedings

 Springer

Volume Editors

Masakatsu Nishigaki
Shizuoka University, Graduate School of Science and Technology
3-5-1 Johoku, Naka, Hamamatsu 432-8011, Japan
E-mail: nisigaki@inf.shizuoka.ac.jp

Audun Jøsang
University of Oslo, UNIK Graduate Center
Gunnar Randers vei 19, 2007 Kjeller, Norway
E-mail: josang@unik.no

Yuko Murayama
Iwate Prefectural University, Faculty of Software and Information Science
152-52 Sugo, Takizawa, Takizawa-mura, Iwate 020-0173, Japan
E-mail: murayama@iwate-pu.ac.jp

Stephen Marsh
Communications Research Centre Canada
3701 Carling Avenue, Ottawa, Ontario K2H 8S2, Canada
E-mail: steve.marsh@crc.gc.ca

CR Subject Classification (1998): K.6.5, C.2, E.3, D.4.6, H.4, H.5

ISSN   1868-4238
ISBN-10   3-642-42234-9 Springer Berlin Heidelberg New York
ISBN-13   978-3-642-42234-8 Springer Berlin Heidelberg New York

springer.com

© IFIP International Federation for Information Processing 2010
Softcover re-print of the Hardcover 1st edition 2010

Typesetting: Camera-ready by author, data conversion by Scientific Publishing Services, Chennai, India
Printed on acid-free paper   06/3180

Preface

This volume contains the proceedings of IFIPTM 2010, the 4th IFIP WG 11.11 International Conference on Trust Management, held in Morioka, Iwate, Japan during June 16-18, 2010.

IFIPTM 2010 provided a truly global platform for the reporting of research, development, policy, and practice in the interdependent arrears of privacy, security, and trust. Building on the traditions inherited from the highly successful iTrust conference series, the IFIPTM 2007 conference in Moncton, New Brunswick, Canada, the IFIPTM 2008 conference in Trondheim, Norway, and the IFIPTM 2009 conference at Purdue University in Indiana, USA, IFIPTM 2010 focused on trust, privacy and security from multidisciplinary perspectives. The conference is an arena for discussion on relevant problems from both research and practice in the areas of academia, business, and government.

IFIPTM 2010 was an open IFIP conference. The program of the conference featured both theoretical research papers and reports of real-world case studies. IFIPTM 2010 received 61 submissions from 25 different countries: Japan (10), UK (6), USA (6), Canada (5), Germany (5), China (3), Denmark (2), India (2), Italy (2), Luxembourg (2), The Netherlands (2), Switzerland (2), Taiwan (2), Austria, Estonia, Finland, France, Ireland, Israel, Korea, Malaysia, Norway, Singapore, Spain, Turkey. The Program Committee selected 18 full papers for presentation and inclusion in the proceedings. In addition, the program and the proceedings include two invited papers by academic experts in the fields of trust management, privacy and security, namely, Toshio Yamagishi and Pamela Briggs.

In the IFIPTM 2010 conference, as well as the tutorials and the demonstration sessions, we had newly established short paper sessions and poster paper sessions. In addition, five related workshops were held with IFIPTM 2010. We believe the deep and wide profiles produced by all of the events helped to solidify IFIPTM 2010 as an international, multidisciplinary trust conference.

Running an international conference requires immense effort from all parties involved. We would like to thank the Program Committee members and external referees for having provided timely and in-depth reviews of the submitted papers. We would also like to thank the Workshop, Tutorial, Poster and Demonstration, Publications, Local Organization, Registration, Publicity, Liaison, Website Chairs, and Advisory Committee, for having provided great help organizing the conference.

We are also grateful to the Japan Society for the Promotion of Science (JSPS), Japan, National Institute of Information and Communications Technology (NICT), Japan, Information-Technology Promotion Agency (IPA), Japan, and Iwate Prefectural University, Japan for their financial support of IFIPTM 2010.

We hope you enjoy the proceedings.

June 2010

Masakatsu Nishigaki
Audun Jøsang
Yuko Murayama
Stephen Marsh

Organization

Executive Committee

General Chairs
Yuko Murayama   Iwate Prefectural University, Japan
Stephen Marsh   Communications Research Centre (CRC), Canada

Program Chairs
Masakatsu Nishigaki   Shizuoka University, Japan
Audun Jøsang   University of Oslo, Norway

Workshop Chairs
Hiroaki Kikuchi   Tokai University, Japan
Justin Zhan   CMU, USA

Tutorial Chair
Ayako Komatsu   Information-Technology Promotion Agency (IPA), Japan

Poster and Demonstration Chair
Katsumi Takahashi   NTT Corp., Japan

Local Organization Chairs
Yasuhiro Fujihara   Iwate Prefectural University, Japan
Norihisa Segawa   Iwate Prefectural University, Japan

Publications Chairs
Tetsutaro Uehara   Kyoto University, Japan
Kanta Matsuura   University of Tokyo, Japan

Registration Chairs
Masato Terada   Hitachi Ltd., Japan
Toyoo Takata   Iwate Prefectural University, Japan

Publicity Chairs
Yuji SUGA   Internet Initiative Japan Inc. (IIJ), Japan
Hidema Tanaka   National Institute of Information and Communications Technology (NICT), Japan

Liaison Chairs

Masayuki Terada	NTT Docomo, Inc., Japan
Kozo Noaki	NTT Docomo, Inc., Japan

Website Chairs

Yoshia Saito	Iwate Prefectural University, Japan
Kentarou Yamaguchi	Institute of Information Security, Japan

Advisory Committee

Yoichi Shinoda	National Institute of Information and Communications Technology (NICT), Japan and Japan Advanced Institute of Science and Technology (JAIST)
Ryoichi Sasaki	Tokyo Denki University, Japan
Eiji Okamoto	University of Tsukuba, Japan
Koji Nakao	National Institute of Information and Communications Technology (NICT), Japan and KDDI CORPORATION, Japan
Katsuya Uchida	Institute of Information Security, Japan
Kenzo Itoh	Iwate Prefectural University, Japan

Program Committee

Elisa Bertino	Purdue University, USA
Gary Bolton	Pennsylvania State University, USA
L. Jean Camp	Indiana University at Bloominton, USA
Licia Capra	University College London, UK
Cristiano Castelfranchi	ISTC-CNR, Italy
Christian Damsgaard Jensen	Technical University of Denmark
Anupam Datta	Carnegie Mellon University, USA
Chrysanthos Dellarocas	University of Maryland, USA
Theo Dimitrakos	BT Innovate & Design, UK
Pierpaolo Dondio	Trinity College Dublin, Ireland
Naranker Dulay	Imperial College London, UK
Sandro Etalle	T.U. Eindhoven and University of Twente, The Netherlands
Rino Falcone	ISTC-CNR, Italy
Elena Ferrari	University of Insubria, Italy
Giusella Finocchiaro	University of Bologna, Italy
Jennifer Golbeck	University of Maryland, USA
Dieter Gollmann	Hamburg University of Technology, Germany
Elizabeth Gray	Accenture, USA
Ehud Gudes	Ben Gurion University of the Negev, Israel
Jochen Haller	SAP Research, Germany

Peter Herrmann   The Norwegian University of Science and
                               Technology
Kevin Hoffman   Purdue University, USA
Steffen Huck   University College London, UK
Roslan Ismail   Universiti Tenaga Nasional
                               (UNITEN), Malaysia
Valerie Issarny   INRIA, France
James Joshi   University of Pittsburgh, USA
Yuecel Karabulut   SAP Office of the CTO, USA
Günter Karjoth   IBM Research, Switzerland
Reid Kerr   University of Waterloo, Canada
Claudia Keser   University of Goettingen, Germany
Hiroaki Kikuchi   Tokai University, Japan
Mark Kramer   MITRE, USA
Adam J. Lee   University of Pittsburgh, USA
Ninghui Li   Purdue University, USA
Tie-Yan Liu   Microsoft Research, China
Stephane Lo Presti   Brunel University, UK
Emiliano Lorini   Institut de Recherche en Informatique de
                               Toulouse (IRIT), France
Xixi Luo   Beihang University, China
Pratyusa Manadhata   Symantec Research, USA
Fabio Massacci   University of Trento, Italy
Kanta Matsuura   University of Tokyo, Japan
D. Harrison McKnight   Michigan State University, USA
Walter Quattrociocchi   ISTC-CNR, Italy
Mark Ryan   University of Birmingham, UK
Jordi Sabater-Mir   IIIA - CSIC, Spain
Kent Seamons   Brigham Young University, USA
Jean-Marc Seigneur   University of Geneva, Switzerland
Simon Shiu   HP Labs, UK
Joel Snyder   Opus One, USA
Jessica Staddon   PARC, USA
Ketil Stolen   SINTEF & University of Oslo, Norway
Vipin Swarup   MITRE, USA
Kenji Takahashi   NTT, Japan
Sotirios Terzis   University of Strathclyde, UK
Mahesh Tripunitara   University of Waterloo, Canada
Tetsutaro Uehara   Kyoto University, Japan
William H. Winsborough   University of Texas at San Antonio, USA
Marianne Winslett   University of Illinois at Urbana-Champaign,
                               USA
Danfeng Yao   Rutgers University, New Brunswick, USA

External Reviewers

Naveed Ahmed
Sruthi Bandhakavi
Rafael Deitos
Changyu Dong
Nurit Gal-Oz
Bin Gao
Ryota Hashimoto
Tormod Havaldsrud
Hiroki Itoh
Kevin Killourhy
Yun Hee Lee
Olav Ligaarden
Amirreza Masoumzadeh

Kazuhiro Minami
Nima Mousavi
Susanta Nanda
Aida Omerovic
Milan Petkovic
Rachid Saadi
Hiroyuki Sato
Hassan Takabi
Xavier Titi
Joana Matos Fonseca da Trindade
Daniel Trivellato
Yue Zhang

Supported by

Japan Society for the Promotion of Science (JSPS)
National Institute of Information and Communication Technology (NICT), Japan
Information-Technology Promotion Agency (IPA), Japan
Iwate Prefectural University, Japan

In Cooperation with

Information Processing Society of Japan

Table of Contents

Privacy and Trust

Schemes for Privately Computing Trust and Reputation 1
  Nurit Gal-Oz, Niv Gilboa, and Ehud Gudes

Self-service Privacy: User-Centric Privacy for Network-Centric
Identity.. 17
  Jose M. del Alamo, Miguel A. Monjas, Juan C. Yelmo,
  Beatriz San Miguel, Ruben Trapero, and Antonio M. Fernandez

Naïve Security in a Wi-Fi World 32
  Colleen Swanson, Ruth Urner, and Edward Lank

Security Through Trust

Securing Class Initialization 48
  Keiko Nakata and Andrei Sabelfeld

xESB: An Enterprise Service Bus for Access and Usage Control Policy
Enforcement 63
  Gabriela Gheorghe, Stephan Neuhaus, and Bruno Crispo

Metric Strand Spaces for Locale Authentication Protocols 79
  F. Javier Thayer, Vipin Swarup, and Joshua D. Guttman

Visitor Access Control Scheme Utilizing Social Relationship in the Real
World 95
  Gen Kitagata, Debasish Chakraborty, Satoshi Ogawa,
  Atushi Takeda, Kazuo Hashimoto, and Norio Shiratori

Trust Models and Management

Impact of Trust Management and Information Sharing to Adversarial
Cost in Ranking Systems 108
  Le-Hung Vu, Thanasis G. Papaioannou, and Karl Aberer

Shinren: Non-monotonic Trust Management for Distributed Systems ... 125
  Changyu Dong and Naranker Dulay

Modeling and Analysis of Trust Management Protocols: Altruism
versus Selfishness in MANETs 141
  Jin-Hee Cho, Ananthram Swami, and Ing-Ray Chen

Trust Models

Trustworthiness in Networks: A Simulation Approach for Approximating
Local Trust and Distrust Values   157
    Khrystyna Nordheimer, Thimo Schulze, and Daniel Veit

Design of Graded Trusts by Using Dynamic Path Validation   172
    Akira Kubo and Hiroyuki Sato

Implementation and Performance Analysis of the Role-Based Trust
Management System, RT^C   184
    Tyler L. Hobbs and William H. Winsborough

A Formal Notion of Trust – Enabling Reasoning about Security
Properties...   200
    Andreas Fuchs, Sigrid Gürgens, and Carsten Rudolph

Experimental and Experiential Trust

Leveraging a Social Network of Trust for Promoting Honesty in
E-Marketplaces   216
    Jie Zhang, Robin Cohen, and Kate Larson

Does Trust Matter for User Preferences? A Study on Epinions
Ratings   232
    Georgios Pitsilis and Pern Hui Chia

Bringing the Virtual to the Farmers' Market: Designing for Trust in
Pervasive Computing Systems   248
    Ian Wakeman, Ann Light, Jon Robinson, Dan Chalmers, and
    Anirban Basu

Incorporating Interdependency of Trust Values in Existing Trust
Models for Trust Dynamics..   263
    Mark Hoogendoorn, S. Waqar Jaffry, and Jan Treur

Author Index   277

Schemes for Privately Computing Trust and Reputation

Nurit Gal-Oz, Niv Gilboa, and Ehud Gudes

Dept. of Computer Science and Deutsche Telekom Laboratories
at Ben-Gurion University
Beer-Sheva, 84105
Israel
galoz@cs.bgu.ac.il, gilboan@bgu.ac.il, ehud@cs.bgu.ac.il

Abstract. Trust and Reputation systems in distributed environments attain widespread interest as online communities are becoming an inherent part of the daily routine of Internet users. Several models for Trust and Reputation have been suggested recently, among them the Knots model [8]. The Knots model provides a member of a community with a method to compute the reputation of other community members. Reputation in this model is subjective and tailored to the taste and choices of the computing member and those members that have similar views, i.e. the computing member's *Trust-Set*. A discussion on privately computing trust in the Knots model appears in [16]. The present paper extends and improves [16] by presenting three efficient and private protocols to compute trust in trust based reputation systems that use any trust-sets based model. The protocols in the paper are rigorously proved to be private against a semi-honest adversary given standard assumptions on the existence of an homomorphic, semantically secure, public key encryption system. The protocols are analyzed and compared in terms of their privacy characteristics and communication complexity.

1 Introduction

Recent years have seen a substantial growth of virtual communities across the Internet. These enable people to gather around some common goal or shared interest. The accessibility of information and services offered by these communities, makes it both possible and legitimate to communicate with strangers and carry out interactions anonymously, as rarely done in "real" life. On the other hand, virtual communities are prone to many types of deception - possibly exposing users to various threats - ranging from people forging their identity and imposing as others, to people giving extremely bad or extremely good ratings to other members unrelated to the service they have received from them. Trust and Reputation systems provide communities with means to reduce the potential risk when communicating with people hiding behind virtual identities. These systems utilize the experience and knowledge accumulated and shared by all participants for assigning reputation values to individuals. Moreover, they attempt to identify dishonest members and prevent their negative effect.

M. Nishigaki et al. (Eds.): IFIPTM 2010, IFIP AICT 321, pp. 1–16, 2010.

Centralized reputation systems, such as the commercial system eBay [1] , collect and store reputation ratings from feedback providers in a centralized reputation database. In eBay, for example, both buyers and sellers participating in a transaction, may provide one of three possible feedbacks: positive (+1), neutral (0), and negative (-1). The reputation score of a user is simply the sum of her accumulated ratings over a period of six months.

Several authors have noted that reputation is a much more complex concept than simply aggregation of ratings. It may depend on interaction of multiple attributes (also exist in eBay), on the certainty of the rating [18], on the time the interaction and rating was performed, and on the trust between members. The last factor, trust between members, is crucial in obtaining reputation which is specifically compatible with a user profile or preferences. One usually gives much higher weight to ratings provided by people she has trust in. Trust between members is considered among others by [5], and when anonymity of users is required, trust between members may be computed based on the similarity of their past ratings. (see [8]).

However, in the above systems and models the reputation engine assumes knowledge of all ratings and other reputation factors, and does the computation centrally. As a result, the raters suffer a severe loss of privacy. An empirical study conducted by [27] on data sets extracted from eBay's reputation system reported a high correlation between buyer and seller ratings. Moreover, most of the feedback provided was positive. A possible explanation for these results is that when feedback providers' identities (or pseudo-identities) are known, reputation ratings are provided based on reasons of reciprocation and retaliation, not properly reflecting the trustworthiness of the rated parties. Thus preserving privacy while computing reputation becomes an important issue.

Decentralized reputation systems, on the other hand, do not make use of a central repository to collect and report reputation ratings [32]. In these types of systems, both the reputation of users and the ratings they have given may be stored locally and known only to the corresponding user. The challenge in these system it to compute the reputation without revealing the private data. Its important to emphasize that depending on the reputation model, there may be different data which may be considered private, such as the rating itself, the weight assigned to any specific rating, the identity of the raters, the trust between members, etc.

A recent paper on this topic [24] suggested several privacy preserving schemes for computing reputation when the reputation computation is very simple (similar to eBay). That is, the reputation is based on the summation of reputation scores.

The current paper advances the state of the art as it uses a more advanced model of reputation computation which considers the trust members have in one another. We use some notations of the *Knots* model [8] to demonstrate and formulate our schemes however it is important to note that the ideas presented may apply to any model in which trust between members is an important factor in computing reputation. Specifically we refer to trust based reputation models that use the feedback of a set of trusted members (trust-set) to compute reputation. We present *three* different methods for computing trust and reputation privately and discuss their comparative advantages and disadvantages. Each method offers a slightly different degree of privacy and communication overhead.

We use the terms *Trust* and *Reputation*, as introduced by [19]. Trust is a subjective expectation a member has about another member's future behavior, based on the history of their encounters, while Reputation is the perception that an agent creates through past actions about its intentions and norms, and is computed by some aggregation of members ratings of previous interactions. Normally, the trust we have in an unknown person is based on their reputation. The exact use of these two terms in our paper will become clearer in Section 3.

The rest of the paper is organized as follows. Section 2 provides an overview of the related work. In section 3, we formally define our trust-set-aware model which is essential for understanding the rest of the paper, while in Section 4 we formally define secure computation in our context. Section 5 describes the three different schemes and in Section 6 we conclude and give some future research directions.

2   Background and Related Work

A community (virtual or online community) is a group of entities (e.g. people, nodes, peers or agents acting on behalf of people), interacting via computer networks for a common interest. Different communities serve various needs of social groups through different levels of interactions. A community of strangers is a community of anonymous entities who would like to participate, i.e. contribute to and benefit from the community activities, without revealing personal information. This is in contrast to the recently popular Internet communities of identified users (e.g. 'Facebook', 'LinkedIn' etc.)

A review on trust and reputation systems is provided by Josang et al. in [2]. Their review discusses the semantics of the trust and reputation concepts and the relations between them. The authors also provide an overview of reputation computation models and existing applications of online reputation systems. Sabater et al [28] also present an overview of several computational trust and reputation models that have been implemented and classify them according to several criteria, such as the source of the information used, the assumptions made on agents behavior, the visibility of trust, and whether reputation is considered as a personal/subjective property or as a global property. The concern for privacy in communities in general, and the privacy of reputation information in particular, was discussed in several papers [19,17,30,26,7] as explained next.

In [19] the authors discuss the issues of privacy in a P2P network where the reputation information is distributed among the P2P nodes. The following aspects are analyzed: How the requirements for fair use practices reflect on the system design? What classes of information may be leaked? How to manage the risks related to social and technical issues? However, a specific method of computing reputation is not discussed. In [17] a distributed trust management system which is constructed from a two level hierarchy is described. The high level is composed of brokers which are responsible for aggregating trust information from their individual local nodes. This provides some privacy from one broker to another, although no privacy is provided at a single broker's network.

Steinbrecher in [30] presents an information theoretic model of reputation privacy. She tries to model the amount of privacy lost when a single user uses different pseudonyms in the same community or in different communities, or when a user change his/her pseudonym. Her measure enables the estimate of unlinkability provided by such a pseudonym change. In [26] the authors discuss the issue of privacy when a single user is a member in multiple communities and requires the transfer of the reputation between these communities creating the concept of cross-community reputation. Cross community reputation requirements were analyzed in [7] including the issues of privacy, user control vs. community control, ontology matching and others.

The closest paper to the present work and the one in [16] is the paper by Pavlov et al. [24] for privately computing reputation information, when the reputation is defined as an additive reputation system (e.g. the Beta reputation system by Josang [18]). The authors present three algorithms for computing additive reputation information with various degrees of privacy and with different abilities for protecting against malicious users. The paper starts with a method for "witness selection" which reduces the risk of selecting dishonest witnesses. Then, a simple scheme is presented which is very efficient but is vulnerable to collusion of even two witnesses. The second scheme is more resilient towards curious users although still vulnerable to collusions and uses a secret splitting scheme. The last method provides the most secure protocol which uses the verifiable secret sharing scheme [25] which is based on Shamir's secret sharing scheme [29]. The complexity of the scheme is quite high since it requires $O(n^3)$ messages where n is the number of contributing nodes. Another relevant paper was presented recently by Nin et al. [21]. [21] also uses Homomorphic encryption similar to two of our schemes, but their reputation model is quite different and is not a Trust-set based model like ours.

Finally, in our previous paper [16] we described three methods for computing reputation privately, where the last one uses the scheme of [24]. The contributions of the present paper over [16] are in two areas:

1. Out of the three presented protocols, two are completely new and use the idea of Homomorphic encryption [23]. In addition, some of the strong assumptions made in [16] are removed here.
2. We present a formal framework for the three protocols and define precisely the concept of privacy in our context. Then, using this framework we prove rigorously the correctness of the three protocols.

3   Computing Reputation Based on Trust Sets

The *Trust-Set* of a member at some point in time is the subset of community members she trusts above some level. The idea behind the trust-set concept is to allow every member to rely on members that provided her with accurate feedback in the past. The benefit of using trust-sets is in limiting the recommendation process to a smaller group of members that are better qualified for the task, while increasing the chance of getting more accurate results. While many trust based reputation systems (e.g. [31,33]) use trust-sets, they differ in two major aspects: the criteria they use to generate these sets and the method for calculating trust in each member of the trust-set. These aspects have no affect on the privacy preserving schemes we present and therefore they are out of the scope of this paper.

The Knots model is a trust-based reputation model introduced in a previous work [8] for large-scale virtual communities. It is designed for communities in which members typically do not reveal their real identities. We consider for example communities in which experts in specific fields offer their advice and consulting services to community members seeking such services. The Knot model uses trust-sets as well as Knots, a relaxed form of trust-set. Knots are designed among other things to cope with the problem of sparsity i.e. insufficient number of trust relations between members in the community. Without loss of generality we adopt the notation form the knot-aware model, however the underlying approach of using trust relations among members as a weight when computing reputation exists in other models as well:

- *TrustMember* (TM) is trust in the context of recommendations. More specifically, it is a trust value that quantifies the extent by which one member relies on another member to rate experts "correctly".
- *TrustExpert* (TE) is trust in the context of experts. More specifically, it is a trust value that quantifies the extent by which a member relies on an expert to successfully provide the service it requires.
- An α - **Trust Set** of a member A, is the set of all members whom A trusts with level α or more.

The motivation for our current paper is to provide trust based reputation models (such as the knot model), with a means to compute reputation in a distributed manner while preserving private information. In this context the trust one member has in another (TM) and the trust a member has in an expert (TE), are considered private information. One would prefer not to reveal her trust in a member from which she gets recommendations since this trust value is used relative importance. On the other hand the recommending party may prefer to keep her recommendation private due to the fear of retaliation. Revealing these values to malicious parties exposes the community to the risk of manipulating recommendations.

The problem of privacy we address can be described as follows. Member A needs to compute its trust in an expert x, based on the experience other members of the community have had with this expert. Using the terms introduced in [8], this trust can vary from using the concept of *Trust Expert* based only on A's own trust-set, to using the expert's local reputation based on the Knot to which A belongs to, to using the expert's global reputation based on the entire community. We focus on Trust-set based computation since the other options are quite similar. The trust of A in x using the experience of her Trust-set can be computed according to:

$$TE(A, x) = \frac{\sum_{\substack{B_i \in TrustSet(A), \\ DTE(B_i, x) \neq \perp}} DTE(B_i, x) \cdot TM(A, B_i)}{\sum_{\substack{B_i \in TrustSet(A), \\ DTE(B_i, x) \neq \perp}} TM(A, B_i)}$$

where:

- $DTE(B_i, x)$ - the trust member B_i has in expert x based on her own accumulated experience.
- $TM(A, B_i)$ - the trust member A has in member B_i.

We assume that $TM(A, B)$ is known to agent A since it reflects her private information. Therefore the denominator in this formula is easy to compute by A without disclosing private information. The nominator is a sum of products of two terms, the first one is assumed to be known only to the individual agents B_i and the second one is known to A. Therefore the challenge we face is to privately compute the following sum of products, denoted by $\rho(A, x)$:

$$\rho(A, x) = \sum_{B_i=1}^{|S|} DTE(B_i, x) \cdot TM(A, B_i)$$

where S denotes the trust-set of A.

Each product in this sum expresses the indirect trust that member A has in expert x based on B_i's direct trust in x, denoted

$$ITM(A, B_i, x) = TM(A, B_i) \cdot DTE(B_i, x)$$

We use this notation in Section 5 to explain our schemes.

4   Formal Framework

We now define the exact notion of secure computation in our context. Members of a trust set wish to jointly compute a function of their private inputs so that one of these members obtains an output, while no member obtains information on the input of other members. We assume that the participants in our protocols are semi-honest. In other words, each player executes the protocol as required, but may attempt to learn information on the input of other parties. Thus, a computation is secure if it is *private* for each of the parties, leaking no unnecessary information about a party's input.

Let Π be a protocol for k parties to compute a function g. The input of the i-th party is denoted x_i and the protocol output $g(x_1, \ldots, x_k)$ is obtained by the first party, denoted by A. An adversary controls a set I of parties and receives the "view" of every party in I. The view of a party includes its input, output (if any) and all intermediate messages that it receives. Informally, we say that a protocol is private if for every adversary there is a probabilistic, polynomial time algorithm with access only to the adversary's input and output, that simulates the view of the adversary. Intuitively, if the view of an adversary can be simulated from this adversary's input and output, then the adversary learns nothing about the input of other parties from an execution of Π.

Our formal definitions follow the full framework set in [10] and [11]. We use only those elements of the definition framework that are necessary in our setting.

Definition 1. *A function* $\mu : I\!N \longrightarrow I\!N$ *is* negligible *if for every polynomial* $p : I\!N \longrightarrow [0,1]$*, there exists* N *such that* $\mu(n) < \frac{1}{p(n)}$ *for every* $n > N$.

Two distribution ensembles are computationally indistinguishable if no efficient algorithm can decide with good probability, whether its input is chosen according to the first distribution or the second distribution. We regard a distribution ensemble as a collection of distributions that are indexed by two parameters: a binary string a and a security parameter n represented in unary form. In our setting, a is the input for a protocol, the distribution is over all the messages of a protocol (for a subset of parties) and is induced by coin tosses of each party as it executes its part of the protocol. The security parameter 1^n determines the required length of cryptographic keys to ensure privacy of the protocol. Formally:

Definition 2. *Let* $X = \{X(a, 1^n)\}_{n \in I\!N, a \in \{0,1\}^*}$ *and* $Y = \{Y(a, 1^n)\}_{n \in I\!N, a \in \{0,1\}^*}$ *be two distribution ensembles. We say that* X *and* Y *are* computationally indistinguishable *if for every probabilistic, polynomial time algorithm* D *, there exists a negligible function* μ *such that for every* $a \in \{0,1\}^*$:

$$|Pr[D(X(a, 1^n)) = 1] - Pr[D(Y(a, 1^n)) = 1]| < \mu(n).$$

We denote computational indistinguishability of two ensembles by $X \overset{c}{\equiv} Y$.

We restrict an adversary to corrupting a subset of parties *statically*. In other words, the adversary controls the same subset of parties throughout the execution of a protocol. The adversary may corrupt only specific subsets of parties.

Definition 3. *Let* Π *be a communication protocol for* k *parties to compute a function* g. *Let* $2^{\{1,\ldots,k\}}$ *be the set of all subsets of parties in the protocol. We say that* U *is the* adversary structure *if* $U \subseteq 2^{\{1,\ldots,k\}}$ *includes exactly all subsets of parties, I, such that the adversary can corrupt all parties in I simultaneously.*

We denote by $\text{view}_I^\Pi(X_I, 1^n)$ the aggregated input, output and protocol messages of all parties in $I = \{i_1, \ldots, i_\ell\}$ as they execute a protocol Π with security parameter 1^n on input $X_I = (x_{i_1}, \ldots, x_{i_\ell})$. Next, we formally define multi-party private computation.

Definition 4. *Let* $g : (\{0,1\}^*)^k \longrightarrow \{0,1\}^*$ *be a function mapping* k *binary strings to a single binary string. Let* Π *be a communication protocol for* k *parties, such that if the i-th party has input x_i for $i = 1, \ldots, k$ then after the parties execute Π, the first party has output $g(x_1, \ldots, x_k)$. Let U be an adversary structure. For every subset of parties I, such that $I = \{i_1, \ldots, i_\ell\}$, denote by X_I the input vector $(x_{i_1}, \ldots, x_{i_\ell})$ and by O_I the output obtained by members of I. Π privately computes g if for every I such that $I \in U$, there exists a probabilistic, polynomial time algorithm S such that when n ranges over $I\!N$ and X_I ranges over $(\{0,1\}^*)^{|I|}$:*

$$\{S(X_I, O_I, 1^n)\} \overset{c}{\equiv} \{\text{view}_I^\Pi(X_I, 1^n)\}$$

We use semantically-secure public-key encryption [14] to construct our protocols is . Semantic security means that a ciphertext does not leak any information about the plaintext when the private key is unknown. Furthermore, even if an adversary has some a-priori knowledge about the plaintext (e.g. a possible range of values for the plaintext) it cannot infer additional information from the ciphertext. Let $f(\cdot)$ be information on the plaintext that the adversary is trying to obtain and let $h(\cdot)$ be information on the plaintext that the adversary already knows.

Let an encryption scheme be three algorithms: a key generation algorithm G, an encryption algorithm E and a decryption algorithm D. On input 1^n, G outputs a randomly chosen key of appropriate length. Intuitively, an algorithm that has an encryption $E(X)$ and $h(X)$ does not have significant advantage computing $f(X)$ compared to an algorithm that has only $h(X)$. The formal definition follows [11]:

Definition 5. *Let (G, E, D) be a public key encryption scheme. (G, E, D) is semantically-secure if for any probabilistic, polynomial time algorithm P there exists a probabilistic, polynomial time algorithm P' such that for probability ensemble $\{X_n\}_{n \in \mathbb{N}}$, with $|X_n|$ polynomial in n, and two polynomially bounded functions f, h, there exists a negligible function μ such that for every n*

$$\left| Pr[P_{X_n}(E, h) = f(X_n)] - Pr[P'_{X_n}(h) = f(X_n)] \right| < \mu(n)$$

where $P_{X_n}(E, h) \stackrel{\triangle}{=} P(1^n, E(X_n), h(X_n))$ and $P'_{X_n}(h) \stackrel{\triangle}{=} P'(1^n, 1^{|X_n|}, h(X_n)) = f(X_n)$

Intuitively, semantic security enables one party in a multi-party computation to send encrypted data to another party without compromising privacy. A simulator for the receiving party can simulate this encrypted data by encrypting some data that it generates. Semantic security ensures that real encrypted data can't be distinguished from simulated encrypted data. This intuition is formalized in Lemma 1. Due to space limitations we leave out the proof of this lemma.

Lemma 1. *Let (G, E, D) be a semantically secure public key encryption scheme, let n be a security parameter and let $x_1, \ldots, x_\ell$ be chosen according to a distribution D that can be efficiently constructed. Let Π be a polynomial time (in n) multi-party protocol to compute a function g and let I be a set of parties, such that $view_I^\Pi(X_I, 1^n)$ is comprised of X_I, O_I and $E(x_1), \ldots, E(x_\ell)$. $G(1^n)$ generates a public and private key pair. Members of I know the public key, but not the private key. Then Π privately computes g for an adversary structure U, $U = \{I\}$.*

5   The Protocols

In this section we present three different schemes for privately computing reputation and we prove the correctness of these schemes based on the above framework under the assumption of semi-honest participants. In all three schemes we compute the reputation of x in the eyes of A $\rho(A, x)$, using input from A's trust-set S (see section 3).

5.1   Scheme 1: An External Party

In this scheme, A learns only $\rho(A, x) = \sum_{B_i=1}^{|S|} DTE(B_i, x) \cdot TM(A, B_i)$ (see section 3), while B_i receives no information at all, for every i. We assume the existence of an additional party Z that must not collude with A.

The main tool we use in this scheme is public-key, homomorphic encryption. In such encryption there is a modulus m and an efficiently computable function ϕ that maps a pair of encrypted values $(E_K(x), E_K(y))$, where $0 \le x, y \le m$, to a single encrypted element $\phi(E_K(x), E_K(y)) = E_K(x + y \bmod m)$. In many homomorphic encryption systems the function ϕ is multiplication modulo some integer N. Given a natural number c and an encryption $E_K(x)$, it is possible to compute $E_K(c \cdot x \bmod m)$, without knowing the private key [1].

There are quite a few examples of homomorphic encryption schemes known in the cryptographic literature, including [14,3,20,22] and [23]. There are also systems that allow both addition and multiplication of two encrypted plaintexts, e.g. [4] (only a single multiplication is possible for a pair of ciphertexts) and [9]. All of these examples of homomorphic cryptosystems are currently assumed to be semantically secure.

We assume that all participants in the protocol know prior to the beginning of the protocol a semantically-secure, public key and homomorphic encryption scheme (G, E, D), an associated function ϕ and a security parameter n. We can assume that the modulus m of the homomorphism is large enough, that is $m > \rho(A, x)$, since in many of the well-known homomorphic cryptosystems the key can be chosen to accommodate an arbitrarily large m. We require that for every i, $TM(A, B_i)$ and $DTE(B_i, x)$ have integral values.

The total computational complexity of this scheme is $O(|S|)$ encryptions, decryptions and multiplications. The total communication complexity is $O(|S|)$ times the size of a ciphertext.

Proposition 1. *Let $A, Z, B_1, \ldots, B_{|S|}$ be the parties, let the input of A be $TM(A, B_1), \ldots, TM(A, B_{|S|})$ and for all $i = 1, \ldots, |S|$ let the input of B_i be $DTE(B_i, x)$. Let g be a function that maps the ordered sequence of pairs $\langle TM(A, B_i), DTE(B_i, x) \rangle_{i=1,\ldots,|S|}$ to the value $\rho(A, x) = \sum_{B_i \in S} ITM(A, B_i, x)$. Let the adversary structure U include all subsets I of $\{A, Z, B_1, \ldots, B_{|S|}\}$ s.t. $|I \bigcap \{A, Z\}| \le 1$. Then, the protocol in Algorithm 1 privately computes g.*

Proof. If the adversary controls $I = \{A, B_{i_1}, \ldots, B_{i_\ell}\}$, then the view of the adversary is identical to its input and output, hence simulation is trivial.

---

[1] Set $\beta = E_K(0)$ and let the binary representation of c be $c = c_k c_{k-1} \ldots c_0$. Go over the bits $c_k, \ldots, c_0$ in descending order. If $c_j = 0$ set $\beta = \phi(\beta, \beta)$ and if $c_j = 1$ set $\beta = \phi(\phi(\beta, \beta), E_K(x))$. If ϕ is modular multiplication, this algorithm is identical to regular modular exponentiation.

Algorithm 1. Computing a scalar product

1: A runs $G(1^n)$ and obtains a private-public key pair.
2: A sends to B_i the ciphertext $E_{K_A}(TM(A, B_i) \bmod m)$, for every $B_i \in S$.
3: **for all** $B_i \in S$ **do**
4:     B_i uses $E_{K_A}(TM(A, B_i) \bmod m)$ and $DTE(B_i, x)$ to compute $E_{K_A}(ITM(A, B_i, x) \bmod m)$.
5:     B_i sends $E_{K_A}(ITM(A, B_i, x) \bmod m)$ to Z.
6: Z uses ϕ to compute $E_{K_A}(\sum_{B_i \in S} ITM(A, B_i, x) \bmod m)$ and sends this encrypted value to A.
7: A obtains $\rho(A, x) = \sum_{B_i \in S} ITM(A, B_i, x)$ by decryption.

If the adversary controls $I = \{B_{i_1}, \ldots, B_{i_\ell}\}$ (without A), then its view includes aside from its input, the elements $\left\{ E_{K_A}(TM(A, B_{i_j}) \bmod m) \right\}_{j=1,\ldots,\ell}$. By Lemma 1, Π privately computes g with respect to I.

If the adversary controls $I = \{Z, B_{i_1}, \ldots, B_{i_\ell}\}$, then its view includes aside from its input, the encrypted elements $\left\{ E_{K_A}(ITM(A, B_{i_j}, x) \bmod m) \right\}_{j=1,\ldots,\ell}$. Again, Lemma 1 shows that Π privately computes g with respect to I. $\qquad\square$

5.2   Scheme 2: No Outside Help

In this scheme, we dispense with the additional party Z. A learns only $\rho(A, x) = \sum_{\forall B \in S} ITM(A, B, x)$, while for every i, B_i receives no information at all. A protocol without Z is obviously desirable for those situations in which such a semi-trusted party is not available. The disadvantage of the current protocol is its greater communication complexity compared to Algorithm 1.

As is often the case in distributed, cryptographic protocols, the parties use secret sharing to distribute the input [29]. The number of distributed shares, and thus the communication complexity depends on the possible number of colluding adversarial parties. We denote this threshold by t and assume that it is part of the protocol's input.

We assume that all participants in the protocol know a semantically-secure, public key and homomorphic encryption scheme (G, E, D), an associated function ϕ and a security parameter n prior to the beginning of the protocol. We assume that the modulus m of the homomorphism satisfies the inequality $m > \rho(A, x)$.

Using algorithm 2, A computes the correct result because:

$$\sum_{j=1}^{t} \sum_{i=1}^{|S|} TM(A, B_i) \cdot r_j^i + q_j^i \bmod m =$$
$$\sum_{i=1}^{|S|} TM(A, B_i) \cdot \left(\sum_{j=1}^{t} r_j^i \right) + \sum_{j=1}^{t} q_j^i \bmod m =$$
$$\sum_{i=1}^{|S|} TM(A, B_i) \cdot DTE(B_i, x) \bmod m =$$
$$\rho(A, x)$$

Denoting the maximum length of a ciphertext in this protocol by $|E(\cdot)|$, the communication complexity of steps 1-4 is $O(|S| \cdot |E(\cdot)|)$, the communication complexity

Algorithm 2. No outside help

1: A runs $G(1^n)$ and obtains a private-public key pair.
2: A sends to B_i the ciphertext $E_{K_A}(TM(A, B_i) \bmod m)$, for every $B_i \in S$.
3: **for all** $B_i \in S$ **do**
4:    B_i chooses $r_1^i, r_2^i, \ldots, r_t^i$ and $q_1^i, q_2^i, \ldots, q_t^i$ uniformly at random from $\{0, \ldots, m-1\}$ so that $\sum_{j=1}^{t} r_j^i \equiv DTE(B_i, x) \bmod m$ and $\sum_{j=1}^{t} q_j^i \equiv 0 \bmod m$.
5: **for all** $B_i \in S$ **do**
6:    B_i computes the values: $E_{K_A}(TM(A, B_i) \cdot r_j^i + q_j^i \bmod m)$, for $j = 1, \ldots, t$.
7:    **for all** $j = 1, \ldots, t$ **do**
8:      B_i sends $E_{K_A}(TM(A, B_i) \cdot r_j^i + q_j^i \bmod m)$ to B_j.
9: **for all** $j = 1, \ldots, t$ **do**
10:    B_j uses ϕ on $E_{K_A}(TM(A, B_1) \cdot r_j^1 + q_j^1 \bmod m), \ldots, E_{K_A}(TM(A, B_{|S|}) \cdot r_j^{|S|} + q_j^{|S|} \bmod m)$ to compute $E_{K_A}(\sum_{i=1}^{|S|} TM(A, B_i) \cdot r_j^i + q_j^i \bmod m)$. B_j sends this value to A.
11: A decrypts and sums up all the values to obtain $\rho(A, x) = \sum_{j=1}^{t} \sum_{i=1}^{|S|} TM(A, B_i) \cdot r_j^i + q_j^i \bmod m$.

of step 5 is $O(t |S| \cdot |E(\cdot)|)$ and the communication complexity of steps 6, 7 is $O(t \cdot |E(\cdot)|)$. Hence the total communication complexity of the protocol is $O(t |S| \cdot |E(\cdot)|)$.

Proposition 2. *Let $A, B_1, \ldots, B_{|S|}$ be the parties, let the input of A be $TM(A, B_1), \ldots, TM(A, B_{|S|})$ and for all $i = 1, \ldots, |S|$ let the input of B_i be $DTE(B_i, x)$. Let g be a function that maps the ordered sequence of pairs $\langle TM(A, B_i), DTE(B_i, x) \rangle_{i=1, \ldots, |S|}$ to the value $\rho(A, x) = \sum_{B_i \in S} ITM(A, B_i, x)$. Let the adversary structure U include all subsets I of $A, B_1, \ldots, B_{|S|}$ such that $|I| \leq t$. Then, the protocol in Algorithm 2 privately computes g.*

Proof. If the adversary controls $I = \{B_{i_1}, \ldots, B_{i_\ell}\}$ then its view includes aside from its input, the following:

- $E_{K_A}(TM(A, B_{i_1}) \bmod m), \ldots, E_{K_A}(TM(A, B_{i_\ell}) \bmod m)$.
- For every B_j such that $j \in \{i_1, \ldots, i_\ell\} \bigcap \{1, \ldots, t\}$, a sequence of encrypted elements: $E_{K_A}(TM(A, B_1) \cdot r_j^1 \bmod m) + q_j^1, \ldots, E_{K_A}(TM(A, B_{|S|}) \cdot r_j^{|S|} + q_j^{|S|} \bmod m)$.

A simulator chooses all the necessary values to simulate $TM(A, B_i)$ and $DTE(B_i, x)$ from an appropriate distribution. The simulator can then encrypt all these $TM(A, B_i)$ and choose uniformly at random $r_1^i, \ldots, r_t^i$ and $q_1^i, \ldots, q_t^i$ from $\{0, \ldots, m-1\}$ so that $\sum_{j=1}^{t} r_j^i \equiv DTE(B_i, x) \bmod m$ and $\sum_{j=1}^{t} q_j^i \equiv 0 \bmod m$. The simulator can then use the homomorphic properties of E to compute $E_{K_A}(TM(A, B_1) \cdot r_j^1 \bmod m) + q_j^1, \ldots, E_{K_A}(TM(A, B_{|S|}) \cdot r_j^{|S|} + q_j^{|S|} \bmod m)$. According to Lemma 1 the result is indistinguishable from the protocol view of I.

If the adversary controls $I = \{A, B_{i_1}, \ldots, B_{i_\ell}\}$, then its view includes aside from its input and output:

- For every B_j such that $j \in \{i_1, \ldots, i_\ell\} \bigcap \{1, \ldots, t\}$, a sequence of encrypted elements: $E_{K_A}(TM(A, B_1) \cdot r_j^1 + q_j^1 \mod m), \ldots, E_{K_A}(TM(A, B_{|S|}) \cdot r_j^{|S|} + q_j^{|S|} \mod m)$.
- $\sum_{i=1}^{|S|} TM(A, B_i) \cdot r_j^i \mod m$, for every $j = 1, \ldots, t+1$.

$|\{i_1, \ldots, i_\ell\}| \leq t - 1$ because $|I| \leq t$ and therefore there exists some $j \in \{1, \ldots, t\}$ such that $j \notin \{i_1, \ldots, i_\ell\}$. Thus, each set $E_{K_A}(TM(A, B_i) \cdot r_{i_1}^i + q_{i_1}^i \mod m)$, $\ldots, E_{K_A}(TM(A, B_i) \cdot r_{i_\ell}^i + q_{i_\ell}^i \mod m)$, is an encryption of at most $t - 1$ random elements in the range $\{0, \ldots, m - 1\}$. Since for each $i = 1, \ldots, |S|$, these sets are chosen independently, a simulator can simulate all these encrypted elements by choosing $|S| \cdot |i_1, \ldots, i_\ell|$ random elements in $\{0, \ldots, m - 1\}$ and encrypting them.

Similar reasoning works for simulating $\sum_{i=1}^{|S|} TM(A, B_i) \cdot r_j^i + q_j^i \mod m$, for every $j = 1, \ldots, t$. For an index η such that $\eta \notin \{i_1, \ldots, i_\ell\}$, each sum $\sum_{i=1}^{|S|} TM(A, B_i) \cdot r_j^i + q_j^i \mod m$ includes a summand q_j^η, which is random (until all the elements $q_1^\eta, \ldots, q_t^\eta$ are summed up). Therefore, the t elements $\sum_{i=1}^{|S|} TM(A, B_i) \cdot r_j^i + q_j^i \mod m$ can be simulated as t random elements in the range $0, \ldots, m - 1$ whose sum modulo m is exactly $\rho(A, x)$. □

5.3   Scheme 3: Improved Online Communication Complexity

A drawback of Algorithm 2 is that if the threshold is linear in the number of participants, $|S|$, then the total communication and the total computational complexity are quadratic in $|S|$. The next scheme improves this result by having two phases, an offline phase and an online phase.

The offline phase occurs only once for each member that enters the system and may be viewed as an initialization phase in which the new member exchanges keys with all other members as a preparation for future information sharing. The online phase occurs whenever a member wishes to compute some other member's reputation. The offline phase requires $O(|S|^2)$ communication and computation, but the online phase requires only linear communication and $O(|S|^2)$ computation.

In this scheme we use a Pseudo-Random Function family, $\mathcal{F} = \{F\}_k$, [12] in addition to homomorphic encryption as in the previous schemes. All the functions in $\mathcal{F}$ have the same domain and range. Additionally, a polynomially bounded adversary can't distinguish between the output of a random function chosen from the family and the output of a completely random function with the same domain and range. There are various theoretical constructions of pseudo-random function families. However, for practical purposes any block cipher can be regarded as such a family, where a function in the family is given by a specific key for the block cipher (such a key determines a function from a block of plaintext to a block of ciphertext).

In the offline phase, each pair of members B_i and B_j chooses a random function $F_{i,j} \in \mathcal{F}$. No one other than B_i and B_j may know the identity of their function. B_i and B_j will each use $F_{i,j}$ in the online phase of the scheme, one of them will use it with a plus sign, and the other with a minus sign. Let $sign_{i,j} = 1$ if $i > j$ and $sign_{i,j} = -1$ if $i < j$.

Algorithm 3 presents the online phase of the scheme. This protocol has two logical stages (although both take place in the same communication round). In the first stage, A and $B_1, \ldots, B_{|S|}$ re-share their values so instead of having to compute a scalar product for $\rho(A, x)$ they have to compute a sum. The second stage involves private and efficient computation of this sum using the functions $F_{i,j}$.

Algorithm 3. Improved communication complexity

1: A runs $G(1^n)$ and obtains a private-public key pair.
2: A chooses a random element RND in the domain of the functions in $\mathcal{F}$.
3: **for all** $B_i \in S$ **do**
4:     A sends to B_i the values RND and $E_{K_A}(TM(A, B_i) \bmod m)$.
5: **for all** $B_i \in S$ **do**
6:     B_i chooses r_i uniformly at random from $\{0, \ldots, m - 1\}$.
7:     B_i computes the value $\rho_i \triangleq E_{K_A}(TM(A, B_i) \cdot DTE(B_i, x) - r_i \bmod m)$.
8:     B_i computes the value $R_i \triangleq r_i + \sum_{j=1, j \neq i}^{|S|} F_{i,j}(RND) \cdot sign_{i,j} \bmod m$.
9:     B_i sends R_i and ρ_i to A.
10: A decrypts the values $\rho_1, \ldots, \rho_{|S|}$.
11: A computes $\rho(A, x) = \sum_{i=1}^{|S|} TM(A, B_i) \cdot DTE(B_i, x) - r_i + R_i \bmod m$.

A computes the correct result because:

$$\sum_{i=1}^{|S|} TM(A, B_i) \cdot DTE(B_i, x) - r_i + R_i \bmod m \quad = $$
$$\rho(A, x) + \sum_{i=1}^{|S|} \sum_{j=1, j \neq i}^{|S|} F_{i,j}(RND) \cdot sign_{i,j} \bmod m = $$
$$\rho(A, x)$$

Each value $F_{i,j}(RND)$ appears exactly twice in the sum, once with a plus sign and once with a minus sign, and thus the contribution of each summand $F_{i,j}(RND)$ to the sum is 0.

The communication complexity of steps 3 and 4 is $O(|S| \cdot |E(\cdot)|)$ and the communication complexity of step 9 is $O(|E(\cdot)|)$ for each of $B_1, \ldots, B_{|S|}$. Thus, the total communication complexity of Algorithm 3 is $O(|S| \cdot |E(\cdot)|)$. The total computational complexity is $O(|S|^2)$ times the time required to compute $F_{i,j}(RND)$, due to step 7.

The privacy of the protocol can be shown against any adversary that controls no more than $|S| - 2$ parties. The proof is very similar to the proof of Algorithm 2 with the pseudo-random values $F_{i,j}(RND)$ replacing the truly random values q_j^i in Algorithm 2.

5.4   Faults and a Malicious Adversary

The protocols we present assume that the adversary is honest-but-curious. That is, even corrupted parties correctly perform the protocols, but may attempt to discover private information about other members. Our protocols can be adapted to be secure in the presence of a malicious adversary as long as there is an honest majority, by using standard methods, e.g. [13].

Even without malicious intent, users in community-based protocols, such as we propose, may often be absent during protocol execution, thus causing unintentional faults (B_i expects that B_j is part of the computation, but B_j is not present). Our first protocol is robust against such faults while the second and third protocols can be extended to be robust by using secret sharing. We will present these robust protocols in the full version of our paper.

A malicious adversary may do more than simply attempt to subvert the protocols we proposed. An adversary that controls A learns $\rho(A, x) = \sum_{i=1}^{|S|} TM(A, B_i) \cdot DTE(B_i, x)$, where A itself determines the values $TM(A, B_i)$. Setting $TM(A, B_i) = 0$ for any i except for $i = i'$ provides A with the exact value of $DTE(B_i, x)$. If A can repeatedly compute $\rho(A, x)$ then the adversary can learn the private values of many participants.

Even if A proves (by a zero-knowledge protocol) that the values $TM(A, B_i)$ do not form a unit vector, the adversary may still learn all the values $DTE(B_i, x)$. Let M be some non-singular $|S| \times |S|$ matrix. A executes the protocol $|S|$, changing the values of $TM(A, B_1), \ldots, TM(A, B_{|S|})$ to be the value of the next row of M. Multiplying the results by M^{-1} yields $DTE(B_1, x), \ldots, DTE(B_{|S|}, x)$.

A possible approach to overcome a malicious adversary is to compute an approximation of $\rho(A, x)$ and achieve differential privacy [6]. The idea is that querying data sets that differ only slightly does not provide information about the data in which they differ. The main tool to achieve differential privacy is by adding noise to the data sets.

In our case, the data sets are the values $TM(A, B_1), \ldots, TM(A, B_{|S|})$ that A holds. The members B_i can add noise to this data in all of our protocols by using the properties of homomorphic encryption.

6   Conclusions

In this paper we discussed the problem of computing reputation of members in a community while preserving the privacy of sensitive information. Such information includes the rating of individual members and the trust that one member has in another. The paper presents three schemes for privacy preserving computation and analyzes their privacy characteristics and communication overhead. The presented schemes apply techniques for secure summation and use these as primitives in a virtual community oriented setting. Our constructions extend state of the art work to elevate existing trust based models in which privacy is a major concern.

Although the reputation computation formula was presented in the context of a specific trust and reputation model, the Knots model, it may be used by any Trust-set based model which take into account the same sensitive information (members ratings and members trust). In future work we will deal with some other privacy issues not dealt with in the current paper. One issue is the frequency of Update. How one can avoid leakage of private rating information if the reputation is updated frequently (e.g. after every expert/member interaction). Another issue is the private computation and presentation (amount of drill-down) of reputation information in case reputation is accumulated from multiple communities (see [15]).

References

1. ebay, http://www.ebay.com/
2. Audun, J., Roslan, I., Colin, B.: A survey of trust and reputation systems for online service provision. Decis. Support Syst. 43(2), 618–644 (2007)
3. Benaloh, J.: Dense probabilstic encryption. In: Proc. of the Workshop on Selected Areas of Cryptography, May 1994, pp. 120–128 (1994)
4. Boneh, D., Goh, E., Nissim, K.: Evaluating 2-dnf formulas on ciphertexts. In: Kilian, J. (ed.) TCC 2005. LNCS, vol. 3378, pp. 325–341. Springer, Heidelberg (2005)
5. Chakraborty, S., Ray, I.: Trustbac: integrating trust relationships into the rbac model for access control in open systems. In: Proc. of the eleventh ACM symposium on Access control models and technologies (SACMAT 2006), pp. 49–58. ACM, New York (2006)
6. Dwork, C.: Differential privacy. In: Bugliesi, M., Preneel, B., Sassone, V., Wegener, I. (eds.) ICALP 2006. LNCS, vol. 4052, pp. 1–12. Springer, Heidelberg (2006)
7. Gal-Oz, N., Grinshpoun, T., Gudes, E., Meisels, A.: Cross-community reputation: Policies and alternatives. In: Proc. of International Conference on Web Based Communities, IADIS - WBC 2008 (2008)
8. Gal-Oz, N., Gudes, E., Hendler, D.: A Robust and Knot-Aware Trust-Based Reputation Model. In: Proceedings of the 2nd Joint iTrust and PST Conferences on Privacy, Trust Management and Security (IFIPTM 2008), Trondheim, Norway, June 2008, vol. 263, pp. 167–182 (2008)
9. Gentry, C.: Fully homomorphic encryption using ideal lattices. In: Proc. of STOC, pp. 169–178 (2009)
10. Goldreich, O.: Foundations of Cryptography: Basic Tools. Cambridge University Press, New York (2000)
11. Goldreich, O.: Foundations of Cryptography: Volume 2, Basic Applications. Cambridge University Press, New York (2004)
12. Goldreich, O., Goldwasser, S., Micali, S.: How to construct random functions. JACM 33(4), 792–807 (1986)
13. Goldreich, O., Micali, S., Wigderson, A.: How to play any mental game (extended abstract). In: STOC 1987, pp. 218–229 (1987)
14. Goldwasser, S., Micali, S.: Probabilistic encryption. Journal of Computer and systems science 28, 270–299 (1984)
15. Grinshpoun, T., Gal-Oz, N., Meisels, A., Gudes, E.: Ccr: A model for sharing reputation knowledge across virtual communities. In: Web Intelligence, pp. 34–41 (2009)
16. Gudes, E., Gal-Oz, N., Grubshtein, A.: Methods for computing trust and reputation while preserving privacy. In: Gudes, E., Vaidya, J. (eds.) Data and Applications Security XXIII. LNCS, vol. 5645, pp. 291–298. Springer, Heidelberg (2009)
17. Yung-Jen Hsu, J., Lin, K., Chang, T., Ho, C., Huang, H., Jih, W.: Parameter learning of personalized trust models in broker-based distributed trust management. Information Systems Frontiers 8(4), 321–333 (2006)
18. Josang, A., Ismail, R.: The beta reputation system. In: proceedings of 15th Bled Electronic Commerce Conference e-Reality: Constructing the e-Economy (June 2002)
19. Mui, L., Mohtashemi, M., Halberstadt, A.: A computational model of trust and reputation for e-businesses. In: Proc. of the 35th Annual Hawaii International Conference on System Sciences (HICSS 2002), Washington, DC, USA, vol. 7, p. 188 (2002)

20. Naccache, D., Stern, J.: A new public key cryptosystem based on higher residues. In: Proc. of ACM Conference on Computer and Communications Security, pp. 59–66 (1998)
21. Nin, J., Carminati, B., Ferrari, E., Torra, V.: Computing reputation for collaborative private networks. In: 33rd IEEE Int. COMPSAC conference, pp. 246–253 (2009)
22. Okamoto, T., Uchiyama, S.: A new public-key cryptosystem as secure as factoring. In: Nyberg, K. (ed.) EUROCRYPT 1998. LNCS, vol. 1403, pp. 308–318. Springer, Heidelberg (1998)
23. Paillier, P.: Public-key cryptosystems based on composite degree residuosity classes. In: Stern, J. (ed.) EUROCRYPT 1999. LNCS, vol. 1592, pp. 223–238. Springer, Heidelberg (1999)
24. Pavlov, E., Rosenschein, J.S., Topol, Z.: Supporting privacy in decentralized additive reputation systems. In: Jensen, C., Poslad, S., Dimitrakos, T. (eds.) iTrust 2004. LNCS, vol. 2995, pp. 108–119. Springer, Heidelberg (2004)
25. Pedersen, T.P.: Non-interactive and information-theoretic secure verifiable secret sharing. In: Feigenbaum, J. (ed.) CRYPTO 1991. LNCS, vol. 576, pp. 129–140. Springer, Heidelberg (1992)
26. Pingel, F., Steinbrecher, S.: Multilateral secure cross-community reputation systems for internet communities. In: Furnell, S.M., Katsikas, S.K., Lioy, A. (eds.) TrustBus 2008. LNCS, vol. 5185, pp. 69–78. Springer, Heidelberg (2008)
27. Resnick, P., Zeckhauser, R.: Trust among strangers in Internet transactions: Empirical analysis of eBay's reputation system. In: Baye, M.R. (ed.) The Economics of the Internet and E-Commerce. Advances in Applied Microeconomics, vol. 11, pp. 127–157. Elsevier Science, Amsterdam (2002)
28. Sabater, J., Sierra, C.: Review on computational trust and reputation models. Artificial Intelligence Review 24(1), 33–60 (2005)
29. Shamir, A.: How to share a secret. Commun. ACM 22(11), 612–613 (1979)
30. Steinbrecher, S.: Design options for privacy-respecting reputation systems within centralised internet communities. In: Proc. of the IFIP TC-11 21st International Information Security Conference (SEC 2006), pp. 123–134 (2006)
31. Xiong, Z., Yang, Y., Zhang, X., Yu, D., Liu, L.: A trust-based reputation system in peer-to-peer grid. In: HCI (15), pp. 228–235 (2007)
32. Yu, B., Singh, M.: Detecting deception in reputation management. In: proceedings of Second International Joint Conference on Autonomous Agents and Multi-Agent Systems, pp. 73–80 (2003)
33. Yu, B., Singh, M.P., Sycara, K.: Developing trust in large-scale peer-to-peer systems. In: Proceedings of First IEEE Symposium on Multi-Agent Security and Survivability, pp. 1–10 (2004)

Self-service Privacy: User-Centric Privacy for Network-Centric Identity

Jose M. del Alamo[1], Miguel A. Monjas[2], Juan C. Yelmo[1], Beatriz San Miguel[1], Ruben Trapero[1], and Antonio M. Fernandez[1]

[1] Universidad Politécnica de Madrid, Ciudad Universitaria s/n, 28040 Madrid, Spain
{jmdela,jcyelmo,smiguel,rubentb,antoniofer}@dit.upm.es
[2] Technology and Innovation Unit, Madrid R&D Center, Ericsson
miguel-angel.monjas@ericsson.com

Abstract. User privacy has become a hot topic within the identity management arena. However, the field still lacks comprehensive frameworks even though most identity management solutions include built-in privacy features. This study explores how best to set up a single control point for users to manage privacy policies for their personal information, which may be distributed (scattered) across a set of network-centric identity management systems. Our goal is a user-centric approach to privacy management. As the number of schemas and frameworks is very high, we chose to validate our findings with a prototype based on the Liberty Alliance architecture and protocols.

Keywords: Privacy, identity management, user-centric, network-centric, user control.

1 Introduction

Being online today means so much more than just being connected to the Internet and browsing simple Web sites. Users join, interact with and enjoy social Web sites and online communities such as Facebook and MySpace, photo and video hosting Web sites such as Flickr and YouTube, streaming music programs such as Spotify and Last.fm, application stores such as the Apple App Store, online banks and e-commerce businesses such as PayPal, e-government sites, and so forth.

The process is quite simple. Users create a new account on any of these feature-rich content and service providers by filling in a registration form and providing a few personal details. Additionally, by accepting the default service privacy policy, users may allow the provider to share these details with the outside world. At the end of the process, the user is allowed to access and enjoy the provider's site.

The amount of scattered personal information begins to grow as users repeat this simple process with different providers. As a result, some undesirable problems can arise: not only the most obvious of bad user experience (users have to remember different logins and passwords), and increased risk of identity theft, but, eventually, data privacy concerns. In this context, we understand privacy as someone's right to keep their personal information and relationships secret and thereby reveal themselves selectively.

M. Nishigaki et al. (Eds.): IFIPTM 2010, IFIP AICT 321, pp. 17–31, 2010.
© IFIP International Federation for Information Processing 2010

In truth, the privacy concerns might not be a problem. Legislation usually forces providers (to different extents, depending on the jurisdiction) to handle user data in accordance with the law. Thus, service providers generally offer different mechanisms and custom tools to manage user data. However, the resulting heterogeneity is a huge disadvantage for users who wish to actively manage and control their personal information. As concluded by a thorough analysis of 45 social networking sites [1], *"privacy in social networks is dysfunctional in that there is significant variation in sites' privacy controls, data collection requirements, and legal privacy policies"*.

In summary, users currently lack a simple mechanism to verify what personal information is available on the Web, how it is used and how they can modify, update or delete it. Our vision is that in the short run privacy awareness will rise much higher as a result of the lack of comprehensive solutions. Thus governments and individuals alike will demand simple tools to govern the use and release of their personal information. In this article, we introduce a solution that aims to address some of these problems by enabling users to manage their personal data privacy in a simple and efficient way.

The remainder of the paper is organized as follows. First, in section 2 and 3 we describe the main approaches to identity management and stress the differences between them regarding privacy control. Then, section 4 details the solution that we have implemented to enable users to manage their personal data privacy in a simple and efficient way. After that, section 5 describes the validation we have conducted. Finally, section 6 analyses the state of the art of the related work and section 7 concludes the paper.

2   Network-Centric Identity Management

Identity Management commonly refers to the processes involved in the management and selective disclosure of user-related identity information, either within an institution or between several entities, while preserving and enforcing both privacy and security requirements. Identity management systems can be classified according to several different criteria. A common taxonomy distinguishes network- from user-centric approaches. With regard to the former, the first comprehensive specifications were created by the Liberty Alliance Project [2], a business alliance established in 2001, which has been recently succeeded by the Kantara Initiative [3]. Its early work was followed by others such as SAML 2.0 (Security Assertion Markup Language) [4] and WS-Federation [5].

The Liberty approach to identity federation and identity-based web services associates service providers with trusted domains (identity networks), which are supported by Liberty technology and operative agreements through which trust relationships are defined between providers. The identity network infrastructure supports users in transacting business with associated providers in a secure and apparently seamless environment. Each company maintains its own customer accounts, including relevant identity resources. Users can federate (link) accounts at different providers using an opaque pseudonym, which enables a single sign-on between providers and allows for the secure sharing of identity information.

Some entities may focus on managing these federations, as well as providing ancillary services:

- Identity Providers (IdP) know all users and service providers within the identity network and their affiliations. They also know how to authenticate users; thus, they can certify a user's identity to any provider. Whenever users want to access a service provider, they will be redirected to the IdP, where they will be authenticated. Once a user has successfully logged in, the IdP will send a statement back to the service provider containing information related to the identity of the user (pseudonym), information about other entities within the identity network and the credentials needed to access them.

- Discovery Services (DS) record where the users' identity resources are stored within the identity network. When a service provider wishes to find any user's information it sends a query to the DS, which returns the endpoint reference for that resource and a valid credential for one-time access.

In the Liberty context, a service provider is a Web service that acts with a certain identity resource to retrieve information about an identity, update information about an identity or perform an action for the benefit of some identity. A service provider may play the roles of both an identity-based Web Service Consumer (WSC) or an identity-based Web Service Provider (WSP). WSPs usually aggregate several identity resources into an identity profile (e.g., a personal profile or address book). The Liberty protocol that allows WSCs to access WSPs to query/update/delete personal data on behalf of a user is called the Data Service Template (DST) [6].

Within a given Liberty-based identity network, privacy is supposed to be handled by the user at each WSP (and not at the IdP/DS level). From that point on, the WSP is responsible for managing user privacy settings and preferences. The method for choosing and recording privacy settings is outside the scope of the Liberty specifications.

3 User-Centric Identity Management

Network-centric identity management approaches, such as the one proposed by the Liberty Alliance, have failed to reach the interest (and trust) of users, becoming constrained to the enterprise or governmental domains. For years, companies (especially telecommunication operators) have controlled user attributes: they know who you are, what is done with some of your identity-related information, who is using it, how and for what. Fortunately now, multiple service providers populate the Internet without being associated to any operator thus bringing the existing identity management systems towards a new scope around the concept of *user centricity*.

The term user-centric was introduced in the identity arena in about 2006. A user-centric identity management system *"needs to support user control and considers user-centric architectural and usability aspects"* [7]. Two main principles support user-centric identity management:

- *The user is in the middle of a data transaction.* Any information that flies between any entity pass through the user as a must condition, who has the power of consenting the transaction.

- *Huge scale advantages*, since the identity provider does not need to know about every service provider, the user directly deals with them. The identity provider can simply be used to validate the information that will be sent to the service provider.

User-centric identity management principles can be implemented by different means but the most popular ones can be divided into two categories, namely: URL- and card-based systems.

- *Simple URL-based systems* are decentralized and use URLs as users' identifiers. Compatible service providers accept identifiers created by a trusted entity (the identity provider); users are free to choose any identity provider to create an identity. The security of the transaction depends on how much the user relies on her identity provider.

  This is precisely one of the drawbacks of this approach. Malicious identity providers may give a false trust feeling, allowing unaware users to gain access to malicious service providers. Once inside the service provider, the victims can be easily cheated taking advantage of a false security feeling. Some examples of URL-based systems are OpenID [8] and LID (Light-Weight Identity) [9].

- *Identity card-based systems* are built using the information card metaphor [10]. Although there are different definitions of this concept, the simplest could be that expressed by the Information Card Foundation [11]: *"Information Cards are the digital version of the cards you carry in your purse or wallet today. You use them with a new kind of digital wallet called a selector."* Selectors are pieces of software that complement Web browsers and allow users to choose the information card that will be supplied to service providers upon access. Depending on the user identity information that the service provider requires, the user chooses a certain information card. In these systems users decide, using a single interface (the card selector), which pieces of their identity they share with a given service provider. This approach gives users excellent control over their identity resources: they can assume at least partial control over their privacy, while enjoying enhanced usability.

  Additionally, card-based systems provide user with a consistent user experience. No matter what service provider is being used or what type of identity information is being enclosed towards them. In general, users interact with the same type of identity managers for every identity transaction they do. This is an important difference with respect to the network centric identity management scenario, where each service provider provides its own user interface which means the user is learning a new interface, sometime simply for using it only one time (for instance, at registration time). Examples of identity card based systems are Higgins [12] and Windows Cardspace [13].

  However, several security and privacy issues arise in information card based systems [14]. Firstly, the identity providers are aware of the service providers to which the user attempts to log in, so malicious identity provider can learn about the behavior of the users on the Web. Secondly, and even more important, is the problem of the reliance on the user's judgment of the trustworthiness of the service provider. This means that if a service provider is not trustworthy, it could gather information about users and potentially use this in unauthorized ways.

In both URL- and card-based approaches, the user identity information sharing happens in the foreground, since the user must be online and the service provider must actively request this information. This might be seen as a major handicap since users must be online and connected with the consumer service provider. Additionally, users cannot configure default privacy preferences to infer automated decisions regarding the release of their identity information. Instead, users must always give explicit permission for the release of information on a per-request basis.

Furthermore, it is unrealistic to expect that all user-related data are reachable through a user agent. Consider, for instance, information such as cellular network-based location information. Moreover, consider identity-based services such as sending an SMS or billing the user on behalf of a third party. These are identity-based services that only a specialized identity-based service provider can offer, preferably within a trusted domain.

4 Self-service Privacy in Practice

We feel that network-centric identity management solutions are essential to manage some identity information and identity-based transactions. However, a user-centric approach to privacy enabling consistent user-experience is still required in order to provide users with adequate control of their information. Therefore we introduce a solution that merges both approaches, providing a user-centric privacy approach to a network-centric identity management solution to put the concept of Self-Service Privacy into practice.

Fig. 1 introduces a high-level view of a network-centric identity management architecture consistent with the Liberty Alliance specifications. A new entity has been added to this architecture, namely *Privacy Controller* (PC). The PC joins the identity network so that its users can federate (link) their accounts with those they have in other providers (using pseudonyms).

Using this new entity users are able to:

1. Retrieve a global view (snapshot) of their identity resources across different nodes of the identity network to understand which identity resources are stored, where they exist and their specific values. Users are also allowed to modify and delete any data.
2. See the history of how their identity resources have been used, i.e., what entities have requested them, when, the outcome of each request, etc.
3. Govern the future use and release of all identity resources by setting privacy preferences.

A generic requirement for all scenarios is that the PC must be authenticated, on behalf of the user, against the identity network in order to gain access to participating entities. The authentication is carried out against the IdP following standard Liberty protocols (Fig. 1, flow 0) using the pseudonyms obtained during the federation process. At the end of the authentication process the PC obtains an endpoint reference and credentials to access the DS.

Apart from these interactions, Fig. 1 also shows some other information flows. There is a communication flow between the user and the PC through a Graphical User

Interface (GUI). The PC shows information to users and, in response, users take certain actions and decisions, which are sent back to the PC in order to drive the aforementioned flows.

Flows labelled A, B and C correspond to standard protocols as defined by the Liberty specifications: (A) a WSP informs the DS that it is storing an identity resource for a certain user; (B) a WSC queries the DS to discover which WSP stores selected identity resources about a user and also asks the DS for credentials to access them; and (C) a WSC uses the credentials retrieved in (B) to attempt to access an identity resource stored in a WSP.

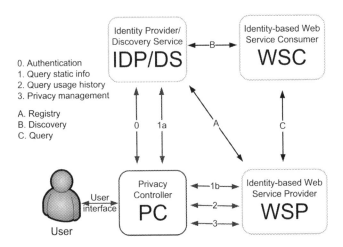

Fig. 1. Overview of the Privacy Controller

The following sections further elaborate on each particular scenario in order to describe the functionality that allows user-centric privacy management of distributed personal information.

4.1   Providing a Snapshot of Distributed User Identity Resources

Our first sample scenario is a combination of two major flows. Firstly, users see an overall picture of the distribution of their identity resources (Fig. 2, steps 0 to 4). Through this flow, the user is able to determine which parties are hosting user resources and what kind of resources are being stored. Once the users have seen the overall set of identity resources, they can choose to manage (modify or delete) any or all of the stored data (Fig. 2, steps 5 to 11).

The PC performs as a Liberty WSC to query or update a WSP using the DST protocol. The PC receives the end-point reference and the credentials needed to access the WSP each time information about identity resources is retrieved (Fig. 2, step 3).

Fig. 3 shows a screenshot of the user interface that we have implemented for the PC. It is an example of the personal data that a user has stored in two different WSPs (iProfile and myPaymentBroker). Specifically, it indicates that myPaymentBroker stores two personal resources (name and credit card) that the user can edit and modify.

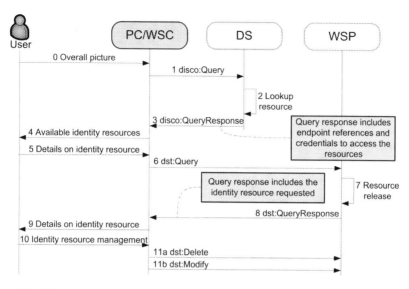

Fig. 2. Sequence diagram for the retrieval and management of identity resources

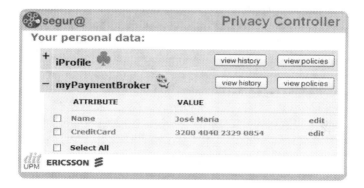

Fig. 3. Screenshot of the PC providing a snapshot of distributed personal data

4.2   Retrieving the Usage History for Identity Resources

In this scenario a user wants to know the usage history of one of their previously obtained identity resources. The PC shows the usage history for that resource with details about the resource type and value, timestamps of access and all WSCs that accessed the resource. Further information can be presented if available, such as privacy protection commitments made by the requestor, or conditions on the release of the information.

Fig. 4 shows a screenshot of the user interface that we have implemented. It shows the services that have requested access to an identity resource (credit card details stored at myPaymentBroker), for what purpose, the timestamp of the request and the outcome of the process (shown with self-explaining icons).

Fig. 4. Screenshot of the PC showing a usage history for a personal data

There are several approaches to gathering usage history. An approach based on proactive notifications from the WSP that stores the identity resource to the PC is not viable because it might cause scalability and performance problems in the event of large bursts of notifications. These problems can be reduced using thresholds and timers to smooth out the data flow. Nevertheless, this mechanism is always WSP-initiated (push mode), preventing the PC from requesting information at will.

A better approach is to extend the Liberty identity profiles with information that registers the use of the identity resources. These records can be considered an extension of the information in a profile since they add relevant information about the retrieval of identity resources. As in the previous scenario, the PC uses the DST protocol to retrieve this information. The main benefit of this approach is that it can be PC-initiated (pull mode). This means that the information is retrieved whenever the PC requires it and is limited to PC requests. Thus, we do not foresee any scalability or performance issues. Additionally, the Liberty specifications for identity services consider extensions of the identity resources, and thus our solution can be considered Liberty-compliant.

We assume at this point that every WSP registers the request and release of the identity resources it stores. This information could be used, for example, for future audits (in fact, this may be compulsory under the laws in certain countries). The minimum information to be recorded at the WSP every time a WSC tries to access an identity resource includes:

- UserID – to identify whose information is being accessed. This is the user alias in the WSP.
- IdentityResourceType – to identify what information has been accessed. This is a subset of the information included within the identity profile.
- WSC – to identify who requested the information.
- Other information – for example, the time of access. Other relevant information that could be useful for future requirements may be the intended use of the information retrieved, whether the WSC will share it with third parties, and the promises the WSC makes about any future use of the requested information.

4.3   Enabling User-Centric Privacy Management

This scenario elaborates on the mechanisms that allow users to centrally manage their privacy preferences. The scenario is composed of four major steps:

1. The user selects a specific identity resource stored in a WSP and reviews its privacy preferences.
2. The PC retrieves and displays the privacy preferences associated with that identity resource.
3. The user modifies the privacy preferences and the PC updates them in the WSP.
4. The WSP enforces the privacy preferences whenever a requestor tries to access the identity resource.

Initial preferences might have been set by the user at the service provider's site or by the service provider itself using default values, or they can even be undefined. Privacy preferences follow a default-deny pattern: An empty set of preferences implies that all requests should be denied (other than those issued by the PC itself). Each preference added to the set grants a specific type of permission.

The PC allows users to change the policy applied to an identity resource by selecting one of a set of pre-defined policies, each of which is described in natural language. This natural language description is mapped to a specific policy described in machine-oriented privacy policy expression language. Policies are hierarchical so that it is easier for users to compare them and choose the one that best meets their needs. This approach benefits from simplicity and usability because users do not have to deal with technical policy details.

Additionally, the PC allows users to define specific options for the use and release of each data element from their profile (Fig. 5). Although this approach provides greater flexibility, it also poses some usability risks, since only advanced users understand (and probably want to know) the detailed meaning of each available policy. Therefore, this is offered only as an advanced option.

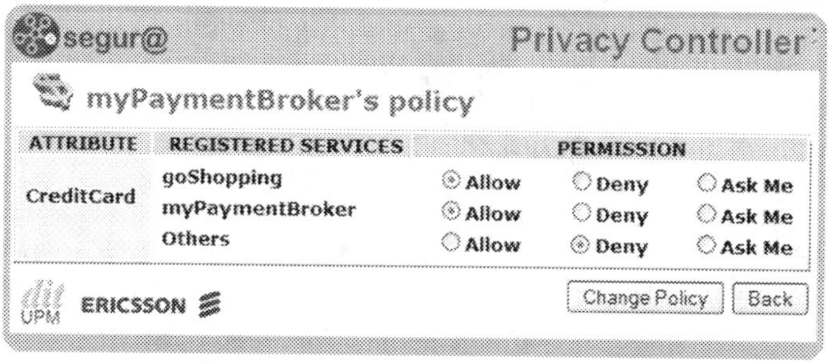

Fig. 5. Screenshot of the PC to control privacy preferences

The variables that define a custom privacy preference include the identity resource, the requestor of the identity resource, the operation requested, the permission level chosen by the user and the resource owner identifier. The identity resource values are constrained to those defined within the identity profile provided by the WSP. The requestor can be any WSC from within the identity network. The operation values might be those defined in a DST protocol (i.e., query, create, delete, modify and subscribe). The permission can be set to grant, deny or askMe, when the user prefers to decide on a per–request basis.

Since the number of rule combinations will increase exponentially (number of requestors multiplied by number of identity resources), we allow for simpler options such as *allow anyone to query this specific identity resource* or *allow just this WSC to update any identity resource*. Therefore, options such as *all* or *just one* are supported.

The solution presented in this article does not impose any specific privacy preference language. However, we have evaluated several different alternatives in terms of the following requirements. On one hand, we must allow users to easily describe their preferences and on the other hand, we have to translate these preferences into policies that a Web service provider can enforce. For our prototype we have chosen the Extensible Access Control Markup Language (XACML) [15] since it allows for easy governance of information once the policy has been defined. However, it poses certain usability difficulties in terms of limiting how a user can express this information. Previous paragraphs have described the measures that we have taken to address these problems.

User-generated privacy preferences (and their expression in the form of privacy policies) govern user identity resources. Thus, privacy policies must be associated with the identity of a user or, more specifically, with the identity resources that they govern. Our solution realizes this association by extending the generic identity profile as defined by Liberty with a privacy policy description schema. Thus, the schema is defined once and can be added to any existing Liberty-based identity profile. Additionally, this approach allows the PC, using the DST protocol, to set (Fig. 6, steps 0 to 3) and query (Fig. 6, steps 4 to 8) the privacy policies associated with a given identity resource.

To set a privacy policy, the PC must play the role of a WSC and include the privacy policy as part of the *Create* or *Modify* element that is sent to the WSP to store the identity resource and its associated privacy policy. This mechanism does not require any changes in current DST protocols, as the policy is transmitted in the same way as any other information, namely, in the body of the message. On arrival, the WSP retrieves the policy and stores it in a policy repository.

The PC retrieves privacy policies that are associated with an identity resource using the DST protocol as well. In this case, however, the PC uses the Query operation. Once the policy has been retrieved, it is translated back into privacy preferences so that the user can understand it.

Finally, privacy policies are enforced whenever a request for an identity resource is received by a WSP. To meet this requirement we have introduced three functions in the WSP (Fig. 7): Policy Enforcement Point (PEP), Policy Decision Point (PDP) and Policy Repository (PR).

The PEP catches the incoming identity resource request and retrieves information about the requesting entity (requestor WSC), the requested identity resource, the operation and the user to whom it refers. Then the PEP creates a request for the PDP with the information retrieved. When the PDP receives the request it retrieves the applicable policies from the PR and compares the request and the policies before sending a decision back to the PEP. When the PEP receives the decision it can allow the requested resource retrieval, deny the operation or pause the operation until further

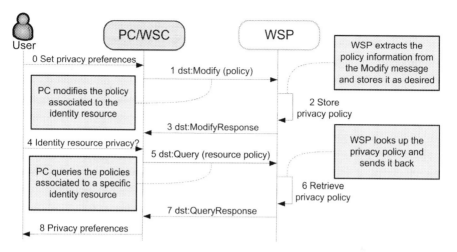

Fig. 6. The Privacy Controller sets and queries privacy policies

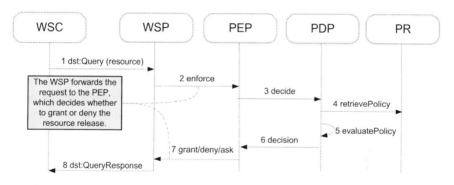

Fig. 7. Sequence diagram for privacy enforcement

actions have been completed (e.g., asking the resource owner for permission). The last step can be implemented using a Liberty Interaction Service [16].

5 Validation

To validate our approach we have developed an identity network made up of five entities (Fig. 8):

- A standard IDP/DS that provides the basic infrastructure as defined by the Liberty Alliance architecture and protocols.
- Two modified identity-based WSPs. The first one, namely iProfile, is a personal profile containing postal address information. The second one, myPaymentBroker, is an identity-based payment service that stores credit card numbers. These WSPs have been modified to incorporate our contributions.

- A standard identity-based WSC; an online shop called goShopping. Once a user selects a product and decides to buy it goShopping queries myPaymentBroker to retrieve the credit card number to charge the user and, if successful, then queries iProfile to retrieve the delivery details.
- A Privacy Controller, which allows users to centrally govern their identity information in the identity network, to trace the use of the information, and to set privacy policies for its future governance.

Our solution does not introduce any impact on standard-based IDP/DS or WSCs implementations. Regarding WSPs, they must enforce privacy policies and log transactions related to the release of personal information, which anyway may be compulsory according to privacy protection laws in some countries. Additionally, an extension to identity data services is needed, which has been done following Liberty recommendations. The extension defines a container for privacy policies governing the use of the information contained within the profile. This extension must be included in any data service supporting privacy policy management.

Liberty-based entities were developed using the open source access management and federation server platform and libraries Open Web SSO (OpenSSO) [17] by Sun Microsystems. With regard to the management and enforcement of privacy policies, we have used an open source implementation of XACML [18], also by Sun Microsystems. This implementation provides support for creating privacy policies in the PC and managing and evaluating requests against policies in the WSPs.

The PC and the WSC were deployed on a Tomcat server, while the IDP/DS and the WSPs were deployed in a Glassfish Server running the OpenSSO platform.

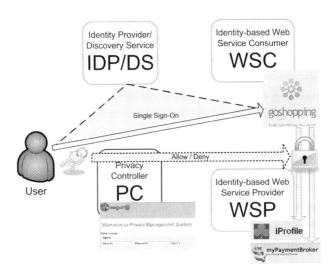

Fig. 8. Demonstration scenario for the prototype validation

In our demonstration scenario, a user firstly signs in the PC to obtain a snapshot of her information distributed in the identity network (Fig. 3), that is, the personal information stored in iProfile and myPaymentBroker. From the PC interface, the user can also modify the values stored.

Additionally, the user can also review the history of use of any piece of this information. For example, Fig. 4 shows the screenshot that the user sees when she chooses to review the history of use of her credit card details stored at myPaymentBroker.

Since goShopping has been denied access to the credit card details, the user is not able to buy at this online shop. Thus, using the PC interface, the user modifies her privacy preferences. Fig. 5 shows the screenshot that the PC presents to set new privacy preferences regarding her credit card details. Once the new preferences are set, the user is able to go back to goShopping and successfully carry out the purchase.

6 Related Work

The approach to identity management described by Liberty Alliance specifications is a solution for the problem of how to manage shared identity resources in a network-centric identity management system. However, this solution does not allow for user-centric management of the scattered users' identity resources and privacy settings in the identity network. The Liberty approach forces users to know where every identity resource is stored and to set privacy preferences for every single node of the identity network. Moreover, it cannot possibly provide overall information about the flows of identity resources among entities since each entity only knows about others to which it has released information or from which it has retrieved information.

Recently, Liberty has announced the release of the Identity Governance Framework (IGF) [19], which aims to describe detailed privacy constraints and the mechanisms by which entities within an identity network can interact. IGF privacy constraints describe fundamental restrictions regarding the propagation, usage, retention, storage and display of identity data for entities involved in consuming and providing them. Unfortunately, the IGF is enterprise-oriented and thus does not allow for user-centric privacy management.

A promising initiative for user-centric privacy management is the PRIME Console [20], which is an interface to the user's identity management system. It allows users to create partial identities (pseudonyms) and associate personal data with each of these identities, assists the user in understanding privacy policies, makes decisions on the basis of the user's preferences and allows users to inspect the transaction history for their personal data. However, sometimes identity information is not initially disclosed by users. For example, in a network-centric identity system some entities can automatically retrieve and offer identity information regarding a user, such as geolocation. Therefore, the PRIME Console is not a comprehensive solution as it focuses only on user-centric identity systems and fails to support network-centric ones.

The HP Virtual Identity and Profile Broker (VIP Broker) [21] provides a single, centralised point of access to distributed identity data, allowing users to monitor relevant information flows. With the VIP Broker, users can also configure release policies, which will be centrally enforced whenever a request for personal information is received. Unlike the VIP Broker, our solution distributes the policies to the custodians of the information. Thus, privacy preferences are applied wherever the information is stored, avoiding the need for an intermediate broker. This is convenient from a business standpoint, since service providers usually want to retain control of the distribution of any information they own. Recently, Google has announced the release of the Google Dashboard [22]. The dashboard lists some of the information associated with the Google services the user has subscribed and provides links to control their personal settings. However, unlike our Privacy Controller, Google Dashboard redirects the user to every service provider in order to modify the privacy preferences. Therefore, users are not provided with a comprehensive tool from where to centrally define their privacy preferences. In addition, users are not able to trace how their information has been used, which is one of the contributions of our proposal.

7 Conclusions

In this article we have presented a comprehensive solution, the Privacy Controller, to help users to actively control the privacy of their personal information while using services in the digital world. The Privacy Controller leverages various identity management technologies (consistent with the Liberty Alliance specifications) to help users understand how much personal information about them is being stored, who has accessed it and how it will be safeguarded in the future.

The lack of simple tools and inadequate privacy-awareness among users are two major obstacles that prevent the involvement of users in privacy control. Therefore, enhanced usability and better default settings play a fundamental role. We have described different measures that our Privacy Controller introduces to support users in defining their own privacy preferences. Nevertheless, we feel that there is room for improvement in this area and thus we are evaluating user modelling techniques that allow the automatic generation of user privacy preferences.

For our solution to be practical, collaboration and coordination with service providers is a must: Service providers would have to provide new interfaces and capabilities to allow external control of personal data. We envision that in the near term governments will force providers to declare the personal information they store and to provide standards-based mechanisms to interact with it. As a matter of fact, in Europe recent privacy protection initiatives [23] have introduced legislative principles such as 'privacy by design' and 'accountability'.

In the future we hope to extend the Privacy Controller to other identity networks such as social networks, which are huge and often unregulated sources of personal information. We feel that such Web sites urgently need mechanisms to provide semantic interoperability between different identity networks. The use of ontologies as information mediators might be a promising future direction.

Acknowledgments

This work has been partially supported by CDTI Ministry of Science and Innovation of Spain, as part of the SEGUR@ project (https://www.cenitsegura.es/), under the CENIT program, CENIT-2007/2004.

References

1. Bonneau, J., Preibusch, S.: The Privacy Jungle: On the Market for Data Protection in Social Networks. In: the 8th Workshop on the Economics of Information Security, WEIS 2009 (2009)
2. Liberty Alliance Project, http://www.projectliberty.org
3. Kantara Initiative, http://www.kantarainitiative.org
4. Cantor, S., et al.: Assertions and protocols for the OASIS Security Assertion Markup Language (SAML) Version 2.0. OASIS Standard. OASIS Security Services TC (2005)
5. Goodner, M., Nadalin, A. (eds.): Web Services Federation Language (WS-Federation) Version 1.2. OASIS Standard. OASIS Web Services Federation (WSFED) TC (2009)
6. Kainulainen, J., Ranganathan, A. (eds.): Liberty ID-WSF Data Services Template Specification, Version 2.1. Liberty Alliance Project (2006)
7. Bhargav-Spantzely, A., Camenisch, J., Gross, T., Sommer, D.: User centricity: A taxonomy and open issues. In: The Second ACM Workshop on Digital Identity Management (DIM 2006), pp. 493–527. IOS Press, Amsterdam (2007)
8. OpenID Web site, http://openid.net/
9. Light-Weight Identity Web site, http://lid.netmesh.org/wiki/Main_Page
10. Jones, M., McIntosh, M. (eds.): Identity Metasystem Interoperability Version 1.0. OASIS Standard. Identity Metasystem Interoperability (IMI) TC (2009)
11. Information Card Foundation, http://informationcard.net
12. Higgins, http://www.eclipse.org/higgins/
13. Windows Cardspace, http://www.microsoft.com/windows/products/winfamily/cardspace
14. Alrodhan, W.A., Mitchell, C.J.: Addressing privacy issues in Cardspace. In: The Third International Symposium on Information Assurance and Security, pp. 285–291. IEEE Computer Society, Washington (2007)
15. Moses, T. (ed.): Extensible Access Control Markup Language (XACML), Version 2.0. OASIS Standard. OASIS eXtensible Access Control Markup Language (XACML) TC (2005)
16. Aarts, R., Madsen, P. (eds.): Liberty Id-WSF Interaction Service Specification, Version 2.0-errata-v1.0. Liberty Alliance Project (2007)
17. OpenSSO, https://opensso.dev.java.net/18
18. Sun's XACML Implementation, http://sunxacml.sourceforge.net/
19. Madsen, P. (ed.): Liberty IGF Privacy Constraints Specification, Version 1.0. Liberty Alliance Project (2009)
20. Leenes, R., Schallaböck, J., Hansen, M.: PRIME White Paper, Version 3. PRIME Project (2008)
21. Hewlett-Packard Development Company: HP Virtual Identity and Profile Broker. Hewlett-Packard (2007)
22. Google Dashboard, http://www.google.com/dashboard/
23. Article 29 of the Data Protection Working Party, The Future of Privacy - Joint contribution to the Consultation of the European Commission on the legal framework for the fundamental right to protection of personal data, 02356/09/EN (December 01, 2009)

Naïve Security in a Wi-Fi World

Colleen Swanson, Ruth Urner, and Edward Lank

David C. Cheriton School of Computer Science
University of Waterloo
Waterloo, Ontario, N2L 3G1, Canada
{c2swanso,rurner,lank}@cs.uwaterloo.ca

Abstract. Despite nearly ubiquitous access to wireless networks, many users still engage in risky behaviors, make bad choices, or are seemingly indifferent to the concerns that security and privacy researchers work diligently to address. At present, research on user attitudes toward security and privacy on public Wi-Fi networks is rare. This paper explores Wi-Fi security and privacy by analyzing users' current actions and reluctance to change. Through interviews and concrete demonstrations of vulnerability, we show that users make security choices based on (often mistaken) analogy to the physical world. Moreover, despite increased awareness of vulnerability, users remain ingenuous, failing to develop a realistic view of risk. We argue that our data present a picture of users engaged in a form of naïve security. We believe our results will be beneficial to researchers in the area of security-tool design, in particular with respect to better informing user choices.

Keywords: Wi-Fi, hotspot, security, behavior, privacy, trust.

1 Introduction

In March 2002, Network World ran an article entitled "Wi-Fi World," in which they hypothesize a world where wireless internet is ubiquitous. They describe a scenario in which people move from wireless at home to wireless at work, at cafés, and at airports. Helped along by inexpensive hardware, we now enjoy near-universal access to 802.11 wireless networks. While wireless hotspots have made accessing the internet more convenient, they also pose significant privacy and security risks to users.

Wireless network communication is particularly susceptible to eavesdropping (or packet sniffing) because an eavesdropper need not physically connect to a hardwired connection. They can sit in secluded locations within range of a wireless access point, but at some distance from their victim, and monitor all internet traffic being transmitted through the wireless signal. This allows them to easily determine websites users are visiting and any files, messages, or passwords used in the event users log into unsecured sites, use unencrypted email protocols (POP3 or IMAP) or unencrypted computer-to-computer connections (e.g. FTP, telnet, remote desktop). Furthermore, recent attacks on the SSL protocol [16] highlight the vulnerability of even encrypted—and therefore supposedly secure—connections.

M. Nishigaki et al. (Eds.): IFIPTM 2010, IFIP AICT 321, pp. 32–47, 2010.

This paper focuses on users' reactions to an awareness of their vulnerabilities when on Wi-Fi networks. To develop an understanding of whether people change with awareness of their vulnerabilities, we conducted a novel two-phase study of Wi-Fi users recruited from public cafés. This study included a demonstration of packet sniffing during the first phase and a follow-up study to determine whether and how users changed behaviors.

While we find that some participants do report an increased awareness of encrypted connections, changes in behavior were generally minor. We found an ingenuousness, a naïveté with respect to existing dangers, both before and after our demonstration of packet sniffing. Participants analyze dangers based on a set of simplistic assumptions: that they have nothing to hide; that no one would care to listen; that others on the network are honest; or that it is unlikely someone would target them. As a result, while they do take some steps to protect themselves, our participants engage in *naïve risk mitigation*, often basing their security strategies on faulty assumptions and analogies to the real world. Finally, we argue that by understanding users' perceptions of security, designers will be better able to train users to be secure and to communicate to users the risks and vulnerabilities that exist on their systems.

This paper is structured as follows. Section 2 contrasts our current research with related work. Section 3 outlines the details of our study. Sections 4 and 5 present the results, and Section 6 the design implications of our work.

2   Related Work

Research often paints a rather pessimistic image of users as having little understanding of current technology and the potential security risks involved. Even informed users often do not use available security tools, pay attention to browser indicators, or use secure passwords [3, 6, 10, 21].

In the past decade, there has been broad interest in user understanding and reactions to privacy and security issues that arise in the online world [1, 8, 9, 10, 11, 13]); we will not attempt to address all related work, but rather highlight the most relevant. Flinn and Lumsden [9] conclude that although users try to educate themselves, they generally lack the basic knowledge necessary to assess privacy and security risks. Viseu [20] briefly touches on the theme of user behavior varying based on location, but only in the context of distinguishing between personal and public computers for online banking. Dourish et al. [8] highlight the need to make security more understandable, a theme we explore in our paper. We, however, focus on public Wi-Fi behavior with respect to both privacy and security, whereas Dourish is interested in security on a much broader level, focusing on how users view security relative to desired tasks. Finally, Dourish and Anderson [7] note that security is more than "economic rationality" and that general models of privacy and security are frequently borrowed from the physical world, a conclusion that echoes our observations of naïve risk management in the Wi-Fi world.

There is a small set of studies that focus on security, privacy and behavior on Wi-Fi connections. Kindberg et al. [12] investigate trust in Wi-Fi hotspots, observing that users willingly provided personal information in order to register for the authors' spoofed wireless service. Kowitz and Cranor [15] explore privacy in a lab setting by projecting excerpts from captured Wi-Fi packets onto a display. They report that participants felt uncomfortable while the display was on, but admit that participants may not have properly understood the relationship of the display to the functioning of the wireless network.

Klasnja et al. [14] investigate user understanding of Wi-Fi technology, current practices, and whether users send information they consider sensitive in the clear (accomplished by installing software to monitor participants' computers). They observe that users do not have a firm understanding of Wi-Fi security issues, and are surprised and concerned when presented with a list of released personal information. Users also indicated an intent to change their practices. Klasnja et al.'s primary focus, however, was on what users currently do to protect their privacy and whether users release information they wish to keep private.

Our study complements Klasnja et al.'s work in three ways. First, while Klasnja et al. look at what users currently do to protect their security, we expand significantly on this, exploring motivations for users' current Wi-Fi behaviors. Second, while Klasnja et al. observe a desire to change, they did not follow up to explore whether users actually changed, and why they did or did not change. Finally, our approach differs significantly from that of Klasnja et al. (and from Kowitz and Cranor) in that we did not involve participants' personal information in the demonstration of vulnerability. There is a distinction between a violation of privacy and an awareness of the possibility of privacy violation, especially with respect to user reactions and potential behavior changes. While both approaches have merit, we are most interested in how to encourage users to improve their privacy and security without first violating their security or privacy. In summary, we go beyond these and other previous works by not only exploring users' understanding of privacy and security practices, but also what effect increased knowledge of Wi-Fi actually has on behavior.

3 Methodology

Participants were recruited by word of mouth at local cafés offering free Wi-Fi and were only told we were interested in gathering information on general Wi-Fi behavior in public places. We interviewed 11 people of varying occupations and computer knowledge, P1–P11, and one security expert, S1, with ages ranging from 22–67; see Table 1. We remark that of the 12 participants, while most used their laptops frequently for work, study, and/or personal use, only S1 had extensive computer knowledge. Local recruitment and sample size may raise some concerns about the generalizability of these results. However, security and privacy researchers have found that geographic location and demographic characteristics have little effect on security/privacy behaviors [10]. As well, our sample size is not particularly small for a qualitative study [7].

Interviews were audio recorded and transcribed. For each round of interviews (initial and follow-up), once the data collection was complete, selected quotes were highlighted and analyzed using open coding; we refer the reader to [19] for a discussion of this technique. Quotes were organized using an affinity diagram by two of the researchers working collaboratively. A third researcher performed a separate coding of transcripts and validated clustering on the affinity diagram.

Table 1. Participant Demographics

ID	Occupation	Age, M/F
P1	Mathematics Ph.D. student	29/M
P2	English student/retail employee	22/M
P3	Retired sales manager	67/M
P4	Government employee	24/M
P5	MBA student	26/F
P6	MBA student	29/M
P7	Chemical engineering/MA student	23/F
P8	Investment analyst	23/M
P9	Physiotherapy/recreation student	24/F
P10	Sociology MA student	26/F
P11	Behavior therapist	30/F
S1	Security expert	35+/M

Our interviews were designed as follows. In the first interview, we gathered demographic information about the participants, as well as information on where participants use wireless internet. We conducted a walk-through of their most recent Wi-Fi session at a public place, then inquired whether and how often participants engage in various online activities at public Wi-Fi locations, all without reference to security. We transitioned into a discussion of privacy and security by asking about privacy and/or security concerns if participants had not already mentioned these topics on their own. We asked whether participants use any sort of protective measures while using wireless internet, explored their understanding and behavior with respect to SSL, and asked what information about their Wi-Fi activities might be available to other people.

We then moved to a brief explanation of how information is sent on wireless networks, introduced the concept of packet sniffing, and gave a brief demonstration using Wireshark (www.wireshark.org), a freeware network-monitoring program. Packet sniffing may be illegal by Canadian law, so we used two computers belonging to the researchers and avoided involving participants' or other café customers' computers. Instead, the demonstration consisted of using one computer to sniff the traffic of the other, while a researcher used the target computer to go to GoogleMaps and type in an address. Participants watched as the first computer captured this information, and were then shown how it was possible to recover exactly what had been typed and submitted to Google. Participants were allowed to ask questions as the demonstration progressed. In case participants did not ask about activities such as online banking or online shopping, we briefly explained how SSL encryption disguises information and noted the URL indicator "https." Following the demonstration, we encouraged participants to discuss what they had seen, how they felt about it, and whether anything they had witnessed was likely to affect their Wi-Fi behavior.

Between 3–4 weeks after the initial interview, we contacted participants for a follow-up. Participants were not informed in advance of the second interview, but had agreed to be contacted in case we had further questions. Out of the participants P1–P11, all but P6 met us for a follow-up[1]. In this interview, we asked participants if they had given the demonstration any further thought and whether their public Wi-Fi behavior had changed in any way. We inquired how likely participants felt a packet-sniffing attack was, and what, if anything, would prompt them to change their behavior. To complete the overall picture of user behavior, we also asked participants about privacy and security programs and whether they would use such tools to protect themselves.

4   Current Wi-Fi Beliefs and Practices

The overwhelming view of our participants, when asked to identify any concerns they might have using Wi-Fi, was that they had none. Most explained that they generally felt safe using public Wi-Fi. P1 explained that while "there is probably some security risk . . . ," he was not concerned, describing himself as a "careless Wi-Fi user." P5 justified her lack of concern by comparing public wireless with her previous work wireless connection: given that "it's secure enough to use Wi-Fi for business purposes," she felt public wireless must also be safe by association. Although P5 was aware that her work laptop had special security features installed, this did not affect her reasoning. Her comment is a first glimpse of participants making choices based on analogy to the real world: while in some circumstances, it might make sense to say that "if A can do activity x safely, so can B", this is often faulty reasoning in reality and certainly does not translate well to the wireless world, as different security settings and software will result in different levels of security.

An analysis of the typical online activities our participants engage in via unsecured wireless, however, reveals a more complicated view of safety and security. Indeed, almost all of our participants (with the exception of P8) acted to protect either their privacy or their security, most commonly in the form of deciding on a set of activities with which they were comfortable, a topic we discuss in Section 4.1. In addition, some of our participants actively sought to protect themselves via awareness of SSL or security certificates; we discuss our participants' behaviors with respect to these security tools in Section 4.2. These results are especially interesting in the context of what types of attacks our participants believed possible before the packet-sniffing demonstration, which ranged from the belief in all-powerful hackers who could access any information

---

[1] We remark that given S1's area of expertise, we only conducted the first part of the initial interview, as we felt the packet-sniffing demonstration and second interview would be inappropriate.

on users' computers to the belief that any attackers would have to physically look at the laptop screen to glean information; a common theme was the idea that any attack beyond shoulder-surfing would require "computer savvy" (P12). Regardless of how extensive participants thought an attacker's reach might be, their security behaviors were surprisingly similar.

4.1 Controlling Risk through Regulation of Online Activities

In the first component of the interview process, we paid special attention to the types of online activities participants engage in while using public Wi-Fi. We were particularly interested in activities participants claimed to avoid and attempted to determine the underlying cause. The overwhelming (and unsurprising) theme emerging from this was that participants were primarily concerned with the security of their financial information and therefore uncomfortable banking or shopping via public Wi-Fi. While this was the main focus of their security concerns, we also observed that participants viewed privacy and security based on a perception of context (i.e., a café) and what was appropriate in that context. Some of these participants were particularly concerned with protecting the impression others would have of them.

As we discuss in the following sections, participants' security choices are frequently informed by an understanding of typical behavior in the real world, a phenomenon we call *naïve risk mitigation*. For example, some think about impression management and try to ensure that nothing scandalous about them is released. Others, conditioned to protect financial information, apply this same notion to the online world. Finally, while many researchers have argued that participants "don't care" enough about security or privacy to alter their actions, it seems that (with the exception of P8) participants we interviewed accept and expect the need to adapt their behavior to protect themselves.

Avoiding Financial Transactions. Almost all of our participants reported avoiding banking and shopping while on public Wi-Fi. P2 even expressed his lack of concern regarding public Wi-Fi in terms of this avoidance:

> [Public Wi-Fi has] never been a concern because ... I don't do online banking in public places or purchase anything in public. (P2)

Two participants who said they did not "really" have concerns about public Wi-Fi immediately mentioned a discomfort in banking while on public Wi-Fi. P6 mentioned that he was unsure whether he would access his online banking over an unsecured wireless connection and that he tried to pay attention to whether the network was "secure" or not, citing fear of identity theft. The other, who said she does occasionally connect to online banking in public if she has forgotten to at home, admitted:

> I feel like I don't want to do my banking, also, like sometimes at a public location, because I don't know how computers work very well. (P10)

Other reasons given for this discomfort or avoidance varied, but most were equally vague in nature. P11, in examining her security concerns, explained that she does not "do banking or anything" when she is at the café, as it "says it's unsecured." P1 said that he did not bank online in public, but rather preferred to connect at home (via his neighbor's unsecured Wi-Fi) or school, explaining that "somehow I think it's more secure, but it probably isn't." Others who expressed clear security concerns about financial transactions—"I do it at home, the same as online banking" (P7)—focused on physical security, not the security of the Wi-Fi connection. P7 worried her account number would be stolen; P5 explained:

> I'm not sure if it's [avoiding online shopping] primarily due to . . . security of the internet connection, or just because I don't like flashing my personal information [in public].

Even the security expert avoids banking online over a wireless connection, explaining that he "know[s] enough of the security to know it's reasonable, but [he] just [does not] do it." S1 further clarified this, mentioning the possible technical attacks on SSL sessions and the potential to be tricked when tired. He concluded the discussion, however, by reiterating the common theme of being more comfortable at a location perceived to be private and controlled: "It's one of those things I just don't bother doing, because I just wait until I get home."

As the security expert notes, it is reasonable to argue that participants' determination to avoid financial transactions is somewhat irrational. Online banking and e-commerce sites use SSL connections to transmit information, so the information is encrypted. However, with limited security knowledge, applying the age-old adage "better safe than sorry" is not an unreasonable choice. Users who do not understand how security works and do not have the knowledge to verify security before entering financial information are nevertheless confronted with the need to make a decision how to behave. "Just as you wouldn't take your wallet [out] to count your cash" (P2), online banking is viewed as an activity more appropriate to the supposedly safe environ of the home. Indeed, P2 gives perhaps the most direct explanation of this phenomenon, describing it as a result of external conditioning to protect one's financial information:

> It just strikes me as something you do in the privacy of your own home. . . . I guess I'm probably conditioned in some way to believe that yeah, you just don't . . . because it's dangerous or whatever. . . . I don't really believe that, but I can't explain why I wouldn't do [online shopping]. That's probably why.

Impression Management. Some participants expressed concern about protecting their privacy while on public Wi-Fi; some of the approaches were rather unique, amounting to impression management. For example, P5 limits the information on her laptop to what she is comfortable sharing with her mother:

> My laptop is mum-safe. . . . There is nothing which I wouldn't show to my mum and my mum is very conservative. There is nothing that couldn't be given to pretty much anyone.

As P5 further explained, she does not perform activities or store information she deems private:

> So like when I'm in a coffee shop right now, I don't do anything really, which is going to be a concern of mine if somebody finds out.

A similar limitation on behavior to protect privacy was echoed by other participants. For example P1, P3, and P7 did not want to be caught doing something that others might consider inappropriate. Both P1 and P3, somewhat tongue-in-cheek, mentioned pornography as something they would not download, and P7 explained that she does not have privacy concerns because she "didn't do anything illegal, you know, anything wrong."

4.2   Views of Security Protocols: SSL and Security Certificates

Although many of our participants' behaviors fit the general impression that the public suffers from lack of awareness and concern, we did see some interesting responses to SSL and security certificate warnings. Of the four participants who actually knew what SSL was, only two, P2 and P4, claimed to actively look for the "https" indicator. Interestingly, the others, P1 and P8, admitted that they never checked, but rather assumed SSL was being used whenever they "needed it"; this reaction of trust was quite similar to other participants' security beliefs and is theme we discuss further in Section 5.3.

Participants had a mixed reaction to security certificate pop-ups. Many, including S1, ignored these warnings either all or "most of the time." Our more security-aware participants, P2 and P4, claimed to pay attention to the pop-up warnings, unless they were viewing websites they "trust" (P4). One participant, P7, said she would "rather just close [the site]." P3 noted he would be reluctant to visit the site, but that he has little of value on his computer, so it would not matter if the site was malicious. P9 said she generally goes to the site, but judges whether to remain by the website's appearance. Finally, P5 ignores the warnings if she recognizes the site and has never had any problems, but otherwise uses a friend's laptop to access the site if her fiancé says it is not safe.

5   Participant Responses to a Demonstration of Risk

One question we asked was how people would respond to a realistic depiction of their vulnerabilities. Does it spur them to learn more about security? To change their behavior? As we note earlier, past results in security research have rarely focused on concrete demonstrations of specific vulnerabilities, or whether such demonstrations have any lasting impact.

5.1   Initial Responses to Demonstration of Packet Sniffing

Beyond general statements of interest—comments like "Cool," "Awesome," or "Neat"—our participants expressed a range of responses to the packet-sniffing demonstration. P1 was surprised by the demonstration, but noted that privacy was not "really a big deal" for him, and that if "something like that happened, I wouldn't really care that much." One participant stated he was "a little perturbed" (P4), but not overly concerned (although this participant later modified his behavior significantly, as described in Section 5.2). Others noted that the demonstration was "kind of scary" (P11) or "super creepy" (P10). Some expressed surprise that "people can actually see my info, personal things" (P9). Others questioned whether we could spy on anyone in the café, and when we explained how we could (though we did not spy on others), commented that this was "not good" (P3). More specific reactions to the demonstration can be grouped into four categories: participants were surprised at how easy packet sniffing was; participants wanted to know how packet sniffing could be prevented; participants had questions about the security of their own activities; and participants appreciated learning about packet sniffing.

Many participants were not surprised by the demonstration itself, but were surprised by how easy it was:

> I probably would have thought something like this is possible. ...I am surprised that there is a program that does that readily for you. (P8)

P2, P4, P5, P6, P8, and P9 all expressed similar sentiments, particularly some surprise at how easy it was for non-technical users. P6, for example, thought that it would "take some ...technical skills, some programming or whatever."

An interesting role reversal took place at this point of the interview, where participants began to interview us. Participants were curious about how to prevent packet-sniffing attacks; they wanted to know "how you prevent that?" (P3), or "what [the café] would have to do to prevent this" (P8). Another common type of query involved the safety of online activities: online banking, e-commerce sites, Facebook, email, and others. Participants questioned us quite carefully on how security for online banking and e-commerce sites works. We provided a basic description of SSL protocols and how this protected participants from such attacks when connecting to these sites. Also, if participants did not ask about online banking or e-commerce, we proactively explained SSL connections to them. Several participants were reassured by this, noting that things were OK "as long as they can't find my banking information" (P10).

Finally, a common response was appreciation. P5 indicated that it "clearly shows that you can pretty much see everything." P4 always "thought it was that easy, but now that you showed me, [I'm more aware]." P2 noted:

> I'll certainly remain conscious of it, which is a good thing, obviously.

Participants also appreciated the ability to be able to act on information from the demonstration. P11 commented on getting laptops with wireless at work with "a lot of client info" on them and intended to verify that "those security measures" would be put in place. Another participant, P6, was concerned about "inside company information," noting that it was a "good thing" to see the demonstration because he was "doing this consulting project now" and "has a lot of financial documents" he sends "back and forth."

5.2 Behavioral Changes: The Plan and the Reality

When queried immediately after the demonstration about whether it would motivate behavior change, participants were split. Some participants expressed a desire to "be more cautious" (P11). Participants who queried us about online banking and security measures noted they would be more aware of the "https" indicator to ensure an SSL connection (P9, P10, P11). P5 explained that she was "probably gonna be a little bit more paranoid in terms of not using any . . . personal information in public locations." Other participants were less concerned. P6 said he would not change his behavior because he does not "really have anything to hide." However, he also notes:

> Certainly if I were to work on some sensitive stuff, then that's definitely what I would probably think of. I would probably not send stuff from here on this wireless network.

P2 explained that despite a desire to remain conscious of the demonstration, "I don't think it would necessarily change my practices." This mixed message was common: participants indicated they were unlikely to change their practices, but also indicated that they would be more aware and take more care.

An analysis of reported participant behavior on follow-up confirms this notion: on the whole, any changes in behavior that occurred were minor and relegated to attempts to be more aware. Our main focus after the initial interview was determining whether participants had actually changed their behavior in any way. We wanted to see what they retained from the demonstration and if they reported being more aware. We conducted our follow-ups after 3–4 weeks, in our estimation enough time for participants to have re-established regular behaviors, but not so much that they would have difficulty recalling the demonstration.

We began the follow-up interviews by asking participants if they had given the demonstration any thought. Several participants mentioned having thought about the demonstration and all but one of the participants had discussed it. Some just told one or two of their friends, an unsurprising result. Some reported using their new knowledge to correct behaviors of their friends:

> I told [two of my friends] how it's not safe [to enter personal information in unsecured websites] because you showed me that what I typed in actually shows on your computer. (P9)

One participant (P11) taught all of her colleagues at work about the SSL protocol, claiming that they had all become more aware of the "s" in the browser and now tried to pay attention to it. P3, P5, P9, and P10 also reported remembering and thinking about SSL when online. Unfortunately, this did not necessarily translate into participants' behavior being more secure. While some (P3, P10, P11) reported checking for SSL when using sites they considered sensitive (e.g. banking), others only mentioned noticing the "https" when it was present:

> I haven't really investigated [whether sites I log into use "https"], but now I know [about "https"] so I probably know when it comes up and I

> feel more safe about it. ... When it comes up it will automatically make
> me think it's a safe site, right. But then I didn't really [look] for it. (P9)

This last observation is particularly concerning, as from a security perspective,
it is more important for users to notice the absence of a secure connection than
its presence. P9's response to learning about SSL was to be reassured if she
happened to notice its presence, rather than to actively check that SSL was
being used. In this case, our user *felt* more safe online because she thought she
was more aware, but in reality she had not improved her security.

Participants' perceptions of security and privacy changed in other ways as
well. Increased knowledge of technology caused some participants to feel less safe
overall, with some expressing doubts about their security even in the presence
of security protocols. P3, at the end of his first interview, captured this feeling
quite well: "I mean even the secure stuff, how secure is it?" P4 became so unsure
of his online safety that he tried to avoid public Wi-Fi entirely, and if he did
use public Wi-Fi did not do "anything that requires a login and a password."
P9 explained that she now felt it was not "really safe to access [her] bank or
you know, personal information," so she tried to avoid these activities while in
public. P5 noted:

> Say if I was about to buy something and I had to enter all my credit card
> information. Although you said that if it says "s" it's safe, I probably
> would think about it twice, whether or not I want to use Wi-Fi.

Finally, nothing had changed for P1, P2, P7, and P8. P2, one of our more
security-conscious participants, stressed that he had no reason to change as he
had already been careful about his online activities. The others were also happy
with their pre-demonstration behavior. As P8 explained:

> Nothing that I saw in there made me feel unsecure or threatened.

Given the limited effect of the demonstration, we asked participants what would
motivate them to change their behaviors online. Most noted that the only thing
that might prompt them to change their behavior would be if someone captured
information from them:

> If I ever had a problem I'd change things, but ... I have no reason to
> think that I'd do anything different right now. (P3)

Many participants echoed the sentiment that they would take action if something happened, but these behaviors were usually discrete, solving that specific
problem rather than protecting themselves more generally. For example, P1 mentioned that if someone hacked into his email account, he would "have to change
the password or something like that." P7 said that if she knew someone was
spying on her, she would be "upset" and would stop using the Wi-Fi connection.

5.3   A Deeper Look: Underlying Motivations for (Lack of) Change

While we saw some change in behavior, we were surprised that, even with an
awareness of how open information is on Wi-Fi, we did not see more awareness of

privacy and security vulnerabilities. On the whole, participants were comfortable with their original Wi-Fi behavior. An analysis of the data reveals the following set of underlying assumptions that helps explain this: participants believed they had nothing to hide; participants felt people would lose interest pretty quickly; participants trusted others to not spy on them or to protect them; participants believed that packet sniffing did not happen often.

Nothing to Hide, Nothing to Fear. Security researchers frequently quote the adage "The honest man has nothing to hide" as motivation for inertia when it comes to self-protection online. P1, P2, P5, P6, P7, P8, and P10 all mentioned variants of this. Participants felt that it was perfectly acceptable for someone to find out what they do online. P8 and P9 shared the sentiment that "if somebody is out there logging what websites I visit and sells it, that's all fine" (P8). P7 characterized her online activities as "not private," saying that she does "nothing super important." P5 echoed this sentiment when she explained that her "personal emails" were not "security sensitive."

I'm Not That Interesting. P1 stated: "I'm not that interesting to begin with." Participants operated under a perception that the things they might reveal would be of limited value to other parties. P1, P2, P5, P6, P7, and P8 all noted the limited payoff someone would get from eavesdropping:

> The general notion of people that are invading your privacy isn't that much of a concern to me . . . I think they would lose interest pretty quickly in my case, anyway. There's not much to [know]. (P2)

I Can Trust Others. There are two dimensions to trust that we found in responses. P1, P7, P9, and P10 all expressed trust that others would not spy— that others would be honest. P7 asked "What's the point of spying on what other people do?", while P1 explained that an eavesdropper would have to have "some psychological problems."

Both P7 and P9 attributed an honesty of intent to others, that people would do "their own stuff" (P9):

> I mean if people come in, they would do their own things, right? Normally people don't spying on purpose. (P7)

This trust extended to companies and institutions. For example, P10 trusted her internet service provider to monitor her home wireless network for intruders. P2 trusted the café to combat eavesdropping. Finally, P1, P4, and P6 assumed universities would protect the security of their communication on campus, an assumption faulty in reality. P1 and P3 both felt online banking must be all right because their banks were "legitimate" institutions.

It Would Never Happen to Me. Some participants assumed the likelihood of network snooping was low, either because of a lack of interesting data or their understanding of the expense of the attack. P8 thought the odds are "slim to none":

> I just don't see what motive somebody would have to do that. To . . . take your time, go out of your way, put all this software on and go to a public [place] . . . and then sniff around.

Only P4 and P5 seemed to think eavesdropping more likely. P4 explained that "Enough of [his] friends have had some sorts of security issues that . . . [he is] not willing to open [himself] up to that," and P5 took it as a "fact of life":

> I'm pretty sure people do it because it's available, it's there. I mean, for crying out loud, people peak on people in the change rooms, why won't they peak on somebody's laptop, which seems to be a little bit more useful to me.

6   Discussion

6.1   Practicing Naïve Security

In our observations, we bring to light two trends. First, we note that many participants' actions are (mis)informed by drawing mistaken analogy to real-world practices. Second, lacking knowledge, our participants believe that they have little of value, trust that others would not victimize them, and believe that something bad is unlikely. Together, these data lead to a view of our participants as both naïve (making decisions based on feelings, impressions, ideas, and not facts) and ingenuous (guided by a false sense of security). We draw a likeness between our participants' views of security and the concept of naïve, or 'folk' physics. Computers and computer security are incomprehensible to our participants. Therefore, our participants exhibit a naïve Wi-Fi behavior—they avoid things that may be dangerous, but they do so without knowing what is truly risky behavior. Participants practice naïve Wi-Fi Security based on their perceptions of risk and vulnerability.

Participants' activities are rife with instances of naïve security. When discussing security certificates, P9 went to websites and trusted the site based on if it "looked safe." P6 stated he would use any unsecured access point he could find to "check email," but not to browse the web. Finally, P8 does not believe people have "time to log hundreds of people." Unfortunately, malicious websites are designed to look trustworthy, unsecured access points are trying to get users to release passwords and other personal information, and logging and then parsing large data sets is trivial with simple scripting. Participants felt snooping did not happen because others would be honest, that their online financial transactions would be all right because they trusted the companies in question. P8, who never looked for SSL, was perfectly comfortable in the assumption that it was there if he "needed it."

Naïve security is also evident when we examine the more complicated behaviors of our participants. For example, recall P5's method of off-loading risk when confronted with security certificate warnings: If she recognizes a site and has never had any problems, she ignores the warnings. Otherwise she asks her more technically-minded fiancé if it is safe to go on, transferring responsibility. If he tells her it is not, she then "call[s] up [her] friend and use[s] his laptop" (P5), thereby transferring risk.

To overcome the misunderstandings in the naïve security paradigm, one valuable avenue for our participants seemed to be interaction with experts. They valued the packet-sniffing demonstration and in some cases acted on it appropriately. Just as concepts from naïve physics are addressed through education and enhanced understanding, additional discussions with experts could help our participants address security issues like email client setup, Gmail and Facebook use, malicious access points, and other potential Wi-Fi threats. However, it is challenging to engage participants to this extent. Beyond the limited resources of computer experts—we cannot spend individual time with everyone who uses public Wi-Fi—participants have an "it won't happen to me" attitude. Like those who believe theorems from folk physics, participants lack interest in developing a full and sophisticated understanding of the Wi-Fi world and how to protect themselves there:

> I did mention [the demonstration] to my fiancé, and I had to stop him at some point, because he ... tried to explain in detail, but .... I'm really not interested in technical details. (P5)

6.2 Creating Wi-Fi Security and Privacy Tools

Participants' reluctance to break from the naïve security paradigm might, at first, seem frustrating. However, through a better understanding of the paradigm of naïve security, one can imagine designing tools that educate users about risks based on analogies that they understand. Moreover, our results suggest that users appreciate learning about security via concrete, non-technical demonstrations, indicating the potential usefulness of such tools. Consider the following example. In spoken communication, we monitor our privacy by looking around to see who is close enough to overhear our conversation. Tools like Wi-Fi Radar that provide users with a radar display of nearby access points and the signal strengths associated with these access points could also display other wireless network interface cards (NICs) on the network. Combining this idea with Kowitz and Cranor's projected packet excerpts [15] could let Wi-Fi users know what others can hear and that others might be listening.

The challenge with tool design is that users still do not place a sufficiently high premium on privacy and security. When we explored attributes of security tools that participants might adopt during our interviews, participants noted that tools need to be cheap. Participants also did not want tools that slow their computer or require frequent interaction, describing security software as "just plain annoying" (P8):

> If [that tool] is not really expensive to buy .... Pretty sure I'll get it. If it's a product like a virus detector, a program that I [just] need to put in my computer. (P9)

I mean, given that nothing happened to me yet, I think my priorities would still be as long as it's convenient, it doesn't slow my computer down, stuff like that, right? (P1)

While challenges in tool design may seem insurmountable, some tools have met with broad consumer acceptance. Most users hate the User Account Control dialog in Vista ("A program needs your permission to continue ...") because it prompts them at what seems to be foolish times, but the "set and forget" attributes of Windows Firewall and most virus scanners have met with broad acceptance. Research has consistently demonstrated that if users can understand explanations, they are much more accepting of software [5]. Coupling explanations that incorporate concepts of naïve security with technologies such as peripheral or ambient displays [17], better awareness of user interruptibility [4], or more intelligent "detail on demand" could enhance acceptance of security tools.

7   Conclusion

In this paper we explore the rationale behind current Wi-Fi security practices and the factors that limit changes in user behavior. Together, our observations of naïve risk mitigation and user ingenuousness depict a domain of naïve security, where users apply superficial concepts of real-world privacy and security and real-world likelihood of risk to the Wi-Fi world. We argue that by understanding how and why users rationalize actions, we can approach security-tool design from a more user-centric perspective, educating users based on their current understanding and presenting information in new, more effective ways.

Acknowledgments. We thank the participants in our study. Funding for this research was provided by the Natural Science and Engineering Research Council of Canada, NSERC.

References

1. Ackerman, M.S., Cranor, L.F., Reagle, J.: Privacy in E-commerce: Examining User Scenarios and Privacy Preferences. In: ACM Electronic Commerce, EC 1999, pp. 1–8 (1999)
2. Acquisiti, A., Grossklags, J.: Privacy and Rationality in Individual Decision Making. In: IEEE Security and Privacy, pp. 26–33 (2005)
3. Adams, A., Sasse, M.A.: Users Are Not the Enemy. ACM Commun. 42(12), 40–46 (1999)
4. Avrahami, D., Fogarty, J., Hudson, S.E.: Biases in Human Estimation of Interruptibility: Effects and Implications for Practice. In: CHI 2007, pp. 50–60 (2007)
5. Bunt, A., Conati, C., McGrenere, J.: Supporting Interface Customization Using a Mixed-initiative Approach. In: IUI 2007, pp. 92–101 (2007)
6. Dhamija, R., Tygar, J.D., Hearst, M.: Why Phishing Works. In: CHI 2006, pp. 581–590 (2006)

7. Dourish, P., Anderson, K.: Collective Information Practice: Exploring Privacy and Security as Social and Cultural Phenomena. Human-computer Interaction 21(3), 319–342 (2006)
8. Dourish, P., Grinter, R., Delgado de la Flor, J., Joseph, M.: Security in the Wild: User Strategies for Managing Security as an Everyday, Practical Problem. Personal Ubiquitous Comput. 8(6), 391–401 (2004)
9. Flinn, S., Lumsden, J.: User Perceptions of Privacy and Security on the Web. In: PST 2005 (2005), http://www.lib.unb.ca/Texts/PST/2005/
10. Friedman, B., Hurley, D., Howe, D.C., Felten, E., Nissenbaum, H.: Users' Conceptions of Web Security: A Comparative Study. In: CHI 2002 Extended Abstracts, pp. 746–747 (2002)
11. Hart, D.: Attitudes and Practices of Students towards Password Security. J. Comput. Small Coll. 23(5), 169–174 (2008)
12. Kindberg, T., O'Neill, E., Bevan, C., Kostakos, V., Stanton Fraser, D., Jay, T.: Measuring Trust in Wi-Fi Hotspots. In: CHI 2008, pp. 173–182 (2008)
13. Kindberg, T., Sellen, A., Geelhoed, E.: Security and Trust in Mobile Interactions: A Study of Users' Perceptions and Reasoning. In: Davies, N., Mynatt, E.D., Siio, I. (eds.) UbiComp 2004. LNCS, vol. 3205, pp. 196–213. Springer, Heidelberg (2004)
14. Klasnja, P., Consolvo, S., Jung, J., Greenstein, B.M., LeGrand, L., Powledge, P., Wetherall, D.: When I am on Wi-Fi, I am Fearless: Privacy Concerns & Practices in Everyday Wi-Fi Use. In: CHI 2009, pp. 1993–2002 (2009)
15. Kowitz, B., Cranor, L.: Peripheral Privacy Notifications for Wireless Networks. In: WPES 2005, pp. 90–96. ACM, New York (2005)
16. Marlinspike, Moxie.: Null Prefix Attacks against SSL/TLS Certificates (2009), http://www.thoughtcrime.org/papers/null-prefix-attacks.pdf
17. Sankarpandian, K., Little, T., Edwards, W.K.: Talc: Using Desktop Graffiti to Fight Software Vulnerability. In: CHI 2008, pp. 1055–1064 (2008)
18. Solove, D.J.: 'I've Got Nothing to Hide' and Other Misunderstandings of Privacy. San Diego Law Review 44 (2007), http://ssrn.com/abstract=998565
19. Strauss, A., Corbin, J.M.: Basics of Qualitative Research: Techniques and Procedures for Developing Grounded Theory, 3rd edn. Sage Publications, Thousand Oaks (2007)
20. Viseu, A., Clement, A., Aspinall, J.: Situating Privacy Online: Complex Perceptions and Everyday Practice. Information Communication and Society 7(1), 92–114 (2004)
21. Wu, M., Miller, R.C., Garfinkel, S.L.: Do Security Toolbars Prevent Phishing Attacks? In: CHI 2006, pp. 601–610 (2006)

Securing Class Initialization

Keiko Nakata[1] and Andrei Sabelfeld[2]

[1] Institute of Cybernetics, Tallinn University of Technology, Tallinn, Estonia
[2] Chalmers University of Technology, Gothenburg, Sweden

Abstract. Language-based information-flow security is concerned with specifying and enforcing security policies for information flow via language constructs. Although much progress has been made on understanding information flow in object-oriented programs, the impact of class initialization on information flow has been so far largely unexplored. This paper turns the spotlight on security implications of class initialization. We discuss the subtleties of information propagation when classes are initialized and propose a formalization that illustrates how to track information flow in presence of class initialization by a type-and-effect system for a simple language. We show how to extend the formalization to a language with exception handling.

1 Introduction

Language-based concepts and techniques are becoming increasingly popular in the context of security [Koz99, SMH00, WAF00, SM03, Ler03, MSL+08, Cro09, Fac09] because they provide an appropriate level of abstraction for specifying and enforcing application and language-sensitive security policies. Popular examples include Java stack inspection [WAF00], which enforces a stack-based access-control discipline, and Java bytecode verification [Ler03], which traverses bytecode and verifies its type safety, as well as web language-based mechanisms such as Caja [MSL+08], ADsafe [Cro09], and FBJS [Fac09], which use program transformation and language subsets in order to enforce sandboxing and separation properties.

Language-based information-flow security [SM03] is concerned with specifying and enforcing security policies for information flow via language constructs. There has been much recent progress on understanding information flow in languages of increasing complexity [SM03], and, consequently, information-flow security tools for languages such as Java, ML, and Ada have emerged [MZZ+10, Sim03, Sys10]. In particular, information flow in object-oriented languages has been an area of intensive development [Mye99, BS99, BCG+02, ABF03, BFLM05, BN05, ABB06, Nau06, BRN06, HS09]. However, it is surprising that the impact of class initialization, being an important aspect of object-oriented programs, has received scarce attention in the context of security. In a language like Java, class initialization is *lazy*: classes are loaded as they are first used. This introduces challenges for information-flow tracking, in particular when class initialization may trigger initialization of other classes, which, for example, may include superclasses. Additional complexity is introduced by exceptions raised during initialization. Exceptions may be exploited to leak secret information.

M. Nishigaki et al. (Eds.): IFIPTM 2010, IFIP AICT 321, pp. 48–62, 2010.

Because of its power, Java's class loading mechanism [LB98] is a target for our model. A class is loaded, linked and initialized lazily on demand when the class is actively used for the first time [LY99] [1]. Moreover the programmer may define application-specific loading policies. Class loading constitutes one of the most compelling features of the Java platform.

This paper turns the spotlight on security implications of class initialization (and loading and liking, which are prerequisites for initialization). We discuss the subtleties of information propagation when classes are initialized. The key issue is that class initialization may perform side effects (such as opening a file or updating the memory). The side effects may be exploited by the attacker who may deduce from these side effects which classes have been (not) initialized, which is sometimes sufficient to learn secret information.

We propose a formalization that illustrates how to track information flow in presence of class initialization by a type-and-effect system for a simple language. By ensuring that classes may not be initialized inside conditionals and loops that branch on secret data, the type-and-effect system guarantees security in a form of *noninterference* [GM82]. We show how to extend the formalization to a language with exception handling. The only approach we are aware of that actually considers class initialization in the context of information-flow security is Jif [Mye99, MZZ$^+$10]. However, Jif's restrictions on code initialization are rather severe: this code is restricted to simple constant manipulation that may not raise any exceptions. Our treatment of class initialization is more liberal than Jif's and yet we demonstrate that it is secure. We argue that this liberty is sometimes desired in scenarios such as server-side code.

2   Background

This section presents informal considerations that lead up to a formalization in the following sections. For illustration purposes, we use a simple subset of Java with classes that contain static fields. We assume variables and class fields are partitioned into *high* (secret) and *low* (public). We assume that l and h are typical low and high variables, respectively. The security goal is to prevent programs from leaking initial values of secret data into final values of public data. The *context* corresponds to a body of a conditional or loop. We say that the context is *high* if the guard depends on a secret (i.e., contains a secret variable or field) and *low* otherwise.

Consider the following two class definitions for class names C and D with low fields g and f, respectively:

$$\text{class } C \{ \, g = 1 \, \}$$
$$\text{class } D \{ \, f = 1/C.g \, \}$$

Certainly the above definitions may be considered secure since no high data is involved. However, an attempt to instantiate an object of D may lead to an information leak:

$$P_0 : \quad C.g := 0;$$
$$\text{if } h = 0 \text{ then new } D \text{ else skip}$$

---

[1] The JVM specification permits the large flexibility as to the timing of loading and linking. But these activities must *appear* as if they happen on the class's (or interface's) first active use.

Indeed, the above program results in an error only when the high variable h initially contains 0, in which case the class D is initialized. Note that in the terminology we have introduced, the initialization occurs in high context. The attacker learns about the secret value of h by observing the termination behavior.

It is illustrative to compare the above program that leaks through termination behavior with the following one that does not:

$$P_1 : \quad \text{new } D;$$
$$C.g := 0;$$
$$\text{if } h = 0 \text{ then new } D \text{ else skip}$$

In this latter program, D is initialized before the assignment. More importantly, D has been initialized before it is used in high context: the second use does not incur any initialization activities.

In Java, when initialization of a class has completed abnormally by throwing some exception, the class is marked as erroneous. Initialization of a class in an erroneous state is not possible [LY99, Ch. 2] [2]. This makes initialization failure persistent in the sense that when initialization of a class failed on it first (active) use, then it will fail on the second use irrespective of the state in which the second initialization is attempted [3]. Catching initialization errors introduces a delicate scenario of information leaks. For instance, consider the following program:

$$P_2 : \quad C.g := 0;$$
$$\text{if } h = 0 \text{ then (try new } D \text{ catch skip) else skip};$$
$$C.g := 1;$$
$$\text{new } D$$

The above program again results in an error only when the high variable h initially contains 0. The next variation of the example shows how to exploit this flow so that the resulting program always terminates normally and reflects the initial value of h in the final value of l. Standard security type systems (e.g., [Mye99, PS03, HS06, AS09]) allow liberate handling of exceptions raised by expressions that are independent of secret data, as long as these expressions are used in public context. Since seemingly neither class definitions of C nor D involves high variables, one may be tempted to consider possible errors caused by initializing D as low. However, the following program illustrates the subtlety of the problem:

$$P_3 : \quad C.g := 0;$$
$$\text{if } h = 0 \text{ then (try new } D \text{ catch skip) else skip};$$
$$C.g := 1;$$
$$\text{try new } D; l := 1 \text{ catch } l := 0$$

The above program successfully terminates irrespective of the initial value at h, and the final value at l indicates whether h was 0 or not.

---

[2] To be precise, the *Class* object representing the class is labeled as erroneous.

[3] Initialization may recover for instance by resorting to garbage collection. But normally a class is eligible for unloading when the running application has no reference to the class.

Security might be compromised within correct, i.e., error-free, programs. Moreover class hierarchy also may impact on the security: before a class is initialized, its super-classes are initialized. For instance, consider class definitions below, involving only low fields.

$$\text{class } C_0 \{ g = 1 \}$$
$$\text{class } D_0 \{ f = C_0.g\text{++} \}$$
$$\text{class } D_1 \text{ extends } D_0 \{\}$$

The next program leaks the initial value of h into the final value of $C_0.g$.

$$P_4 : \quad \text{new } C_0;$$
$$\qquad \text{if } h = 0 \text{ then new } D_1 \text{ else skip}$$

Combining the two previous programs yields a scenario, where class hierarchy and persistence of initialization failure cooperate to leak information:

$$\text{class } C_0 \{ g = 1 \}$$
$$\text{class } D_0 \{ f = 1/C_0.g \}$$
$$\text{class } D_1 \text{ extends } D_0 \{\}$$

$$P_5 : \quad C_0.g := 0;$$
$$\qquad \text{if } h = 0 \text{ then } (\text{try new } D_1 \text{ catch skip}) \text{ else skip};$$
$$\qquad C_0.g := 1;$$
$$\qquad \text{try new } D_0; l := 1 \text{ catch } l := 0$$

Again the resulting program always terminates normally and reflects secret input values in the public results.

The bottom line is that class initialization may perform side effects, causing information to leak. One rather conservative approach to securing class initialization is to eliminate any possibilities of side effects during initialization and disallow errors due to initialization to be caught, an approach taken in Jif [Mye99, MZZ+10]. This approach rules out, among other, read and write access to instance as well as static fields, method calls and object creation during initialization. For example, a static field of a reference type may only be initialized to null, which would exclude some standard Java APIs [Sun], such as *(java.lang.)Boolean* and *String*, etc. Indeed Jif restricts (class) field initializers to simple constant manipulation that may not raise any exceptions. While it is rarely good practice to catch initialization errors within ordinary methods, such as methods in libraries, there are several scenarios where it is good practice to catch them, such as in server applications to avoid crashing the entire system due to third party applications or to log messages. For instance, Fortress, the primary product from the Excalibur software project [Exc], catches *LinkageError* and rethrows an object of a subclass of *Exception*, which may in turn be caught and logged.

This paper goes ahead to propose and formalize a different approach: we restrict class initialization in high contexts but allows side effects during initialization. Section 4 develops a type-and-effect system for a simple language, defined in Section 3. The type-and-effect system ensures a class has been initialized before it is used in high contexts and, as we show, guarantees information-flow security. Moreover, Section 5 shows how to scale our approach, when initialization errors are permitted to be caught. Section 6 discusses related work, and Section 7 concludes.

3   Language

We define the language for our formal study by the following syntax:

Expressions	$e ::= n \mid x \mid e_0 \; op \; e_1 \mid C.f$
Statements	$s ::= \mathsf{skip} \mid s_0; s_1 \mid x := e \mid C.f := e \mid \mathsf{if} \; e \; \mathsf{then} \; s_t \; \mathsf{else} \; s_f$
	$\mid \mathsf{while} \; e \; \mathsf{do} \; s_t$
Class definitions	$CL ::= \mathsf{class} \; C \; \{f_0 = e_0, \; \ldots, f_k = e_k\}$

Metavariables x, n, C and f range over variables, integers, class names and field names, respectively. We assume given a binary partial operator op on integers, i.e., op may signal an error. We write $n_0 \; op \; n_1 = \bullet$ when op signals an error on operands n_0 and n_1. A class definition class $C \; \{f_0 = e_0, \; \ldots, f_k = e_k\}$ declares a class name C consisting of the (static) fields f_i's with e_i's being initializing expressions. Then a class table CT is a (finite) mapping from class names to class definitions. A program is a pair (CT, s) of a class table and a statement. To lighten the notation, we assume a fixed class table CT hereafter.

A *state* (or *store*), ranged over by σ, maps variables to integers and class names to *abstract class objects*. An abstract class object, or simply class object, denotes the loaded status of a class name C in a state σ: C is uninitialized in σ when $\sigma(C) = \circ$; initialization is in progress or has been successfully completed when $\sigma(C) = \{f_0 = n_0, \ldots, f_k = n_k\}$, where f_i's are the fields of the class C; C has failed to initialize when $\sigma(C) = \bullet$. We write $uninitialized(\sigma)$ to denote the set of uninitialized classes in σ, i.e., $\{C \mid \sigma(C) = \circ\}$, $initialized(\sigma)$ the set of classes of which initialization is in progress or has been completed in σ, i.e., $\{C \mid \sigma(C) = \{f_1 = n_1, \ldots, f_k = n_k\}$ for some $f_1, \ldots, f_k, n_1, \ldots, n_k$, and $failed(\sigma)$ the set of classes that have failed to initialize, i.e., $\{C \mid \sigma(C) = \bullet\}$. When the context ensures C is in $initialized(\sigma)$, we may write $\sigma(C.f)$ to denote f-field of the class object for C in σ, i.e., $\sigma(C.f) = n$ where $\sigma(C) = \{\ldots, f = n, \ldots\}$, and $\sigma[C.f \mapsto n]$ to denote the update of f-field of the class object for C in σ by n.

Evaluation of expressions is given in Fig. 1. The relation $(\sigma, e) \downarrow (\sigma', n)$ states that the expression e in the state σ evaluates to the result n with the state being σ'. The relation $(\sigma, e) \uparrow \sigma'$ states that evaluating the expression e in the state σ fails in the state σ', signaling an error.

The inference rules in Fig. 1 are straightforward except those for reading from a field of a class. Both read and write access to a field of a class C triggers initialization of C. Class initializer $\rho(C, \sigma)$, to be defined below, initializes the class C in the state σ. If the initialization is in progress or has been successfully completed, written $\rho(\sigma, C) \downarrow \sigma'$, σ' contains a class object for C and evaluation of $C.f$ returns f-field of the class object. If the initialization fails, written $\rho(\sigma, C) \uparrow \sigma'$, so does the evaluation of $C.f$.

The small-step operational semantics for the statements is given in Fig. 2. The one-step reduction relation $\langle \sigma, s \rangle \rightarrow \langle \sigma', s' \rangle$ states that in the state σ the statement s one-step reduces to s' with the next state being σ'. The relation $\langle \sigma, s \rangle \rightarrow \langle \sigma', \bullet \rangle$ states that the statement s in the state σ signals an error in the state σ'. We write $\langle \sigma, s \rangle \downarrow \sigma'$, stating that s in the initial state σ successfully terminates in the final state σ'. Or, $\langle \sigma, s \rangle \downarrow \sigma'$ if $\langle \sigma, s \rangle \rightarrow^* \langle \sigma', \mathsf{skip} \rangle$, where $\rightarrow^*$ denotes the reflexive and transitive closure of $\rightarrow$.

$$\overline{(\sigma, n) \downarrow (\sigma, n)} \quad \overline{(\sigma, x) \downarrow (\sigma, \sigma(x))}$$

$$\frac{(\sigma, e_0) \downarrow (\sigma', n_0) \quad (\sigma', e_1) \downarrow (\sigma'', n_1) \quad n_0 \ op \ n_1 = n}{(\sigma, e_0 \ op \ e_1) \downarrow (\sigma'', n)}$$

$$\frac{(\sigma, e_0) \uparrow \sigma'}{(\sigma, e_0 \ op \ e_1) \uparrow \sigma'} \quad \frac{(\sigma, e_0) \downarrow (\sigma', n_0) \quad (\sigma', e_1) \uparrow \sigma''}{(\sigma, e_0 \ op \ e_1) \uparrow \sigma''}$$

$$\frac{(\sigma, e_0) \downarrow (\sigma', n_0) \quad (\sigma', e_1) \downarrow (\sigma'', n_1) \quad n_0 \ op \ n_1 = \bullet}{(\sigma, e_0 \ op \ e_1) \uparrow \sigma''}$$

$$\frac{\rho(\sigma, C) \downarrow \sigma'}{(\sigma, C.f) \downarrow (\sigma', \sigma'(C.f))} \quad \frac{\rho(\sigma, C) \uparrow \sigma'}{(\sigma, C.f) \uparrow \sigma'}$$

Fig. 1. Expression evaluation

Similarly we write $\langle \sigma, s \rangle \uparrow \sigma$, stating that s in the initial state σ abnormally terminates at the state σ'. Or, $\langle \sigma, s \rangle \uparrow \sigma'$ if $\langle \sigma, s \rangle \rightarrow^* \langle \sigma', \bullet \rangle$.

The inference rules for the one-step reduction relation are again straightforward. Assignment to a field of a class triggers initialization of the class, and thus may fail if the initialization fails.

Finally Fig. 3 defines the class initializer. If initialization of the class has been initiated and has not failed, i.e., $\sigma(C) = \{f_0 = n_0, \ldots, f_n = n_k\}$, then the initializer immediately returns. This covers both the cases that initialization is in progress and that initialization has been successfully completed. If initialization has previously failed, therefore the class object is in erroneous state, i.e., $\sigma(C) = \bullet$, then initialization is not possible. Otherwise, the initialization is initiated: the fields are first set to default values, namely 0, then updated according to their initializing expressions. The initialization may fail, in which case the class object is marked erroneous.

4 Specifying and Enforcing Security

We now introduce a security condition for our language and then develop a security type system for statically guaranteeing this condition.

4.1 Security Condition

As before, we assume a simple security lattice [Den76] consisting of only two levels *low* (public) and *high* (secret), with $low \sqsubseteq high$. Metavariables ℓ and pc range over security levels. Then a *security environment* Γ is a finite mapping from variables and pairs (C, f) of a class name and a field name of the class to their security levels. We extend Γ to expressions by assuming an expression is mapped to the least upper bound of the security levels that occur in it. Again, for the sake of notational simplicity, we assume a fixed security environment Γ in what follows.

$$\frac{(\sigma, e) \downarrow (\sigma', n)}{\langle \sigma, x := e \rangle \rightarrow \langle \sigma'[x \mapsto n], \mathsf{skip} \rangle}$$

$$\frac{(\sigma, e) \downarrow (\sigma', n) \quad \rho(\sigma', C) \downarrow \sigma''}{\langle \sigma, C.f := e \rangle \rightarrow \langle \sigma''[C.f \mapsto n], \mathsf{skip} \rangle}$$

$$\frac{(\sigma, e) \uparrow \sigma'}{\langle \sigma, C.f := e \rangle \rightarrow \langle \sigma', \bullet \rangle} \qquad \frac{(\sigma, e) \downarrow (\sigma', n) \quad \rho(\sigma', C) \uparrow \sigma''}{\langle \sigma, C.f := e \rangle \rightarrow \langle \sigma'', \bullet \rangle}$$

$$\overline{\langle \sigma, \mathsf{skip}; s \rangle \rightarrow \langle \sigma, s \rangle}$$

$$\frac{\langle \sigma, s_0 \rangle \rightarrow \langle \sigma', s_0' \rangle}{\langle \sigma, s_0; s_1 \rangle \rightarrow \langle \sigma', s_0'; s_1 \rangle} \qquad \frac{\langle \sigma, s_0 \rangle \rightarrow \langle \sigma', \bullet \rangle}{\langle \sigma, s_0; s_1 \rangle \rightarrow \langle \sigma', \bullet \rangle}$$

$$\frac{(\sigma, e) \downarrow (\sigma', n) \quad n \neq 0}{\langle \sigma, \mathsf{if}\ e\ \mathsf{then}\ s_t\ \mathsf{else}\ s_f \rangle \rightarrow \langle \sigma', s_t \rangle} \qquad \frac{(\sigma, e) \downarrow (\sigma', 0)}{\langle \sigma, \mathsf{if}\ e\ \mathsf{then}\ s_t\ \mathsf{else}\ s_f \rangle \rightarrow \langle \sigma', s_f \rangle}$$

$$\frac{(\sigma, e) \downarrow (\sigma', n) \quad n \neq 0}{\langle \sigma, \mathsf{while}\ e\ \mathsf{do}\ s_t \rangle \rightarrow \langle \sigma', s_t; \mathsf{while}\ e\ \mathsf{do}\ s_t \rangle} \qquad \frac{(\sigma, e) \downarrow (\sigma', 0)}{\langle \sigma, \mathsf{while}\ e\ \mathsf{do}\ s_t \rangle \rightarrow \langle \sigma', \mathsf{skip} \rangle}$$

$$\frac{(\sigma, e) \uparrow \sigma'}{\langle \sigma, Q[e] \rangle \rightarrow \langle \sigma', \bullet \rangle}$$

where $Q ::= x := [] \mid \mathsf{if}\ []\ \mathsf{then}\ s_t\ \mathsf{else}\ s_f \mid \mathsf{while}\ []\ \mathsf{do}\ s_t$

Fig. 2. Operational semantics for statements

$$\frac{\sigma(C) = \{f_0 = n_0, \dots, f_k = n_k\}}{\rho(\sigma, C) \downarrow \sigma} \qquad \frac{\sigma(C) = \bullet}{\rho(C, \sigma) \uparrow \sigma}$$

$$\frac{\sigma(C) = \circ \quad CT(C) = \mathsf{class}\ C\ \{f_0 = e_0, \dots, f_k = e_k\}}{\langle \sigma[C \mapsto \{f_0 = 0, \dots, f_k = 0\}], C.f_0 := e_0; \dots; C.f_k := e_k \rangle \downarrow \sigma'}{\rho(\sigma, C) \downarrow \sigma'}$$

$$\frac{\sigma(C) = \circ \quad CT(C) = \mathsf{class}\ C\ \{f_0 = e_0, \dots, f_k = e_k\}}{\langle \sigma[C \mapsto \{f_0 = 0, \dots, f_k = 0\}], C.f_0 := e_0; \dots; C.f_k := e_k \rangle \uparrow \sigma'}{\rho(C, \sigma) \uparrow \sigma'[C \mapsto \bullet]}$$

Fig. 3. Class initialization

Two states σ and σ' are *low-equivalent*, written $\sigma =_{low} \sigma'$, if they agree on low variables and fields and on class objects. Formally, $\sigma =_{low} \sigma'$ if the following three conditions hold:

- for any x such that $\Gamma(x) = low$, $\sigma(x) = \sigma'(x)$;
- *uninitialized*$(\sigma) = $ *uninitialized*(σ'), *initialized*$(\sigma) = $ *initialized*(σ'), and also *failed*$(\sigma) = $ *failed*(σ');
- for any C and f such that $\Gamma(C, f) = low$ and C is in *initialized*(σ), $\sigma(C.f) = \sigma'(C.f)$.

We adopt a commonly-used baseline policy of *termination-insensitive noninterference* [VSI96, SM03, PS03]. Intuitively, a program satisfies noninterference if for any two initial memories that agree on public data, whenever the program runs that start in these memories terminate, then these runs result in the memories that also agree on public data. This policy is an appropriate fit for batchjob programs, where leaks due to (non)termination are ignored because they may leak at most one bit per execution [AHSS08].

Definition 1. *A statement s satisfies termination-insensitive noninterference if, for any low-equivalent states σ_0 and σ_1, $\langle \sigma_0, s \rangle \downarrow \sigma_0'$ and $\langle \sigma_1, s \rangle \downarrow \sigma_1'$ imply $\sigma_0' =_{low} \sigma_1'$.*

4.2 Type System

Class initialization potentially performs low side effects. Therefore, we are going to prohibit class initialization in high contexts. Our type system essentially performs a must-analysis: a class must have been initialized before it is used in high contexts.

Fig. 4 presents typing rules for expressions. The judgment $pc \vdash e : \delta \hookrightarrow \delta'$ states that the expression e is typable at the security level pc with the effect type $\delta \hookrightarrow \delta'$. The pretype δ and the posttype δ', respectively, represent the classes that must have been initialized before and after the expression is evaluated. Effectively $pc \vdash e : \delta \hookrightarrow \delta'$ is read that the class names that occur in e must be in δ when pc is *high*, and δ' is the union of the class names that occur in e and δ. The type system may be made more permissive by computing, for each class C, the set of the classes that are necessarily initialized during the initialization of C.

Fig. 5 presents typing rules for statements. The judgment $pc \vdash s : \delta \hookrightarrow \delta'$ is read similarly to that for expressions. For example, the rule for assignment prevents explicit flows (such as $l := h$), *implicit* flows [DD77] via control structure (as in if $h = 0$ then $l := 0$ else $l := 1$) in a standard fashion [DD77, VSI96, SM03]. In addition, the effect type information is propagated from the expression to command level, and class initialization in high contexts is ruled out. For the posttype of if-statement, we take the intersection of the posttypes of the branches, collecting classes that must have been initialized irrespective of which branch is taken. Similarly, the posttype of while-statement only includes classes initialized by evaluating the boolean guard, since the loop-body might not be executed at all.

To state soundness with respect to the security condition, we must ensure that the type environment Γ is consistent with the class table CT.

Definition 2. *A type environment Γ is well-formed with respect to a class table CT if, for any class name C and a field f of C, $\Gamma(e) \sqsubseteq \Gamma(C, f)$ where $CT(C) = $ class $C \{\ldots, f = e, \ldots\}$.*

The existence of a well-formed environment ensures typability of the class table.

The type system is sound with respect to termination-insensitive noninterference:

Lemma 1. *Suppose Γ is well-formed with respect to CT. If $pc \vdash s : \delta \hookrightarrow \delta'$ and $\sigma_0 =_{low} \sigma_1$ and $\delta \subset initialized(\sigma_0) \cup failed(\sigma_0)$ and $\langle \sigma_0, s \rangle \downarrow \sigma_0'$ and $\langle \sigma_1, s \rangle \downarrow \sigma_1'$, then $\delta' \subseteq initialized(\sigma_0') \cup failed(\sigma_0')$ and $\sigma_0' =_{low} \sigma_1'$.*

Corollary 1. *If $pc \vdash s : \emptyset \hookrightarrow \delta$ then s satisfies noninterference.*

$$\overline{pc \vdash n : \delta \hookrightarrow \delta} \quad \overline{pc \vdash x : \delta \hookrightarrow \delta}$$

$$\frac{pc \vdash e_0 : \delta \hookrightarrow \delta_0 \quad pc \vdash e_1 : \delta \hookrightarrow \delta_1}{pc \vdash e_0 \; op \; e_1 : \delta \hookrightarrow \delta_0 \cup \delta_1}$$

$$\overline{low \vdash C.f : \delta \hookrightarrow \delta \cup \{C\}} \quad \frac{C \in \delta}{high \vdash C.f : \delta \hookrightarrow \delta}$$

Fig. 4. Typing of expressions

$$\overline{pc \vdash \mathsf{skip} : \delta \hookrightarrow \delta} \quad \frac{pc \vdash e : \delta \hookrightarrow \delta' \quad \Gamma(e) \sqsubseteq \Gamma(x) \quad pc \sqsubseteq \Gamma(x)}{pc \vdash x := e : \delta \hookrightarrow \delta'}$$

$$\frac{low \vdash e : \delta \hookrightarrow \delta' \quad \Gamma(e) \sqsubseteq \Gamma(C.f)}{low \vdash C.f := e : \delta \hookrightarrow \delta' \cup \{C\}}$$

$$\frac{C \in \delta \quad high \vdash e : \delta \hookrightarrow \delta' \quad \Gamma(e) \sqsubseteq \Gamma(C.f) \quad high \sqsubseteq \Gamma(C.f)}{high \vdash C.f := e : \delta \hookrightarrow \delta'}$$

$$\frac{pc \vdash s_0 : \delta_0 \hookrightarrow \delta_1 \quad pc \vdash s_1 : \delta_1 \hookrightarrow \delta_2}{pc \vdash s_0; s_1 : \delta_0 \hookrightarrow \delta_2}$$

$$\frac{pc \vdash e : \delta \hookrightarrow \delta' \quad pc \sqcup \Gamma(e) \vdash s_t : \delta' \hookrightarrow \delta_0 \quad pc \sqcup \Gamma(e) \vdash s_f : \delta' \hookrightarrow \delta_1}{pc \vdash \mathsf{if} \; e \; \mathsf{then} \; s_t \; \mathsf{else} \; s_f : \delta \hookrightarrow \delta_0 \cap \delta_1}$$

$$\frac{pc \vdash e : \delta \hookrightarrow \delta' \quad pc \sqcup \Gamma(e) \vdash s_t : \delta' \hookrightarrow \delta''}{pc \vdash \mathsf{while} \; e \; \mathsf{do} \; s_t : \delta \hookrightarrow \delta'}$$

Fig. 5. Typing of statements

5   Exception Handling

This section extends our system with an exception handling mechanism. The Java virtual machine throws an object that is an instance of a subclass of *LinkageError* when a loading, linkage, preparation, verification or initialization error occurs [GJSB96, Ch. 11]. *LinkageError* is a subclass of *Error*, rather than *Exception*. *Error* is designed in principle to indicate serious problems, and ordinary applications, such as library programs, are not expected to catch *Error*. However, as we argued in Section 2, there are several scenarios where catching *Error* is desirable such as in server applications to avoid crashing the entire system or to log messages. Therefore, we are motivated to develop a security type system which allows errors due to class initialization to be caught, while rejecting attacks that leak information through exception handling.

5.1   Operational Semantics

We extend the syntax of the statements with try s_0 catch s_1, whose operational semantics is given in Fig. 6.

$$\overline{\langle \sigma, \text{try skip catch } s \rangle \rightarrow \langle \sigma, \text{skip} \rangle}$$

$$\frac{\langle \sigma, s_0 \rangle \rightarrow \langle \sigma', s_0' \rangle}{\langle \sigma, \text{try } s_0 \text{ catch } s_1 \rangle \rightarrow \langle \sigma', \text{try } s_0' \text{ catch } s_1 \rangle}$$

$$\frac{\langle \sigma, s_0 \rangle \rightarrow \langle \sigma', \bullet \rangle}{\langle \sigma, \text{try } s_0 \text{ catch } s_1 \rangle \rightarrow \langle \sigma', s_1 \rangle}$$

Fig. 6. Operational semantics for exception handling

$$\overline{pc \vdash n : \delta \hookrightarrow \delta :: low} \qquad \overline{pc \vdash x : \delta \hookrightarrow \delta :: low}$$

$$\frac{pc \vdash e_0 : \delta \hookrightarrow \delta_0 :: \ell_0 \quad pc \vdash e_1 : \delta \hookrightarrow \delta_1 :: \ell_1}{pc \vdash e_0 \; op \; e_1 : \delta \hookrightarrow \delta_0 \cup \delta_1 :: pc \sqcup \ell_0 \sqcup \ell_1 \sqcup \Gamma(e_0) \sqcup \Gamma(e_1)}$$

$$\overline{low \vdash C.f : \delta \hookrightarrow \delta \cup \{C\} :: \Gamma(C)}$$

$$\frac{C \in \delta}{high \vdash C.f : \delta \hookrightarrow \delta :: high}$$

Fig. 7. Typing of expressions for exception handling

$$\overline{pc \vdash \text{skip} : \delta \hookrightarrow \delta :: low}$$

$$\frac{pc \vdash e : \delta \hookrightarrow \delta' :: \ell \quad \Gamma(e) \sqsubseteq \Gamma(x) \quad pc \sqsubseteq \Gamma(x)}{pc \vdash x := e : \delta \hookrightarrow \delta :: \ell}$$

$$\frac{low \vdash e : \delta \hookrightarrow \delta' :: \ell \quad \Gamma(e) \sqsubseteq \Gamma(C.f)}{low \vdash C.f := e : \delta \hookrightarrow \delta' \cup \{C\} :: \ell \sqcup \Gamma(C)}$$

$$\frac{C \in \delta \quad high \vdash e : \delta \hookrightarrow \delta' :: \ell \quad \Gamma(e) \sqsubseteq \Gamma(C.f) \quad high \sqsubseteq \Gamma(C.f)}{high \vdash C.f := e : \delta \hookrightarrow \delta' :: high}$$

$$\frac{pc \vdash s_0 : \delta_0 \hookrightarrow \delta_1 :: \ell_0 \quad pc \sqcup \ell_0 \vdash s_1 : \delta_1 \hookrightarrow \delta_2 :: \ell_1}{pc \vdash s_0; s_1 : \delta_0 \hookrightarrow \delta_2 :: \ell_0 \sqcup \ell_1}$$

$$\frac{pc \vdash e : \delta \hookrightarrow \delta' :: \ell \qquad \Gamma(e) \sqcup \ell \sqcup pc \vdash s_t : \delta' \hookrightarrow \delta_0 :: \ell_0 \quad \Gamma(e) \sqcup \ell \sqcup pc \vdash s_f : \delta' \hookrightarrow \delta_1 :: \ell_1}{pc \vdash \text{if } e \text{ then } s_t \text{ else } s_f : \delta \hookrightarrow \delta_0 \cap \delta_1 :: \ell \sqcup \ell_0 \sqcup \ell_1}$$

$$\frac{pc \vdash e : \delta \hookrightarrow \delta' :: \ell \quad \Gamma(e) \sqcup \ell \sqcup pc \vdash s_t : \delta' \hookrightarrow \delta'' :: \ell'}{pc \vdash \text{while } e \text{ do } s_t : \delta \hookrightarrow \delta' :: \ell \sqcup \ell'}$$

$$\frac{pc \vdash s_0 : \delta \hookrightarrow \delta' :: \ell_0 \quad pc \sqcup \ell_0 \vdash s_1 : \delta \hookrightarrow \delta' :: \ell_1}{pc \vdash \text{try } s_0 \text{ catch } s_1 : \delta \hookrightarrow \delta' :: \ell_1}$$

Fig. 8. Typing of statements for exception handling

5.2 Type System

Fig. 7 and Fig. 8 give typing rules for expressions and statements, respectively. We extend the type environment Γ to map class names to the security levels of the exceptions that may be raised during initialization. We have to adjust the definition of well-formed type environments:

Definition 3. *A type environment Γ is well-formed with respect to a class table CT if, for any class name C and a field name f of C such that $CT(C) =$ class C $\{\ldots, f = e, \ldots\}$, we have*

- $\Gamma(e) \sqsubseteq \Gamma(C, f)$;
- *if $low \vdash e : \delta \hookrightarrow \delta' :: \ell$ then $\ell \sqsubseteq \Gamma(C)$.*

We note that initialization failure of a class having high fields may be low and a class having only low fields may be high, as the following example illustrates:

$$\text{class } C_0 \ \{ \ g = 4, \ f = 1 \ op \ 0 \ \}$$
$$\text{class } C_1 \ \{ \ g = 1 \ op \ 0, \ f = 1 \ \}$$
$$\text{class } C_2 \ \{ \ f = C_1.f \ \}$$

A type environment Γ such that $\Gamma(C_0) = \Gamma(C_0, f) = \Gamma(C_1, f) = \Gamma(C_2, f) = low$ and $\Gamma(C_1) = \Gamma(C_2) = \Gamma(C_0, g) = \Gamma(C_1, g) = high$ is well-formed with respect to the class table corresponding to the above class definitions.

Having noticed the above subtlety, the typing rules in Fig. 7 and Fig. 8 are straightforward adaptation from type systems that track information flow in the presence of exceptions (e.g., [Mye99, PS03, HS06, AS09]). The new form of judgment $pc \vdash e : \delta \hookrightarrow \delta' :: \ell$ for expressions (resp. $pc \vdash s : \delta \hookrightarrow \delta' :: \ell$ for statements) indicates the level ℓ of an exception that the expression e (resp. the statement s) may throw in the context pc.

For expression typing, $pc \vdash e : \delta \hookrightarrow \delta' :: low$ is derivable if either e does not throw an exception, or else pc is low and for any class C that occurs in e, $\Gamma(C) = low$ and, for any subexpression e' of e that is an operand of op, $\Gamma(e') = low$. Suppose $\Gamma(x) = high$, for instance, then $high \vdash x : \emptyset \hookrightarrow \emptyset :: low$ and $low \vdash x \ op \ n : \emptyset \hookrightarrow \emptyset :: high$ are derived. Notice that the security level of x is propagated to the security level of an exception only if the value of x may affect whether or not an exception is thrown.

We look at the inference rules for typing of statements. Since skip does not throw an exception, its exception level is low. The exception level of an assignment $x := e$ is that of the expression e at pc. For the exception level of an assignment to a field of a class, $C.f := e$ at low program context, we take the upper bound of the exception level of e at low and $\Gamma(C)$. More importantly, the exception level of $C.f := e$ in high program context is necessarily $high$, even if e does not throw an exception. This is because initialization of C may be triggered *and* fail, if it has previously failed, as illustrated by the following program, where f is low and g is high.

$$\text{class } C \ \{ \ f = 1/0, \ g = 1 \ \}$$

```
try C.f := 1 catch skip;
try (if h = 0 then C.g := 0 else skip) catch l := 1
```

The above program is insecure and indeed rejected by our type system.

For the sequence statement, we prohibit s_1 from performing side effects lower than the level of exceptions that s_0 may throw. Rules for if- and while-statements are similar. The exception levels of the boolean guards are propagated to branches. In try-statement, the catch clause must not perform side effects lower than the exception level of the try block. Note that the exception level of the whole statement is ℓ_1, the exception level of the catch clause.

Proposition 1. *If* $pc \vdash s : \emptyset \hookrightarrow \delta :: \ell$ *then* s *satisfies noninterference.*

We now come back to the examples in Section 2. Since none of the class definitions from Section 2 involves high fields, they are typable with respect to an obvious type environment Γ mapping all the classes and class-field pairs to low. We keep the convention that $\Gamma(l) = low$ and $\Gamma(h) = high$. All the programs but P_1 are not typable. For P_1, we have $low \vdash P_1 : \emptyset \hookrightarrow \{D\} :: high$. Note that the programs P_0, P_1 and P_2 satisfy noninterference, but P_3, P_4 and P_5 do not (assuming the operational semantics is appropriately extended to take class hierarchy into account).

6 Related Work

A survey [SM03] on language-based information-flow security contains an overview of the area. Most related to ours is work on tracking information flow in object-oriented languages and on information-flow controls in the presence of exceptions.

Objects. To the best of our knowledge, the only information-flow mechanism that addresses class initialization is the one implemented by Jif [Mye99, MZZ+10], a compiler for Java extended with security types. As discussed earlier, Jif is rather conservative about class initialization code. This code is restricted to simple constant manipulation that may not raise any exceptions. As mentioned earlier, sometimes it is desirable to lift these restrictions.

Much other work has been done on information-flow security for object-oriented languages. Although none of the approaches directly addresses problems with class initialization, we nevertheless discuss some recent highlights.

Barthe and Serpette [BS99] present a type system for enforcing information-flow security in a simple object-oriented language based on the Abadi–Cardelli functional object calculi [AC96]. Bieber et al. [BCG+02] apply model-checking for securing information flow in smartcard applets.

Avvenuti et al. [ABF03] suggest an information-flow analysis in a language similar to Java bytecode. Bernardeschi et al. [BFLM05] check information-flow security in Java bytecode by a combination of program transformation and bytecode verification. These two approaches assume fixed security levels for classes. This might not be a flexible choice since it forces all instances and attributes to conform to the class level. Another concern is the scalability of this choice in presence of inheritance.

Banerjee and Naumann [BN05] show how to guarantee noninterference by a type-based analysis for a Java-like imperative language with objects. Amtoft et al. [ABB06] present a flow-sensitive logic for reasoning about information flow in the presence of pointers. Naumann [Nau06] investigates invariant-based verification of information-flow properties in a language with heaps. Barthe and Rezk [BR05] consider type-based enforcement of secure information flow in Java bytecode-like languages. Barthe et al. [BRN06] extend this work to derive an information-flow certifying compiler for a Java-like language.

Hammer and Snelting [HS09] develop a flow-sensitive, context-sensitive, and object-sensitive framework for controlling information flow by program dependence graphs. This approach takes advantage of similarities of information-flow and slicing analyses.

Exceptions. As noted earlier, our treatment of exception handling draws on standard approaches from the literature (which we extend with the must-analysis). The intuition is if an occurrence of an exception in a statement may carry sensitive information, then there must be no publicly-observable side effects in either the code that handles the exception or in the code between the statement and the exception-handling block. Jif [Mye99, MZZ+10] implements such a discipline. Based on a similar discipline, Pottier and Simonet [PS03] propose a sound treatment of exceptions for ML.

Barthe and Rezk [BR05] treat a single type of exceptions in a JVM-like language. Barthe et al. [BPR07] extend this approach to multiple types of catchable exceptions. Connecting this with security-type preserving compilation, Barthe et al. [BRN06] show how to securely compile a source language with a single type of catchable exceptions to the low-level language of Barthe and Rezk [BR05].

Hedin and Sands [HS06] prove a noninterference property for a type system that tracks information flow via class-cast and null-pointer exceptions in a language with non-opaque pointers. Askarov and Sabelfeld [AS09] show how to achieve permissive yet secure exception handling by providing the choice for each type of exception: either the traditional discipline discussed above or by consistently disallowing to catch exceptions. The actual choice for each kind of exception is given to the programmer.

7   Conclusion

Seeking to shed light on a largely unexplored area, we have presented considerations for and a formalization of secure class initialization. Our considerations highlight that class initialization poses challenges for security since controlling (the order of) side effects performed by class initialization is challenging. Hence, great care needs to be taken by information-flow enforcement mechanisms to guarantee security. One path, taken by Jif [Mye99, MZZ+10], is to severely restrict class initialization code so that it may only manipulate constants in an exception-free manner. Arguing that it is sometimes too restrictive, we have explored another path: allow powerful initialization code, but disallow class initialization inside conditionals and loops that branch on secret data. This approach has the advantage that the side effects in class initialization do not have to be predicted since they may not carry sensitive information in the first place: the attacker may not deduce anything interesting from observing these side effects anyway.

Our formalization demonstrates the idea by a type-and-effect system for a simple language that enforces noninterference. To the best of our knowledge, it is the first formal approach to the problem of secure class initialization. (Soundness of Jif's class initialization is yet to be established).

Future work includes an extension to handle class hierarchies. We believe our approach of ruling out class initialization in high contexts is sound in the presence of class hierarchies. To extend our technical results to class hierarchies, we only need to adjust the operational semantics so that when a class is initialized, all its (uninitialized) super classes are initialized. Based on the results of the paper, we are currently working on more sophisticated type systems that allow initialization of *high* classes in high contexts.

Acknowledgments. K. Nakata acknowledges the support of action IC0701 of COST, the Estonian Centre of Excellence in Computer Science, EXCS, financed mainly by ERDF, and the Estonian Science Foundation grant no. 6940. A. Sabelfeld is supported by the Swedish research agencies SSF and VR.

References

[ABB06]   Amtoft, T., Bandhakavi, S., Banerjee, A.: A logic for information flow in object-oriented programs. In: Proc. ACM Symp. on Principles of Programming Languages, pp. 91–102 (2006)

[ABF03]   Avvenuti, M., Bernardeschi, C., De Francesco, N.: Java bytecode verification for secure information flow. SIGPLAN Notices 38(12), 20–27 (2003)

[AC96]   Abadi, M., Cardelli, L.: A Theory of Objects. Monographs in Computer Science. Springer, New York (1996)

[AHSS08]   Askarov, A., Hunt, S., Sabelfeld, A., Sands, D.: Termination-insensitive noninterference leaks more than just a bit. In: Jajodia, S., Lopez, J. (eds.) ESORICS 2008. LNCS, vol. 5283, pp. 333–348. Springer, Heidelberg (2008)

[AS09]   Askarov, A., Sabelfeld, A.: Catch me if you can: Permissive yet secure error handling. In: Proc. ACM Workshop on Programming Languages and Analysis for Security (PLAS) (June 2009)

[BCG+02]   Bieber, P., Cazin, J., Girard, P., Lanet, J.-L., Zanon, G.: Checking secure interactions of smart card applets: extended version. J. Computer Security 10(4), 369–398 (2002)

[BFLM05]   Bernardeschi, C., De Francesco, N., Lettieri, G., Martini, L.: Checking secure information flow in java bytecode by code transformation and standard bytecode verification. Software: Practice and Experience 34, 1225–1255 (2005)

[BN05]   Banerjee, A., Naumann, D.A.: Stack-based access control and secure information flow. Journal of Functional Programming 15(2), 131–177 (2005)

[BPR07]   Barthe, G., Pichardie, D., Rezk, T.: A certified lightweight non-interference java bytecode verifier. In: De Nicola, R. (ed.) ESOP 2007. LNCS, vol. 4421, pp. 125–140. Springer, Heidelberg (2007)

[BR05]   Barthe, G., Rezk, T.: Non-interference for a jvm-like language. In: Proc. Types in Language Design and Implementation, pp. 103–112 (2005)

[BRN06]   Barthe, G., Rezk, T., Naumann, D.: Deriving an information flow checker and certifying compiler for java. In: Proc. IEEE Symp. on Security and Privacy, pp. 230–242 (2006)

[BS99]   Barthe, G., Serpette, B.: Partial evaluation and non-interference for object calculi. In: Middeldorp, A. (ed.) FLOPS 1999. LNCS, vol. 1722, pp. 53–67. Springer, Heidelberg (1999)

[Cro09]   Crockford, D.: Making javascript safe for advertising. adsafe.org (2009)

[DD77]   Denning, D.E., Denning, P.J.: Certification of programs for secure information flow. Comm. of the ACM 20(7), 504–513 (1977)

[Den76]   Denning, D.E.: A lattice model of secure information flow. Comm. of the ACM 19(5), 236–243 (1976)

[Exc]   Excalibur. Documentation and Software,
            http://excalibur.apache.org/index.html
[Fac09]   Facebook. FBJS (2009),
            http://wiki.developers.facebook.com/index.php/FBJS
[GJSB96]   Gosling, J., Joy, B., Steele, G., Bracha, G.: The Java^{TM} Language Specification.
            Addison-Wesley, Reading (1996)
[GM82]   Goguen, J.A., Meseguer, J.: Security policies and security models. In: Proc. IEEE
            Symp. on Security and Privacy, April 1982, pp. 11–20 (1982)
[HS06]   Hedin, D., Sands, D.: Noninterference in the presence of non-opaque pointers. In:
            Proc. IEEE Computer Security Foundations Workshop, pp. 255–269 (2006)
[HS09]   Hammer, C., Snelting, G.: Flow-sensitive, context-sensitive, and object-sensitive in-
            formationflow control based on program dependence graphs. International Journal
            of Information Security 8(6), 399–422 (2009); Supersedes ISSSE and ISoLA 2006
[Koz99]   Kozen, D.: Language-based security. In: Kutyłowski, M., Wierzbicki, T., Pacholski,
            L. (eds.) MFCS 1999. LNCS, vol. 1672, pp. 284–298. Springer, Heidelberg (1999)
[LB98]   Liang, S., Bracha, G.: Dynamics class loading in the Java virtual machine. In: Proc.
            ACM SIGPLAN Conference on Object-Oriented Programming Systems, Languages
            & Applications, pp. 36–44 (1998)
[Ler03]   Leroy, X.: Java bytecode verification: algorithms and formalizations. J. Automated
            Reasoning 30(3–4), 235–269 (2003)
[LY99]   Lindholm, T., Yellin, F.: The Java^{TM} Virtual Machine Specification, 2nd edn.
            Addison-Wesley, Reading (1999)
[MSL^{+}08]   Miller, M., Samuel, M., Laurie, B., Awad, I., Stay, M.: Caja: Safe active content in
            sanitized javascript (2008)
[Mye99]   Myers, A.C.: JFlow: Practical mostly-static information flow control. In: Proc. ACM
            Symp. on Principles of Programming Languages, January 1999, pp. 228–241 (1999)
[MZZ^{+}10]   Myers, A.C., Zheng, L., Zdancewic, S., Chong, S., Nystrom, N.: Jif: Java informa-
            tion flow. Software release (2001– 2010),
            http://www.cs.cornell.edu/jif
[Nau06]   Naumann, D.: From coupling relations to mated invariants for checking informa-
            tion flow. In: Gollmann, D., Meier, J., Sabelfeld, A. (eds.) ESORICS 2006. LNCS,
            vol. 4189, pp. 279–296. Springer, Heidelberg (2006)
[PS03]   Pottier, F., Simonet, V.: Information flow inference for ML. ACM TOPLAS 25(1),
            117–158 (2003)
[Sim03]   Simonet, V.: The Flow Caml system. Software release (July 2003),
            http://cristal.inria.fr/~simonet/soft/flowcaml
[SM03]   Sabelfeld, A., Myers, A.C.: Language-based information-flow security. IEEE J. Se-
            lected Areas in Communications 21(1), 5–19 (2003)
[SMH00]   Schneider, F.B., Morrisett, G., Harper, R.: A language-based approach to security.
            In: Wilhelm, R. (ed.) Informatics: 10 Years Back, 10 Years Ahead. LNCS, vol. 2000,
            pp. 86–101. Springer, Heidelberg (2001)
[Sun]   Java 2 platform, standard edition 5.0, API specification,
            http://java.sun.com/j2se/1.5.0/docs/api/
[Sys10]   Praxis High Integrity Systems. Sparkada examinar. Software release (2010),
            http://www.praxis-his.com/sparkada
[VSI96]   Volpano, D., Smith, G., Irvine, C.: A sound type system for secure flow analysis. J.
            Computer Security 4(3), 167–187 (1996)
[WAF00]   Wallach, D.S., Appel, A.W., Felten, E.W.: The security architecture formerly known
            as stack inspection: A security mechanism for language-based systems. ACM Trans-
            actions on Software Engineering and Methodology 9(4), 341–378 (2000)

xESB: An Enterprise Service Bus for Access and Usage Control Policy Enforcement*

Gabriela Gheorghe, Stephan Neuhaus, and Bruno Crispo

Università degli Studi di Trento, I-38100 Trento, Italy
First.Last@disi.unitn.it

Abstract. Enforcing complex policies that span organizational domains is an open challenge. Current work on SOA policy enforcement splits security in logical components that can be distributed across domains, but does not offer any concrete solution to *integrate* this security functionality so that it works across security services for organization-wide policies. In this paper, we propose xESB, an enhanced version of an Enterprise Message Bus (ESB), where we monitor and enforce preventive and reactive policies, both for access control and usage control policies, and both inside one domain and between domains. In addition, we introduce indicators that help SOA administrators assess the effectiveness of their policies. Our performance measurements show that policy enforcement at the ESB level comes with only moderate penalties.

1 Introduction

As Service-oriented architectures (SOAs) expand, they need to interconnect and adapt to increasing business and infrastructural demands. These intercommunication and interconnection requirements are met by a piece of middleware called the Enterprise Service Bus (ESB). The ESB offers a standard way to connect services by acting as a message hub, making interservice communication smooth and painless. But this ease of use comes with a downside: when businesses expose their services in order to participate in an SOA, they face increased risks of misuse or abuse. What is therefore needed is a way to formulate and enforce policies that make such misuse or abuse impossible.

However, ESBs do not address non-functional aspects such as security, so what protects messages in transit and makes security decisions based on them? Since ESB components are using the bus as a low-level service which abstracts communication details from the higher-level services, we believe that it is the ESB that should be in charge of enforcing message-level policies.

There are two main aspects in which current work in SOA policy enforcement falls short of this expectation. First, the majority of existing work locates policy enforcement inside an orchestration engine such as BPEL, but such a view is not suited to scenarios where policies concern the service request or response

---

* This work is supported by the European Commission under the project EU-FP7-IST-IP-MASTER.

M. Nishigaki et al. (Eds.): IFIPTM 2010, IFIP AICT 321, pp. 63–78, 2010.

messages themselves instead of the effect they have on the business process. Second, current approaches focus mostly on simple access control policies instead of complex organization-wide policies that also include usage control.

Another problem, one that plagues administrators of SOAs, is whether security policies perform as they should. The state of the art is to pepper the deployed services with debugging output, but this is clearly unsatisfactory, if not completely infeasible, for example when using third-party services.

This paper addresses all three issues by implementing flexible, instrumentable, and highly configurable policy enforcement mechanisms at the ESB level. We also cover access as well as usage control policies that can span the entire organization: our enforcement mechanisms implement *reactions* to violations in addition to traditional access control. Additionally, we augment policies with *indicators* that our ESB continuously monitors in order to measure how well the policies perform. By providing a unified and service-independent way to aggregate data, indicators help administrators understand, at run-time, why policies fail.

Besides addressing the issues of regulating message flow and allowing organisation-wide policies, our work also decouples the enforcement logic from the business logic. This way, process and application designers can focus on the business aspects of their applications and how they must be used, but not how this is technically enforced. Thus our contributions can be summarized as follows:

- A *new approach* for security policy enforcement for SOA (Sect. 4).
- A *working prototype implementation of* xESB, (Sect. 5), that has *low overhead* (Sect. 8).
- Support for *reactive policies*, and for *usage control policies* (Sect. 6).
- Support for *indicators* to help monitoring policies (Sect. 7).

The remainder of this paper is organized as follows. After showing our supporting case study (Sect. 2) and some background on the ESB platform (Sect. 3), we motivate why policy enforcement on the ESB is needed (Sect. 4). After that, we introduce our xESB prototype (Sect. 5) and briefly present the language we used to write our policies (Sect. 6). We next give an overview of some possible enforcement indicators (Sect. 7), and present a performance evaluation (Sect. 8). We finish with a review of related work (Sect. 9) and a discussion of future work and conclusions (Sect. 10).

2   Motivating Example

As motivating example to illustrate the design and features of xESB, we consider a hypothetical company 'Foo.uk', providing VoIP-based services using a communication platform implemented as a SOA using an ESB. While Foo.uk is hypothetical, the problems it faces definitely are not. For example, Zimmermann et al. published a large case study in which a "large telecommunication wholesaler" switches to BPEL and SOA, so it is clear that the wholesaler will also have to face security issues at the SOA level [1]. However, giving examples from actual companies would give much extraneous detail not relevant to this paper, and we have therefore stripped the examples down so that the relevant problems and their solutions can be exposed more clearly.

Since Foo.uk operates in the UK, it must comply with regulations such as those described in the Statutory Instrument 2003 No. 2426 [2] implementing the Privacy and Electronic Communications EC Directive [3]. In order to do so, the Foo.uk platform must be able to enforce policies such as "Log starting time and duration of incoming calls" or "Hide initiator number in outgoing calls".

For the first policy, a simple mechanism should signal the start of a call and its duration. Capturing and logging these events should leave the application unaltered. What is therefore required is a control that is able to *filter* messages and to *duplicate* them to a logging service. For the second policy, a mechanism is needed to *filter* outgoing calls from incoming ones. This can be achieved simply by looking at the type and parameters of the event (either a service invocation or a service response) and then *modifying* those that identify the initiator. In addition, for business purposes Foo.uk must be able to enforce also policies like:

Silver customers can use premium services only for 3 hours a month.
If the control service assigns special message identification that can easily differentiate between subscriber types and call types, Foo.uk needs logic to infer the duration of a call for a specified amount of time. Anytime a silver customer would request a video call, the request should not be serviced unless the 3 hours a month have not been exceeded. Thus, the service response depends on whether a predicate is satisfied or not.

Process collect calls only after destination has agreed to pay. Similar to the previous case, verifying a condition in this case means ensuring that something has happened in the past: the VoIP destination must have accepted to pay for the call. This predicate needs to be checked only before replying to a collect call request: the response is delayed until the destination either explicitly accepts or rejects the payment or times out (which should be construed as rejection).

Delay high-quality calls until resources are available. Assuming a VoIP user requests high quality parameters for a call, a load-balancer component of the SOA would have the authority to *delay* the service request until it allocates the resources needed for such a situation.

Enacting the rules above can be done by a dedicated component acting as gateway for rule compliance: as an infrastructure component, it would interpose between the VoIP provider and the service clients. Having an application-level module in charge of this would be inefficient because the above policies do not directly relate to application logic; they concern legal issues that the VoIP communication protocol should obey, irrespective of its conceptual design or its architecture. These issues, or constraints, can be more frequently subject to change (or update), than the overall SOA application. We argue that it is best to separate the constraint checking functionality from the business application in such a way that the former can easily *adapt to new organizational requirements*. If a new business or regulatory policy would replace an existing one (e.g., not hide, but *encrypt* initiator number in outgoing calls), then the changes on the enforcement logic should be as light as changing a service endpoint (from one that hides data to one that encrypts data). This behavior would be in complete resonance with the concepts of service-orientation and reuse, because it brings a clear decoupling between service logic and service security. Such a separation has not been previously addressed at the message level, and our solution benefits from this approach in that the prototype is not *hardcoded* to a specific decision making or enforcement component; any trusted security components of these types can be plugged in.

3   The ESB in the Service-Oriented Architecture

The ESB is a middleware placed between the various services of an SOA application. It offers a layer of communication and integration logic in order to mitigate technology disparities between communication parties, ranging from intelligent routing to XML data transformation.

Java Business Integration (JBI) [4] standardizes deployment and management of services deployed on an ESB. It describes how applications need to be built in order to be integrated easily. The generic JBI architecture is shown in Figure 1 (left). Since the primary function of the ESB is message mediation, the Normalized Message Router (NMR) is the core of the JBI-ESB and provides the infrastructure for all message exchanges once they are transformed into a normalized form. Components deployed onto the bus can be either service engines, which encapsulate business logic and transformation services; or binding components, which connect external services to the JBI environment.

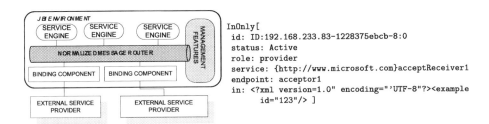

Fig. 1. The architecture of the JBI system (left) and example of a normalized message in an InOnly exchange (right)

4   The Enforcement Process

The runtime enforcement process starts the moment a message is intercepted. Once obtained, the event is evaluated against the deployed security policies; the result is a decision that the enforcer translates into a series of actions; the enforcement process is in charge of performing those actions (either directly or by delegating them to a trusted third party). This section describes how we modeled the policy enforcement process that we later implemented in xESB.

The policy language and its interpretation are the subject of Section 6.

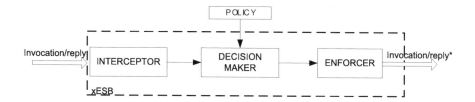

Fig. 2. The enforcement process behind xESB

4.1   Interception

Enforcement starts by intercepting messages to which at least one policy applies. The policies dictate what message types and parameters to look at: message destination, source, size, or metadata like annotation information. Irrespective of the message format (usually XML-based), the elements described above are usually easy to inspect on every message simply because all messages on the bus have the same format. A prefiltering mechanism can help the interceptor catch messages with a higher probability of being relevant than any other message; for instance, if a policy refers to requests that are simultaneously outgoing *and* have a valid security signature, then the interceptor could just check if the current call is outgoing. This is a condition which is inexpensive to check compared to the validity of the signature, and if it does not hold then the signature need not be validated. Figure 1 (right) shows the format of a message on the NMR; because of the normalized format, split into structured metadata and payload, the message destination and the direction of the message can be easily extracted and compared against given data.

This simple mechanism is an easy way to separate incoming calls from outgoing ones, based on message metadata.

4.2   Decision

Once a policy-relevant message is intercepted, it needs to be evaluated against the applicable policy (see Fig.2). The decision component does policy matching: it examines all policies in the policy base (or policy repository) by evaluating them against the current message. The evaluation is done by comparing message context and actual parameters (e.g., destination service, source service, message type, etc) with the conditions required by interested policies. We considered the simple case of comparing the message against all policies in the policy base, until the first match is found.

The output of the decision phase is called the *verdict*. This enforcement decision is binary: either the message is legitimate, or it is a policy violation. While the first case implies that there will be no consequences onto the message flow, the second case calls for one or more enforcement actions. These actions are detailed below.

4.3   Actions

The third step of enforcement is to take action based on the verdict that was reached in step 2. We have implemented five basic enforcement actions that implement the four mechanisms formalized by Pretschner et al. [5] to approach usage control enforcement:

The acceptor accepts whole messages. If the verdict does not indicate any policy violation, then the acceptor is invoked, with the effect that the message is allowed without any modification.

The blocker rejects whole messages. Contrary to the previous case, the blocker mechanism is invoked to react to a policy violation by rejecting the entire message and sending back an error message.

The modifier pertains to the class of mechanisms that modify a message. The point is to go beyond the classic "all or nothing" enforcement approach and modify the message so that it conforms to the given policy.

The delayer refers to the class of mechanisms that postpone a message until a condition is satisfied. This mechanism maps to the idea of obligation enforcement, where an actor would be allowed to perform an action only after a condition has been verified. For instance the policy "Delete all traces of a call after the call has been terminated and paid" can be implemented by delaying the deletion of call traces until the arrival of a message that signals a call that is terminated and paid for.

The executor enables complex actions. In some cases, the reaction to a violation may require the execution of a complex recovery process that requires more than the basic mechanisms implemented by xESB. Implementing these mechanisms in xESB would make it inflexible, so xESB uses the executor to invoke an external service or process, which can also be an orchestration engine.

Actions can be differentiated as *preventive* or *corrective*. Preventive actions ensure that a policy violation will not happen: prior to allowing a sensitive action, they check its compliance with the policies. Corrective actions, on the other hand, try to compensate a violation that already happened. The blocker is a preventive mechanism: if a message on the ESB is not allowed to reach its destination, then it is simply dropped. The other actions—modifying, delaying, calling an external entity—are by their nature compensatory: if an intercepted message or a group of messages already constitute a policy violation, an appropriate action must be taken to *correct* the respective message or message flow (e.g., reroute to a secure service, deny further messages on that route until next day, etc.). The executor mechanism can be both preventive and reactive.

We see the actions described above as *enforcement primitives* on ESB messaging. Because implementing a blocking, modifying, delaying and executing mechanism should be different from application to application, we argue that our design caters to a *customizable* ESB enforcement framework. Our model provides a set of basic components – the interceptor, the decision maker, the action performer – and the wiring between them; the semantic behind the enforcement actions and the policies are independent of the solution design.

5 The Design of xESB

In a JBI service bus, the component that mediates all communication is the normalized message router (NMR). It is therefore natural to embed an *interposition mechanism* within the NMR, in order to capture incoming messages on their way to their destination, be it before being processed (service requests) or after being processed (service replies).

Once the message has been intercepted, the next step is to *analyze* the messages just captured. The JBI standard helps us again: the messages being routed are normalized before they get to the router; this means that they are transformed to a fixed format that separates clearly the XML payload of a message, the message context (metadata) and message attachments (the format is given in Figure 1). This feature makes it feasible to analyze parts of a normalized message. In order to derive a verdict, we designed the analysis component to compare the metadata of a current message with the metadata specified by the policies in the policy base. By metadata, we mean information such as message source and destination; by context we mean any flow-related condition, such as a constraint that pertains to message flow precedence (e.g., an incoming call was not logged before it was accepted), or usage control-specific constraints that mainly involve counting (e.g., a silver customer has used 2 hours of premium services this month) or obligations (e.g., silver customers can use video calls for

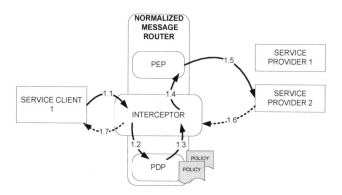

Fig. 3. The xESB enforcement architecture. The solid arrows indicate the invoke chain, while the dotted arrows show the response chain. Both request and response are intercepted. The policy is only on requests from Client 1 to Provider 2, hence the interceptor gives the request to the PDP, and then passes the response from the PDP to the PEP.

no more than 3 hours a month). With some information on the state of a service or a message, the problem of comparing the current intercepted message against the business constraints in the policy base is described in Sect. 6.

Once a verdict is reached, the *action performing* phase consists of one of the actions given in Sec. 4.3. xESB implements message blocking by sending the current message not to its desired endpoint but to a loopback interface (the request initiator can receive nothing or a fault message); the xESB modifier simply replaces parts of the message header as specified by the policy; the delayer routes the message to a delayer component that puts the message in a queue and removes it again when the condition associated with it is satisfied (be it time or a boolean condition); lastly, the executor is implemented by routing the current message to the endpoint of the desired service. An underlying assumption of the design is that the xESB mechanism is always invoked because the NMR processes every message. The xESB is trusted to always invoke the PEP, and the enforcement actions are on services that are deployed on the ESB (hence a service not deployed on the bus is not known to xESB). Therefore, xESB acts as a reference monitor.

Performance considerations made us embed the modifying and rerouting functionality into the component that does message interception on the bus. The specific delaying and blocking behavior were implemented as separate components (namely, plain Java objects) to which the NMR would direct messages. Thus, while the intercepting mechanism is ESB platform-specific, we aimed to make the analysis and action hooks reusable across applications. The logic to decide on the enforcement verdict can be reused irrespective of the deployed policies, but the actions matching this verdict are application-dependent. This design has *flexibility* as its greatest advantage; for instance, it does not rule out the call-back to an analysis component that is application-logic aware, and that might be interested to analyze message payload in order to make an enforcement decision. In addition to this aspect, we have also incorporated support for indicators within our xESB. Section 7 will discuss indicators in greater detail.

6   Enforcement Language

As we have shown in Sect. 4.3, we wish to enforce not only by control, but also by reaction. Reaction covers temporal and transient obligations to which any entity in the distributed environment can be bound. Existing languages and language frameworks address only some of these aspects (see Sect. 9). Consequently, we have created our own policy language.

A policy is written as text, which is compiled into binary form. During execution, the compiled policy file resides in memory and is interpreted by a stack machine. Policy turnover is at the moment not implemented, but we do not see large technical difficulties in doing so: turnover is problematic only for enforcement on message *exchanges* or *sessions*, where different policies may have to be applied to different messages. Since we enforce policies one message at a time, such problems do not exist in xESB.

6.1   Policy Files

Policies are expressed as a sequences of rules, expressed in Event-Condition-Action form. A message is sequentially checked against the rules until either a rule applies or there are no more rules. Figure 4 shows how the policy "Silver customers can use video calls for no more than 3 hours a month" would be expressed in this language. From this example, we can see that the policy language contains the following components:

```
default-action { allow; }
// Total duration of video calls, in seconds
hash videoDuration = 0;
timer resetDuration = next month;
obligation {
  if invocation
  when { resetDuration.fired }
  do {
    clear videoDuration;
    arm resetDuration fire next month;
  }
}
obligation {
  if response
  when { h "Type" equals "video-call" && h "Success" equals "True"
    && h "Customer-Type" equals "Silver" }
  do { update-counter videoDuration[source] += h "Duration"; }
}
rule {
  if invocation
  when { h "Type" equals "video-call" && h "Customer-Type" equals "Silver"
    && videoDuration[source] > 10800 }
  do { block; }
}
```

Fig. 4. Policy for "Silver customers can use video calls for at most 3 hours a month"

Default Action. This allows *allow-based* or *deny-based* policies.

Counters, Timers, and Hashes. These declare items of state, which are pieces of data that keep their values across policy checks. There are three types of state: *counters*, *timers*, and *hashes*. The latter keep arrays of state, thus allowing state per user or state per messge source etc.

Rules and Obligations. Rules and obligations are very similar. However, *rules* compute verdicts such as block, allow and so on. When a rule that carries a verdict matches a message, the action part of that rule is executed and processing is stopped. On the other hand, *obligations* exist solely for the purpose of updating state, so processing continues.

Event, Condition and Action Specifications. The event part of a rule or obligation checks if the message is a *request* or a *response*. Conditions are part of a rule or obligation and *checks whether the rule or obligation applies* to the current message. The action specification of a rule or obligation can *update state* (both rules and obligations) or *return a verdict* (rules only).

What is the overall effect of this policy file? The first obligation takes care of rearming the timer if it has fired. The second obligation updates the length of video calls, and the rule blocks video calls in excess of three hours. Identifiers such as 'type', 'source', 'destination', etc. refer to names of the metadata fields in the normalized message.

While this example illustrates the main features of the language, some other features of interest include:

Modifying message metadata. The language construct "modify h *metadata-name = string-expression*" modifies parts of a message's metadata, i.e., anything outside the message payload. Modification lets the message pass after modification.

Delaying a message. One possible verdict is "delay *n*", which means to delay the message by a specified amount of time. This implies allowing the message to pass eventually.

Delay until a condition is met. Another innovative verdict is "delay until *condition*", which will delay a message until a certain condition is met. The condition can be any boolean expression on the state (but not on any message headers). This is not the same as bocking a message, since a message is completely *discarded* when it is blocked, whereas here it is merely *delayed*.

6.2   Cross-Service Policies

To show that we can use xESB to enforce cross-service and hence potentially inter-organisational policies, let us consider the regulatory requirement to hide initiator numbers in outgoing calls. Since this policy holds for video, audio and ordinary phone calls, it affects potentially many services and therefore also potentially different organisations within Foo.uk. Figure 5 shows how to express this policy. Note how simple this policy is to implement on the ESB level. On the BPEL level, it would be much more complicated, because a generic anonymisation service would have to be written and deployed, and message transformation would have to be performed at the BPEL level.

```
default-action { allow; }
rule {
  if invocation
  when { h "Type" equals "start-call" }
  do { modify h "Initiator" = "000000"; }
}
```

Fig. 5. Policy expressing "Initiator numbers need to be anonymized for outgoing calls"[2]

Figure 6 shows the two remaining policies from Sect. 2, namely "log start time and duration of calls", and "accept collect calls only after destination explicitly accepts to pay".

---

[2] The modify action implies a verdict, hence this is indeed a rule, not an obligation.

```
default-action { allow; }              default-action { allow; }
rule {                                 hash payAccepted = 0;
  if invocation                        obligation {
  when { h "Type" equals "start-call"    if request
      || h "Type" equals "end-call" }    when { h "Type" equals "collect-payment" }
  do { duplicate                         do { update-counter payAccepted[destination] := 0; }
    "http://internal.foo.uk/log"; }    }
}                                      obligation {
                                         if response
                                         when { h "Type" equals "collect-payment"
                                             && h "Success" equals "True"
                                             && h "PaymentAgreed" equals "True" }
                                         do { update-counter payAccepted[destination] := 1; }
                                       }
                                       rule {
                                         if invocation
                                         when { h "Type" equals "call-collect"
                                             && payAccepted[destination] == 0 }
                                         do { block; }
                                       }
```

Fig. 6. Policies expressing "log start time and duration of calls" (left), and "accept collect calls only after destination accepts to pay" (right)

7 Enforcement Indicators

As previously mentioned, we want indicators to give a quantitative measure of the quality of the enforcement process. We will provide some examples of possible ESB-level indicators that have an impact over the assessment of policy enforcement. We split them in two basic types:

Indicators for misconfiguration. By counting repeated violations from a particular service, an indicator can show that the service always violates the policy no matter the user on whose behalf it works. This would mean that the cause is not the user nor the way the service is used, but rather the way in which the service is configured. Another example is an indicator that can quantify how many services do not follow deployment or runtime constraints such as: using disallowed protocol versions, being in disallowed service states or deploying services that should not have been deployed. That may be a more general indicator for misconfiguration of the overall application. We show two simple examples in Fig. 7.

Indicators for reaction to misuse/attacks. Recursion in service chains can impact service availability because it can lead to deadlocks. Counting and limiting the number of times this happens may be an indicator of service availability. An example of an indicator preventing attacks is disabling access to services based on security parameters or on the history of requests from a caller. For example, if a caller is denied access three times in a row, we block access permanently. Limiting the number of requests from a particular client to a particular service can prevent DoS attacks; see Fig. 8.

It can be noticed from the examples above that we can derive a number of useful indicators by combining mechanisms for counting, using flags for flow precedence, inspecting message types, sizes and message parts. Our language

```
counter violations = 0;               counter violations = 0;
rule {                                obligation {
  if request                            if request
  when { ... }                          when { h "Protocol-Version" != "1.3"
  do {                                      || h "Service-Type" != "ShoppingCart" }
    update-counter violations += 1;     do { update-counter violations += 1; }
    block;                            }
  }
}
```

Fig. 7. Indicators for misconfiguration: Counting repeated violations (left), counting deployment errors (right)

```
counter recursion = 0;                 hash fails = 0;
counter aCalledB = 0;                  obligation {
obligation {                             if response
  if request                             when { source = "Payment" && h "Status" = "Fail" }
  when { source = "a"                    do { update-counter fails[destination] += 1; } }
      && destination != "b" }          rule {
  do { update-counter aCalledB := 0; } }   if response
obligation {                             when { source = "Payment" && h "Status" = "Success" }
  if request                             do { update-counter fails[destination] := 0; } }
  when { source = "a"                  rule {
      && destination = "b" }             if response
  do { update-counter aCalledB := 1; } }   when { source = "Fail-Admin" && h "Status" = "Success" }
obligation {                             do { pass;
  if request                                 update-counter fails[h "Subject"] := 0; } }
  when { source = "b"                  rule {
      && destination = "a" && aCalledB }   if request
  do { update-counter recursion += 1; } }   when { destination = "Payment" && fails[source] > 3 }
                                         do { block; } }
```

Fig. 8. Indicators for misuse or attack: counting recursions (left), preventing DoS or password guessing (right)

and our intercepting mechanism can be used to count specific events and reason on message precedence, as well as inspecting message properties.

8   Performance Evaluation

To implement xESB, we chose Apache Servicemix 3.3, a JBI-compliant open source ESB. We used the Servicemix API to intercept messages according to Fig. 3. This section describes the evaluation of our prototype implementation.

We followed a capacity testing model [6] to measure the lower bound of the instrumentation overhead. We used the sample SOAP that come with ServiceMix 3.3, and soapUI as a tool for load generation[3]. We used SOAP messages of 8 Kb size and a varying number of parallel clients. Our testbed PC was a 32-bit system with a 2.6GHz processor and 3GB of RAM. The JVM was allowed 1280MB of memory, with a ServiceMix queue size of 256 requests.

To answer the question "how does the number of rules in a policy file affect the round-trip time (RTT) of messages?", we constructed policy files of 0, 5, 10, 25, 50, 100, and 200 rules such that in all files, only the last rule would ever match. Therefore we are actually measuring the effect of checking the rules, not simply

---

[3] http://www.soapui.org/

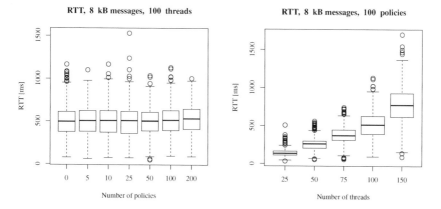

Fig. 9. RTT for varying policy file sizes (left) and varying number of parallel connections (right), for 8 Kb messages. The x axes are not uniformly spaced.

loading a larger ruleset, which would have almost no effect. For each policy file, we then used SoapUI to send 8 Kb messages to xESB using 100 parallel threads for 3 minutes. We repeated this process 3–5 times. Since SoapUI does not return the RTT for individual messages, we looked at the average RTT. The results are plotted in Fig. 9, left. The most important conclusion is that xESB is almost unaffected by the size of the policy file: the main delay seems to be in message processing, not policy enforcement. In fact, profiling shows that policy enforcement takes only about 0.2% of CPU time.

The next question we asked is "How does the number of parallel clients affect the RTT?". Using a similar method as above (8 Kb messages using 100 rules for 3 minutes, repeat 3–5 times, then look at the average RTTs), we arrived at Fig. 9, right. As expected, both the average RTT and the variability rise linearly.

A curious feature that can be seen in the figure is the tremendous variability in RTT. Since this variability also shows in the uninstrumented ServiceMix, we conclude that policy enforcement is not responsible for this. We conjecture that this is due to the staged-event architecture of ServiceMix, where processing is done in bursts because computation happens in stages[4].

9 Related Work

There is a large number of security standards that cover XML message validation, authorization, encryption or even federated authentication: OASIS's WS-Security, SAML, XACML[5], and other WS-* specifications. These standards only deal with particular narrow issues of SOA scenarios (point-to-point authentication, authorization, message integrity, etc.) and not with SOA policy compliance.

---

[4] Staged Event-Driven Architecture http://www.eecs.harvard.edu/~mdw/proj/seda/
[5] These OASIS standards can be found at http://docs.oasis-open.org

The work on enforcing security at the message-level is limited to considering access control policies. The solution of Svirskas et al. [7] is limited to controlling service access and logging on the ESB. A similar approach [8] suggests several infrastructure security services to act on different types of events by means of a gateway, but the separation between business and security concerns is not clear. Maierhofer et al. [9] describe a dynamic enforcement framework for security at the message-level, but do not discuss interoperability nor implementation. Another solution [10] suggests a custom security service bus for enforcement of complex policies. Other conceptual approaches based on law-governed interactions [11] aim to model enforcement of laws onto communication between servers and clients, but they consider generic distributed dedicated entities to perform the law realization. Our assumption differs in that it uses the ESB as a centralized mechanism that either performs on-the-fly enforcement or delegates it to a trusted entity. We explicitly focus on access and usage control policies, and unlike other approaches, we offer a concrete model and a proof-of-concept implementation.

Concerning the policy language, elaborate access control languages (e.g., Ponder [12], EPAL [13], SPL [14]) are unable to express obligations that pertain to usage control. More generic usage control centric languages are POLPA [15] and OSL [16]; while the former does not explicitly address obligations, the latter is not supported by an implementation. Unaware of any implementation of a generic usage control language that supports compensations, we have developed a proof-of-concept policy language fit for the ESB. Compared to theoretic works on access control compensations [17], violation management [18] and obligation assessment [19,20], we go beyond access control and provide an implementation of compensations on the fly. This means that whenever a violation of some service usage rule is detected, the correction happens as the event travels through the system, before it reaches some interested party.

In usage control enforcement [21], Katt et al. [22] add the notion of post-obligations to the obligation model; they consider and implement a mechanism for ongoing enforcement. The work of Pretschner et al. [5,23] describes a formalized usage control language and the mechanisms to enforce such a language, but do not cover an enforcement model for SOA. xESB reuses these enforcement mechanisms as well as idea of post-obligations but applies them for the first time to the ESB level.

10   Conclusion and Future Work

The paper presented xESB, an instrumented JBI ESB for the enforcement of security policies that are organization-wide. xESB is able to enforce both access and usage controls policies. The rich enforcement semantics of xESB allows not only to reject ESB messages that violate a policy but also to compensate that violation. xESB also introduces and supports indicators aiming to help the security administrator analyze and derive useful information about policy violations (e.g., discover configuration mistakes) and their impact to the overall security of the organization. While initial performance tests are very promising, we are planning to use xESB with a commercial SOA application and run more extensive tests to validate the initial results.

We are currently working to extend xESB on four aspects:

Optimization. In a large policy file a lot of time is spent evaluating conditions in order to find those rules or obligations that apply to a given message. To improve this, we will implement some form of the Rete algorithm [24], or select rules according to which message parts appear in `where`-clauses.

Conditions on message payload. We will extend xESB so that complex conditions on the message payload can also be evaluated. We will most likely base this capability on XPath.

Performance measurements. Apart from measuring the performance impact of the executor and modifying mechanism, we plan to evaluate different policy engines against our enforcement design, thus checking its extensibility.

Performance indicators. We will implement performance indicator support in order to derive general information on the runtime enforcement process (e.g., statistics on the rules that are frequently enforced or violated).

References

1. Zimmermann, O., Doubrovski, V., Grundler, J., Hogg, K.: Service-oriented architecture and business process choreography in an order management scenario: rationale, concepts, lessons learned. In: OOPSLA 2005: Companion to the 20th annual ACM SIGPLAN conference on Object-oriented programming, systems, languages, and applications, pp. 301–312. ACM, New York (2005)
2. UK Government: The privacy and electronic communications (ec directive) regulations (June 2003), http://www.opsi.gov.uk/si/si2003/20032426.htm
3. European Parliament: Directive 95/46/ec of the european parliament and of the council (June 2009),
   http://ec.europa.eu/justice_home/fsj/privacy/docs/95-46-ce/
   dir1995-46_part1_en.pdf
4. Sun, Java Community Process Program: Sun JSR-000208 Java Business Integration (August 2005),
   http://jcp.org/aboutJava/communityprocess/final/jsr208/index.html
5. Pretschner, A., Hilty, M., Basin, D., Schaefer, C., Walter, T.: Mechanisms for usage control. In: Proc. ASIACCS 2008, pp. 240–244. ACM, New York (2008)
6. Ueno, K., Tatsubori, M.: Early capacity testing of an enterprise service bus. In: ICWS 2006: Proceedings of the IEEE International Conference on Web Services, pp. 709–716. IEEE Computer Society, Los Alamitos (2006)
7. Svirskas, A., Isachenkova, J., Molva, R.: Towards secure and trusted collaboration environment for european public sector. In: International Conference on Collaborative Computing: Networking, Applications and Worksharing, CollaborateCom 2007, November 2007, pp. 49–56 (2007)
8. Leune, K., van den Heuvel, W.J., Papazoglou, M.: Exploring a multi-faceted framework for soc: how to develop secure web-service interactions? In: Proc. 14th Intl. Workshop on Research Issues on Data Engineering, March 2004, pp. 56–61 (2004)

9. Maierhofer, A., Dimitrakos, T., Titkov, L., Brossard, D.: Extendable and adaptive message-level security enforcement framework. In: Networking and Services, ICNS 2006, pp. 72–72 (2006)
10. Goovaerts, T., De Win, B., Joosen, W.: Infrastructural support for enforcing and managing distributed application-level policies. Electron. Notes Theor. Comput. Sci. 197(1), 31–43 (2008)
11. Lam, T., Minsky, N.: A collaborative framework for enforcing server commitments, and for regulating server interactive behavior in soa-based systems. In: Proceedings of the 5th International Conference on Collaborative Computing: Networking, Applications and Worksharing, November 2009, pp. 1–10 (2009)
12. Damianou, N., Dulay, N., Lupu, E., Sloman, M.: The ponder policy specification language. In: Sloman, M., Lobo, J., Lupu, E.C. (eds.) POLICY 2001. LNCS, vol. 1995, pp. 18–38. Springer, Heidelberg (2001)
13. Backes, M., Pfitzmann, B., Schunter, M.: A toolkit for managing enterprise privacy policies. In: Snekkenes, E., Gollmann, D. (eds.) ESORICS 2003. LNCS, vol. 2808, pp. 162–180. Springer, Heidelberg (2003)
14. Ribeiro, C., Zquete, A., Ferreira, P., Guedes, P.: Spl: An access control language for security policies with complex constraints. In: Proceedings of the Network and Distributed System Security Symposium, pp. 89–107 (1999)
15. Baiardi, F., Martinelli, F., Mori, P., Vaccarelli, A.: Improving grid services security with fine grained policies. In: Meersman, R., Tari, Z., Corsaro, A. (eds.) OTM-WS 2004. LNCS, vol. 3292, pp. 123–134. Springer, Heidelberg (2004)
16. Hilty, M., Pretschner, A., Basin, D., Schaefer, C., Walter, T.: A policy language for distributed usage control. In: Biskup, J., López, J. (eds.) ESORICS 2007. LNCS, vol. 4734, pp. 531–546. Springer, Heidelberg (2007)
17. Povey, D.: Optimistic security: A new access control paradigm. In: Proceedings of 1999 New Security Paradigms Workshop, pp. 40–45. ACM Press, New York (1999)
18. Brunel, J., Cuppens, F., Cuppens, N., Sans, T., Bodeveix, J.P.: Security policy compliance with violation management. In: FMSE 2007, pp. 31–40. ACM, New York (2007)
19. Irwin, K., Yu, T., Winsborough, W.H.: Assigning responsibility for failed obligations. IFIP Intl. Federation for Information Processing 263, 327–342 (2008)
20. Irwin, K., Yu, T., Winsborough, W.H.: On the modeling and analysis of obligations. In: CCS 2006, pp. 134–143. ACM, New York (2006)
21. Park, J., Sandhu, R.: The UCON$_{ABC}$ usage control model. ACM Trans. Inf. Syst. Secur. 7(1), 128–174 (2004)
22. Katt, B., Zhang, X., Breu, R., Hafner, M., Seifert, J.P.: A general obligation model and continuity: enhanced policy enforcement engine for usage control. In: Proc. SACMAT 2008, pp. 123–132. ACM, New York (2008)
23. Pretschner, A., Schütz, F., Schaefer, C., Walter, T.: Policy evolution in distributed usage control. In: 4th Intl. Workshop on Security and Trust Management (June 2008)
24. Forgy, C.: A network match routine for production systems. Working paper. Carnegie-Mellon University (1974)

Metric Strand Spaces for Locale Authentication Protocols*

F. Javier Thayer, Vipin Swarup, and Joshua D. Guttman

The MITRE Corporation, USA
{jt,swarup,guttman}@mitre.org

Abstract. Location-dependent services are services that adapt their behavior based on the locations of mobile devices. For many applications, it is critical that location-dependent services use trustworthy device locations, namely locations that are both accurate and recent. These properties are captured by a security goal called *locale authentication* whereby an entity can authenticate the physical location of a device, even in the presence of malicious adversaries. In this paper, we present a systematic technique for verifying that location discovery protocols satisfy this security goal. We base our work on the strand space theory which provides a framework for determining which security goals a cryptographic protocol achieves. We extend this theory with a metric that captures the geometric properties of time and space. We use the extended theory to prove that several prominent location discovery protocols including GPS do not satisfy the locale authentication goal. We also analyze a location discovery protocol that does satisfy the goal under some reasonable assumptions.

1 Introduction

Location-dependent services have been well-studied and are widely expected to become an integral part of the pervasive computing infrastructure. These services adapt their behavior depending on the current locations of mobile devices. Device locations are provided by location discovery protocols. Security is a major concern in these systems and a wide variety of security goals have been studied in the literature, e.g., the privacy, freshness, and availability of location information. In this paper, we focus on the threat of malicious users deceiving location-dependent services by providing incorrect or stale location data. They may do this by subverting or bypassing the location discovery protocols.

Robustness against this threat is captured by the security goal of *locale authentication* whereby an entity can authenticate the physical location of a device, even in the presence of malicious adversaries. The entity can then issue a *locale certificate* that asserts that principal P has a physical presence at location (or within region) x at some time during a time interval t. A node that wishes to

---

* This work was supported by the MITRE-Sponsored Research Program.

M. Nishigaki et al. (Eds.): IFIPTM 2010, IFIP AICT 321, pp. 79–94, 2010.

use this attribute certificate must verify the certificate by checking its signature and determining whether the creator is trusted to have used a secure locale authentication protocol to authenticate the stated location.

Locale certificates are indeed feasible. Consider a person P who needs a certificate stating that she is at the physical address x at time t. P contacts a certificate granting authority which then dispatches a human agent to P's claimed location. The agent validates P's identity and secret key (which we assume P has previously obtained), verifies P's location at time t, and issues a document to P with this information and bearing the certificate authority's signature. Clearly this scheme is impractical since it requires a human to service each request, but it illustrates that the concept of a locale certificate is feasible.

A potentially better alternative is to provide each user with a tamper-proof GPS locator device that discovers and certifies the user's location. Such devices have been developed [4]. However, as we show in Section 7.2, any GPS device which relies exclusively on the commercial GPS external signal can be attacked and hence is inadequate for locale authentication in sensitive applications.

In this paper, we provide a precise definition of locale authentication and we present a systematic technique for proving whether or not location discovery protocols satisfy the locale authentication goal. Our work is based on the strand space theory which provides a framework for determining what security goals a cryptographic protocol achieves. Strand spaces are a special-purpose execution model for security protocols, based on a Lamport-style causal partial ordering. Behaviors of some principals, "regular principals," are assumed to follow the rules of the protocol, while others, adversarial principals, do whatever they like, constrained by cryptography and the secrets they possess.

The key notion is a possible global execution, or "bundle," namely a causally well-founded directed acyclic graph, in which the nodes are message transmissions or receptions. The nodes may lie on any number of regular or adversarial behaviors. Every message reception must be explained by some earlier transmission of the same message. Causal well-foundedness justifies a principle of induction for bundles, which is the basis of powerful and reusable proof techniques. Strand spaces were intended to capture a minimal view of protocol behavior, leading to conceptually spare and focused analysis techniques.

Secure location protocols combine cryptography with the physics of message transmission. The cryptographic operations authenticate the principals and preserve confidentiality, while the physics of message transmission constrain their possible locations. We enrich the strand space model by associating a space-time location with each node. The strands follow the world lines of principals. Some bundles are compatible with the physics of message transmission – e.g. the maximum message transmission speed – while others are not. An assertion true in every bundle compatible with the physics is a valid conclusion of a secure location protocol. We use this extended theory to prove that several prominent location discovery protocols including GPS do not satisfy the locale authentication goal. We also analyze a location discovery protocol that does satisfy the goal under some reasonable assumptions.

The remainder of this paper is organized as follows. In Section 3, we review related work. In Section 4, we summarize a broad range of security goals for location discovery protocols. We then focus on the goal of locale authentication and we describe our threat model and attack classes that compromise this goal. In Section 5, we present the metric strand space model. In Section 6, we consider four prominent location discovery protocols and we use the metric strand space model to examine whether they provide locale authentication under a specified threat model. Section 8 concludes the paper with a discussion of future directions for this novel line of work.

2   Some Examples

Consider a client device intended to participate in secure location protocols. It contains a private asymmetric key, and the manufacturer provides a certificate binding the public part of the same key pair to the identity of the purchaser. The device has some tamperproofing, to ensure that it is unlikely to have been subverted without effort on the part of the owner, and certainly not unbeknownst to the owner. The behavior of the device is as follows. When the owner specifies a number of location servers, the device interacts with them so that they can jointly provide evidence of the device's location.

The interaction between the device and the servers consists of two phases. First, a cryptographic protocol allows the device and server to agree on a pair of new shared secrets. This phase uses asymmetric cryptography and is thus expected to be slow. Second, the server transmits a random bitstring; when the device receives it, the device does a bitwise exclusive *or* with one shared secret, and replies with the result. This operation is very fast. The device also emits an estimate of the time t_δ elapsed between receipt and reply; the estimate is encrypted with the other shared secret. The server calculates the elapsed time t_ϵ between transmitting the challenge and receiving the *xored* response; it then certifies that the distance to the device is approximately $c \cdot (t_\epsilon - t_\delta)/2$, where c is the transmission speed in this medium. If the location of each server is known, and the device interacts with a suitable number of servers within a short period of time, then the location of the device on the surface of the earth or in three-dimensional space may be determined.

For the first phase of interaction, we use the Needham-Schroeder-Lowe protocol, taking the resulting shared secrets to be the two nonces. The full protocol is shown in Figure 1. Evidently, if it were possible for a third party to determine the nonces, then with judicious jamming, it may be possible for the third party to convince L that D is at the third party's location. For instance, if the protocol were based on the original, flawed Needham-Schroeder protocol instead of the version as fixed by Lowe, then an attack would be possible (Figures 2, 3). In this scenario, the owner has asked its device to determine its distance from P, a location server that turns out to act fraudulently; P can then surely convince an honest location server that D is where P is. By suitable choices of t_δ, probably any distance can be established.

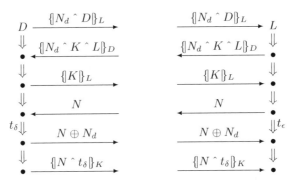

Fig. 1. A Distance-determining Protocol

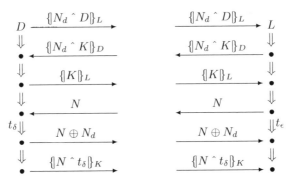

Fig. 2. A Flawed Distance-determining Protocol

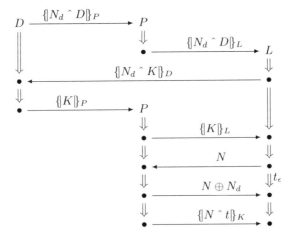

Fig. 3. An Attack on the Protocol of Figure 2

Thus, in protocols of this kind, there is a tight interconnection between the structure of the cryptographic protocol—the way that it uses cryptography to establish authentication and shared secrets—and its usefulness to determine location.

3   Related Work

A wide variety of location discovery protocols (e.g., [8]) have been proposed in the literature. Some protocols let a device compute its own location, some let a server compute the location of a device for the server's own use, and some let a server or device convince a third party of a device's location. The protocols may be passive where the load on location servers is independent of the number of protocol runs, or active where the server load is a function of the number of protocol runs (e.g., if the server has to respond to messages sent by devices).

Location discovery protocols compute the location of a device by using a distributed set of servers whose locations are known precisely. Distance bounding protocols [2] typically use distance or angle measurements of signal transmissions between the servers and the device, and they solve for the unknown location using triangulation (or multilateration) techniques. Distance measurements are made by either measuring the signal strength of a received signal or by measuring the arrival times of one or more signals. Signal strength measurements are converted to distance measurements by knowing the power of the transmitted signal and by modeling its expected strength at various locations [1]. Arrival times are converted to distance measurements by knowing the time of signal transmission and the propagation speed within the transmission medium [6]. Alternatively, if two signals with different propagation speeds are transmitted simultaneously, then the distance can be computed without knowing the actual transmission time of the signals [9]. Angle measurements are made by using special antenna configurations that measure the angle of arrival of a signal.

The most prominent location discovery system is the Global Positioning System (GPS). In this scheme, multiple synchronized satellites transmit periodic messages; a device that receives transmissions from several satellites can use the signals to triangulate its own position. Denning and MacDoran [4] have proposed building a locale authentication service using GPS signals. They suggest that a device can capture the signals it receives from multiple satellites and can package the received signals into a credential. A trusted server can verify that the signals have not been tampered with, and can use the signals to compute the device's position. As we prove in Section 7.2, such a scheme is not secure if the GPS geometry is public knowledge, e.g., as with commercial GPS.

Sastry et al [10] and Capkun et al [3] analyze protocols that can securely verify certain location claims. Their analyses are specific to their respective proposed protocols. Further, they only address the question of whether some arbitrary user is in a designated physical region. In contrast, in this paper we present a general, systematic model for verifying the security properties of any location discovery protocol. We apply this technique to several protocols, including a protocol that addresses the question of whether a specific user (i.e., a user with a specific secret key) is in a designated physical region. Meadows et al [7] present a qualitative framework for analyzing distance bounding protocols based on extending an authentication logic and is closest in spirit to our work.

4   Security for Location Discovery Protocols

Let N, M, P, and Q be principals (e.g., cryptographic keys, mobile nodes with identities, etc.), L be a physical location (or region), and t be a time interval. Some of N, M, P, and Q may possibly be the same principal. If a principal P has a physical presence at a location L (e.g., if P has access to a node at L), then we say that "P is at L" or that "P controls L".

The purpose of a location discovery protocol is to enable M to determine the location of N during t. However, location discovery protocols are subject to attacks by malicious penetrators. In this section, we examine a range of desirable security goals for location discovery protocols, and a set of attacks that may compromise those goals.

4.1   Security Goals

Desirable security goals for location discovery protocols include:

Locale Occupancy Authentication: If M determines that some principal was at L during t, then there was indeed a principal at L during t.

Locale Authentication: If M determines that N was at L during t, then N was indeed at L during t. Thus, a penetrator cannot make M believe that N is at a location other than N's true location.

Privacy: An unauthorized penetrator (e.g., an eavesdropping node) cannot obtain location information via a location discovery protocol. For instance, if M uses a location discovery protocol to determine that N is at L during t, then penetrator P should not be able to learn that N is at L during t.

Availability: An authorized principal M can determine N's location at any time. Thus, a penetrator cannot prevent M from determining N's location.

Nonrepudiation: Evidence that N was at L during t is irrefutable. With such evidence, M can prove to Q that N was at L during t.

Most of the literature on location discovery protocols addresses the functionality of the protocols, namely enabling M to determine the location of N during time interval t. Some techniques enable a node to determine its own location (e.g., [6], [9]), while others enable a node to determine the location of another node (e.g., by measuring signal strengths [1] or round-trip ping times). Some techniques address the privacy and availability goals, but most do not satisfy the goals of authentication or nonrepudiation.

4.2   Threat Model and Attacks

We distinguish between various threats based on the locations that are controlled by penetrators. Control of a location may enable a penetrator to monitor, delay, alter, delete, redirect, or replay any signals (message transmissions) that traverse that location or its immediate neighborhood. However, in this paper, we assume that a penetrator cannot block broadcast transmissions between two neighboring nodes that the penetrator does not control. Note that some penetrators may only control a small number of locations (e.g., a soldier in enemy territory). Some penetrators may control an entire physical region (e.g., an enemy state that controls some territory). Some penetrators ("insiders") may control some nodes used by location discovery protocols, e.g., trusted location servers.

Location discovery protocols are subject to a wide range of attacks. For instance, a penetrator may deny that he was at location L during time t, a penetrator may prevent M from determining N's location, a penetrator may monitor the location discovery protocol to learn the location of a user, etc. In this paper, however, we focus only on attacks on authentication. There are two broad types of attacks.

Location integrity attacks may cause M to believe that N is at location L, even though N does not have a physical presence at L. Two special cases of this attack are: (a) *deception attacks* where a penetrator P causes M to believe that P is at location L, even though that is not the case; and (b) *positioning attacks* where a penetrator P causes M to believe that M is at location L, even though that is not the case. Note that, depending on the attack, the penetrator may or not be able to select the location L.

Masquerade attacks by a penetrator P at L may cause M to believe that the penetrator is N at L. Note that a penetrator P at L may launch a combination masquerade and location integrity attack to cause M to believe that N is at L'.

5   Metric Strand Spaces

We now extend the formalism of strand spaces [11] (see Appendix A for a summary of the strand space theory). The extended theory will enable us to prove whether a location discovery protocol is secure against location integrity and masquerade attacks. In our intended application, a strand will model a sequence of events in a process or in a processor.

We assume that all nodes are subject to physical constraints dictated by the laws of nature as we understand them. We use two laws in this paper. First, a message must be sent before it is received. Second, messages cannot travel faster than the signal speed in the medium of transmission (e.g., the speed of sound in water, or the speed of light). We also assume an idealized model of message transmission; specifically, we assume that broadcast messages are transmitted by a spherical wavefront.

A *partial pseudometric* on a set X is a partial function d with non-negative real values on $X \times X$ such that $d(x, x) = 0$, $d(x, y) = d(y, x)$ when either side is defined, and the triangle inequality

$$d(x, y) \leq d(x, z) + d(z, y)$$

holds when $d(x, y)$, $d(x, z)$, $d(z, y)$ are all defined.

A *time elapse function* on a partially ordered set $(X, \preceq)$ is a partial function e with non-negative real values defined on pairs x, y where $x \preceq y$ such that $\mathrm{e}(x, x) = 0$ and with the additivity property:

$$\mathrm{e}(x, y) = \mathrm{e}(x, z) + \mathrm{e}(z, y) \tag{1}$$

whenever $x \preceq z \preceq y$.

Recall that for nodes m, m' in a single strand of a strand space, $m \Rightarrow^* m'$ means there is a sequence of intermediate nodes $m \Rightarrow m_1 \Rightarrow m_2 \Rightarrow \cdots \Rightarrow m'$, all on the same strand.

Definition 1. *A geometric bundle is a tuple* $(\mathcal{B}, \mathrm{dist}, \mathrm{elapse}, c)$ *where $\mathcal{B}$ is a bundle,* dist *is a partial pseudometric on* $\mathrm{nodes}(\mathcal{B})$*,* elapse *is a time elapse function on pairs* $m, n \in \mathrm{nodes}(\mathcal{B})$ *such that* $m \Rightarrow^* n$*, and c is a positive real.*

Notice that it is possible for different nodes m, n to be within 0 distance of each other. For instance, if the strand s is associated to a static object, then all nodes on s are within 0 distance of each other. However, we can obtain a metric space $\tilde{X}$ from $X = \mathrm{nodes}(\mathcal{B})$, by identifying points m, n which are at 0 distance from each other. The space $\tilde{X}$ and the quotient map $x \mapsto \tilde{x}$ completely determine X. We will refer to $\tilde{X}$ as the geometry of the bundle, c as the message propagation speed, and elapse as the elapsed time between successive events on a strand. We need to relate the metric and the elapsed time function:

Axiom 1. *Suppose* $m_1 \rightarrow n_1 \Rightarrow^* m_2 \rightarrow \cdots \Rightarrow^* m_k \rightarrow n_k$ *is a path in the bundle such that* m_1, n_k *are on the same strand and* $\mathrm{dist}(m_k, n_k)$ *are all defined. Then*

$$\mathrm{elapse}(m_1, n_k) = \frac{1}{c} \sum_{i=1}^{k} \mathrm{dist}(m_i, n_i) + \sum_{\ell=1}^{k-1} \mathrm{elapse}(n_\ell, m_{\ell+1}). \tag{2}$$

In this paper, elapse will be interpreted as elapsed time with respect to a global clock. A *global time* on a bundle is a function $\mathrm{T} : \mathrm{nodes}(\mathcal{B}) \rightarrow \mathbb{R}$ such that

$$\mathrm{elapse}(m, n) = \mathrm{T}(m) - \mathrm{T}(n).$$

Given a geometric bundle with global time, we will use terms such as propagation time, propagation distance, etc.

If strands may be associated with mobile objects, we need to relate the metric and the elapsed time function for nodes on a single strand: $\mathrm{dist}(m, n) \leq v \times \mathrm{elapse}(m, n)$ where $m \Rightarrow^* n$ and where v is a positive real that represents the maximum speed of any object. However, for simplicity, we assume in this paper that all nodes on a strand have the same location (the results in this paper can be extended easily to deal with mobile objects by using the above axiom). This corresponds to strands being associated with static objects and is captured by the following definition:

Definition 2. *A static geometric bundle is a geometric bundle* $(\mathcal{B}, \text{dist}, \text{elapse}, c)$ *where for all pairs* $m, n \in \text{nodes}(\mathcal{B})$ *such that* $m \Rightarrow^* n$, $\text{dist}(m, n) = 0$.

6   Security Analysis of Location Protocols

We now give several illustrative examples of protocols, with precise locale authentication claims and proofs.

6.1   Protocol 1

This first protocol is ancient. It is typically used in the inverse direction to empirically determine the medium propagation speed c from the known distance.

The initiator A sends a nonce N_a and expects return N_a. Responder returns N_a. There are thus two kinds of strands in this protocol:

1. Initiator strands $s = \langle m_1, m_2 \rangle \in \text{Init}[N_a]$ with trace $\langle +N_a, -N_a \rangle$.
2. Responder strands $t = \langle n_1, n_2 \rangle \in \text{Resp}[N_a]$ with trace $\langle -N_a, +N_a \rangle$.

Proposition 1. *Suppose $\mathcal{C}$ is a static geometric bundle. If $\mathcal{C}$ contains a strand $s = \langle m_1, m_2 \rangle \in \text{Init}[N_a]$ of height 2 and N_a uniquely originates on s, then $\mathcal{C}$ contains a strand whose distance from the nodes of s is at most $c/2 \times (\text{elapse}(m_1, m_2))$.*

PROOF. Let $s = (m_1, m_2)$. Since N_a uniquely originates on m_1, there is a path $p_1 \to q_1 \Rightarrow^* p_2 \to \cdots \Rightarrow^* p_k \to q_k$ from m_1 to m_2 (i.e., $p_1 = m_1$ and $q_k = m_2$). Now:

$$\text{elapse}(m_1, m_2) \geq \frac{1}{c} \sum_{i=1}^{k} \text{dist}(p_i, q_i) \geq \frac{1}{c}(\text{dist}(p_1, p_2) + \text{dist}(p_2, q_k))$$

$$= 2 \times \frac{1}{c} \times \text{dist}(m_1, p_2) \quad (\text{since } p_1 = m_1 \text{ and } q_k = m_2)$$

Thus, $\text{dist}(m_1, p_2) \leq c/2 \times \text{elapse}(m_1, m_2)$. ∎

Since the strand whose existence is claimed may be a penetrator strand, this protocol gives no information about who is within the specified distance.

6.2   Protocol 2

The purpose of this protocol is to provide A with a number $r > 0$ and the following guarantee to A: B is within distance r from A. A generates a nonce value which it signs and sends to B. B receives N_a and determines a time delay T to allow for processing time. B signs $N_a \,\hat{}\, T$ and after an elapsed time of T sends $N_a \,\hat{}\, T$ with its signature to A.

Schematically, the protocol can be described thus:

$$
\begin{array}{ccc}
A & & B \\
\bullet & \xrightarrow{\{\!|N_a|\!\}_{K_A^{-1}}} & \bullet \\
\Big\| & & \Big\| \\
\bullet & \xleftarrow{\{\!|N_a \,\hat{}\, T|\!\}_{K_B^{-1}}} & \bullet
\end{array}
$$

Note that we are modeling a message accompanied by a hash as an encryption with a private key. After running this protocol A should have B's reply. Let T_{elapsed} be the time interval A observes between the transmission of the nonce N and receipt of the response from B. A then computes the value:

$$r = \frac{1}{2} \times \left(T_{\text{elapsed}} - T\right) \times c$$

Of course an attacker could still be present, but the claim is that A has received a guarantee that B, an honest participant, is within a ball of radius r of A.

There are two kinds of strands in this protocol:

1. Initiator strands $s = \langle m_1, m_2 \rangle \in \text{Init}[B, N_a, T]$ with trace

$$\langle +N_a, -\{\!|N_a \,\hat{}\, T|\!\}_{K_B^{-1}} \rangle.$$

2. Responder strands $t = \langle n_1, n_2 \rangle \in \text{Resp}[B, N_a, T]$ with trace

$$\langle -N_a, +\{\!|N_a \,\hat{}\, T|\!\}_{K_B^{-1}} \rangle$$

for which $\text{elapse}(n_1, n_2) \geq T$.

We need to assume the hash-key mapping $A \mapsto K_A^{-1}$ is injective.

Proposition 2. *Suppose C is a static geometric bundle. Suppose also that the set of penetrator keys is empty. If C contains a strand s in $\text{Init}[B, N_a, T]$ of height 2 and N_a uniquely originates on s, then C contains a strand t in $\text{Resp}[B, N_a, T]$ of height 2. Moreover the distance from the nodes of s to the nodes of t is at most $1/2 \times \left(\text{elapse}(m_1, m_2) - T\right) \times c$.*

PROOF. Let $s = \langle m_1, m_2 \rangle$. The term $\{\!|N_a \,\hat{}\, T|\!\}_{K_B^{-1}} = \text{term}(m_2)$ originates on at least one strand t. t is regular, since the set of penetrator keys is empty. Thus t must be the second node n_2 of a regular strand in $\text{Resp}[B, N_a, T]$. In particular there is a path $q = \langle q_0, q_1, \ldots, q_{\ell(q)} \rangle$ from n_2 to m_2. Since N_a is uniquely originating at s, there is a path $p = \langle p_0, p_1, \ldots, p_{\ell(p)} \rangle$ from the first node m_1 of s to the first node n_1 of t. The paths p, q may traverse intermediate nodes on various strands. However, by the definition of geometric strand space and Axiom 1:

$\text{elapse}(m_1, m_2) \geq$

$$\geq \frac{1}{c} \sum_{k=0}^{\ell(p)-1} \text{dist}(p_k, p_{k+1}) + \text{elapse}(n_1, n_2) + \frac{1}{c} \sum_{k=0}^{\ell(q)-1} \text{dist}(q_k, q_{k+1})$$

$$\geq \frac{1}{c} \left(\text{dist}(m_1, n_1) + \text{dist}(m_2, n_2)\right) + T = 2 \times \frac{1}{c} \times \text{dist}(m_1, n_1) + T$$

Thus, $\text{dist}(m_1, n_1) \leq 1/2 \times \left(\text{elapse}(m_1, m_2) - T\right) \times c$. ∎

6.3   Clock Distortion

The preceding protocol has two related problems:

1. The condition that the reported delay time T be less than the elapsed time for the initiator is too severe;
2. The requirement that principals have exact clocks is unrealistic.

We briefly indicate a simple refinement of the model that can deal with bounded time drift and distortion. The main idea here is that the time variation is bounded:

Definition 3. *A time elapse function τ_s on a strand s is α bounded iff*

$$\mathrm{elapse}(m, n) \leq \alpha\ \tau(m, n).$$

Having these distortion bounds allows us to introduce locale certificates with specified tolerances. We leave the details to future work.

7   Noninteractive Schemes

The previous locale schemes were based on the pessimistic assumption that the attacker may actually block all messages. We now consider schemes in which this capability is weakened or eliminated altogether. The impossibility of blocking messages is formulated as follows:

Definition 4. *A bundle $\mathcal{C}$ in a geometric strand space with global time* T *is radial iff for every positive node m and every strand s there is a negative node n on s such that $m \to n$ and* $\mathrm{T}(n) = \mathrm{T}(m) + \frac{1}{c}\ \mathrm{dist}(m, n)$

The property expressed in this definition implies that messages sent are always received by all principals and in particular, that messages cannot be destroyed by the attacker. Questions of system failure are not an issue here since there is no intermediate hardware between sender and receiver to required for message delivery. A weaker property which allows for failure conditions for strands is also possible, but our goal here is to consider questions of authenticity not of liveness.

7.1   Protocol 3

Consider the following protocol: A generates a nonce value N, attaches a signature and emits the signed term $\{|N|\}_{K_A^{-1}}$. The value $\{|N|\}_{K_A^{-1}}$ is received by a set of location servers B_i. We assume the location servers B_i have access to universal time T. B_i notes the time $T_i = \mathrm{T}(m_i)$ it first receives the signal $\{|N|\}_{K_A^{-1}}$. We note that B_i may receive the signal more than once since an attacker may attempt to confuse the location servers by delay and retransmission,

The servers B_i send the values $\{\!\{\{\!|N|\!\}_{K_A^{-1}} \,\hat{}\, T_i\}\!\}_{K_i^{-1}}$ to a central server, who creates a certificate with information on A's location.

$$
\begin{array}{ccc}
A & B_i & S \\[2pt]
& \{\!|N|\!\}_{K_A^{-1}} & \\
n_A & \xrightarrow{} m_i & \\
& \| & \\
& \Big\downarrow & \\
& \bullet \xrightarrow{\;\{\!\{\{\!|N|\!\}_{K_A^{-1}} \,\hat{}\, T_i\}\!\}_{K_i^{-1}}\;} \bullet
\end{array}
$$

Proposition 3. *The following relations hold:*

$$
\frac{1}{c}\Big(\mathrm{dist}(n_A, m_i) - \mathrm{dist}(n_A, m_j)\Big) = T_i - T_j. \tag{3}
$$

PROOF. Suppose A generates the message at time $T_A = \mathrm{T}(n_A)$ then by the definition of global time, for every B_i we have the identity:

$$
T_i - T_A = \frac{1}{c}\,\mathrm{dist}(n_A, m_i),
$$

from which formula (3) follows immediately by subtraction.

Corollary 4. *Suppose the underlying geometry is $\mathbb{R}^3$ with Euclidean distance. Then the distance equation for each pair of servers constrains n_A to be on a hyperboloid.*

PROOF. This follows from the fact that the locus of points z whose distances from points a_0, a_1 satisfy "$\mathrm{dist}(z, a_0) - \mathrm{dist}(z, a_1) = \text{constant}$" is a hyperboloid.   ∎

This scheme is impractical since it requires that all servers respond to each request for locale authentication.

7.2   Protocol 4

We now describe a passive scheme much like GPS. The scheme is passive in the sense that the location servers just transmit signals instead of responding to clients. The protocol we describe is an idealized form of the actual protocol because we assume transmissions are continuous. For each time value t the server A_i generates a nonce N_{t,A_i} and at time t transmits $\{\!|N_{t,A_i}|\!\}_{K_{A_i}^{-1}}$. The client collects all signals received at a single time instant and packages the messages into a vector $\langle \{\!|N_{t,A_i}|\!\}_{K_{A_i}^{-1}}, \ldots, \{\!|N_{t,A_i}|\!\}_{K_{A_i}^{-1}}\rangle$. This vector is used as a locale certificate. It would appear to constrain the client to be on an intersection of balls whose centers are the locations of the servers.

Unfortunately, this scheme does not appear to be much better than saying "I am here", because nothing enforces the client to package the messages actually received at a single instant, even if the servers encrypt the signals. Encryption of the nonces adds no security to this protocol, since an attacker may determine beforehand which value of t to use for each server.

To analyze this protocol with encrypted nonces, we associate to each server A_i the function $\mu_i : t \mapsto \{N_{t,A_i}\}_{K_{A_i}}$. For each time instant t, the value of this function is the encrypted value of the nonce transmitted at time t by the server A_i. Let us consider a fixed client B with location x. Since we are assuming the underlying geometry is radial, any signal transmitted by the server is received by the client after propagation delay. Denoting the signal propagation delay to x from the location of A_i by $\tau_{A_i,x}$, we have

$$\tau_{A_i,x} = \frac{1}{c}\operatorname{dist}(A_i, x) \tag{4}$$

Thus the client sees a time translate of the server generated function μ_i

$$\phi_{A_i,x}(t) = \mu_i(t - \tau_{A_i,x}). \tag{5}$$

The goal of this protocol, ostensibly, is to provide a principal at x the data to assemble a locale certificate that binds that principal to location x at time t. The client is expected to package the sequence of values corresponding to messages received at time t, into a vector $\langle \phi_{A_1,x}(t), \ldots, \phi_{A_n,x}(t) \rangle$. which he can then use as a certificate. However, a malicious client may package some other sequence of signals received at different times $t_1, \ldots, t_n$ into a bogus certificate $\langle \phi_{A_1,x}(t_1), \ldots, \phi_{A_n,x}(t_n) \rangle$.

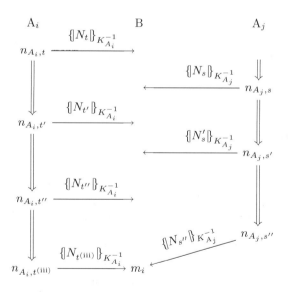

In the following proposition we use the expression "complete knowledge of the underlying geometry" whose meaning is explained in the context of the proof.

Proposition 5. *Under free encryption, if B has complete knowledge of the underlying geometry, of its own location and that of all the servers, then B can falsify any location.*

PROOF. B is at location x. Let y be some arbitrary location. Since the locations of the servers are known to B, the distances $\text{dist}(A_i, y)$ are known to B. It follows that the propagation times

$$\tau_{A_i,y} = \frac{1}{c}\,\text{dist}(A_i, y)$$

from location of A_i to y are also known to B. Note

$$\begin{aligned}
\phi_{A_i,y}(t) &= \mu_i(t - \tau_{A_i,y}) \\
&= \mu_i((t + \tau_{A_i,x} - \tau_{A_i,y}) - \tau_{A_i,x}) \qquad (6) \\
&= \phi_{A_i,x}(t + \tau_{A_i,x} - \tau_{A_i,y}).
\end{aligned}$$

Every term in this last expression is accessible to B. Thus B can claim the vector

$$\langle \phi_{A_1,x}(t + \tau_{A_1,x} - \tau_{A_1,y}), \ldots, \phi_{A_n,x}(t + \tau_{A_n,x} - \tau_{A_n,y}) \rangle.$$

as a time t location certificate, thus asserting to be at location y. ∎

We leave open the more general question of whether it is possible to have a passive location discovery protocol that satisfies the locale authentication goal.

8   Conclusion

We identified the security goal of locale authentication and provided a systematic technique for proving that location protocols satisfy that goal. The technique is based on extending the well-developed strand space theory with a metric that captures the geometric properties of time and space. We used the metric strand space theory to prove that several prominent location discovery protocols including GPS do not satisfy the locale authentication goal. We also analyzed a location discovery protocol that does satisfy the goal under some reasonable assumptions.

There are occasions in which certificates for physical parameters other than location would be desirable. For instance, a regulatory agency may require certification that certain parameters (level of contaminants, radiation, temperature) in a production facility are within legal tolerances. In principle, this can be done in much the same way by a certification authority by dispatching a human agent to the site. This can also be done by a tamper-proof gauge which issues an electronic certificate or prints out a paper one. However, there is no obvious way to exploit some physical resource such as geometry so that these certificates can be issued remotely without tamper-proof gadgetry. At this point the remote construction of such certificates remains an open problem. Another interesting question is whether it is possible to have a passive location discovery protocol that satisfies the locale authentication goal.

References

1. Bahl, P., Padmanabhan, V.N.: Radar: An in-building RF-based user location and tracking system. In: Proceedings of IEEE INFOCOM, vol. 2, pp. 775–784 (2000)
2. Brands, S., Chaum, D.: Distance-bounding protocols. In: Helleseth, T. (ed.) EU-ROCRYPT 1993. LNCS, vol. 765, pp. 344–359. Springer, Heidelberg (1994)
3. Capkun, S., Buttyan, L., Hubaux, J.P.: SECTOR: Secure tracking of node encounters in multi-hop wireless networks. In: Proceedings of the ACM Workshop on Security of Ad hoc and Sensor Networks, SASN (2003)
4. Denning, D.E., MacDoran, P.F.: Location-based authentication: Grounding cyberspace for better security. Computer Fraud & Security (February 1996)
5. Guttman, J.D., Thayer Fábrega, F.J.: Authentication tests and the structure of bundles. Theoretical Computer Science 283(2), 333–380 (2002)
6. Hofmann-Wellenhof, B., Lichtenegger, H., Collins, J.: The Global Positioning System: Theory and Practice. Springer, Wien (20014b)
7. Meadows, C., Poovendran, R., Pavlovic, D., Chang, L., Syverson, P.: Distance bounding protocols: Authentication logic analysis and collusion attacks. In: Advances in Information Security, vol. 30, pp. 279–298. Springer, Heidelberg (2007)
8. Poovendran, R., Wang, C., Roy, S. (eds.): Secure Localization and Time Synchronization for Wireless Sensor and Ad Hoc Networks. Advances in Information Security, vol. 30. Springer, Heidelberg (2007)
9. Priyantha, N.B., Miu, A.K.L., Balakrishnan, H., Teller, S.J.: The cricket compass for context-aware mobile applications. In: MOBICOM, pp. 1–14 (2001)
10. Sastry, N., Shankar, U., Wagner, D.: Secure verification of location claims. In: Proceedings of the ACM Workshop on Wireless Security, WiSe (2003)
11. Thayer Fábrega, F.J., Herzog, J.C., Guttman, J.D.: Strand spaces: Proving security protocols correct. Journal of Computer Security 7(2/3), 191–230 (1999)

A   Strand Space Definitions

This appendix, derived from [11,5], defines the basic strand space notions.

A.1   Strands, Strand Spaces, and Origination

Consider a set A, the elements of which are the possible messages that can be exchanged between principals in a protocol. We will refer to the elements of A as *terms*. In a protocol, principals can either send or receive terms. We represent transmission of a term as the occurrence of that term with positive sign, and reception of a term as its occurrence with negative sign.

Definition 5. *A signed term is a pair $\langle \sigma, a \rangle$ with $a \in A$ and σ one of the symbols $+, -$. We will write a signed term as $+t$ or $-t$. $(\pm A)^*$ is the set of finite sequences of signed terms. We will denote a typical element of $(\pm A)^*$ by $\langle \langle \sigma_1, a_1 \rangle, \ldots, \langle \sigma_n, a_n \rangle \rangle$.*

A strand space over A is a set Σ with a trace mapping $\mathrm{tr} : \Sigma \to (\pm A)^*$.

By abuse of language, we will still treat signed terms as ordinary terms. For instance, we shall refer to subterms of signed terms. We will usually represent a strand space by its underlying set of strands Σ.

Definition 6. *Fix a strand space* Σ.

1. *A node is a pair* $\langle s, i \rangle$, *with* $s \in \Sigma$ *and* i *an integer satisfying* $1 \leq i \leq$ $length(tr(s))$. *The set of nodes is denoted by* $\mathcal{N}$. *We will say the node* $\langle s, i \rangle$ *belongs to the strand* s. *Clearly, every node belongs to a unique strand.*
2. *If* $n = \langle s, i \rangle \in \mathcal{N}$ *then* $index(n) = i$ *and* $strand(n) = s$. *Define* $term(n)$ *to be* $(tr(s))_i$, *i.e. the* ith *signed term in the trace of* s. *Similarly,* $uns\_term(n)$ *is* $((tr(s))_i)_2$, *i.e. the unsigned part of the* ith *signed term in the trace of* s.
3. *There is an edge* $n_1 \rightarrow n_2$ *if and only if* $term(n_1) = +a$ *and* $term(n_2) = -a$ *for some* $a \in \mathsf{A}$. *Intuitively, the edge means that node* n_1 *sends the message* a, *which is received by* n_2, *recording a potential causal link between those strands.*
4. *When* $n_1 = \langle s, i \rangle$ *and* $n_2 = \langle s, i+1 \rangle$ *are members of* $\mathcal{N}$, *there is an edge* $n_1 \Rightarrow n_2$. *Intuitively, the edge expresses that* n_1 *is an immediate causal predecessor of* n_2 *on the strand* s. *We write* $n' \Rightarrow^+ n$ *to mean that* n' *precedes* n *(not necessarily immediately) on the same strand.*
5. *An unsigned term* t *occurs in* $n \in \mathcal{N}$ *iff* $t \sqsubset term(n)$.
6. *Suppose* I *is a set of unsigned terms. The node* $n \in \mathcal{N}$ *is an* entry point *for* I *iff* $term(n) = +t$ *for some* $t \in I$, *and whenever* $n' \Rightarrow^+ n$, *term*$(n') \notin I$.
7. *An unsigned term* t *originates on* $n \in \mathcal{N}$ *iff* n *is an entry point for the set* $I = \{t' : t \sqsubset t'\}$.
8. *An unsigned term* t *is* uniquely originating *in a set of nodes* $S \subset \mathcal{N}$ *iff there is a unique* $n \in S$ *such that* t *originates on* n.
9. *An unsigned term* t *is* non-originating *in a set of nodes* $S \subset \mathcal{N}$ *iff there is no* $n \in S$ *such that* t *originates on* n.

If a term t originates uniquely in a suitable set of nodes, then it can play the role of a nonce or session key, assuming that everything that the penetrator does in some scenario is in that set of nodes.

$\mathcal{N}$ together with both sets of edges $n_1 \rightarrow n_2$ and $n_1 \Rightarrow n_2$ is a directed graph $\langle \mathcal{N}, (\rightarrow \cup \Rightarrow) \rangle$.

A *bundle* is a finite subgraph of $\langle \mathcal{N}, (\rightarrow \cup \Rightarrow) \rangle$, for which we can regard the edges as expressing the causal dependencies of the nodes.

Definition 7. *Suppose* $\rightarrow_{\mathcal{C}} \subset \rightarrow$; *suppose* $\Rightarrow_{\mathcal{C}} \subset \Rightarrow$; *and suppose* $\mathcal{C} = \langle \mathcal{N}_{\mathcal{C}}, (\rightarrow_{\mathcal{C}}$ $\cup \Rightarrow_{\mathcal{C}}) \rangle$ *is a subgraph of* $\langle \mathcal{N}, (\rightarrow \cup \Rightarrow) \rangle$. $\mathcal{C}$ *is a bundle if:*

1. $\mathcal{N}_{\mathcal{C}}$ *and* $\rightarrow_{\mathcal{C}} \cup \Rightarrow_{\mathcal{C}}$ *are finite.*
2. *If* $n_2 \in \mathcal{N}_{\mathcal{C}}$ *and* $term(n_2)$ *is negative, then there is a unique* n_1 *such that* $n_1 \rightarrow_{\mathcal{C}} n_2$.
3. *If* $n_2 \in \mathcal{N}_{\mathcal{C}}$ *and* $n_1 \Rightarrow n_2$ *then* $n_1 \Rightarrow_{\mathcal{C}} n_2$.
4. $\mathcal{C}$ *is acyclic.*

In conditions 2 and 3, it follows that $n_1 \in \mathcal{N}_{\mathcal{C}}$, because $\mathcal{C}$ is a graph.

Definition 8. *A node* n *is in a bundle* $\mathcal{C} = \langle \mathcal{N}_{\mathcal{C}}, \rightarrow_{\mathcal{C}} \cup \Rightarrow_{\mathcal{C}} \rangle$, *written* $n \in \mathcal{C}$, *if* $n \in \mathcal{N}_{\mathcal{C}}$; *a strand* s *is in* $\mathcal{C}$ *if all of its nodes are in* $\mathcal{N}_{\mathcal{C}}$.

If $\mathcal{C}$ *is a bundle, then the* $\mathcal{C}$-height *of a strand* s *is the largest* i *such that* $\langle s, i \rangle \in \mathcal{C}$. $\mathcal{C}$-trace$(s) = \langle tr(s)(1), \ldots, tr(s)(m) \rangle$, *where* $m = \mathcal{C}$-height(s).

We say that $s \in \mathcal{C}$ *if the* $\mathcal{C}$-height *of* s *equals* $length(s)$.

Visitor Access Control Scheme Utilizing Social Relationship in the Real World

Gen Kitagata[1], Debasish Chakraborty[1], Satoshi Ogawa[1], Atushi Takeda[2], Kazuo Hashimoto[3], and Norio Shiratori[1]

[1] Research Institute of Electrical Communication, Tohoku University
2-1-1 Katahira, Aoba-ku, Sendai 980-8577, Japan
[2] Tohoku Bunka Gakuen University, Sendai, Japan
[3] Graduate School of Information Sciences, Tohoku University, Sendai, Japan

Abstract. Access control to resources is one of the most important technologies for supporting human activities in the digital space. To realize the control two schemes were proposed: RBAC (Role-Based Access Control) and TRBAC (Temporal Role-Based Access Control) by adding time constraints and role dependencies to RBAC. However, these methods are not effective for temporal activities such as visitor access because of maintenance costs and inadequacy in safeness. In this paper, we focus on a visitor access control in the real world, by utilizing relationship with users and situations, and propose a novel access control scheme which is effective for temporal activities.

Keywords: Access control, socialware, symbiotic computing, collaborative work.

1 Introduction

Growth of ubiquitous computing technology make people's activities in digital space more popular than ever. Digital space is a kind of societies where people participate and interacts. Same as in real space, people in digital space should recognize society, and be able to take actions without anxiety and discomfort. Socialware [1] is a software technology to support people's activities in digital space by enhancing social reality. Socialware has two goals: to apply existing rules and knowledge used in real space to activities in digital space, and to create new and knowledge specific rules to digital space. In social knowledge, where knowledge involved with social activities, is an important information source to enhance people's social reality in digital space. In this paper, focusing on access control to resources in digital space, which is indispensable for activities in digital space, we propose a novel access control scheme based on the concept of Socialware.

RBAC (Role-Based Access Control) [2] is one of the existing access control schemes, where users are assigned with roles, and roles with access rights. This scheme has an advantage of management cost because roles are, in general, likely to be associated with positions in an organization. However, this scheme requires static configuration of acceptable roles in ACL (Access Control List). So to add, change, and delete users and roles, it has to be done manually. Therefore, this scheme is effective where roles are

M. Nishigaki et al. (Eds.): IFIPTM 2010, IFIP AICT 321, pp. 95–107, 2010.

semi-static. But some users accesses should be enabled temporarily. This is because, in the latter case, administrator will be burdened by frequent manual management of ACL, and also there might be an issue of safety if administrator forgot to disable temporal access rights afterwards. TRBAC (Temporal Role-Based Access Control) [3] is an access control scheme for dynamic and temporal changes to access rights assigned to roles. TRBAC is effective for activities with clear action times, such as a task starting from a fixed time. However, TRBAC can not deal with occasional meetings and unexpected activities caused due to emergency situation. Therefore, it is necessary to dynamically control access rights for activities with no clear action time.

In this paper, we propose automated visitor access control scheme to control third person's access right by utilizing social relationship. Our scheme flexibly gives access rights in response to situation of workplace and social relationship. This realizes temporal grant of access to resources for irregular activities that do not have explicit action times such as occasional meeting. It is to be noted that 'right' and 'authentication' has been used to represent the same meaning throughout this paper if not otherwise mentioned.

The remainder of this paper is organized as follows. In Section 2, we introduce related works on access control and issues. The proposed scheme and its model are described in Section 3. Section 4 presents a collaborative work support system with the proposed scheme, and Section 5 presents experiments and discussion with the system. In Section 6, we compare our scheme with existing access control scheme utilizing social relationship. We conclude our work in Section 7.

2   Related Works

TRBAC (Temporal Role-Based Access Control) [3] introduces time constraint and role dependencies to its scheme, to deal with temporal roles. For example, assume that a part-time staff works with some company from 9 a.m. to 1 p.m., and a role 'part-time-staff' is assigned to the staff. In this case, an administrator can activate the role 'part-time-staff' from 9 a.m. to 1 p.m. in order to give the staff an access right to the company's system with some time constraint. In addition, validity of a certain role can be controlled in response to the condition of other role, which is called role dependencies. For example, a role 'nurse' can be active only if a role 'doctor' is active. With time constraint and role dependencies, TRBAC effectively deal with regular activities. However, administrator has to make changes to roles for temporal or emergency activities, and higher the frequency of such activities, heavier the workload. Therefore, it is necessary to realize temporal access grant for temporal and emergency activities.

3   Access Control Proposal Based on Real Space Social Interactions

3.1   Access Control in Real Space

This paper introduces the notion of temporary access control based on irregular time stamps. This concept is difficult to apply in the existing TRBAC. In real world, there is a need to grant temporary access control during undetermined time stamps, as shown

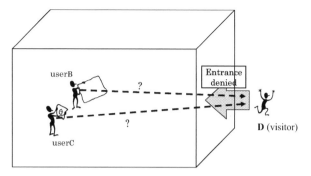

(a) No member has social relationship with the visitor

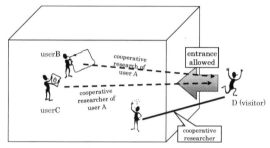

(b) Person *User A* has social relationship with the visitor

Fig. 1. Access control in real-space

in Fig. 1. In this case, *User A*, *User B* and *User C* are members of the laboratory *L*, whereas *User D* (visitor) is not a member. However, *User D* involves in a cooperative research project with *User A*. Let us suppose *User D* is going to *L*. As shown in Fig. 1(a), due to the fact that *User A* is not in the laboratory, *User B* and *User C* are unable to identify *User D*. Therefore, *User D* will not be allowed inside. Since *User A* is not present, *L* infers that there is no cooperative project in development and so *User D* would not receive the permission to enter the laboratory. On the other hand, as shown in picture Fig. 1(b), when *User A* is in the laboratory, it creates an environment in which *User D* is authenticated as socially related with *User A*. Therefore, *User D* is allowed inside the room. In this way, rooms that normally would be out of reach for an outsider, can be accessed due to the social relationship.

While inside the laboratory, person *User A* becomes responsible of *User D*'s behavior. For that reason, *User D* can have same or less access privileges than *User A*. In this similar way we introduce the term of social relationship based access control authority delegation.

3.2 Proposal

As we presented in the previous chapter, we introduce the notion of automatic temporary access control based on irregular time stamps. This concept is difficult to implement by using only TRBAC. We intend to implement in the digital space the same concept regarding access control permissions as in the real world. The spectrum of our access control permissions greatly depends on the existence of a guarantor at the location where a certain job or task is being undertaken.

Therefore, we consider the following two conditions as important:

- T1 - selection of the socially related user from inside the working place (L)
- T2 - delegation of rights based on social relationship

Based on the previous two conditions, we propose the following:

- S1 - Implementation of the workplace.
- S2 - Social relationship based access control filter and delegation of rights.

We will explain in detail about S1 and S2 in the next chapters.

The introduction of a work place. In real space, depending on the existence of a guarantor, in other words if there is no social relationship, our access to certain resources in a certain environment are limited or completely restricted. In order to introduce this concept into the digital world, we have to explicitly state the existence of a working place. So far, this was not considered by the existing access control models. Because of the existence of the working place we can now define the relationship between the users that activate within its boundaries. The working place in this case is what we defined in Section 3(A) as L. Inside the working place, there are several resources like printer, projector etc., which can be accessed by outsiders only with the explicit permission of an insider with the right permissions and the right social relationship.

Delegation of access control based on social relationship. A couple of events occur when $User\ A$, the user that delegates the access rights transfers its rights to $User\ D$, the user that receives the delegated rights.

- The delegation of rights occurs in conformity with the social relationship between the two.
- The person that receives the rights cannot have more rights that the person that delegates the rights.

In order to meet the previous two requirements, we propose an authentication filter whose role is to delegate only the necessary rights from $User\ A$ to $User\ D$. The access rights of $User\ D$ will be the intersection between the set of rights of $User\ A$ and set of rights accepted by the filter. The control knowledge (access control rules) is given by the pair of social relationship and permission filter. As shown in Fig. 2, in order to delegate access control rights based on social relationships, we need to setup the access control filter based on access control knowledge. The filter will therefore set the terms of access control rights.

If the permission delegation does not occur in a hierarchical manner, from the security point of view we do not have a trustworthy environment. Therefore, we introduce the concept of allowing rights which enables the user with access permissions to delegate his rights to others. To fulfill this we employ two types of filters:

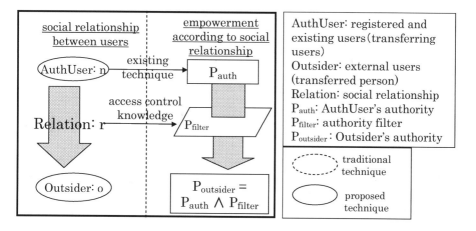

Fig. 2. Delegation of access authorization

1. Filter A - which will give right to delegate even to the outsiders if they are trustworthy.
2. Filter B - which will give only specific rights to outsiders, but not the right to delegate.

3.3 The Concept in Detail

Factors (components) and models. In this proposal we introduced seven components of the access control model: *resources, users (visitor and member), access (authority) rights, (permission) rights filter, social relationship, work place and access control knowledge.* Fig. 3 shows our access control model. We will explain them in detail as follows.

- Resource I: computing resources or secret information which fall into the authority of access control.
- Outsider O: a visitor who wants to use resources but not having permission regularly.
- Member M: a member of organization who has regular permission for resource usage.
- Access authority (permission, rights) P: the set of rules against the resources utilized by users.
- Permission filter F: the set of access permissions that can be delegated.
- Social relationship R: the link between users (e.g. if there is a cooperative project under development, the participating members are bound by social links).
- Workplace W: the place where resources are located.
- Access control knowledge K: this knowledge is used to choose authority filter which is used for authority transferring utilizing social relationships among users.

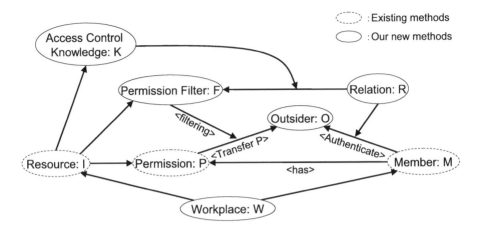

Fig. 3. Access control model of our scheme

Workplace (attribute value; property value). In our proposal, considering the importance to retrieve information about the status of a user, we define the workplace as follows:

$$w = \langle u_{list}, i_{list} \rangle$$
$$u_{list} = \langle u_0, u_1, ..., u_n \rangle$$
$$i_{list} = \langle i_0, i_i, ..., i_m \rangle$$
$$w \epsilon W, u_n \epsilon R, i_m \epsilon I$$

In this case, the u_{list}, and i_{list} are set of users and resources in a certain workplace. In other words, our workplace is formed of users and existing resources. The user's status with regard to the workplace might change. Therefore w changes with time. User u is defined as:

$$u = \langle d_u, ru_{list}, p_{list} \rangle$$
$$ru_{list} = \langle ru_0, ru_1, \cdots, ru_n \rangle$$
$$ru_k = \langle r_k, u_k \rangle$$
$$p_{list} = \langle p_0, p_1, \cdots, p_n \rangle$$
$$r_k \in R, u_k \in U, p_k \in P$$

In this case, d_u represents the user's data and ru_{list} represents the set of social relationships of the user. For example, in case of a cooperative project, we can identify it as social relationship between the coworkers.

Delegation of access control. We propose a system in which a user u_u wishing to utilize a workplace w is looking for a user u_a with whom u_u has a social relationship r and it is being identified by the latter. The permission filter is based on the access control knowledge and the social relationship. As a result, the permission p_a, held by the user u_p intersected with the permission filter set f, produces the set of permissions

```
authorize(u_u){
    (u_a, r_{a-u}) := decideDelegater(u_u, w);
    p_u := delegatePermissions(u_a, r_{a-u});
    allow(p_u);
}

delegatePermissions(u_a, r_{a-u}){
    f := getPermissionFilter(r_{a-u});
    p := u_a.p_{list} ∧ f;
    return  p;
}
```

Fig. 4. Algorithm for access delegation

```
getPermissionFilter(r_{a-u}){
    if (r_{a-u} == "cooperative researcher")
        return [p1, p2, p3, p4];
    elseif (r_{a-u} == "OB")
        return [p3, p4];
    elseif (r_{a-u} == "visiting Lab.")
        return [p4];
    else
        return [];
}
```

Fig. 5. Access control knowledge for a laboratory

p_u of user u_u. The process of granting access permission p to user u_u is shown in Fig. 4. The algorithm starts with the selection of the socially related user (*decideDelegater*) which can delegate permissions. In order to do that, the *delegatePermissions* function is applying the *getPermissionFilter* and returns the proper access control rights. In Fig. 5 we show how the access knowledge works.

3.4   The Process of Granting Access Permission

We explain the process of granting access permission with Fig. 6. In this example we portray user *UserD* who is not a part of the laboratory L but has the intent of activating for a while there. The users *UserA* and *UserB* are members of laboratory L. *UserD* and *UserA* are socially linked through a common (cooperative) project and the former has *rwa (read, write, allow)* rights for the resource 1. Socially linked users as co-researchers are empowered by the access control knowledge with *rw* rights for resource 1. We present the process of granting permissions to *UserD* as follows:

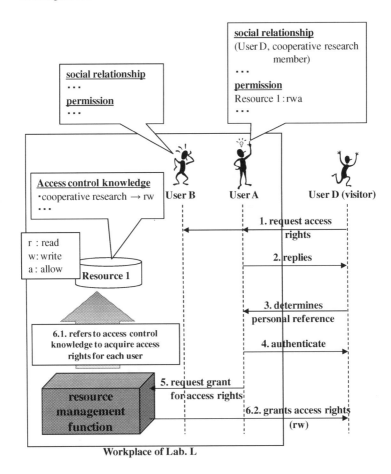

Fig. 6. Flow of access authorization

1. *UserD* asks for access permission from the workplace - in this case the laboratory L.
2. The users that have any social link with *UserD* reply to it.
3. *UserD* finds *UserA* as being socially related.
4. Based on the predetermined rules, *UserA* becomes the guarantor of *UserD* .
5. If the authentication process is successful, *UserA* requests access permissions from the resource administrator.
6. The resource administrator checks all the resource access knowledges, passes them through permission filter and intersects them with the set of *UserA* 's permissions resulting in *UserD* 's permissions.

In this way, utilizing our concept, even if *UserD* does not have permissions to access resources, due to the social link with *UserA* , the former will be granted temporary access rights to the resources that make the object of the common goal.

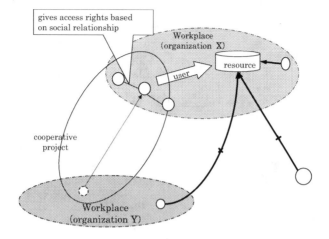

Fig. 7. Cooperative work support system

4   Cooperative Work Support System

4.1   Summary of the System

To confirm effectiveness of our proposal, we design a cooperative work support system. This system realizes access control for resources owned by organizations, and also the system can be applied for temporal activities of users by utilizing social relationships. Fig. 7 shows summary of the system. In Fig. 7, there are two organization X and Y. These organizations proceed cooperative project. Social relationship such as "cooperative project member" are constructed among users who are joined the project. Due to this social relationship, users belonging to organization Y and are joined the project can use resource in organization X. By contrast, users belonging to organization Y but are not joined the project and has no relationship with member of organization X cannot use the resource in organization X. Also a visitor who does not belong to both organization X and Y, and has no relationship with member of organization X cannot use the resource in organization X.

4.2   Agent Composition

We design the system based on agent-oriented computing and introduce the following three agents:

1. User Agent: This agent is a delegate of a user in digital space. This agent uses resources instead of real user according to the user's request.
2. Resource Agent: This agent agentificates resources and has access control knowledge and an authority filter. For instance, we designed a printer agent ($printerAg$) and a projector agent ($projectorAg$).
3. Workplace Agent: This agent administrates user agents and resource agents in workplace. It delegate access authority to a user according to social relationships by referring access control knowledge held in resource agent.

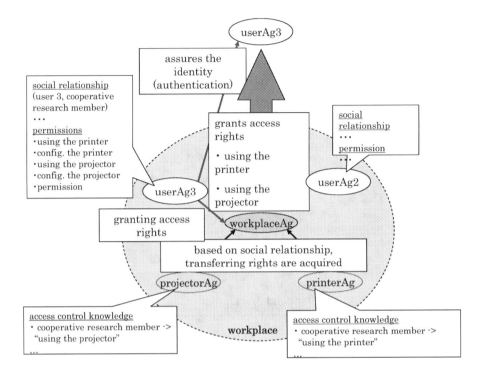

Fig. 8. Agent composition

Fig. 8 shows agent composition of our system. *userAg1* to *userAg3* represents user agents; *printerAg* and *projectorAg* are resource agents. And *workplaceAg* is a workplace agent. And workplace in Fig. 8 represents the space where user works. The field is administrated by *workplaceAg*. Here, presence of a user is expressed as presence of a user agent in workplace. For example, when a user sends a request for authority delegation but no response is returned by any user agents, it implies that there are no member who has social relationship with the user, and as a result access for requested resource is denied.

4.3 Environment of Implementation

We implemented the system by using DASH [5] system which is rule-based agent framework, and IDEA [6] which is an integrated design environment for DASH. We used Java language to implement base processes controlled by DASH agents.

5   Experiment and Evaluation

To evaluate our proposal, we conducted experiments with some scenarios under certain conditions depicted in Fig. 9. *User C* and *User D* are member of laboratory, and *User A* and *User B* are visitors. *User C* proceeds a cooperative research with *User A*.

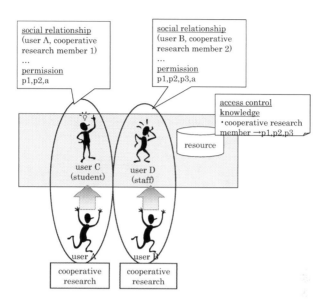

Fig. 9. Precondition of operation scenario

$User\ D$ also does another cooperative research with $User\ B$. So there are social relationships according to these cooperative researches. In addition, $User\ C$ is a student and $User\ D$ is a staff, so $User\ D$ has much authority than $User\ C$. We assume situations that a visitor, $User\ A$ and $User\ B$, comes to laboratory's workplace to proceed cooperative research. Here, we conducted 4 experiments as following scenarios: (1) no one is in the laboratory, (2) only $User\ C$ is present, (3) only $user\ D$ is present, (4) both $User\ C$ and $User\ D$ are present.

Fig. 10 shows experimental results. We confirmed that both $User\ A$ and $User\ B$ got access authority by social relationship as "cooperative research member", but the authorities of $User\ A$ and $User\ B$ are not same. This is because they are delegated authorities by different user. Also in some scenarios, we found cases when authority is not delegated. In these scenarios, because a member who has social relationship with the visitor, $user\ A$ or $User\ B$, is absent and the system cannot verify identity of the visitor, and no authority is delegated. In other words, absent of $User\ C$ means that cooperative work of $User\ A$ and $User\ C$ are not proceeded. Therefore $User\ A$ cannot get authority while $User\ C$ is absent.

By the above results, we confirmed that our system is useful to delegate authority for temporal activities by utilizing social relationship of users presented in field of activity.

6   Discussion

Visitor access control schemes utilizing social relationship was proposed in previous works [4]. In this access control scheme, access rights are statically configured based on social relationship. Because of static configuration, administrator has to configure

Cases scenario (Users in Workplace)	User A requests access rights	User B requests access rights
(1) None	X	X
(2) User C	p1, p2	X
(3) User D	X	p1, p2, p3
(4) User C & D	p1, p2, p3	p1, p2, p3

X: no access right is granted due to lack of personal reference

Fig. 10. Evaluation results

multiple access rules for each social relationships. For example, necessary rules for a relationship of 'co-researcher' are professor, associate professor, student and so on. In contrast, the proposed scheme gives an access right to a user by applying authentication filter to the right of who offer the user's personal reference. Therefore, administrator only needs to configure authentication filter and access control rules for each relationship. For example, one set of them for the 'co-researcher' relationship. In addition, existing scheme uses social relationship of all users regardless of existence of them. This can realize temporal access grant with time constraint for regular activities, but unable to deal with irregular ones. In contrast, proposed scheme can effectively control access rights even if temporal grant of access is necessary.

7   Conclusion

In this paper, we proposed a novel access control scheme to automatically grant accesses for irregular activities such as resource usage of visitor which TRBAC cannot deal with. This scheme achieves to control access rights in digital space as in real space.

Acknowledgement

This work is partially supported by the Research and Development of Dynamic Network Technology program of NiCT.

References

1. Kinoshita, T., Konno, S., Kitagata, G., Uchiya, T., Hara, H.: Symbiotic System: Co-existence and Mutual Respect of Human, Society, Environment, and Information System, Forward: Socialware. IPSJ 47(8), 817–824 (2006)
2. Sandhu, R.S., Coyne, E.J., Feinstein, H.L., Youman, C.E.: Role-Based Access Control Model. Computer 29(2), 38–47 (1996)
3. Bertino, E., Bonatti, P.A., Ferrari, E.: TRBAC: A Temporal Role-Based Access Control Model. ACM Trans. Information and System Security 4(3), 191–233 (2001)
4. Nagao, M., Keeni, G.M., Ishigaki, M., Togashi, A., Noguchi, S.: A Secure Distributed Database System with Time-series Data and Social-Relation Based Information Access Control. IEICE Technical Report 107(6), 55–60

5. Fujita, S., Hara, H., Sugawara, K., Kinoshita, T., Shiratori, N.: Agent-based design model of adaptive distributed systems. The International Journal of Artificial Intelligence, Neural Networks and Complex Problem-Solving Technologies 9(1), 57–70 (1998)
6. Uchiya, T., Maemura, T., Sugawara, K., Kinoshita, T.: Interactive Design Environment for Agent-Based System. Transaction of the Institute of Electronics, Information and Communication Engineers. D-I J88-D-I(9), 1344–1355

Impact of Trust Management and Information Sharing to Adversarial Cost in Ranking Systems

Le-Hung Vu, Thanasis G. Papaioannou, and Karl Aberer

School of Computer and Communication Sciences
École Polytechnique Fédérale de Lausanne (EPFL)
CH-1015 Lausanne, Switzerland
{lehung.vu,thanasis.papaioannou,karl.aberer}@epfl.ch

Abstract. Ranking systems such as those in product review sites and recommender systems usually use ratings to rank favorite items based on both their quality and popularity. Since higher ranked items are more likely selected and yield more revenues for their owners, providers of unpopular and low quality items have strong incentives to strategically manipulate their ranking. This paper analyzes the adversary cost for manipulating these rankings in a variety of scenarios. Particularly, we analyze and compare the adversarial cost to attack ranking systems that use various trust measures to detect and eliminate malicious ratings to systems that use no such a trust management mechanism. We provide theoretical results showing the relation between the capability of the trust mechanism in detecting malicious ratings and the minimal adversarial cost for successfully changing the ranking. Furthermore, we study the impact of sharing trust information between ranking systems to the adversarial cost. It is proved that sharing information between two ranking systems on common user identities and malicious behaviors detected can increase considerably the minimal adversarial cost to successfully attack the two systems under certain assumptions. The numerical evaluation of our results shows that the estimated adversary cost for manipulating the item ranking can be made significant when proper trust mechanisms are employed or combined.

Keywords: Trust; information sharing; open systems; adversarial cost; ranking systems; dishonesty detection.

1 Introduction

Ranking has become a popular and important feature of online business applications. A ranking system enables users to rate their favorite items based on item quality and also according to their own preferences. Items may represent services, products, sellable articles, digital content, or search results in different application scenarios. To facilitate the searching of users, these ratings are then used to rank a large number of items of the same category according to both their quality and popularity, e.g. ranking of digital content in social sites (Digg.com) or products in recommender systems (Amazon.com).

M. Nishigaki et al. (Eds.): IFIPTM 2010, IFIP AICT 321, pp. 108–124, 2010.

The impact of user online opinions on sales and profits is significant [1]. One can reasonably expect that items with higher ranks are more likely to be selected by clients and thus to produce more value for their providers. Consequently, there is a clear incentive for owners of unpopular and bad items to employ malicious identities to promote (i.e. "ballot-stuff") their own items and demote (i.e. "badmouth") competing ones to generate higher revenue. In real applications these issues are inevitable. For example, sellers can pay people for posting positive reviews on their products, as in [2] where Amazon reviews are bought with 65 cents each. Botnets can even be hired to conduct the attacks [3].

Regarding manipulation-resistance of ranking metrics, there have been a large number of works on studying resistance of Web page ranking algorithms, such as by throttling Web spams via link structure and link credibility analysis [4,5]. These works are applicable to large scale ranking systems that sort Web pages based on various criteria, such link quality and credibility of provider sites [6,7]. The application of trust mechanisms [8,9] to improve the robustness of a ranking system under adversarial attacks, such as ballot-stuffing and badmouthing is also well-explored [5,10]. However, the impact of the capability of a trust mechanism in detecting malicious ratings to the robustness of the ranking system using such mechanisms has not been analyzed yet.

To this end, we present in this paper an analytical approach to evaluate the robustness of a ranking system under attack by an intelligent adversary with limited resources. Particularly, we analyze the cost of an adversary to successfully manipulate the item ranking in smaller-scale systems, such as product review sites and recommender systems. The adversarial cost is estimated as the number of identities and ratings that need to be employed by the adversary to successfully change the ranks of specific targeted items. In practice, this cost may represent the cost of hiring people or botnets to post fake ratings on the targets [3]. We compare the adversary costs when specific trust mechanisms to eliminate biased ratings are employed or not. Thus, we provide theoretical results showing the relation between the capability of the trust mechanism being used to detect malicious ratings and the adversarial cost to attack a ranking system. By numerically evaluating our results, we show that the improvement in robustness of a ranking system using a trust mechanism with a given capability to detect dishonest ratings can be significant under certain assumptions.

Moreover, we extend our analysis to quantify the adversarial cost in an interesting scenario where two similar ranking systems share information regarding common users and the detection of malicious ratings. This scenario is realistic for the following reasons. On one hand, building applications that allows better exchanges of information on user activities with similar systems is an emerging trend adopted by many research and commercial initiatives, e.g., the on-going standardization of the OASIS committee on information exchange across reputation systems[1] and the OpenSocial API for better sharing information among

---

[1] www.oasis-open.org/committees/orms

online social networks. Commercial initiatives that are capable of collecting user activities across virtual communities are already available, some examples of which include Spokeo[2] and Reputation Defender[3]. On the other hand, malicious providers may want to publish their items in different systems for higher profits. To reduce cost, an adversarial provider may reuse a number of malicious identities across systems when posting bogus votes to manipulate the ranking of their items in different systems, e.g., by hiring only one botnet. Hence, by sharing the detection of malicious behaviors across systems, more malicious users are discovered and eliminated, which in turn helps to improve the robustness of the participating systems. We prove that, under certain realistic assumptions, two systems sharing information on common user identities and detected malicious ratings can increase the attack cost of an adversary considerably.

The remainder of this paper is organized as follows: in the next section, we describe the problem of ranking items in the presence of malicious raters. In Section 3, we analytically derive the minimum cost for the adversary to manipulate the ranking of the items under a trust mechanism that detects malicious votes with a certain effectiveness. In Section 4, we prove that the adversarial cost for manipulating the ranking of items increases when two systems exchange information regarding user identities and detected malicious ratings. Our results are numerically evaluated in Section 5, in Section 6 we discuss the related work before concluding the paper in Section 7.

2   Problem Formulation

Consider a ranking system with a set S of items (e.g. products or services), each having a binary static quality (good or bad). A user may rate the quality of the item after buying it. Let U be the set of honest raters. We denote as $r(u, s) \in \{1, 0, -1\}$ the value of a rating from a user $u \in U$ for an item $s \in S$, where a value $r(u, s) = 0$ implies that u does not rate s. In general, a user $u \in U$ reports accurately the item quality. However, due to some observation noise, u may rate an item inaccurately with a small probability $0 < \varepsilon \ll 1$, e.g. a bad item is rated positively or vice versa. The items are ranked by their quality and popularity score (*QP-score*) $f(s)$ defined for any item $s \in S$ as:

$$f(s) = \sum_{u \in U} r(u, s), \tag{1}$$

where a rating $r(u, s)$ is counted only once for each user u and each item s.

Let $S = \{s_i, 1 \leq i \leq M\}$ be the set of all items, where s_i has an original rank i according to the formula (1). Intuitively, $i < j$, or the item s_i is said to have a higher rank than s_j iff $f(s_i) > f(s_j)$.

The simple ranking function in (1) that only counts the number of positive and negative votes on an item is already effective to rank items in terms of their quality and popularity, provided that no adversary is present. In fact such a

---

[2] www.spokeo.com
[3] www.reputationdefender.com

metric has been used for ranking the digital contents on various Web 2.0 sites, e.g., to identify the most popular videos or blog entries. The use of sophisticated ranking metrics in more complex business applications, e.g. by considering credibility of the raters, belongs to the class of trust-based ranking functions that we will consider later on. We note that our approach to estimate the adversarial cost as presented in this work can even be extended to arbitrary ranking functions, although a closed-form solution cannot be easily obtained.

Suppose that there is an adversary who wants to boost the rank of an item s_k to the highest rank $k^* = 1 < k$. Herein, we use $k^* = 1$ to reduce the number of notations, but it is trivial to extend our analysis for any $k^* < k$. The same analytical reasoning could also be applied to the case that the adversary wanted to raise or lower the rank of a set of items instead of a single one. In order to promote item s_k, the adversary uses a set D of malicious user identities to post positive ratings on s_k and negative ratings on competing items, i.e. $s_i, 1 \leq i \leq k - 1$. The total number of malicious ratings is C, and the cost of the adversary includes both components C and $|D|$.

For each item $s_i, 1 \leq i \leq k$, denote as U_i and D_i the set of honest and malicious users who rate on s_i, respectively. The number of ratings on an item s_i by a honest and malicious users are respectively $x_i = |U_i|$ and $y_i = |D_i|$. Depending the true quality (high or low) of s_i, the majority of x_i honest ratings on s_i would be positive or negative. Naturally, $\bigcup_{i=1}^{k} D_i = D$ and $\sum_{i=1}^{k} y_i = C$, since ratings items ranked lower than s_k does not help boosting the rank of the target item s_k but increase the cost of the adversary. Note that the adversary can observe, prior to his attack, the set U_i of any item s_i. We assume the worst case scenario where the adversary can estimate the numerical ranking score of every item, apart from the ranking, and thus can derive the cost C and $|D|$ to strategically change the ranking of items.

The system designer wants the ranking to reflect the true quality and popularity of items, so that the system is useful to its users. One naive approach that is often followed would be to simply ignore the presence of a possible adversary, and the items to be ranked according to the QP-score of each item s as in (1): $f_N(s) = \sum_{u \in U \cup D} r(u, s)$. To restrict the effect of the malicious ratings posted by the adversary, a preferable approach is to rank items based on the following trust-based QP score:

$$f_T(s) = \sum_{u \in U \cup D} r(u, s) t(u, s), \qquad (2)$$

where $0 \leq t(u, s) \leq 1$ is the estimated trustworthiness of the rating $r(u, s)$ and it is measured differently based on the trust management approach employed.

We focus in the comparison of the optimal cost of the adversary in terms of its minimal numbers of ratings C and malicious identities $|D|$, to successfully boost the rank of the item s_k in many situations where different QP scores $f_T(s), f_N(s)$ are used to rank items, and under different possible approaches to evaluate the trustworthiness of ratings. Note that without the adversary $D = \emptyset$, we have $f_T(s) = f_N(s) = f(s)$. Since $r(u, s)$ can be considered as a random variable, i.e., subject to observation noise or the honesty of the rating user, we estimate the expected values $E[f(s)], E[f_N(s)], E[f_T(s)]$, whenever the exact rating $r(u, s)$ is unknown. Regarding the quality of the other items, we only consider the most important case where items in the competing set $s_i, 1 \leq i \leq k - 1$ are of good quality (and thus they should be highly ranked for the benefit of the users). The other cases can be similarly analyzed.

3   Adversarial Cost under Trust-Based Ranking

3.1   Uniform Detection Capability of Malicious Ratings

Consider the system as described in Section 2, with approximate $x_i = |U_i|$ honest ratings (both positive and negative ones) on an item $s_i, i = 1, ..., |S|$. With the trust-based QP-score (2) as a ranking metric, the minimal cost of the adversary to manipulate the ranking is given by Proposition 1.

Proposition 1. *Suppose that the system uses a trust mechanism that can detect malicious ratings on any item with a probability $0 < \gamma < 1$. It is possible to design a ranking system in which the minimal adversarial cost, in expectation, to boost the rank of an item from k to 1 includes the cost of creating $|D_T|$ identities and posting $C_T = |D_T|$ ratings on the target item s_k, where:*

$$|D_T| = (x_1 + x_k)\frac{1 - 2\varepsilon + \varepsilon\gamma}{1 - \gamma} \tag{3}$$

Proof. First, we prove that there exists a simple trust management approach that is capable of detecting malicious ratings on any item with a probability $0 < \gamma < 1$. The following naive trust management approach to define the trustworthiness $t(u, s)$ of a rating satisfies such a requirement (see Fig. 1):

- A trusted rater e is used to monitor the quality of a (uniformly) randomly selected set of items $E \subseteq S$, where $|E| = \gamma|S|$.
- For any $u \in U \cup D$, if there exists some item $s \in S$ such that the rating $r(u, s) \neq r(e, s)$, and $r(u, s)r(e, s) \neq 0$, we define $t(u, s) = 0$.
- Each remaining rating $r(u, s)$ has its trustworthiness proportional to the number of ratings with the same value. Formally, $t(u, s) = |Ut(s)|/|U(s)|$, where $U(s) \subseteq U \cup D$ is the group of users who rate on s, and $Ut(s) \subseteq U(s)$ is the users with ratings $r(u, s)$ on s.

Apparently, the above trust mechanism can detect malicious ratings on any item $s \in S$ with a probability γ, at the cost of the system designer evaluating $|E| = \gamma|S|$ items to learn of their true quality. Of course there may exist other trust mechanisms that are more cost-efficient, i.e., require the evaluation of less than $\gamma|S|$ services for a given capability of detection γ. The designing of such a trust mechanism is out of the scope of this analysis.

Recall that U_i and D_i are correspondingly the sets of honest and cheating raters on s_i. The trust-based QP score of an item $s_i, 1 \leq i \leq k$ is $f_T(s_i) = \sum_{u \in U_i \cup D_i} r(u, s_i)t(u, s_i)$. To effectively boost the rank of s_k, the adversary needs to post *at least* y_i negative ratings on each item $s_i, 1 \leq i \leq k - 1$ and *at least* y_k positive ratings on the item s_k. The goal of the adversary is to ensure the

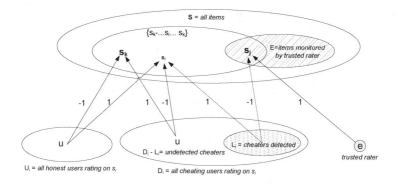

Fig. 1. Detection possibly malicious ratings on items by using a trusted rater

expected trust-based QP-score of the target item s_k to be as high as that of every other item of higher rank, i.e., $E[f_T(s_k)] \geq E[f_T(s_i)], 1 \leq i \leq k-1$.

Consider any item s_i, $1 \leq i \leq k-1$ with a good quality. Due to observation noise, among honest users U_i, a subset $U_i' \subseteq U_i$ may give unfair (negative) ratings on s_i. A smaller subset $U_i'' \subseteq U_i'$ may be detected by the trust management approach as cheater. Similarly, a subset of malicious users D_i who rate s_i negatively (to favor s_k) would be detected by the trust management mechanism. Denote as $L_i \subseteq D_i$ the set of malicious raters that are not detected. Then, users in the group $P_i = U_i - U_i'$ vote positively and those in the group $N_i = (U_i' - U_i'') \cup L_i$ vote negatively on s_i. Note that $P_i \cup N_i = (U_i - U_i'') \cup L_i$, as in Fig. 2(a). The trustworthiness $t(u, s_i)$ of a rating $r(u, s_i)$ is estimated as:

- For $u \in U_i'' \cup (D_i - L_i) : t(u, s_i) = 0$, i.e., users with erroneous observation and malicious users are marked as cheaters.
- For $u \in P_i = U_i - U_i' : t(u, s_i) = \frac{|P_i|}{|P_i \cup N_i|}$. Similarly, for $u \in N_i = (U_i' - U_i'') \cup L_i$, $t(u, s_i) = \frac{|N_i|}{|P_i \cup N_i|}$.

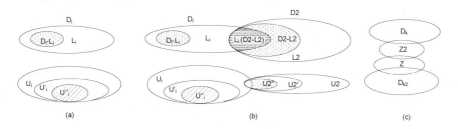

Fig. 2. (a) Venn diagram of the set of malicious and honest users detected by a trust mechanism. (b) The set of malicious and honest users detected by combining two trust management mechanisms. (c) Different sets of malicious users used by the adversary.

Eliminating ratings with 0 trustworthiness, i.e., those of users in the shaded parts of Fig. 2(a), the trust-based QP-score of any $s_i \in S, i = 1, ..., k - 1$ becomes:

$$f_T(s_i) = \sum_{u \in P_i} 1 \cdot \frac{|P_i|}{|P_i| + |N_i|} + \sum_{u \in N_i} (-1) \frac{|N_i|}{|P_i| + |N_i|} = |P_i| - |N_i|$$

Since with a probability γ, malicious ratings on any item will be detected by the trust mechanism, we have:

- $E[|U_i'|] = |U_i|\varepsilon = x_i\varepsilon$, and $E[|U_i''|] = E(|U_i'|)\gamma = x_i\varepsilon\gamma$.
- $E[|D_i - L_i|] = E[\sum_{u \in D_i} 1_{\{u \text{ detected}\}}] = \sum_{u \in D_i} E[1_{\{u \text{ detected}\}}] = |D_i|\gamma$. It follows that $E|L_i| = |D_i|(1 - \gamma) = y_i(1 - \gamma)$.

As a result $E[|P_i|] = E[|U_i - U_i'|] = E[|U_i| - |U_i'|] = x_i(1 - \varepsilon)$ and $E[|N_i|] = E[|(U_i' - U_i'') \cup L_i|] = E[|U_i'| - |U_i''| + |L_i|] = x_i\varepsilon - x_i\varepsilon\gamma + y_i(1-\gamma) = (1-\gamma)(x_i\varepsilon + y_i)$. Therefore, for any $1 \leq i \leq k - 1$:

$$E[f_T(s_i)] = E[|P_i|] - E[|N_i|] = x_i(1 - \varepsilon) - (1 - \gamma)(x_i\varepsilon + y_i) = x_i(1 - 2\varepsilon + \varepsilon\gamma) - y_i(1 - \gamma)$$

Similarly for the target item s_k, noting that honest users mostly rate negatively and malicious users rate positively on s_k, we have:

$$E[f_T(s_k)] = -E[|P_k|] + E[|N_k|] = -x_k(1-\varepsilon) + (1-\gamma)(x_k\varepsilon + y_k) = -x_k(1-2\varepsilon + \varepsilon\gamma) + y_k(1-\gamma)$$

The item s_k has a higher rank than s_i iff $E[f_T(s_k)] \geq E[f_T(s_i)]$, or:

$$y_k + y_i \geq (x_k + x_i)\frac{1 - 2\varepsilon + \varepsilon\gamma}{1 - \gamma}$$

The minimal number of ratings the adversary needs to insert into the system is the solution of the following integer program:

$$C_T = \min\{y_1 + y_2 + ... + y_k\}$$
$$\text{s.t. } y_k + y_i \geq (x_i + x_k)(1 - 2\varepsilon + \varepsilon\gamma)/(1 - \gamma), i = 1, ..., k - 1 \qquad (4)$$

where all x_i, y_i are non-negative integers, x_is are fixed. One can also verify that as the first $k - 1$ items are assumedly good, the number of ratings on them satisfies $x_i \geq x_{i+1}$, for $i = 1, ..., k - 2$. This program has the following complete set of solutions[4]:

$$y_k = (x_1 + x_k)(1 - 2\varepsilon + \varepsilon\gamma)/(1 - \gamma) - d; y_1 = d; y_i = 0, 2 \leq i \leq k - 1,$$
$$\text{where } 0 \leq d \leq d_{max} = (x_1 - x_2)(1 - 2\varepsilon + \varepsilon\gamma)/(1 - \gamma) \qquad (5)$$

Each solution above (for each $0 \leq d \leq d_{max}$) requires the adversary to post the same total number of ratings $C_T = \sum_{i=1}^{k} y_i = (x_1 + x_k)\frac{1 - 2\varepsilon + \varepsilon\gamma}{1 - \gamma}$. For each d, a corresponding attack strategy is to create at least $\max\{C_T - d, d\} = C_T - d$ identities[5]. Each of these $C_T - d$ identities posts a positive rating on the target item s_k; d identities are then reused to post negative ratings on the highest

---

[4] For clarity, we omit rounding operators $\lceil . \rceil$ from the right side of equations (5).

[5] Without loss of generality, we assume that $x_1 + x_k \geq 2(x_1 - x_2)$, hence $C_T - d_{max} \geq d_{max}$ and thus $\max\{C_T - d, d\} = C_T - d$.

ranked item s_1. With the attack strategy of $d = 0$, the adversary needs to create C_T identities, and the probability the attack is successful is $1 - \gamma$. For $d > 0$, the adversary needs to create fewer $(C_T - d)$ identities, since he can use the same user to post ratings on both items s_1 and s_k. However, a strategy with $d > 0$ leads to higher chance that these identities are detected, and the probability that the attack is successful in this case becomes smaller, i.e., $(1 - \gamma)^2 < 1 - \gamma$. Formally, considering the expected gain and the risk of the adversary being detected, we can prove that the utility of the adversary is maximized at $d = 0$ in any of the two cases (1) γ is within a certain range or (2) the gain of the adversary if the attack is success is very large compared to its cost of creating d_{max} malicious identities. The proof is skipped due to space limitation. If we assume the case that the adversary cares most about the probability of success of the attack, the optimal strategy of the adversary is when $d = 0$, which incurs the following cost of creating at least $|D_T| = (x_1 + x_k)\frac{1 - 2\varepsilon + \varepsilon\gamma}{1 - \gamma}$ identities and posting at least $C_T = |D_T|$ ratings on the item s_k, as claimed by the proposition.   □

In this paper, we refrain from presenting the analysis for the general case where an item $s_i, 1 \le i \le k$ has a true quality $q_i \in \{1, 0\}$ (high or low) for clarity reasons. This general result can be obtained by similar reasoning and by replacing the factor $x_1 + x_k$ in (3) with $(-1)^{1-q_1}x_1 - (-1)^{1-q_k}x_k$. Also by analogy, one can verify that the adversarial cost for promoting the target item to a desired rank $k^* < k$ can be obtained from (3) after replacing x_1 with x_{k^*}.

Following immediately from Proposition 1, we have an estimate of the extent of rank manipulation that can be done by an adversary.

Corollary 1. *If the system uses a trust mechanism that can detect malicious ratings on any item with probability $0 < \gamma < 1$, an adversary with capability to create at most $|D|$ identities and posts C ratings may manipulate the rank of a favorite item from the origin k to the highest rank $k^* \le k$ defined by:*

$$k^* = \min_{k'=1}^{k}\{k' : (x_{k'} + x_k)\frac{1 - 2\varepsilon + \varepsilon\gamma}{1 - \gamma} \le \min(C, |D|)\} \tag{6}$$

By similar reasoning, we obtain another result on the minimal adversarial cost when no trust mechanism is employed in the system (see Proposition 2).

Proposition 2. *In a system with no trust management mechanism to detect malicious users and eliminate their ratings, the minimal cost of the adversary to boost an item with rank k to rank 1 includes:*

- *The cost to create $|D| = (x_2 + x_k)(1 - 2\varepsilon)$ identities.*
- *The cost to post $C = (x_1 + x_k)(1 - 2\varepsilon)$ ratings on the two items s_1 and s_k.*

The optimal attack strategy is to post $d_{max} = (x_1 - x_2)(1 - 2\varepsilon)$ negative ratings on the top item s_1 and post $C - d_{max}$ positive ratings on the target item s_k.

The proof is similar to that of Proposition 1 for $\gamma = 0$. The difference is in the optimal attack strategy of the adversary. If the system uses no trust mechanism to detect malicious users and eliminate their ratings, the optimal strategy of the adversary to boost an item with rank k to rank 1 is attained at $d = d_{max}$, for which the adversary needs to create only $C - d_{max}$ identities and uses them to vote negatively for s_1 and rate positively on the target item s_k.

From Proposition 2, we can also estimate to which extent an adversary with a fixed cost may manipulate the rank of his or her favorite items (Corollary 2).

Corollary 2. *Consider a system with no trust management mechanism to detect malicious users and eliminate their ratings. An adversary with capability to create at most $|D|$ identities and posts C ratings to the system may manipulate the rank of its favorite item from k to the highest rank $k^* \leq k$ defined by:*

$$k^* = \max\{\min_{k'=1}^{k}\{k' : (x_{k'+1} + x_k)(1 - 2\varepsilon) \leq |D|\}, \min_{k'=1}^{k}\{k' : (x_{k'} + x_k)(1 - 2\varepsilon) \leq C\}\} \tag{7}$$

Compared between the cost in Proposition 1 and Proposition 2, using a trust management mechanism that detects malicious ratings on any item with a probability γ would increase the minimal adversarial cost by some magnitudes:

$$|D_T|/|D| \simeq \frac{(x_1 + x_k)(1 - 2\varepsilon + \varepsilon\gamma)}{(x_2 + x_k)(1 - 2\varepsilon)(1 - \gamma)} > 1 \tag{8}$$

$$C_T/C \simeq \frac{1 - 2\varepsilon + \varepsilon\gamma}{(1 - 2\varepsilon)(1 - \gamma)} > 1 \tag{9}$$

Our analysis is general as the notion of γ include the capability of the trust mechanism to detect malicious on any item. There may exist other trust mechanisms that are more efficient in terms of guaranteeing a higher detection probability γ. These mechanisms might consider the reputation of the raters, credibilities of the item providers, and the correlation of ratings among raters to each others, etc. Designing such trust mechanism is, however, orthogonal to our work.

The cost of attacking the system also strongly depends on the set of votes by honest users, i.e., x_i. In systems where honest users outnumber the malicious users deployed by the adversary, manipulation of the trust-based ranking is much more costly to the adversary. Existing techniques to restrict the number of identities created by the adversary can be easily integrated to our analytical framework to restrict the capability of the adversary to manipulate the ranking.

3.2   Non-uniform Detection Capability of Malicious Ratings

Generally, the probability that the trust mechanism detects malicious ratings on different items may be non uniformed. For example, the trust mechanism may focus more on protecting of popular (and usually higher ranked) items, thereby increasing the probability of detecting unreliable ratings on these items. Let γ_i be the probability that malicious ratings on an item $s_i \in S$ are detected and eliminated. As a generalization of the analysis in Section 3.1, the optimal cost of the adversary to successfully manipulate the rank of the item s_k is the solution to the following integer program:

$$C_{ext} = \min\{y_1 + y_2 + \ldots + y_k\}$$

$$\text{s.t. } y_k(1 - \gamma_k) + y_i(1 - \gamma_i) \geq x_i(1 - 2\varepsilon + \varepsilon\gamma_i) + x_k(1 - 2\varepsilon + \varepsilon\gamma_k) \stackrel{\triangle}{=} \phi_i, i = 1, \ldots, k - 1$$

where all $0 < \gamma_i < 1$ are fixed, all x_i are fixed non-negative integers, and $x_i \geq x_{i+1}$, for $i = 1, ..., k - 2$.

The probabilities γ_i are inherent to the trust mechanism, possibly determined by the system designer, while unknown to the adversary. The solution to the above optimization problem is the lower bound of the cost of the adversary. It is also our interest to evaluate which setting of $\gamma_1, ..., \gamma_k, ..., \gamma_{|S|}$ would result in a higher minimal cost of the adversary. Finding closed-form solutions for these cases is non-trivial and thus it is done numerically in Section 5.

4   The Benefits of Sharing Trust across Ranking Systems

This section presents the analysis of the adversarial cost in a system that uses an open trust management approach for detection and elimination of malicious ratings. That is, the system exchanges information on the identities of malicious users detected with another ranking system. Let $S2$ be the item set of the second system. Given any item $s'_j \in S2$, define $U2_j$ the set of honest users with ratings on s'_j, and $U2 = \bigcup_{s'_j \in S2} U2_j$. Also, let $D2_j$ be the set of malicious users with ratings on s'_j, and also define $D2 = \bigcup_{s'_j \in S2} D2_j$.

Assume that the second system uses another trust management approach that can detect malicious ratings on any item with a probability $0 < \gamma_2 < 1$. We assume that the two ranking systems are designed to automatically and reliably share the identities of malicious users detected to each other, and the system managers have low incentive to modify the software implementation to tamper such information. Fair and reliable information sharing between systems is an important issue that is beyond the scope of this paper and subject to future work. The identification of common users (in a privacy-preserving way) can be done via alias detection and entity resolution methods, e.g., based on credential attributes of the users. This problem is, however, orthogonal to the current analysis and thus is not further discussed.

For the case where two systems do not share any information, the adversary would need a set of D users to post a minimal number of C_T ratings to boost his favorites item s_k in the first system. Suppose that the goal of the adversary when attacking the second system is to boost the rank of an item $s'_{k_2} \in S2$ from k_2 to $k_2^* = 1$[6]. Then, the adversary would use another set of malicious users $D2$ to post a minimal number of C'_T ratings on his favorite items s_{k_2} in the second system. According to the analysis in Section 3.1:

$$C_T = (x_k + x_1)\frac{1 - 2\varepsilon + \varepsilon\gamma}{1 - \gamma} = |D| \text{ and } C'_T = (x'_{k_2} + x'_1)\frac{1 - 2\varepsilon + \varepsilon\gamma_2}{1 - \gamma_2} = |D2| \quad (10)$$

where $x'_i, i = 1, ..., k_2$ have similar meanings to those of the first system.

Suppose that the adversary is able to create up to $N = |D \cup D2|$ identities in two systems for its malicious purposes. It is required that $N > \max\{C_T, C'_T\}$, otherwise with all N identities the adversary is still unable to attack both systems successfully. We will evaluate the benefit of sharing information between two

---

[6] Again we use $k_2^* = 1$ to reduce the notations without loss of generality of the analysis.

systems where such sharing is beneficial to both. That happens if the adversary does not have enough resources and needs to use a certain number of identities in both systems for its attacks, i.e., when $\max\{C_T, C'_T\} < N < C_T + C'_T$. Under this restriction, the adversary would use C_T among N identities to post C_T ratings on the first system. The posting of C'_T ratings in the second system will be done by employing: (1) the unused $N - C_T$ identities; (2) $C_T + C'_T - N$ among those C_T identities already used in the first system.

Hence, the cost of the adversary in case of no information sharing is:

- The cost of creating N identities, where $\max\{C_T, C'_T\} \leq N \leq C_T + C'_T$.
- The cost of posting $C_T + C'_T$ ratings in both systems.

When the two systems share trust evaluation results, the adversarial cost is:

- The same cost of N identities as in the case of not sharing information.
- The cost of posting $R_{\widehat{T}}$ ratings, which would be defined later on.

We want to analyze how the adversarial cost in the case of sharing trust evaluation result differs from the case of not sharing any information, i.e., to quantify $R_{\widehat{T}} - C_T - C'_T$.

Denote as $\tau_i =| U_i \cap U2 |, 1 \leq i \leq k$ the number of honest users who post ratings on s_i and also appear in the second system. We may approximate that $\tau_i =| U_i \cap U2 | \approx \tau / | S |, 1 \leq i \leq k$, where τ is the number of common honest users who post ratings in both systems. Similarly define $\tau'_i =| U2_i \cap U | \approx \tau / | S2 |, 1 \leq i \leq k_2$ the number of honest users who post ratings on $s'_i \in S2$ and also appear in the first system. The following main result gives us an estimation of the benefit of sharing information between the two systems.

Proposition 3. *Consider two ranking systems with capabilities γ, γ_2 of detection malicious ratings, where $0 < \gamma \leq \gamma_2 < 1$. Assume Δ be the number of identities the adversary needs to reuse in two systems, in the best case for the adversary, we have:*

$$0 \leq \Delta \leq \min\{(x_k + x_1)\frac{1 - 2\varepsilon + \varepsilon\gamma}{1 - \gamma}, (x'_{k_2} + x'_1)\frac{1 - 2\varepsilon + \varepsilon\gamma_2}{1 - \gamma_2}\} \tag{11}$$

If the two systems share trust evaluation information to each other, then the difference of the adversary cost to attack the two systems between two cases of sharing vs. non-sharing of information is bounded below by:

$$R_{\widehat{T}} - C_T - C'_T > \frac{\Delta\gamma}{1 - \gamma} - \frac{\varepsilon\gamma_2(\tau_k + \tau_1)(1 - 2\varepsilon + \varepsilon\gamma)}{(1 - \gamma)^2} - \frac{\varepsilon\gamma(\tau'_{k_2} + \tau'_1)(1 - 2\varepsilon + \varepsilon\gamma_2)}{(1 - \gamma_2)^2} \tag{12}$$

Proof. We provide here a sketch of the proof (the full proof can be found in [11]). Let $z_i =| D_i \cap D2 | \leq y_i, 1 \leq i \leq k$ be the number of malicious raters who appear in both systems and rate an item $s_i \in S$ (of the first system). Similarly denote $z'_j =| D2_j \cap D | \leq y'_j, 1 \leq j \leq k_2$ the number of cheating users present in both systems and rate an item $s'_j \in S2$ (of the second system). Proceed as in Proposition 1, the minimal number of ratings $C_{\widehat{T}}$ by the adversary to successfully attack the first systems is the solution to the following integer program:

$$C_{\widehat{T}} = \min\{y_1 + y_2 + ... + y_k\} \text{ subject to:}$$

$$y_k + y_i \geq (x_k + x_i - \varepsilon\gamma_2(\tau_k + \tau_i))\frac{1 - 2\varepsilon + \varepsilon\gamma}{1 - \gamma} + (z_k + z_i)\gamma_2, i = 1, ..., k - 1$$

$$y_i \geq z_i, i = 1, ..., k$$

where $x_j, y_j, \tau_j, z_j, j = 1, ..., k$ are non-negative integers, all $x_i, \tau_i, z_i, i = 1, ...k$ is fixed, $x_i \leq x_j$, for $i \leq j, i, j = 1, ..., k - 1$.

For $i = 1, ...k$, define $g_i = (x_k + x_i - \varepsilon\gamma_2(\tau_k + \tau_i))\frac{1 - 2\varepsilon + \varepsilon\gamma}{1 - \gamma} - (z_k + z_i)(1 - \gamma_2)$. One may verify that any solution of the above program results in the same optimal number of ratings $C_{\widehat{T}} = \max\{0, \max_{i=1}^{k-1} g_i\} + \sum_{i=1}^{k} z_i$.

Similar to the previous section, if we assume that the adversary cares most about the probability of success of the attack, the optimal attack strategy is:

- for the item s_k: the adversary uses a set of users D_k from the first system and z_k identities from the second system to post $\widehat{y}_k = | D_k | + z_k$ ratings on s_k. We have $| D_k | = \max\{0, \max_{i=1}^{k-1} g_i\}$, and thus $C_{\widehat{T}} = | D_k | + \sum_{i=1}^{k} z_i$.
- for the items $s_i, i = 1, ..., k - 1$: the adversary uses z_i identities from the second system to post z_i ratings on each s_i.

The set of malicious users to be used by the adversary in the first system is then $D = D_k \cup Z$, where $Z \subseteq D2$ is set of identities borrowed from the set of malicious users $D2$ in the second system. These borrowed identities are used by the adversary to post a total of $\sum_{i=1}^{k} z_i$ ratings on those items $s_i, i = 1, ..., k$. Likewise, the set of malicious users in the second system is $D2 = D_{k_2} \cup Z2$, where $Z2 \subseteq D$ is set of identities borrowed from the first system to rate on items in the second system. D_{k_2} is the set of malicious users who are only present in the second system and rate the target item $s'_{k_2} \in S2$.

The set of malicious users used by the adversary to attack both systems is thus $D_{\widehat{T}} = D_k \cup Z \cup D_{k_2} \cup Z2$. Fig. 2(c) illustrates the relation among different sets $D_k, Z, Z2, D_{k_2}$. Clearly, the malicious set $D_{\widehat{T}}$ is smallest iff $Z \subseteq D_{k_2}$ and $Z2 \subseteq D_k$. That is, the same malicious users in one system, e.g., D_{k_2}, are used to rate items in the other system, e.g., to rate item $s_i \in S, i = 1, ..., k$. Under such a situation, the total minimal number of identities the adversary needs to create in the two systems is $| D_{\widehat{T}} | = | D_k | + | D_{k_2} |$.

Similarly, the minimal number of ratings to be posted in the second system is $C'_{\widehat{T}} = | D_{k_2} | + \sum_{i=1}^{k_2} z'_i$. Thus the total cost of the adversary to attack both systems includes two cost: (1) to create $| D_{\widehat{T}} |$ identities and (2) to post $R_{\widehat{T}} = C_{\widehat{T}} + C'_{\widehat{T}}$ ratings in the two systems. Given a fixed number of identities N, the goal of the adversary is to determine the number of common users $z_i \geq 0, z'_j \geq 0, i = 1, ..., k, j = 1, ..., k_2$ such that $R_{\widehat{T}}$ is minimized. In other words:

$$R_{\widehat{T}} = \min\{| D_k | + | D_{k_2} | + \sum_{i=1}^{k} z_i + \sum_{j=1}^{k_2} z'_j\} \text{ subject to: } | D_{\widehat{T}} | = | D_k | + | D_{k_2} | = N$$

$$\text{where } | D_k | = \max\{0, \max_{i=1}^{k-1}\{(x_k + x_i - \varepsilon\gamma_2(\tau_k + \tau_i))\frac{1 - 2\varepsilon + \varepsilon\gamma}{1 - \gamma} - (z_k + z_i)(1 - \gamma_2)\}\}$$

$$\text{and } | D_{k_2} | = \max\{0, \max_{1 \leq i \leq k_2 - 1}\{(x'_{k_2} + x'_i - \varepsilon\gamma(\tau'_k + \tau'_i))\frac{1 - \varepsilon + 2\varepsilon\gamma_2}{1 - \gamma_2} - (z'_k + z'_i)(1 - \gamma)\}\}$$

Solving this program give us $R_{\widehat{T}} \geq -\frac{N\gamma}{1-\gamma}+\max_{i=1}^{k-1}\{\frac{f_i}{1-\gamma}\}+\max_{j=1}^{k_2-1}\{\frac{f'_j}{1-\gamma}\}$, where for simplicity we define $f_i \overset{\triangle}{=} (x_k + x_i - \varepsilon\gamma_2(\tau_k + \tau_i))\frac{1-2\varepsilon+\varepsilon\gamma}{1-\gamma}, i = 1, ..., k-1$ and $f'_i \overset{\triangle}{=} (x'_{k_2} + x'_i - \varepsilon\gamma(\tau'_{k_2} + \tau'_i))\frac{1-2\varepsilon+\varepsilon\gamma_2}{1-\gamma_2}, i = 1, ..., k_2 - 1$.

Since $\max\{C_T, C'_T\} \leq N < C_T + C'_T$, there are at least $\Delta = C_T + C'_T - N$ identities used by the adversary in the two systems, where:

$$0 \leq \Delta \leq \min\{C_T, C'_T\} = \min\{(x_k + x_1)\frac{1-2\varepsilon+\varepsilon\gamma}{1-\gamma}, (x'_{k_2} + x'_1)\frac{1-2\varepsilon+\varepsilon\gamma_2}{1-\gamma_2}\}$$

The bound of Δ is for the best case of the adversary, when he can estimate the cost C_T, C'_T to successfully attack the two systems. Given Δ defined as above, with basic computations we obtain:

$$R_{\widehat{T}} - C_T - C'_T > \frac{\Delta\gamma}{1-\gamma} - \frac{\varepsilon\gamma_2(\tau_k + \tau_1)(1-2\varepsilon+\varepsilon\gamma)}{(1-\gamma)^2} - \frac{\varepsilon\gamma(\tau'_{k_2} + \tau'_1)(1-2\varepsilon+\varepsilon\gamma_2)}{(1-\gamma_2)^2} \tag{13}$$

and Proposition 3 follows naturally. $\square$

The cost difference $R_{\widehat{T}} - C_T - C'_T$ in Proposition 3 mostly depends on the shortage of identities Δ of the adversary. The fewer number of identities the adversary has, the higher number of common identities it shall reuse across the two systems, and the more ratings it needs to insert into both systems to successfully manipulate the ranks of its favorite items. For most Δ and where the noise ε is negligible, it is apparent that $R_{\widehat{T}} - C_T + C'_T > 0$, or the adversarial cost to manipulate the ranking in both systems in the case of sharing trust information between the two systems is higher than the adversarial cost $C_T + C'_T$ where no information is shared. The capabilities of the two trust mechanisms in detecting malicious ratings, i.e. the probability γ, γ_2 also play an important rule in increasing this total adversarial cost. The sharing of information, however, may also lead to some false positives when estimating common users as cheating. This observation noise however plays a minor role, as the two negative terms on the right hand side of (12) are small, given small values of ε. Note that this cost difference $R_{\widehat{T}} - C_T - C'_T$ is estimated in the worst case where the adversary knows the common users (τ_i, τ'_i) and is aware of the effectiveness of the two system at detecting malicious activities (γ, γ_2) to develop an optimal strategy of placement malicious ratings in the two systems.

5   Numerical Evaluation

In this section, we numerically evaluate our results. All items including the target items are assumed to be good (but differ in popularity), which can be proven as even less costly for the adversary to promote them, and with the least difference between the number of ratings between items (hence the minimum adversarial cost is the lowest possible). The estimates are for $\varepsilon = 0.05$ and $M = |S| = 100$ items. There are $x_i = M - i$ honest ratings for each item with rank $1 \leq i \leq M$. Fig. 3 evaluates the increase in the minimal adversarial cost $|D_T|/|D|$ with respect to uniform detection capabilities γ of the trust management and with various values of the original rank k and desired rank $k^* < k$ of the target item. We observe that even in this pessimistic scenario, the use of a trust mechanism with reasonable detection capability $\gamma = 0.5$ doubles the adversarial cost to manipulate the rankings in terms of the number of identities, irrespective of the original rank of the target item. The increase in adversarial cost by the number of malicious ratings C_T/C has a similar trend. Also, the raise of the adversarial cost for promoting the lowest ranked item can be achieved by increasing the detection capability of the trust mechanism being used γ (Fig. 3).

Next, we consider the impact to the minimal adversarial cost of a trust mechanism with non-uniform detection capabilities γ. For simplicity, we assume linear ascending and descending γ functions with respect to the item original rank and numerically solve the linear program of Section 3.2. The adversarial identities and ratings ratios ($|D_T|/|D|$ and C_T/C respectively) with respect to the initial item rank are depicted in Fig. 4. Thus, an ascending γ distribution increases the minimum adversarial cost for promoting lower ranked services. Then, we consider multiple *permutations* of the γ values for the items of various ranks and we observe that a trust mechanism that focuses more on detecting malicious ratings on lower ranked items increases the minimal adversarial cost to promote their ranking. In Fig. 5 the permutations corresponding to to the highest cost are those with γ ascending w.r.t the item rank.

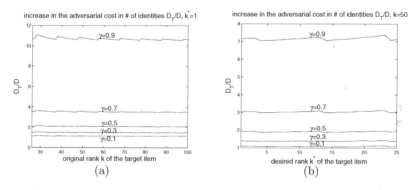

Fig. 3. Identities cost by a trust mechanism with different detection capabilities γ: (a) the target has variable original rank k and desired rank $k^* = 1$; and (b) the target has original rank $k = M/2$ and variable desired rank k^*

The impact of sharing trust information to the overall robustness of the two systems for an example case is given in Fig. 6, measured in the increase of adversarial cost (the number of ratings the adversary needs to insert into both systems). The two systems are assumed to use trust management mechanisms with similar detection capabilities $\gamma = \gamma_2$, have two similar item sets $|S| = |S2| = M$ with roughly $\tau = 10\%$ common honest users. The measurements are done in two representative cases where the target items have different original ranks in the two systems. The estimates are based on Eq. (12) in the worst case scenario with the least difference between the item popularity, $x_i = M - i, 1 \leq$

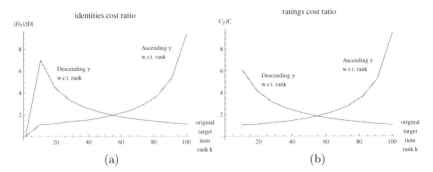

Fig. 4. Identities (a) and ratings (b) cost ratio for promoting an item with rank k with or without a trust mechanism employing an ascending or descending γ distribution

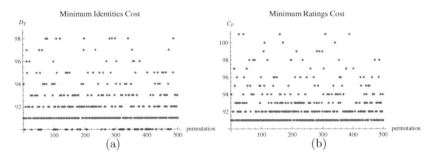

Fig. 5. Identities (a) and ratings (b) minimum cost for promoting an item initially ranked last with different γ distributions

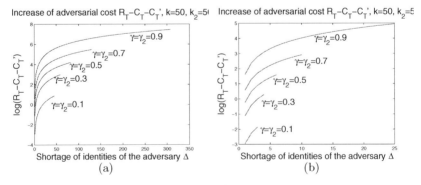

Fig. 6. Impact of the trust information sharing to the increase of adversarial cost (in log scale) where: (a) the (origin) rank of the target is average in both systems; (b) the rank of the target in one system is high. The results in other cases are similar.

$i \leq M, x'_j = M - j, 1 \leq j \leq M$. Observe that the sharing of information between two systems helps to significantly raise the total cost of the adversary to attack the two systems, thus strengthening both systems significantly. The conditions for this sharing of trust information to be beneficial to both systems, i.e., $log(R_{\widehat{T}} - C_T - C'_T) > 0$ are: (1) the detection capabilities of the two systems are sufficiently high, and (2) the resources of the adversary are limited, e.g., $\gamma, \gamma_2 > 0.5$ and $\Delta > 5$ in the case of Fig. 6.

6   Related Work

The works most related to ours include existing research on resilience of Web page ranking algorithms against Web spams, via link structure and credibility analysis, namely [4, 5]. The use of trust and reputation mechanisms to minimize the influence of adversarial attacks in ranking systems has also attracted much effort [8, 9]. EigenTrust [12] presents a global trust metric to measure the credibility to a node in a network based on inter-connecting links among nodes. Other works, as [5], use reputation-based trust management techniques to improve the robustness of ranking systems but with little analysis on the impact of trust mechanisms to the adversarial cost for strategic manipulation the system. A more recent work [10] studies vulnerabilities and attacks by an adversary with a given cost to voting systems and propose defense mechanisms based on item popularity. This work is different from ours as it only considers the binary voting result on item quality while our work is more general: we consider ranking systems that use both popularity and quality of items as ranking metrics.

7   Conclusion

This paper analyzes the minimum adversarial cost to manipulate the ranking of items in systems where a trust mechanism is employed for detecting unfair and biased ratings. We provide theoretical results showing the relation between the capability of the trust mechanism being used to detect malicious ratings and the minimal adversarial cost to successfully attack a ranking system. Moreover, we have proved that, under certain realistic assumptions, two systems with shared information on malicious user activities can increase the minimal successful attack cost of an adversary considerably. Our analysis indicates that the cost of the system designer to prevent attacks from the adversary with a certain power, is related to the cost of implementing a trust management mechanism with a certain capability of detecting malicious rating behaviors. The analytical framework in the paper can be extended to estimate the robustness of more complex ranking score metrics against the adversary. It may also be our interest to analyze the cost and the influence on the final ranking result in presence of many competing adversaries with different powers.

References

1. Chevalier, J.A., Mayzlin, D.: The effect of word of mouth on sales: Online book reviews. Journal of Marketing Research 43(9) (2006)
2. Parsa, A.: Belkins Development Rep is Hiring People to Write Fake Positive Amazon Reviews (2009)
3. Namestnikov, Y.: The economics of Botnets (2009), http://www.viruslist.com/analysis?pubid=204792068
4. Caverlee, J., Webb, S., Liu, L., Rouse, W.B.: A parameterized approach to spamresilient link analysis of the web. IEEE Trans. Parallel Distrib. Syst. 20(10), 1422–1438 (2009)
5. Gyongyi, Z., Garcia-Molina, H., Pedersen, J.: Combating web spam with trustrank. In: Proceedings of the 30th International Conference on Very Large Data Bases (VLDB), pp. 271–279 (2004)
6. Page, L., Brin, S., Motwani, R., Winograd, T.: The pagerank citation ranking: Bringing order to the web. Technical report, Stanford University (1998)
7. Kleinberg, J.M.: Authoritative sources in a hyperlinked environment. J. ACM 46(5), 604–632 (1999)
8. Golbeck, J.: Trust on the world wide web: A survey. Foundations and Trends in Web Science 1(2), 131–197 (2006)
9. Jøsang, A., Ismail, R., Boyd, C.: A survey of trust and reputation systems for online service provision. Decis. Support Syst. 43(2), 618–644 (2007)
10. Feng, Q., Sun, Y., Liu, L., Yang, Y., Dai, Y.: Voting Systems with Trust Mechanisms in Cyberspace: Vulnerabilities and Defenses. IEEE Transactions on Knowledge and Data Engineering (to appear, 2010)
11. Vu, L.H., Papaioannou, T.G., Aberer, K.: Impacts of trust management and information sharing to adversarial cost in ranking systems. Technical Report LSIR-REPORT-2010-001 (2010), http://infoscience.epfl.ch/record/143071
12. Kamvar, S.D., Schlosser, M.T., Molina, H.G.: The EigenTrust algorithm for reputation management in P2P networks. In: Proc. of WWW 2003 (2003)

Shinren: Non-monotonic Trust Management for Distributed Systems*

Changyu Dong and Naranker Dulay

Department of Computing
Imperial College London
180 Queen's Gate, London, SW7 2AZ, UK
{changyu.dong,n.dulay}@imperial.ac.uk

Abstract. The open and dynamic nature of modern distributed systems and pervasive environments presents significant challenges to security management. One solution may be trust management which utilises the notion of trust in order to specify and interpret security policies and make decisions on security-related actions. Most logic-based trust management systems assume monotonicity where additional information can only result in the increasing of trust. The monotonic assumption oversimplifies the real world by not considering negative information, thus it cannot handle many real world scenarios. In this paper we present Shinren[1], a novel non-monotonic trust management system based on bilattice theory and the any-world assumption. Shinren takes into account negative information and supports reasoning with incomplete information, uncertainty and inconsistency. Information from multiple sources such as credentials, recommendations, reputation and local knowledge can be used and combined in order to establish trust. Shinren also supports prioritisation which is important in decision making and resolving modality conflicts that are caused by non-monotonicity.

1 Introduction

The advances in communications and computing research have brought distributed systems and pervasive environments to new prominence. Applications are now distributed across the boundaries of networks, organisations, even countries and deployed on smaller mobile devices. The increasing scope of distributed applications also implies that applications must deal with "strangers" from other organisations and places. This leads to new challenges. How does the security system determine whether or not a request should be allowed if the request comes from an unknown user? The system must be able to decide without pre-knowledge of the user in order to authorise/deny the access. In other words, the system must determine whether and by how much does it trust a user. Trust management [1] was introduced in response to the challenges posed by modern distributed systems and pervasive environments.

In real-life, trust is normally **non-monotonic**. Consider the following:

---

* This research was supported by the UK's EPSRC research grant EP/C537181/1 (Caregrid) and EU FP7 research grant 213339 (ALLOW).

[1] Shinren: the pronunciation of trust in Chinese.

M. Nishigaki et al. (Eds.): IFIPTM 2010, IFIP AICT 321, pp. 125–140, 2010.

*"You are the CEO of a bank and looking for someone to manage a multi-billion pounds investment fund. A CV arrives on your computer. You quickly read through it: worked for the UK's oldest investment bank (interesting), had more than ten years experience as a derivatives trader (**good**), was the Chief Trader and General Manager of operations in futures markets on the Singapore Monetary Exchange (**great**), made £10 million a year which accounted for 10% of former employer's annual income (**excellent**). You almost make up your mind. Then you see the candidate's name: Nick Leeson[2]. Everything is turned upside down. You trash the email."*

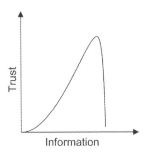

Fig. 1. Non-monotonic trust for CV

If we draw a diagram of this trust-information relation, it might look like Figure 1. From the diagram we can see that when new information comes in, trust can decrease, as well as increase, sometimes drastically. In other words, trust is non-monotonic. The non-monotonicity of trust is a natural consequence of the existence of both goodness and badness in the world. Trust, as defined by Mayer and Davis [2], is "the willingness of a party to be vulnerable to the actions of another party". To trust someone, the trustor needs to judge how competent, how honest, how dependable the trustee is, but more importantly, how incompetent, how dishonest and how undependable the trustee is. Positive information tells us how much we may gain from a trust relationship, while negative information tells us how much we may lose from it. Ignoring negative information may result in misplaced trust which may in turn cause serious damage to the trustor.

Although trust is non-monotonic, mainstream logic-based trust management systems [1,3,4,5,6,7] are monotonic. The reason is that complete knowledge is hard to achieve in large distributed systems and also that those systems are based on classical logic which cannot cope with this situation. Classical logic is monotonic which means a conclusion will never be retracted with new information, i.e. if $\Gamma \models \phi$ then $\Gamma \cup \gamma \models \phi$. To model trust with classical logic, a monotonic assumption is introduced to solve the problem and simplify the design by not using negative information about the world. Monotonic systems do not have problems with incomplete information because all missing information is positive and every decision that they make can only be more "correct" with more information. Accepting the monotonic assumption means accepting the world is always positive (however if there were no negative things in the world, do we still need

---

[2] Nicholas Leeson, the infamous rogue trader who caused the collapse of Barings Bank.

trust management systems?). Monotonic trust management systems have many advantages, but the monotonic assumption is too limiting for many scenarios.

The gap between real world requirements and the current design of trust management systems motivates our work. A more realistic solution is needed for managing trust in distributed systems. In this paper, we describe Shinren, a novel non-monotonic trust management system based on bilattice theory and the any-world assumption. Shinren can make reasonable decisions even with incomplete information. Moreover, it can also utilise unreliable information which makes it more suitable for open distributed systems where reliable information is often hard to come by. Shinren does not just simply make use of the existing theories, it also supports prioritisation, which is achieved by a non-trivial extension of the original theories. Prioritisation is important in resolving conflicts and providing support for decision making.

This paper is organised as follows: We first summarise and compare existing non-monotonic trust management systems with Shinren in section 2. Then we discuss the motivation of this work in section 3. In section 4 we introduce bilattice theory and the any-world assumption. In section 5, we describe Shinren, its policy language and present an example to show the details of policy evaluation in Shinren. In section 6 we show a prototype implementation. Section 7 concludes the paper.

2   Non-monotonic Trust Management Systems

Shinren is not the first logic-based non-monotonic trust management system. Rule-Controlled Environment For Evaluation of Rules and Everything Else (REFEREE) [8], the Trust Establishment System (TES) from IBM [9] and $RT_\ominus$ [10] are also non-monotonic.

The main problem of existing logic-based non-monotonic trust management systems is semantics. A well-defined formal semantics is a critical part of any policy language. However, REFEREE and TES do not have formally defined semantics. $RT_\ominus$ is based on the well-founded semantics which is a non-monotonic semantics proposed originally for logic programming with negation [11]. The problem with using well-founded semantics in trust management is that it is based on the closed world assumption (CWA) and the uniformity of CWA may lead to counter-intuitive results. For example, here is a simple trust policy $trust(a) : -\neg bad(a)$. Under the well-founded semantics, when $bad(a)$ is missing or not provable, it is falsified and thus makes $trust(a)$ true. However, this decision may seem too casual, especially when it is related to security. In Shinren, policy makers can use $unknown$ as the default value for $bad(a)$ while still use $false$ as the default value for other positive atoms.

Existing non-monotonic trust management systems are also less expressive than Shinren. For example, $RT_\ominus$ can only express policies using credentials. Among them, REFEREE is the most expressive one. It is capable of expressing policies utilising evidence from different sources, but it is incapable of distinguish decisions based on information of different quality. REFEREE is based on 3-valued logic, therefore there is no difference between a decision based on a statement from an authority and a decision based on rumour. The users of REFEREE may be given an unreliable trust decision without warning. In Shinren, a trust decision comes with a value which tells the user not only how true the decision is, but also how reliable it is.

Many systems attempt to assign real values to trust and develop sophisticated mathematical models to calculate trust values [12,13,14]. The values are usually based on past experience. Although they are also called trust management systems, we view them as a totally different approach from the trust management systems presented above which rely mostly on logical reasoning and view trust decisions as logical consequences of certain facts and theories. Quantitative trust management systems are usually nonmonotonic and can provide valuable information. However, the accuracy of the trust values largely depends on the amount of data input and may take a long time to get enough data. To differentiate, we call them reputation systems and Shinren can include such systems as subsystems.

3   Why Non-monotonic? Why Shinren?

So why do we need non-monotonic trust management systems? This is because (1) in the real world trust is non-monotonic and therefore a trust management system should be able to capture this; (2) monotonic assumption is not necessary in trust management, it is introduced merely because systems reasoning with classical logic cannot cope with the non-monotonicity in trust. The assumption does not solve the problem, it just makes systems ignore the problem. There are at least two bad consequences of monotonic assumption: first, a trust management system which can be proved correct under the monotonic assumption may not be correct in the real world because the assumption does not hold in general; second, it makes trust management systems incapable of handling certain real world scenarios.

Under the monotonic assumption, monotonic trust management systems do not consider negative information. Syntactically, this is achieved by not allowing negations in the policies. Negation-free policies work fine in some cases, however they reflect a limited view of the world and are inappropriate in many cases. For example, negation-free policies are quite inconvenient in handling *exceptions*. In the world modelled by negation-free policies, it is quite hard to express, "trust all the police officers except the bad ones" because without negations, we would be allowed to say "trust police officers" but not "**do not** trust the bad police officers". In the extreme case, we must specify for each individual good police officer a trust policy in order to exclude the bad ones. Lacking the ability for specifying exceptions can be dangerous particularly in trust management systems where delegations are used. No exceptions means that decisions have to be fully delegated to a delegatee, and the system must fully accept the delegatee's opinions. No exceptions also means that the system cannot accept part of the delegatee's decision while declining other parts. In other words, the system loses control after delegation. Another case is that negation-free policies cannot handle *mutual exclusion*. Coke is tasty, orange juice is tasty too. But the mixture of the two does not taste so pleasant. There are many examples that are mutually exclusive. However, with negation-free policies, there is no way to express "A is good, B is good, but A+B is **not** good". In terms of security policies, separation of duties and conflict of interests are the most significant examples of this type of policy.

One may argue that in the real world, people try to hide their negative aspects. Therefore, even if policies are allowed to use negative information, if the system cannot find it, the non-monotonic feature is useless. It is true that the information we can collect is always limited. But consider the following:

In monotonic trust management systems : $trust$:$-good$

In Shinren : $distrust$:$-bad$

$trust$:$-good$

What is the difference? When the system cannot find bad, i.e. the negative information, Shinren can behave exactly as the monotonic ones. However, because it is not possible to use negative information in monotonic trust management systems, their decisions will still be trust even if bad is presented! In contrast, Shinren's decision will no longer be trust because the distrust policy is applied. Although not guaranteed, Shinren aims to limit any damage with its best effort approach rather than silently ignoring it.

By using bilattices, Shinren suffers less from a dilemma which all trust management systems must face: on the one hand, in order to make a correct trust decision, a large amount of information is needed; on the other hand, in order to make the decision correct, most of the information available cannot be used because it is not reliable. Shinren can reason with unreliable information even with contradictory information. Monotonic trust management systems cannot. This ability is especially important in acquiring negative information.

Prioritisation is not present in any trust management systems. The philosophy is that sometimes trust is not just a Yes/No decision, but also a choice. You might want to follow one rule even if there are multiple rules you can follow, you might trust someone even if there are several persons you can trust. Prioritisation allows policy makers to specify their preferences and thus make complex policies possible. And also, in the presence of modality conflicts, prioritisation seems to be the only way to resolve them. Although there are overheads in defining and managing policies when using prioritisation, the overheads are minimised in Shiren because policy makers only assign priorities to local policies and only trust (distrust) policies are prioritised.

4   Preliminaries

4.1   Bilattices

Bilattice theory [15] was introduced by Ginsberg in the 1980s, and has been widely used in non-monotonic reasoning, knowledge representation and artificial intelligence. Bilattice is a non-empty, possibly infinite set of values with two partial orders, each one giving the set the structure of a lattice. A lattice $\langle L, \preceq \rangle$ is a non empty set L along with a partial order $\preceq$ where any pair of elements $l_1, l_2 \in L$ has a least upper bound (join) and a greatest lower bound (meet) in terms of $\preceq$. We write $l_1 \prec l_2$ if $l_1 \preceq l_2$ and $l_1 \neq l_2$.

A bilattice, denoted by $\langle \mathcal{B}, \preceq_t, \preceq_k \rangle$ where $\mathcal{B}$ is a non-empty set and $\preceq_t, \preceq_k$ are two partial orders called the truth-order and the knowledge-order respectively. $\preceq_t$ is an ordering on the "degree of truth". $b_1 \preceq_t b_2$ means b_2 represents at least as much truth as

b_1 (and possibly more). Meet and join under $\preceq_t$ are denoted by $\wedge$ and $\vee$ and correspond to the classical conjunction and disjunction. $\preceq_k$ is an ordering on the "degree of knowledge". Meet and join under $\preceq_k$ are denoted by $\otimes$ and $\oplus$. $b_1 \otimes b_2$ corresponds to the maximal information b_1 and b_2 can agree on, while $b_1 \oplus b_2$ combines the information represented by b_1 and b_2.

The class of bilattice that we consider in this paper is restricted to *interlaced* bilattices. Interlaced bilattices are bilattices which satisfy the following: (1) if $b_1 \preceq_t b_2$ then $b_1 \otimes b_3 \preceq_t b_2 \otimes b_3$ and $b_1 \oplus b_3 \preceq_t b_2 \oplus b_3$; (2) if $b_1 \preceq_k b_2$ then $b_1 \wedge b_3 \preceq_k b_2 \wedge b_3$ and $b_1 \vee b_3 \preceq_k b_2 \vee b_3$. Thus in an interlaced bilattice an operation associated with one of the lattice orderings is required to be monotonic with respect to the other lattice ordering. This relates the two orderings. An alternative way of connecting the two orderings is via negation which reverses the truth ordering and is monotonic regarding the knowledge ordering.

Such bilattices can be constructed in a natural way by combining two lattices. Given two lattices $\langle L_1, \preceq_1 \rangle$ and $\langle L_2, \preceq_2 \rangle$, we can construct an interlaced bilattice as $\langle L_1 \times L_2, \preceq_t, \preceq_k \rangle$, where $(x_1, y_1) \preceq_t (x_2, y_2)$ if $x_1 \preceq_1 x_2$ and $y_2 \preceq_2 y_1$, $(x_1, y_1) \preceq_k (x_2, y_2)$ if $x_1 \preceq_1 x_2$ and $y_1 \preceq_2 y_2$. Negation can be defined as $\neg(x, y) = (y, x)$ if $L_1 = L_2$. As we will see later, the bilattice used in our system is constructed in this way. We will expand on this later.

4.2 Any-World Assumption

Non-monotonic logics allow a conclusion to be drawn on incomplete information. One way of doing such reasoning is to complete the missing part by *assumptions*. Taking into account assumptions means assigning truth values, implicitly or explicitly, to the unknown facts. The assumptions are usually based on the estimated states of the facts. One of the most common assumptions is the *Closed World Assumption* (CWA). It assumes the default truth states of atoms to be $false$, therefore any atoms that cannot be proved to be $true$ are taken as $false$. Another well-known assumption is the *Open World Assumption* (OWA). OWA is a more cautious assumption in the sense that it assumes the default truth states of atoms to be $unknown$. Therefore, any atoms that cannot be proved to be $true$ are taken as $unknown$. However it also gives us less useful conclusions. Using only one of these assumptions to represent the world uniformly is usually not appropriate.

The *Any-World Assumption* (AWA) [16] unifies and extends the CWA and OWA by taking truth values from an arbitrary bilattice truth space and allow the default value of an atom to be any one of them. If in the assumptions, all the atoms are assigned to $false$, then it becomes CWA which says everything that cannot be inferred is false. If in the assumptions, all the atoms are assigned to $unknown$, then it becomes OWA which says everything cannot be inferred is unknown. The advantages are obvious: the truth, incompleteness and uncertainty can be represented in a finer granularity according to the experience and background information, therefore the assumptions we make carry more knowledge than before which in turn leads to more informed conclusions. The assumptions can be non-uniform which means the default truth values can vary for different atoms. This allows us to form more realistic assumptions.

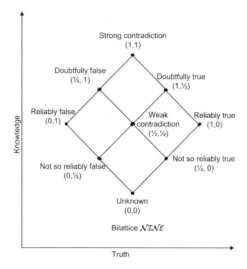

Fig. 2. The bilattice NINE

5   Shinren

5.1   Bilattice $\mathcal{NINE}$

As introduced in Section 4.1, a standard way of constructing an interlaced bilattice is by combining two lattices. The bilattice we employ, $\mathcal{NINE}$, is also built in this standard way. $\mathcal{NINE}$ is obtained by combining two identical lattices $L_1 = L_2 = \langle \{0, \frac{1}{2}, 1\}, \leq \rangle$ where $\leq$ is "less than or equal". The structure of $\mathcal{NINE}$ is shown in Figure 2. The truth values are represented as tuples (x, y) where $x, y \in \{0, \frac{1}{2}, 1\}$. The two orderings, $\preceq_t, \preceq_k$ are defined as:

$$(x_1, y_1) \preceq_t (x_2, y_2) \text{ if } x_1 \leq x_2 \text{ and } y_2 \leq y_1$$
$$(x_1, y_1) \preceq_k (x_2, y_2) \text{ if } x_1 \leq x_2 \text{ and } y_1 \leq y_2$$

Given a statement with a truth value of the form (x, y), the intuitive meaning of the truth value is that x represents how much the statement is true (or you believe it is true), and y represents how much the statement is false (or you believe it is false). For example, $(1, 0)$, i.e. reliably true, is given to a statement supported by very strong and reliable evidence. The possibility of the statement is actually false can be neglected.

From the above it is easy to understand the two orderings. For example, a statement which is reliably true contains more truth (or is more likely to be true) than a statement which is not so reliably true, i.e. $(\frac{1}{2}, 0) \preceq_t (1, 0)$. On the other hand, a reliably true statement gives us more information than a not so reliably true statement, i.e. $(\frac{1}{2}, 0) \preceq_k (1, 0)$. It is possible to extend the bilattice to a finer model of reliability or uncertainty. For example, using a lattice with the value domain $\{0, \frac{1}{3}, \frac{2}{3}, 1\}$, we can create a bilattice with 16 truth values that can represent more reliability levels. However, we do not do so for two reasons: first, enlarging the bilattice also increases the computational complexity. With enough expressiveness, we would like to avoid unnec-essary cost; second, things like reliability and uncertainty cannot typically be measured precisely. There are no metrics and instruments we can use to standardise the measure-ment. A finer scale does not help in solving this problem, even worse, it may bring a false sense of precision. For these reasons, we stay with this basic form and extend it when it is necessary and possible.

Let us also explain the rationale behind this multi-valued truth space. Classical logic, which is the basis of many trust management systems, is bivalent, i.e. the only possi-ble truth values are $true$ and $false$. It gives rise to "black and white thinking" where every proposition must be ascribed to "absolutely true" or "absolutely false". However, in the real world, many would agree with the statement "the only certainty is nothing is certain"[3]. Because classical logic lacks the ability of coping with the uncertainty in truth, mainstream trust management systems restrict the information that can be taken into account to "credentials". A credential is a statement signed by an issuer containing certain information about the credential holder and is believed to be highly reliable. The problems with credentials are two-fold: first, credentials are not able to carry every bit of information about the holder. We may find that signed information is just a very small fraction of all the information we can get. Second, in practice we do not encode negative information about the holder in credentials. The reason is simple: no one both-ers to ask for a credential which is useless or has a negative effect to him. Again, we usually recognise a rogue merchant not from a "rogue merchant" credential signed by a government agency, but from various other sources like reviews in internet forums. If we want a more complete view of the trustee, using only credentials is not sufficient. We need to consider more information, possibly even that from the sources which are not so reliable. The multi-valued truth space gives Shinren the ability to represent and differentiate information with different qualities. And makes it possible for Shinren to utilise unreliable information.

The meet and join operators in terms of both orderings and the negation operator are then defined as follows:

$$(x_1, y_1) \vee (x_2, y_2) = (max(x_1, x_2), min(y_1, y_2))$$
$$(x_1, y_1) \wedge (x_2, y_2) = (min(x_1, x_2), max(y_1, y_2))$$
$$(x_1, y_1) \oplus (x_2, y_2) = (max(x_1, x_2), max(y_1, y_2))$$
$$(x_1, y_1) \otimes (x_2, y_2) = (min(x_1, x_2), min(y_1, y_2))$$
$$\neg(x, y) = (y, x)$$

We will explain these with some examples. Given a statement p which is reliably true and q that is not so reliably true, the truth value of their conjunction is $p \wedge q = (1, 0) \wedge (\frac{1}{2}, 0) = (min(1, \frac{1}{2}), max(0, 0)) = (\frac{1}{2}, 0)$, i.e. not so reliably true. This is easy to understand. Let p be "Alice is a student" and q be "Alice is a research assistant", then the statement "Alice is both a student and a research assistant" cannot be very reliable because we are not quite sure about the fact that she is a research assistant. Consider another example: in the court of a murder case, the prosecutor submits a CCTV record as evidence showing that the suspect was at the crime scene when the murder was happening, while the counsel of the suspect has a witness, who is a friend of the suspect,

---

[3] Pliny the Elder, Roman scholar (23-79 AD).

to certify that the suspect was in a pub 50 km away from the scene at the same time. It turns out the conclusion of whether the suspect was at the scene after we combine these two pieces of evidence is: $(1, 0) \oplus (0, \frac{1}{2}) = (max(1, 0), max(0, \frac{1}{2})) = (1, \frac{1}{2})$. That is, although doubtful, we would believe the suspect is at the scene. The reason is that the video record is more reliable evidence.

5.2   Shinren Policy Language

The syntax of Shinren is based on the logic programming language Datalog [17], with certain extensions. As in Datalog, we do not have function symbols. The restriction is necessary to ensure finiteness of models and termination of inference. A rule, or policy, is of the form:

$$A :- \varphi_1, ..., \varphi_n.$$

where A is an atom and each φ_i is a literal, a consensus formula or a gullibility formula. ": –" is taken as "←" and "," is taken as "∧". The atom A on the left-hand side of the rule is called its *head* and the conjunction $\varphi_1, ..., \varphi_n$ on the right-hand side is called its *body*. Certain types of rules may also have a priority label $\langle lab \rangle$ attached before the rules (will explain later). An *assertion* is a special type of rule defined as:

$$A :- b.$$

where A is a ground atom and b is a truth value. An assertion can be understood as A has a truth value b. A *fact set* is a finite set of assertions. An *assumption set* is also a finite set of assertions. The difference is that the fact set contains the real truth values for the atoms while the assumption set contains the assumptions, i.e. assertions about the default values of the atoms. The assumptions are used only when no facts about the atoms can be found in the fact set or be inferred. We do not need to explicitly represent assumptions of the form $A :- (0, 0)$. If no assumption about an atom can be found in the assumption set, the default value is $(0, 0)$. A *program* is the union of a finite set of rules, a fact set and an assumption set.

By using the Shinren trust policy language, policy makers can define both trust policies and distrust policies, i.e. rules whose heads are $trust$ or $distrust$ predicates. They can also label the policies with *priority levels*. The priority levels express how preferable a policy is. The priority levels in Shinren language are defined as a finite set of non-negative integers $\{0, 1, ..., n\}$. 0 is reserved for default assignment rules. The higher the number is, the higher the priority is. For each priority level, policy makers also define two thresholds in terms of $\preceq_t$ or $\preceq_k$ or both, one for distrust policies and one for trust policies. The thresholds are used to filter poor answers. Answers that satisfy the threshold are called *admissible answers*. Note that only trust or distrust policies need labels, the other policies are not prioritised. When the system is asked to evaluate trust, it starts from policies with the highest priority. At the same level, distrust policies are evaluated before trust policies. In other words, distrust policies have a higher priority than trust policies at the same priority level. If an admissible answer can be found, then the evaluation ends. Otherwise it continues to evaluate the trust policies at the same level. If there are still no admissible answers, the system continues with the policies at the next level. When an admissible answer is found with truth value b, an answer for its counterpart is asserted with a truth value $\neg b$. For example, if the evaluation ends with an admissible answer $distrust(a) = (\frac{1}{2}, 0)$, we also have $trust(a) = (0, \frac{1}{2})$. If after evaluating all the policies at higher priority levels, an admissible answer is still not found, the default value is applied. The default value assignment rules may be omitted, in this case the default value is $(0, 0)$.

The prioritisation mechanism can be used to resolve modality conflicts introduced by trust and distrust policies. Trust and distrust are semantically opposite and it is possible in some situations that both are true based on the policies. Therefore we need to handle the possible conflicts. With priority levels, the conflicts can be resolved by "interlacing" distrust and trust policies and the decisions are governed by the policies with the highest priority levels which give admissible answers. The priority levels can also be used to order trust decisions. For example, if we have decided both Alice and Bob can be reliably trusted, we may prefer Alice if the decision about her came from a trust policy with a higher priority level, i.e. a more preferable policy. The truth values and priority levels can give hints to the decision maker. If the decision is not reliable or from a less preferable policy, it may indicate that the decision is not favourable and may be risky. The decision maker can activate some compensative controls based on the truth value and priority levels.

In order to achieve prioritisation, we require the program to be locally stratified, i.e. there are no cyclical dependencies between ground atoms. This syntactical restriction is needed to guarantee the policies can be evaluated correctly.

Due to space limit, the formal semantics of Shiren is omitted here but is available in the full version [18]. In next section, we will show the policy language by an example. Another example can be found in the appendix.

5.3   Example 1: Electronic Marketplace

Alice is a big fan of Internet shopping and she often visits a website called tBay which is an electronic marketplace like e-bay. Although she has bought a lot of items with very low prices, she also had several unpleasant experiences. So she wants to be cautious before she bids on anything from the website. She decides that she will only bid on items from sellers who live in the UK, have been registered no less than 6 months and have at least 80% positive feedback. She will also ask her friend Bob about his opinion and will not consider a seller if Bob does not like him. However, she knows tBay has a special procedure for items with bid prices lower than £20: in case of dispute, tBay will fully refund the buyer. Since she is not going to lose money, Alice is willing to bid in such situations regardless of her other constraints above. But Alice also has a more important principle: she will never trade with someone who has cheated her. She has a blacklist of such sellers. Alice's policies are:

$\langle 3 \rangle\ distrust(X, bid, Item) :- inBlackList(X).$

$\langle 2 \rangle\ trust(X, bid, Item) :- soldBy(X, Item), itemPrice(Item, Price), Price \leq 20.$

$\langle 1 \rangle\ distrust(X, bid, Item) :- \neg recommendation(bob, X, bid, Item).$

$\langle 1 \rangle\ trust(X, bid, Item) :- seller(tBay, X, Location, RegisterPeriod),$
$\qquad Location = uk, RegisterPeriod \geq 6, soldBy(X, Item),$
$\qquad reputation(X, goodSeller, tBay, Y), Y \geq 0.8.$

Alice's policies have 3 priority levels. At the highest level is the policy which should not be overridden by any other policies. At the second level is a trust policy that allows her to interact with any seller when there is no risk. The lowest level has two policies for general cases. In the policies, $seller(tBay, X, Location, RegisterPeriod)$ represents a seller credential signed by tBay. $soldBy(X, Item)$, $itemPrice(Item, Price)$ and $inBlackList(X)$ are local knowledge predicates supplying useful information. For each priority level, Alice defines thresholds for admissible answers to be $(0,0) \prec_t$, which means only answers somehow true (reliably true, not so reliably true, doubtfully true) will be admissible.

Along with the policies, Alice also has a set of assumptions:

$soldBy(X, Item) :- (0,1).$

$itemPrice(Item, Price) :- (0,1).$

$inBlackList(X) :- (0,1).$

Recall that $(0,1)$ means "reliably false". Alice's assumptions are: if she cannot find any information that says an item is sold by seller X, then this item is not sold by X; if she cannot find any information that says an item is sold for a certain price, then it is not sold for this price; if she cannot find a seller in her blacklist, then he is not in her blacklist. These are easy to understand. All the other predicates are left with default values of $(0,0)$, i.e. unknown. Different default values may make a big difference. For example, if Alice assumes $recommendation(bob, X, bid, Item)$ to be false, i.e. add $recommendation(bob, X, bid, Item) :- (0,1)$ to her assumption set, then she cannot bid anything with a price higher than £20 when she cannot contact Bob. In such cases, since she cannot get recommendations from Bob, the default value will be used and the policy

$distrust(X, bid, Item) :- \neg recommendation(bob, X, bid, Item).$

will always give results of "distrust" with truth value $(1,0)$.

More complicated policies are also possible. For example, if Alice has another policy which says she will bid if at least two of her friends recommend the seller. This can be written as:

$trust(X, bid, Item) :- friend(F1), friend(F2),$
$\qquad recommendation(F1, X, bid, Item) \otimes recommendation(F2, X, bid, Item).$

Alice collects the following facts when she tries to find a cheap iPod on tBay:

$soldBy(carol, ipod) :- (1,0).$

$seller(tBay, carol, uk, 12) :- (1,0).$

$reputation(carol, goodSeller, tBay, 0.9) :- (\frac{1}{2}, 0).$

$itemPrice(ipod, 80) :- (1,0).$

Although not signed, Alice considers the information about who is the seller and the price of the item as reliable. However, the reputation is not. Alice knows at least ten ways which sellers can boost their reputation quickly.

When evaluating the policies, only the assumptions:

$$recommendation(bob, carol, bid, ipod) :- (0,0)$$
$$inBlackList(carol) :- (0,1)$$

are used. This is because Alice does not have any relevant information. The other assumptions are not used because Alice has collected the facts and therefore does not need to assume anything.

Let us also explain how the trust (distrust) policies are evaluated. Shinren starts from priority level 3. For the distrust policy at this level, the body is $inBlackList(carol)$ with truth value $(0,1)$ in the interpretation. Therefore $distrust(carol, bid, ipod)$ is evaluated to be $(0,1)$, according to this policy. Because $(0,0) \not\preceq_t (0,1)$, this answer is not admissible and is discarded. The policy with priority 2 does not have an admissible answer either. Given $itemPrice(ipod, 80) = (1,0)$, the constraint $Price \leq 20$ is not satisfied because the price is £80. This constraint is linked to $itemPrice(ipod, 80)$, so its truth value is $\neg(1,0) = (0,1)$. Overall, $trust(carol, bid, ipod)$ is evaluated to $(0,1)$ according to this policy. The answer is also discarded. Because Alice cannot get a recommendation from Bob, the default value is used and the distrust policy at priority level 1 is evaluated to $(0,0)$. The answer is also not admissible. The last policy is evaluated to $(\frac{1}{2},0)$ and therefore is admissible. Because it is a trust policy, we add $trust(carol, bid, ipod) = (\frac{1}{2},0)$ and also $distrust(carol, bid, ipod) = (0,\frac{1}{2})$ to the model. Alice now knows that although Carol can be trusted, she might still be cheated.

6   Implementation

We have implemented a prototype of Shinren. As shown in Figure 3, Shiren consists of five major modules. Among the five modules, the credential module, the recommendation module, the reputation module and the state module are responsible for retrieving and interpreting information from different sources, and the policy interpreter module is responsible for making decisions according to the policies and the information gathered.

The Shinren prototype is implemented in Java 1.5. The policy interpreter evaluates queries in a bottom-up fashion as in many other datalog-based systems. Policies are loaded into the policy interpreter as plain text files. The rules are stratified when they are loaded by analysing the predicate dependency relationships. To answer a query, the interpreter first initialises an interpretation which is an instance of the Assertion-Set class. The interpreter queries the other four modules in order to gather facts, i.e. ground instances of the predicates with truth values, which are needed for policy evaluation. The facts are stored in tables related to the predicates in the interpretation. After the interpreter obtains all facts, it constructs the Herbrand universe by collecting all the constants from the query, rules and facts. The interpreter then puts into the initial interpretation assumptions for all the other ground atoms which are in the Herbrand base. It then starts evaluating policies iteratively from the lowest strata. Each rule in the stata is grounded with regard to the Herbrand base and then the interpreter applies the immediate consequence operator to each ground instance. The immediate consequence operator retrieves the truth values for the ground atoms in the rule body from

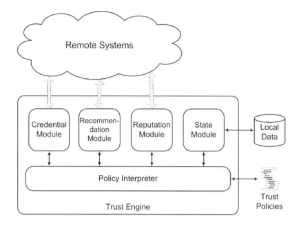

Fig. 3. Shinren Trust Engine

the current interpretation and passes them through the evaluation tree of the rule to obtain the truth value of the ground head atom. The ground atom along with the truth value is a newly generated fact and the table for the head predicate in the interpretation is updated. If an entry with the same ground tuple is already in the table, the truth value of the old entry is ORed with the truth value of the new entry; otherwise the new entry is inserted into the table. Trust (distrust) policies in the same strata are evaluated sequentially by priority level until an admissible answer, i.e. an answer that satisfies the threshold defined for this level, is found. The evaluation of the strata ends when the interpretation does not change anymore. Then the interpreter evaluates the rules in the next strata. The evaluation of the query ends after the interpreter evaluates all the strata containing the rules with the queried atoms as heads.

7   Conclusion and Future Work

In this paper, we have presented Shinren, a novel non-monotonic trust management system based on bilattices and the any-world assumption. The syntax of the Shinren policy language is based on Datalog with certain extensions such as negation, constraints and prioritisation. Shinren can utilise unreliable even contradictory information and supports prioritisation which resolves conflicts and provides decision support. We demonstrated the power of Shinren by two comprehensive examples and outlined its implementation. The semantics of Shiren extends the Kripke-Kleene semantics over bilattices and is given in [18].

One aspect that we would like to investigate further is prioritisation. The current prioritisation mechanism in Shinren is at the meta-level. It works but is not convenient in practice because it is external to the bilattice. However, prioritisation can also be viewed as another ordering. We would like to extend our bilattice, so that a third ordering could be integrated into the theory. This would make prioritisation a built-in feature.

The any-world assumption uses the concept of non-uniform assumption. However, its assumptions are static. We are interested in researching dynamic assumptions which would mean that changes in knowledge could lead to the change of the assumptions. Dynamic assumptions would enable a trust management system to generate more accurate conclusions according to the context. Previous works in belief revision [19] and dynamic prioritisation [20] are possible stepping stones in this direction.

References

1. Blaze, M., Feigenbaum, J., Lacy, J.: Decentralized trust management. In: IEEE Symposium on Security and Privacy, pp. 164–173. IEEE Computer Society, Los Alamitos (1996)
2. Mayer, R.C., Davis, J.H., Schoorman, D.F.: An integrative model of organizational trust. The Academy of Management Review 20(3), 709–734 (1995)
3. Blaze, M., Feigenbaum, J., Ioannidis, J., Keromytis, A.D.: The keynote trust-management system, version 2. RFC 2704 (1999)
4. Jim, T.: Sd3: A trust management system with certified evaluation. In: SP 2001: Proceedings of the 2001 IEEE Symposium on Security and Privacy, Washington, DC, USA, pp. 106–115. IEEE Computer Society, Los Alamitos (2001)
5. Li, N., Mitchell, J.C., Winsborough, W.H.: Design of a role-based trust-management framework. In: IEEE Symposium on Security and Privacy, pp. 114–130 (2002)
6. Hess, A., Seamons, K.E.: An access control model for dynamic client-side content. In: SACMAT 2003: Proceedings of the eighth ACM symposium on Access control models and technologies, pp. 207–216. ACM Press, New York (2003)
7. Carbone, M., Nielsen, M., Sassone, V.: A formal model for trust in dynamic networks. In: SEFM, pp. 54–61 (2003)
8. Chu, Y.H., Feigenbaum, J., LaMacchia, B.A., Resnick, P., Strauss, M.: Referee: Trust management for web applications. Computer Networks 29(8-13), 953–964 (1997)
9. Herzberg, A., Mass, Y., Mihaeli, J., Naor, D., Ravid, Y.: Access control meets public key infrastructure, or: Assigning roles to strangers. In: IEEE Symposium on Security and Privacy, pp. 2–14 (2000)
10. Czenko, M., Tran, H., Doumen, J., Etalle, S., Hartel, P., den Hartog, J.: Nonmonotonic trust management for P2P applications. Electronic Notes in Theoretical Computer Science 157(3), 113–130 (2006)
11. Gelder, A.V., Ross, K.A., Schlipf, J.S.: Unfounded sets and well-founded semantics for general logic programs. In: PODS, pp. 221–230. ACM, New York (1988)
12. Marsh, S.P.: Formalising Trust as a Computational Concept. PhD thesis, University of Stirling (1994)
13. Jøsang, A.: A logic for uncertain probabilities. International Journal of Uncertainty, Fuzziness and Knowledge-Based Systems 9(3), 279–212 (2001)
14. Yu, B., Singh, M.P.: Detecting deception in reputation management. In: AAMAS, pp. 73–80. ACM, New York (2003)
15. Ginsberg, M.L.: Multivalued logics: a uniform approach to reasoning in artificial intelligence. Computational Intelligence 4, 265–316 (1988)
16. Loyer, Y., Straccia, U.: Any-world assumptions in logic programming. Theor. Comput. Sci. 342(2-3), 351–381 (2005)
17. Ceri, S., Gottlob, G., Tanca, L.: What you always wanted to know about datalog (and never dared to ask). IEEE Trans. Knowl. Data Eng. 1(1), 146–166 (1989)
18. Dong, C., Dulay, N.: Shinren: Non-monotonic trust management for distributed systems. Technical Report DTR10-5, Department of Computing, Imperial College London (March 2010)
19. Alchourrón, C.E., Gärdenfors, P., Makinson, D.: On the logic of theory change: Partial meet contraction and revision functions. J. Symb. Log. 50(2), 510–530 (1985)
20. Brewka, G.: Reasoning about priorities in default logic. In: AAAI, pp. 940–945 (1994)

A   Example 2: Healthcare in the Community

Dr Taylor runs a medical clinic in a small town. An unconscious patient is brought to the clinic. From the driver's licence, Dr Taylor learns that the patient is called Mr Johnson. Mr Johnson is a tourist and stayed in a local hotel before he was brought here. The owner of the hotel, who brought Mr Johnson in, tells Dr Taylor that the patient experienced breathing difficulties during breakfast and then passed out a few minutes later. Dr Taylor examines the patient's trachea and hears the lung sound. He decides to intubate the patient in order to let air pass freely to and from the lungs. The patient's temperature is normal and the results of a blood test show no signs of infection. Blood pressure and heart rate are also normal. Dr Taylor decides to check the patient's medical history in order to see whether the symptoms were caused by drugs or allergies. From his computer, Dr Taylor sends a request to the Smith GP practice, found in documents in Mr Johnson's wallet.

The electronic medical record system of the Smith GP practice uses the Shinren trust management system to control who can access patients' medical histories. The policies which regulate the access to a patient's medical history are shown blow:

$\langle 3 \rangle$ $distrust(X, read, med\_history, Y) :- \neg doctor(bma, X)$.

$\langle 3 \rangle$ $trust(X, read, med\_history, Y) :- consent(Y, X, read, med\_history)$

$\langle 3 \rangle$ $trust(X, read, med\_history, Y) :- agent(Y, Z), consent(Z, X, read, med\_history)$

$\langle 2 \rangle$ $trust(X, read, med\_history, Y) :- answer(X, DOB, ADDRESS),$
$\qquad personal\_info(Y, DOB2, ADDRESS2), DOB = DOB2,$
$\qquad ADDRESS = ADDRESS2.$

$\langle 1 \rangle$ $trust(X, read, med\_history, Y) :- collocated(X, Y)$.

Patients' medical histories are sensitive and should only be revealed to doctors who are treating the patients. The distrust policy at level 3 says that X is not allowed to read patient Y's medical history if X does not have a doctor credential signed by the BMA (British Medical Association). The second trust policy at the same level says X is trusted to read patient Y's medical history if Y gives his consent. However, in real-life, it is not always possible to get the patient's consent, e.g. in the case that the patient is in coma. Then a third party consent from the patient's agent, usually the next of kin, also has the same effect. In emergency situations where no consent can be obtained, it is necessary to verify that the doctor is indeed treating the patient before letting the doctor access the information without consent. For example, the verification might be done by letting the doctor provide the patient's personal information and comparing it with the data stored, or using a location service to verify that the doctor is co-located with the patient. Accesses without consent are logged and audited.

Dr Taylor provides his doctor credential and also supplies information about Mr Johnson's birthday and address correctly. The access is granted and logged. Alas the medical history does not provide too much useful information. At the same time, Mr Johnson's condition becomes worse. He starts to have seizures and EEG (electroencephalogram) shows abnormal brain activities.

Dr Taylor suspects that the problem may be in Mr Johnson's brain. However, he is not a neurologist and needs someone to help in diagnosing the patient. Dr Taylor starts looking for help. He searches the NHS database using Shinren with the policies shown below:

⟨2⟩ $trust(X, specialist, neurology)$:$-consultant(Hos, X, neurology)$,
    $hospital(NHS, Hos), member(aon, X, Level), Level >= 2$.

⟨1⟩ $trust(X, specialist, neurology)$:$-consultant(Hos, X, neurology)$,
    $hospital(NHS, Hos), member(aon, X, 1), member(aon, Y, Level), Level >= 2$,
    $recommendation(Y, X, specialist, neurology)$.

The first policy says that Dr Taylor will trust X as a specialist in neurology if X has a consultant credential signed by an NHS hospital which states that X is a consultant in neurology. X must also be a member of the Association of Neurologists with level no lower than senior member. The second policy says almost the same except that if the level of X in the Association of Neurologists is not high enough, he needs a recommendation from a senior member or higher.

Dr Taylor finds 20 doctors who fit his requirements. Among them, he selects Dr Ford, a senior member of the Association of Neurologists who works for Victoria Hospital. Dr Ford is also willing to offer assistance. Dr Taylor sets up a video conference with Dr Ford. After hearing the observations and checking the examination results, Dr Ford suggests that the problem could be caused by a clot in the patient's brain. However, a brain tumour also fits the symptoms. The diagnosis can be confirmed by an MRI (Magnetic Resonance Imaging) scan or a brain biopsy. However, the clinic does not have the equipment and the patient's condition is not suitable for transportation. Dr Ford then suggests that in this situation, Dr Taylor should immediately treat the patient with tPA (tissue Plasminogen Activator), a medicine which helps resolving blood clots, because a long delay could cost the patient's life. If the patient's condition gets better, then the diagnosis of a blood clot can be confirmed, otherwise it suggests a brain tumour.

Dr Ford's plan could be quite dangerous. So Dr Taylor wants to hear a second opinion. To ensure the opinion is independent and fair, Dr Taylor adds another policy before he searches for the second specialist. The policy rules out all the specialists working in the same hospital as Dr Ford.

⟨2⟩ $distrust(X, specialist, neurology)$:$- consultant(victoria, X, neurology)$.

This time Dr Taylor finds Dr Grant, a senior member of the Association of Neurologists who works for the Albert Hospital. Dr Grant confirms that there is no better solution in this situation. Dr Taylor starts to treat the patient with tPA, and watches him closely. 24 hours later, the patient wakes up. After the patient's condition is stabilised, he is transferred to the nearest major hospital for further diagnosis and treatment.

Modeling and Analysis of Trust Management Protocols: Altruism versus Selfishness in MANETs

Jin-Hee Cho[1], Ananthram Swami[1], and Ing-Ray Chen[2]

[1] U.S. Army Research Laboratory
Computational and Information Sciences Directorate
{jinhee.cho,ananthram.swami}@us.army.mil
[2] Virginia Tech
Department of Computer Science
irchen@vt.edu

Abstract. Mobile ad hoc and sensor networks often contain a mixture of nodes, some of which may be selfish and non-cooperative in providing network services such as forwarding packets in order to conserve energy. Existing trust management protocols for mobile ad hoc networks (MANETs) advocate isolating selfish nodes as soon as they are detected. Further, altruistic behaviors are encouraged with incentive mechanisms. In this paper, we propose and analyze a trust management protocol based on the demand and pricing theory for managing group communication systems where system survivability is highly critical to mission execution. Rather than always encouraging altruistic behaviors, we consider the tradeoff between a node's individual welfare (e.g., saving energy for survivability) versus global welfare (e.g., providing service availability) and identify the best design condition so that the system lifetime is maximized while the mission requirements are satisfied.

Keywords: Trust, trust metrics, trust management, mobile ad hoc networks, demand and pricing theory, altruism, selfishness.

1 Introduction

Most existing trust management protocols in mobile ad hoc networks (MANETs) encourage cooperative behaviors while discouraging selfish behaviors of participating nodes, so as to achieve a prescribed system goal such as high service availability. A common approach is to isolate selfish nodes as soon as they are detected and to reward altruistic nodes with incentives to encourage cooperation. However, in MANET environments where resources (e.g., bandwidth, memory, computational power, and energy) are severely constrained, only encouraging altruistic behaviors may adversely shorten the system lifetime. This is because altruistic nodes may die quickly due to energy depletion, thereby possibly resulting in loss of connectivity and system services.

Thomas *et al.* [18] studied system performance in such a scenario, and noted that there is a tradeoff between energy saved by selfish nodes and service availability provided by cooperative nodes. However, no analysis of the tradeoff was given. Papadimitriou [13] coined the term *the price of anarchy* to describe the two conflicting

M. Nishigaki et al. (Eds.): IFIPTM 2010, IFIP AICT 321, pp. 141–156, 2010.

goals of individual welfare versus global welfare, i.e., the local goal of a selfish node to save its energy versus the global goal of an altruistic node to provide high service availability. Similar issues arise in routing in MANETs (e.g., a local goal through selfish routing versus a global goal for service availability) [15]. The price of anarchy was defined as the performance difference between a system run by an all-knowing benign dictator who can make the right decisions to optimize system performance, versus a system run by a selfish anarchy. We postulate that there should be a tradeoff between system survivability and service availability in terms of these two conflicting goals. As Thomas *et al.* [18] indicated, each node can make a decision for its own benefit as well as for global interest by considering the dynamics of the network as well as its own conditions (e.g., energy level).

We propose and analyze a trust management protocol that trades off node altruism for system survivability for mission-driven group communication system (GCS) in MANETs based on the concept of cognitive networks. In a cognitive network, each node has intelligence to adapt to dynamically changing MANET environments through a learning process, by adjusting its altruistic and selfish behaviors in response to network dynamics. We seek to identify the optimal design settings that maximize system lifetime while satisfying performance requirements such as service availability.

Our trust management protocol adopts *demand and pricing (DP)* theory originally derived from economics [4]; under DP a node decides whether it should behave selfishly or altruistically based on the balance between individual welfare (i.e., saving energy) and global welfare (i.e., providing services). A node's decision may depend on its own energy level, 1-hop neighbors' selfishness levels (i.e., to judge whether the system still has sufficient resources such as an adequate number of cooperative neighboring nodes), and the degree of node importance to mission success (e.g., to judge whether a node's selfish behavior would have a significant detrimental impact on the mission success rate). Social scientists have addressed the tradeoff between local/individual utility and global/collective interest in the area of collaboration theories using the concept of *trust* in groups, teams, and organizations [7]. However, no prior work addresses this tradeoff in the context of trust management in MANETs. A number of prior studies have also taken economic perspectives in modeling communication networks [2, 9, 10, 14, 22]. Unlike these prior studies, our work concerns trust management and we specifically adopt DP theory.

Many routing protocols for MANETs have been developed to isolate selfish nodes and to encourage collaborations among participating nodes [11, 20, 21, 23, 24]. Wang *et al.* [20] devised an efficient incentive mechanism to encourage cooperative behaviors in multipath routing. Zhao [23] investigated the optimal transmission probability and Yan *et al.* [21] developed incentive mechanisms using game theoretic approaches. Miranda *et al.* [11] proposed an algorithm in which routing behaviors are monitored; selfish nodes are penalized (their packets are not forwarded) so as to discourage selfish behaviors, and nodes making heavy demands for services are also penalized to ensure faire allocation of resources. Different from the above work, Zhang *et al.* [24] considered the positive aspect of having selfish nodes in terms of traffic reduction, and established bounds on the probability of a node being selfish to optimize system metrics. Our work in this paper is different in that we investigate and identify the best balance between individual welfare via selfish behaviors versus global interest via altruistic behaviors so as to prolong the system lifetime.

Routing protocols have also been proposed based on the concept of trust (or reputation) to isolate selfish nodes [1, 12, 16] using incentive mechanisms that discourage selfish behaviors. However, the trust metric used often does not adequately consider important properties of trust in a MANET environment, including subjectivity, asymmetry, incomplete transitivity, dynamicity, and context-dependency [5]. Our work takes these properties into consideration by adopting a composite trust metric that incorporates both *social trust* and *QoS* (quality-of-service) *trust*. The QoS and social components capture different aspects of trust that are important from the perspective of the user and the end-goal of the mission.

The contributions of this work are as follows. First, we propose a novel composite trust metric encompassing social trust explaining the aspects of internal, interpersonal, and mental aspects of an entity [7] and QoS trust indicating competence for task performance. Second, we develop and analyze a trust-based protocol for a mission-driven GCS in MANETs where nodes may behave selfishly. We use DP theory to quantify the conflicts between individual welfare and global welfare and identify the conditions that best prolong the system lifetime for successful mission execution while satisfying performance requirements. Third, we develop a mathematical model to describe the behaviors of a GCS based on hierarchical stochastic Petri nets (SPN), allowing optimal conditions to be identified to answer what-if type of questions in response to changing operational and environmental conditions. Lastly, through numerical data, we demonstrate that our trust management protocol based on DP theory is capable of maintaining an acceptable trust level for successful mission execution while prolonging system lifetime, when compared with a traditional all-altruistic system.

The rest of this paper is organized as follows. Section 2 describes the system model including the assumptions, trust metric, and energy model. Section 3 develops a performance model to describe the behaviors of a GCS based on hierarchical stochastic Petri nets. Further, Section 3 describes DP theory being applied for the formulation of trust management. Section 4 presents numerical data obtained from the evaluation of our performance model. In particular, we compare the performance of a GCS operating under our proposed trust protocol versus a solely altruistic GCS. Finally, Section 5 concludes the paper and outlines future work.

2   System Model

Due to the unique characteristics of MANETs and unreliable communication in wireless networks, trust management for MANETs should encompass the following trust concepts. Trust should be dynamic to account for uncertainty. Trust should be context-dependent, and subjective, and cannot be assumed to be transitive or reciprocal. To address these unique trust properties, trust management for MANETs should consider the following design features: trust metrics must be customizable, evaluation of trust should be fully distributed without reliance on a centralized authority, and trust management should cope with dynamics and adverse behaviors in a tactical MANET [6].

Cognitive networks are able to reconfigure the network based on past experiences by adapting to changing network behaviors to improve scalability (e.g., reducing complexity), survivability (e.g., increasing reliability), and QoS (e.g., facilitating cooperation among nodes) [18]. We use this concept to indicate a node's ability to adapt to changing network conditions, such as a node's selfish behavior, node failure or mobility, energy exhaustion of a node, or voluntary disconnection for energy savings.

In the initial network deployment, we assume that there is no predefined trust. Without prior interactions, the initial bootstrapping will establish a shallow level of trust based only on indirect information (e.g., reputation from historically collected data or recommendation by third parties) and authentication by a challenge/response process (e.g., public key authentication). Over time, participating nodes will establish a stronger trust level with more confidence based on direct or indirect interactions. Our trust management protocol allows each node to evaluate the trust levels of other nodes as well as to be evaluated by other nodes based on two factors, social trust and QoS trust. *Social trust* includes trust properties for "sociable" purposes (e.g., intimacy) while *QoS trust* includes trust properties for mission execution purposes (e.g., energy level or cooperation) [5].

Trust decays over time without further updates or interactions between entities. Node mobility also hinders continuous interactions with other group members, lowering the chances of evaluations of each other in the group. This includes cases such as a node moving to other areas causing its disconnection from the current group, leaving a group for mission reasons, voluntary disconnection for saving power or involuntary disconnection due to physical terrain or low energy. We use the concept of a *trust chain* [3] to describe propagation of trust. For example, when *A* trusts *B*, *B* trusts *C*, *C* trusts *D*, and *D* trusts *E*, then, *A* may trust *E* over a trust chain of length 4. However, the longer the trust chain is, the more is the decay in the degree of trust [3].

Our target system is a mission-driven GCS in tactical military MANETs where a symmetric key, called the group key, is used as a secret key for group communications between group members [5]. Upon a node's disconnection from the group, the system generates and redistributes a new key so that non-member nodes will not be able to access a valid secret group key. Nevertheless, each group member keeps old trust information even for non-member nodes so that the information can be reused for future interactions, possibly preventing a newcomer attack.

2.1 Assumptions

We assume that the GCS is in a MANET environment without any centralized trusted authority. Nodes communicate with each node through multiple hops. Nodes have different levels of energy, thus reflecting node heterogeneity. Each node periodically beacons its *id* and *location* information so that node failure is easily detected and accordingly rekeying is done immediately upon every membership change.

We assume that mobile devices are carried by human such as dismounted soldiers. A node dynamically adopts selfish or altruistic behavior depending on the remaining energy level, difficulty level of the given mission (i.e., a tougher mission requires a higher workload), and selfishness level of 1-hop neighbors. That is, a node will behave selfishly when it has low energy, the mission assigned to it is not difficult, and/or there is a sufficient number of cooperating 1-hop neighbors. We consider a node to be selfish when the node drops group communication packets transmitted by other nodes. Even though the node is selfish, we assume that it cooperates to perform rekeying operations upon a membership change. The energy level of each node is adjusted depending on its status. For simplicity, we only consider energy consumption due to packet transmission and reception. Thus, if a node becomes selfish, the rate of energy consumption is slowed down.

We consider a redemption mechanism by which a selfish node can become a normal cooperative node again. Specifically, a selfish node reevaluates its status at the end of each trust update interval and decides whether it will become altruistic or stay selfish. This is described in Section 3.2. A non-member will not consume as much energy as a member because of less involvement with group activities. Upon every membership change due to group join/leave, a rekeying operation will be performed to generate a new group key based on a distributed key agreement protocol such as GDH (Group Diffie-Hellman) [17].

We assume that a node's trust value is evaluated based on direct observations (e.g., packet dropping) as well as indirect observations. Indirect observations are recommendations obtained from 1-hop neighbors whom the evaluator trusts the most. If enough recommenders cannot be found, recommendations from all 1-hop neighbors can be used. A node's trust value may be updated after each status exchange period. A status exchange packet includes a node's own information as well as information of nodes on its trust chain for possible use as recommendations on distant nodes to its 1-hop neighbors.

We assume that existing prevention techniques such as encryption, authentication, or rekeying inhibit outsider attacks. We consider the presence of selfish nodes among legitimate group members. We model the selfish behaviors of a node by DP theory as described in Section 3.2.

2.2 Trust Metric

We consider a trust metric that spans two aspects of the trust relationship [5]. First, we consider intimacy (or friendliness) for *social trust* where intimacy is measured by the degree that two nodes are 1-hop neighbors. Second, *QoS trust* accounts for the capability of a node to complete a given mission. We consider the energy level and degree of unselfishness (or cooperation) to estimate the QoS trust level of a node. A node's trust value changes dynamically to account for trust decay over time due to node mobility or failure, as the trust chain becomes longer, as the node's energy level changes, and as the node becomes selfish or cooperative.

We define a node's trust level as a continuous real number in the range of [0, 1], with 1 indicating complete trust, 0.5 ignorance, and 0 complete distrust. The overall trust value is calculated based on three components: energy level, unselfishness, and intimacy. As will be evident, other components could be added if desired. Based on the trust value calculated by 1-hop neighbors, the trust value can be calculated by n-hop neighbors over a trust chain.

The information used for trust evaluation of a particular node j includes probability of being alive, e.g., remaining energy > threshold, ($P_j^{energy}(t)$), probability of being unselfish ($P_j^{unselfish}(t)$), and probability of being located in a particular area ($P_j^{loc=k}(t)$) where k indicates area *id*, and t is time. These three values are obtained from SPN subnets shown in Fig. 2 and the technical method for obtaining them from the SPN subnets is explained in Section 3. We use the term "probability" in a loose sense; one should interpret "probability" here as "value associated with a particular aspect" rather than in the frequentist or Bayesian interpretation.

Now we address how the trust value is calculated. The three trust components, namely, energy level, unselfishness, and intimacy, capture MNAET dynamics. The trust value $(T_{i,j}^{n-hop}(t))$ of node j as evaluated by node i where n indicates the trust chain length used by a node is given by:

$$T_{i,j}^{n-hop}(t) = e^{-\gamma}\left[P_{i,j}^{n-hop,unselfish}(t) + P_{i,j}^{n-hop,energy}(t) + P_{i,j}^{intimacy}(t)\right]/3 \qquad (1)$$

The n-hop trust component X, where X represents unselfishness or energy, is calculated based on the trust values obtained from the trust chain with lengths 1 to n-1 and is given by:

$$P_{i,j}^{n-hop,X}(t) = \sum_{m=2}^{n}\left(\beta\,P_{i,j}^{(m-1)-hop,X}(t) + (1-\beta)\,P_{i,j}^{m-hop,indirect-X}(t)\right) \qquad (2)$$

$$where\quad P_{i,j}^{m-hop,indirect-X}(t) = \frac{\sum_{k\in S_i}(P_{i,k}^{(m-1)-hop,\;X}(t)\,P_{k,j}^{(m-1)-hop,\;X}(t))}{k_{recom}} \qquad (3)$$

Here β is used as a weight for the node's "self-information" and $(1-\beta)$ is a weight for "other-information." The self-information $(P_{i,j}^{(m-1)-hop,X}(t))$ can be obtained recursively by using Equation 2. In Equation 3, S_i is the set of 1-hop neighbors of node i, excluding node j, that forward recommendation of node j and $|S_i| = k_{recom}$ the number of recommender nodes that have the highest trust values among all 1-hop neighbors on the trust chain of the evaluator. Notice that when calculating the trust value of node j via node k's recommendation, node i's trust value on node k is used as a weight; this causes trust to decay as the trust chain increases.

Since the n-hop trust values are computed based on the basis of $(n$-$1)$-hop trust values as shown in Equations 2 and 3, the 1-hop trust values are the basis of all trust values and are computed by:

$$P_{i,j}^{1-hop,X}(t) = \left(\beta\,P_{i,j}^{direct-X}(t) + (1-\beta)\,P_{i,j}^{1-hop,indirect-X}(t)\right) \qquad (4)$$

$$P_{i,j}^{1-hop,indirect-X}(t) = \frac{\sum_{k\in S_i}\left(P_{i,k}^{1-hop,\;X}(t-\Delta t)\,P_{k,j}^{1-hop,\;X}(t-\Delta t)\right)}{k_{recom}} \qquad (5)$$

$$P_{i,j}^{1-hop,unselfish}(0) = 0.5, \qquad P_{i,j}^{1-hop,energy}(0) = 0.5 \qquad (6)$$

The direct information for the trust component X of node j evaluated by node i $(P_{i,j}^{direct-X}(t))$ is obtained, by dividing node j's trust component by node i's trust component, $min\left[P_j^X(t)/P_i^X(t), 1\right]$; it is thus a subjective relative evaluation. Note that $P_i^X(t)$ for all i where X indicates a trust component obtained from our SPN model as explained in Section 3.3. We assume that the local trust component value of a node at time $t = 0$ are set to ignorance (i.e., ignorance value 0.5 in the trust range of $[0, 1]$) during the network bootstrapping period, as shown in Equation 6.

In Equation 1, $e^{-\gamma}$ represents a function of $P_{i,j}^{n-hop}(t)$, the probability that nodes i and j are within n hops. $P_{i,j}^{n-hop}(t)$ is computed as:

$$P_{i,j}^{n-hop}(t) = \sum_{k=1}^{n} q_{i,j}^{k-hop}(t)\;where\;\;q_{i,j}^{k-hop}(t) = \sum_{(l,m)\in S_k}\left(P_i^{loc=l}(t)\,P_j^{loc=m}(t)\right) \qquad (7)$$

Here $P_j^{loc=m}(t)$ is the probability that node j is in location m at time t, and S_k is a set covering all (l, m) pairs with the distance between l and m being k hops. Assuming that nodes move independently, we can verify that $P_{i,j}^{n-hop}(t)$ is the probability that nodes (i, j) are within n hops of each other at time t.

In $e^{-\gamma}$, we define γ by:

$$\gamma = \frac{1}{a * P_{i,j}^{n-hop}(t)} \tag{8}$$

where a is a positive constant. The decay factor $e^{-\gamma}$ increases monotonically with $P_{i,j}^{n-hop}(t)$, implying that the trust evaluation is higher if it is more likely that the nodes are closer. The value of the constant a ($a < 1$ versus $a > 1$) dictates whether the decay function is convex or concave increasing in $P_{i,j}^{n-hop}(t)$. The value of the constant a affects the propagation of trust; guidelines for choosing this parameter will be discussed elsewhere. Note that we use Equations 2-6 to compute trust component values of unselfishness and energy.

$P_{i,j}^{intimacy}(t)$, the third component of Equation 1, can be obtained without the help of other nodes' recommendations since each node can detect and keep track of information on who has been with them as 1-hop neighbors through the beacon messages disseminated by each node periodically. $P_{i,j}^{intimacy}(t)$, the degree that nodes I and j are 1-hop neighbors, is computed by:

$$P_{i,j}^{intimacy}(t) = P_{i,j}^{1-hop}(t) / P_i^{max-intimacy}(t) \tag{9}$$

$$where \ P_i^{max-intimacy}(t) = max\left[P_{i,1}^{1-hop}, ..., P_{i,n}^{1-hop}\right] \tag{10}$$

In Equation 9, the normalization by $P_i^{max-intimacy}(t)$ provides relative weights to intimacy, now ranging from 0 to 1. Note that $P_{i,j}^{intimacy}(0)$ can be calculated based on the location information preloaded in the initial network deployment.

We also derive the objective trust values of each node in order to compare it against the trust value calculated by each node, called *subjective trust*. The objective trust is calculated without considering any network dynamics such as node mobility, trust decay over time, and trust decay as the trust chain becomes longer. The objective trust of node i is calculated by:

$$T_i^{obj}(t) = \left[P_i^{unselfish}(t) + P_i^{intimacy}(t) + P_i^{energy}(t)\right]/3 \tag{11}$$

$$P_i^{intimacy}(t) = \frac{\left(\sum_{j \in S} P_{i,j}^{1-hop}(t)/N\right)}{P^{avg-obj-intimacy}(t)} \tag{12}$$

Here $P_i^{unselfish}(t)$, $P_i^{intimacy}(t)$, and $P_i^{energy}(t)$ are the three components of trust derived from the SPN subnets explained in Section 3. Ideally, the objective trust value $T_i^{obj}(t)$, of node j, would be known to all other nodes. In practice, node i estimates the trust value via the subjective trust value $T_{i,j}^{n-hop}(t)$ as discussed earlier in Equation 1. As discussed by Josang et al. [8], it is desirable that the subjective trust value is below the objective trust value; this ensures that agents are not exposed to unnecessary risk, but clearly there will be missed reward. We will consider objective intimacy based on the average intimacy degree on node i evaluated by all other nodes divided by the average intimacy probability (i.e., the average probability that two nodes will be located as 1-hop neighbors in the operational area). See Section 3 for a specific numeric example. We can then evaluate how accurately subjective trust values are calculated by varying the length of the trust chain through Equation 1, and comparing them with the objective trust shown in Equation 11. Note that the objective trust is not known in real situations, and so it is predicted and used to conservatively evaluate the validity of the proposed scheme.

In Equation 1, we derive a in order for a trust-based system lifetime based on subjective trust to be at least equal to or less than one based on objective trust. Here by the system lifetime, we mean the the accumulated ime period over which the system trust values are above a certain system drop dead trust level, say T_{value}, as used in Section 4.

2.3 Energy Model

We associate the energy level of a node with its state: selfish or group member. Depending on its remaining energy, a node acts differently. The degree of energy consumption is also affected by the node's state. Thus, these parameters are interwoven and affect a node's lifetime significantly.

A GCS in MANETs must handle events such as beaconing, group communication, rekeying, and status exchange. In particular, after a status exchange event, trust evaluation of 1-hop neighboring nodes as well as of distant nodes is performed. Each node may transmit its own status (e.g., information providing the trust values) as well as status of other nodes (i.e., trust values) on its trust chain. Recall that we use recommendations from 1-hop neighbors for trust evaluation and each status message is disseminated periodically. Due to space constraints, we omit the detail of the energy consumption model and refer the reader to [5].

3 Performance Model

This section describes how our analytical model is developed using SPN and how trust values are obtained from the SPN models.

3.1 Hierarchical Modeling Using SPNs

We develop a mathematical model based on SPN to analyze a GCS with nodes switching between selfish and altruistic behaviors based on the theory and identify design conditions under which the selfish versus altruistic behaviors can be balanced. With system lifetime and mission success probability as our reliability metric, we show that our trust management protocol operating under identified design conditions outperforms one that only encourages altruistic behaviors. We use SPN due to its efficient representation of a large number of states where the underlying models are Markov or semi-Markov models. We develop a hierarchical modeling technique to

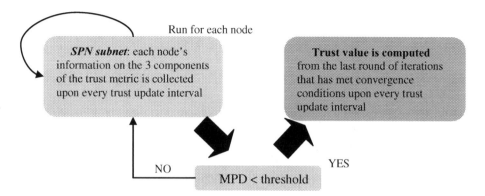

Fig. 1. Hierarchical modeling using SPN subnets

avoid state explosion problems and to improve solution efficiency for realizing and describing a large scale GCS.

We use an SPN subnet to describe each node's lifetime. The square-shaped operational area consists of $m \times m$ sub-grid areas with the width and height equal to wireless radio range (R). Initially the location of each node is randomly distributed over the operational area based on the uniform distribution. A node randomly moves to one of four locations in four directions (i.e., north, west, south, and east) in accordance with its speed. The speed of each node S_{init} is chosen uniformly over $[0, v_{max})$ m/s where v_{max} is the maximum possible speed, and S_{init} is then fixed during the node's lifetime. The boundary grid areas are wrapped around (i.e., a torus is assumed) to avoid end-effects. The SPN subnet for node i computes the probability that node i is in a particular grid area j at time t. This information along with the information of other nodes' location at time t provides the information about a node's n-hop neighbors at time t, which we will use to compute the trust metric (see Section 2.2). Since node movements are assumed to be independent, the probability that two nodes are in a particular location at time t, is given by the product of the two individual probabilities. The SPN subnet also describes a node's lifetime and can be used to obtain each node's information (amount of energy, unselfishness, and intimacy) to derive the trust relationship with other nodes in the system. This process is done by running the SPN subnet N times for the N nodes in the network.

In the first round of iteration, since there is no information available about 1-hop neighbors, it is assumed that each area has an equal number of nodes and all nodes are unselfish. In the second round of iteration, based on the information collected (e.g., number of unselfish or selfish 1-hop neighbors) from the first round, each node knows how many nodes are 1-hop neighbors that can directly communicate with it, and whether or not they are members of the GCS or selfish. A node also knows how many n-hop neighbors it has at time t. It then adjusts its perceived status of 1-hop neighbors at time t with the output generated from the jth round of iteration as input to the $(j+1)^{th}$ round of iteration. This process continues until a specified convergence condition is met. The Mean Percentage Difference (MPD) is used to measure the difference between critical design parameter values, including a node's energy level, the selfish probability, and the unselfish probability of a node at time t in two consecutive iterations. The iteration stops when the MPD is below a threshold 1 percent (%) for all nodes in the system. The calculation of the MPD of parameter X for node i is given by:

$$MPD_i^X = \frac{\sum_t^{max} D_i^X(t)}{N_{interval}} \quad where \quad D_i^X(t) = \frac{\left| X_i^{j+1}(t) - X_i^j(t) \right|}{X_i^j(t)} \tag{13}$$

where $X_i^j(t)$ indicates the value of parameter X of node i at time t in the jth round of iterations, max is the maximum time measured, and $N_{interval}$ the number of time points. We compute MPD for each node's probabilities of being alive, selfish, and unselfish. The node SPN subnet after convergence yields the trust probabilities for three trust components (i.e., unselfishness, energy, and intimacy). The trust metric is then calculated as explained in Section 2.2.

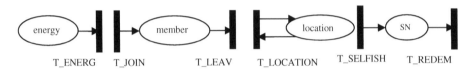

T_ENERG   T_JOIN   T_LEAV   T_LOCATION   T_SELFISH   T_REDEM

Fig. 2. SPN subnet for describing the status of a node

Fig. 2 shows the *SPN subnet*. The subnet describes a node's mobility behavior, join and leave events (i.e., GCS membership status), energy consumption, and selfish behaviors with a redemption mechanism provided. The transition T_LOCATION is triggered when a node moves to a randomly selected area in one of four different directions from its current location with the rate calculated as S_{init}/R based on an initial speed (S_{init}) and wireless radio range (R). We assume that inter-arrival times of a node's join and leave requests are exponentially distributed with rates λ and μ respectively. Place *energy* represents the current energy level of a node.

An initial energy level is assigned according to node heterogeneity information. In our analytical model, we randomly generate a number E_{init} in the range of $[E_{min}, E_{max}]$ based on the uniform distribution. A token is taken out when transition T_ENERGY fires. The transition rate of T_ENERGY is adjusted on the fly based on a node's state; it is lower when a node becomes selfish to save energy or when a node changes from a member to a non-member, following the energy consumption model in [5]. We assume that T seconds will be taken to consume one energy token when a member node has no selfish 1-hop neighbors. We use this energy consumption model for adjusting the time taken to consume one token in place *energy* based on a node's status. Therefore, depending on the node's status, its energy consumption behavior is dynamically changed.

Place *SN* represents whether a node is selfish or not. If a node becomes selfish, a token goes to *SN* by triggering T_SELFISH. When a node becomes altruistic again, transition T_REDEMP is triggered. A node switches between selfish and altruistic following the demand and pricing theory described in Section 3.2 below. The SPN model in Fig. 2 yields the trust components $P_j^X(t)$ where X = energy, unselfishness, and location (to derive intimacy), from which the n-hop trust components and the trust metric can be computed via Equations 1-10.

3.2 Demand and Pricing Model

The basic formula to represent the relationship between demand and pricing in a market is given by [4, 2]:

$$\lambda_i = \alpha_i(v_i)^{-\varepsilon_i} \ where \ \varepsilon_i > 1, \alpha_i > 0 \tag{14}$$

where λ_i is the demand arrival rate and v_i is the pricing of service i while α_i and ε_i are constants correlating λ_i and v_i. Service demand is affected by pricing changes where the elasticity constant ε_i is a key determinant. A market is said to be elastic if $\varepsilon_i > 1$, as assumed here. In such a case lowering the price leads to increase in demand. The elasticity ε_i can be obtained from statistical data describing past market conditions.

We adopt DP theory to decide whether a node should behave selfishly or altruistically based on both individual benefit (i.e., saving energy) and global interest (i.e., serving tasks). We use transition T_SELFISH in our SPN model (described in Section 3) to model a node's changing behavior from altruistic to selfish. Note that remaining energy of a node, mission difficulty, and degree of unselfishness of 1-hop neighbors are used for the place of "price" to apply DP theory in Equation 14. The transition rate to transition T_SELFISH is modeled by:

$$rate(T\_SELFISH) = \frac{f(E_{remain})f(M_{difficulty})f(S_{degree})}{T_{gc}} \tag{15}$$

where $f(x) = \alpha x^{-\varepsilon}$, E_{remain} is the level of current energy (indicated as $mark(energy)$ in SPN model of Section 3), $M_{difficulty}$ is the difficulty level of a given mission where a higher value indicates a tougher mission, and S_{degree} is the degree of selfishness where a higher number refers to more selfishness. We define S_{degree} as the ratio of selfish nodes to unselfish nodes among 1-hop neighbors (refer to [5] for the calculation of the number of selfish/unselfish 1-hop neighboring nodes). T_{gc} is the interval for disseminating a group communication packet where a node's selfishness can be observed. In the context of DP theory, residual energy, mission difficulty and neighborhood selfishness are the prices, and the transition rate from altruistic to selfish is the demand. Equation 15 implies the following:

- $f(E_{remain})$: If a node has a higher level of energy, it is less likely to be selfish.
- $f(M_{difficulty})$: If a node is assigned a tougher mission, it is less likely to be selfish.
- $f(S_{degree})$: If a node observes high selfishness among its 1-hop neighbors, it is less likely to be selfish.

Similarly, we use a transition T_REDEMP in the SPN model (shown in Fig. 2 of Section 3.1) to model the redemption of a node, changing its behavior from selfish to altruistic. The rate to transition T_REDEMP is modeled as:

$$rate(T\_REDEMP) = \frac{f(E_{consumed})f(M_{easiness})f(H_{degree})}{T_{status}} \tag{16}$$

where $f(x) = \alpha x^{-\varepsilon}$, $E_{consumed}$ is the level of consumed energy ($E_{init} - E_{remain}$) where E_{remain} refers to the remaining energy, $M_{easiness}$ is the easiness level of a given mission where a higher number indicates an easier mission (e.g., $M_{max-difficulty} - M_{difficulty}$), and H_{degree} is the degree of unselfishness where a higher number means more unselfishness among 1-hop neighbors. We define $H_{degree} = 1/S_{degree}$ as the ratio of unselfishness to selfishness (refer to [5] for the calculation of the number of selfish/unselfish 1-hop neighboring nodes). A node is given a chance to be redeemed (from selfish to altruistic) in every reevaluation period T_{status} corresponding to the status exchange interval for trust evaluation. Equation 16 implies the following:

- $f(E_{consumed})$: If a node has consumed more energy, it is less likely to redeem itself. This means that if a node has low energy, it may want to further save its energy by staying selfish.
- $f(M_{easiness})$: If a node is assigned an easier mission, it is less likely to redeem itself.
  - $f(H_{degree})$: If a node observes high unselfishness among its 1-hop neighbors, it is less likely to redeem itself and may continue to stay selfish in order to save its energy.

3.3   Calculation of Trust Components

The trust value of node j by node i is calculated based on the information on nodes collected from the *SPN subnet* upon convergence. We calculate the trust probabilities for the three components (i.e., $P_j^X(t)$) of trust based on a reward assignment technique described below. Specifically, the average value, $X(t)$, of a physical property at time t, is the state probability weighted sum of the values at various states, i.e.,

$$X(t) = \sum_{i \in S} (r_i * P_i(t)) \tag{17}$$

where S is a set of states that meet particular conditions, $P_i(t)$ is the probability that the system is in state i at time t, and r_i is the reward or value assigned to the physical property in state i. The reward assignment technique allows us to compute a node's trust component values, say P_j^X where X can be unselfishness and energy, and location information $P_j^{loc=m}$ to derive intimacy trust component values at time t. We use the same reward assignment technique to obtain $P_{j,unselfish}^{loc=k}(t)$ and $P_{j,selfish}^{loc=k}(t)$, the probability that node i is located in area k as being selfish or unselfish.

Table 1. Reward functions

Component	Conditions Satisfied in S
$P^{energy}(t)$	$mark(energy) > 0$
$P^{unselfish}(t)$	$(mark(member) > 0)$ & $(mark(SN) == 0)$ & $(mark(energy) > 0)$
$P^{loc=k}(t)$	$(mark(location) == k)$ & $(mark(member) > 0)$ & $(mark(energy) > 0)$
$P_{unselfish}^{loc=k}(t)$	$(mark(member) > 0)$ & $(mark(SN) == 0)$ & $(mark(energy) > 0)$ & $(mark(location) == k)$
$P_{selfish}^{loc=k}(t)$	$(mark(member) > 0)$ & $(mark(SN) > 0)$ & $(mark(energy) > 0)$ & $(mark(location) == k)$

Table 1 specifies the conditions to be satisfied for states in set S in calculating $P^{energy}(t)$, $P^{unselfish}(t)$, $P^{loc=k}(t)$, $P^{loc=k}_{unselfish}(t)$, and $P^{loc=k}_{selfish}(t)$. When the specified conditions are satisfied, a reward of a 1 is assigned. Based on $P^{loc=k}_j(t)$ so obtained, various k-hop trust probabilities can be computed. For example, the trust value for the intimacy component when i and j are 1-hop apart, $P^{intimacy}_{i,j}$, can also be obtained as described in Section 2.2.

4   Numerical Results and Analysis

This section shows the results obtained through the evaluation of our hierarchical SPN model. Table 2 summarizes the parameters and their default values used in this case study.

Table 2. Default parameter values used

Param	Value	Param	Value	Param	Value
k_{recom}	3	N	150	α, ε	0.01, 2
R	250 m	T_{status}	60*10 s	E_{init}	[6, 12] hrs
λ	1/(60*60)	T_{beacon}	60*2 s	T^{M1}_{gc}	60*10 s
μ	1/(60*60*4)	T	60*60 s	T^{M2}_{gc}	60*5 s
β	0.8: 0.2	S_{init}	(0, 2) m/s	T^{M3}_{gc}	60 s

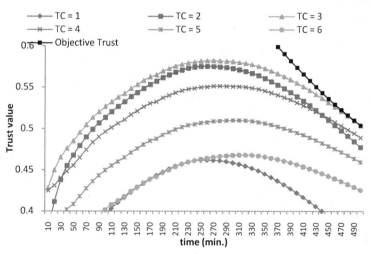

Fig. 3. System trust value versus time, for various trust chain lengths

As shown in Table 2, we set the elasticity constant ε to 2. To maintain a sufficient number of active nodes in the network, the ratio of node join and leave is set to 4:1. The energy level assigned to each node has an average value of 9 hours, representing a reasonable average battery life for mobile devices.

Fig. 3 shows the average trust values of all nodes evaluated by all nodes (hereafter called "system trust") over time parameterized by the length of the trust chain (labeled as TC) under M1. We notice that the maximum trust values are obtained with TC = 3. The effect of using different lengths of TC on trust levels is already examined in our prior work

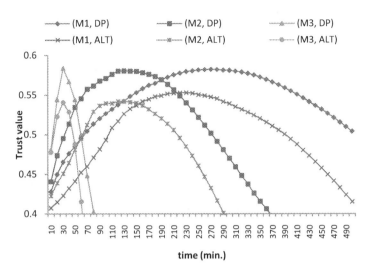

Fig. 4. System trust value over time under DP and ALT, and for various missions with TC = 3

[5]. Note that objective trust predicted via Equation 11 is always larger than the subjective trust computed via Equations 1-10. Thus units are not exposed to unnecessary risk (as noted by Josang *et al.* [8]); but this also implies that there is some missed reward.

Fig. 4 depicts the maximum system trust values identified by TC = 3. We compare the demand and pricing based system (labeled as DP) with the solely altruistic system (labeled as ALT) when different missions are given (labeled as M1, M2, and M3, where M3 requires the highest workload in this case study). As expected, the system assigned M3 has the lowest trust values while the system assigned M1 performs the best, showing the highest trust values. Further, DP significantly performs better than ALT for the same mission M1 or M2 and its effect is more pronounced as time progresses. Our composite trust metric takes into account both the energy level as well as the degree of unselfishness (or cooperation). As a result, the use of DP yields higher trust values. Under M3, the mission difficulty is increased; hence, nodes do not behave selfishly in the beginning. Thus, we note that DP performs only slightly better than ALT in the beginning. Because of the increased workload, energy consumption is larger, and the system lifetime is correspondingly shorter under M3 when compared with M1 and M2.

Selfish behaviors can increase system lifetime by saving energy; on the other hand, if too many nodes are selfish, there will be not an adequate number of cooperative nodes, and the mission will fail. Next we examine the maximum degree of selfishness that can be allowed in order to improve successful mission completion. Suppose the mission can be executed successfully as long as there is at least one cooperative node in an area and a node maintains its trust level at least above the ignorance level, 0.5.

Table 3. Percentage of cooperative nodes versus system lifetime when $T_{value} > 0.5$

	(M1, DP)	(M1, ALT)	(M2, DP)	(M2, ALT)	(M3, DP)	(M3, ALT)
% of cooperative nodes when $T_{value} > 0.5$	> 27%	> 65%	> 35%	> 54%	> 25%	> 78%
Lifetime when $T_{value} > 0.5$	26400 s	17400 s	14400 s	9600 s	3200 s	1800 s

Table 3 shows the percentage of cooperative nodes when the system drop dead trust value (T_{value}) is at least above 0.5 under DP and ALT for various types of missions. Table 3 also shows the system lifetime, the total time when T_{value} is above 0.5. ALT has a larger number of cooperative nodes; but unlike DP, it does not take into account energy, and thus it is unable to maintain a high trust level. We also see that as the mission difficulty decreases, the system is able to prolong its lifetime under DP, maintaining at least the minimum required number of cooperative nodes.

5 Conclusions

In this paper, we developed and analyzed a trust management protocol for a mission-driven GCS in MANETs; we used demand and pricing theory to model selfish and altruistic behaviors to balance individual welfare (i.e., saving energy) versus global welfare (i.e., serving tasks and completing the mission). Our trust management protocol based on DP theory allows each node to dynamically decide if it should stay selfish or altruistic in response to changing environmental conditions so that the overall system trust level can be maximized. We developed a probability model based on SPN to describe the behavior of a large scale GCS operating under the proposed trust management protocol. The results show that our trust management protocol outperforms one that only encourages altruistic behaviors, especially when the mission assigned to the GCS demands light to medium workloads; under these cases our protocol can best explore the tradeoff between energy saved due to selfishness versus quick energy drainage due to altruism.

As future work, we plan to (1) examine the sensitivity of the results obtained with respect to α and ε which are two important parameters in the demand and pricing theory underlying our trust management protocol; (2) develop a more sophisticated mission model considering the effect of mission attributes such as risk, deadline, and workload requirements; (3) analyze the impact of imperfect detection of node failures and attacks; and (4) consider group-based mobility models.

Acknowledgement

This project is supported in part by an appointment to the U.S. Army Research Laboratory Postdoctoral Fellowship Program administered by the Oak Ridge Associated Universities through a contract with the U.S. Army Research Laboratory.

References

1. Adams, W.J., Hadjichristofi, G.C., Davis, N.J.: Calculating a node's reputation in a mobile ad hoc network. In: Proc. of the 24th IEEE Int'l Performance Computing and Communications Conf. (IPCCC 2005), Phoenix, AX, April 2005, pp. 303–307 (2005)
2. Aldebert, M., Ivaldi, M., Roucolle, C.: Telecommunications demand and pricing structure: an economic analysis. Telecommunication Systems 25(1-2), 89–115 (2004)
3. Capra, L.: Toward a human trust model for mobile ad-hoc networks. In: Proc. of the 2nd UK-UbiNet Workshop. Cambridge University, Cambridge (May 2004)
4. Case, K.E., Fair, R.C.: Principles of Economics, 5th edn. Prentice-Hall, Englewood Cliffs (1999)
5. Cho, J.H., Swami, A., Chen, I.R.: Modeling and analysis of trust management for cognitive mission-driven group communication systems in mobile ad hoc networks. In: 2009 IEEE/IFIP Int'l Symposium on Trusted Computing and Communications, Vancouver, Canada (August 2009)

6. Cho, J.H., Swami, A.: Towards trust-based cognitive networks: a survey on trust management for mobile ad hoc networks. In: 14th Int'l Command and Control Research and Technology Symposium, Washington D.C., USA (June 2009)
7. Falcone, R., Castelfranci, C.: Social trust: a cognitive approach. Trust and Deception in Virtual Societies, pp. 55–90. Kluwer Academic Publishers, Dordrecht (2001)
8. Josang, A., LoPresti, S.: Analyzing the relationship between risk and trust. In: Jensen, C., Poslad, S., Dimitrakos, T. (eds.) iTrust 2004. LNCS, vol. 2995, pp. 135–145. Springer, Heidelberg (2004)
9. Li, M., Kamioka, E., Yanada, S.: Pricing to stimulate node cooperation in wireless ad hoc networks. IEICE Transactions on Communications E90-B (7), 1640–1650 (2007)
10. Marbach, P., Qiu, Y.: Cooperation in wireless ad hoc networks: a market-based approach. IEEE/ACM Transactions on Networking 13(6), 1325–1338 (2005)
11. Miranda, H., Rodrigues, L.: Friends and foes: preventing selfishness in open mobile ad hoc networks. In: Proc. of the 23rd Int'l Conf. on Distributed Computing Systems Workshops, May 2003, pp. 440–445 (2003)
12. Moe, M.E.G., Helvik, B.E., Knapskog, S.J.: TSR: Trust-based secure MANET routing using HMMs. In: Proc. of the 4th ACM Symposium on QoS and Security for Wireless and Mobile Networks, Vancouver, Canada, October 2008, pp. 83–90 (2008)
13. Papadimitriou, C.H.: Algorithms, games, and the Internet. In: Proc. of the 33rd Annual ACM Symposium on Theory of Computing, Hersonissos, Crete, Greece, July 2001, pp. 749–753 (2001)
14. Rappaport, P., Alleman, J., Taylor, L.D.: Household demand for wireless telephony: an empirical analysis. In: Proc. of the 31st Annual Telecommunications Policy Research Conf., Arlington, VA (September 2003)
15. Roughgarden, T.: Selfish routing and the price of anarchy. The MIT Press, Cambridge (2005)
16. Soltanali, S., Pirahesh, S., Niksefat, S., Sabaei, M.: An efficient scheme to motivate cooperation in mobile ad hoc networks. In: Int'l Conf. on Networking and Services (ICNS 2007), Athens, Greece, June 2007, pp. 98–103 (2007)
17. Steiner, M., Tsudik, G., Waidner, M.: Diffie-Hellman key distribution extended to group communication. In: CCS 1996 Proc. 3rd ACM Conf. on Computer and Communications Security, New York, NY, USA, pp. 31–37 (1996)
18. Thomas, R.W., Friend, D.H., DaSilva, L.A., MacKenzie, A.B.: Cognitive networks: adaptation and learning to achieve end-to-end performance objectives. IEEE Communications Magazine: Topics in Radio Communications 44(12), 51–57 (2006)
19. Virendra, M., Jadliwala, M., Chandrasekaran, M., Upadhyaya, S.: Quantifying trust in mobile ad-hoc networks. In: Proc. of the Int'l Conf. Integration of Knowledge Intensive Multi-Agent Systems (KIMAS), April 2005, pp. 65–70 (2005)
20. Wang, Y., Giruka, V.C., Singhal, M.: Truthful multipath routing for ad hoc networks with selfish nodes. Journal of Parallel and Distributed Computing 68(6), 778–789 (2008)
21. Yan, L., Hailes, S.: Designing incentive packet relaying strategies for wireless ad hoc networks with game theory. In: IFIP Int'l Federation for Information Processing: Wireless Sensor and Actor Networks II, vol. 264, pp. 137–148 (2008)
22. Yilmaz, O., Chen, I.R.: Elastic threshold-based admission control for QoS satisfaction with reward optimization for servicing multiple priority classes in wireless networks. Information Processing Letters 109(15), 868–875 (2009)
23. Zhao, D.: Access control in ad hoc networks with selfish nodes. Wireless Communications and Mobile Computing 6(6), 761–772 (2006)
24. Zhang, Q., Agrawal, D.P.: Impact of selfish nodes on route discovery in mobile ad hoc networks. In: IEEE Global Telecommunications Conf. (GLOBECOM 2004), December 2004, vol. 5, pp. 2914–2918 (2004)

Trustworthiness in Networks: A Simulation Approach for Approximating Local Trust and Distrust Values

Khrystyna Nordheimer[1], Thimo Schulze[1,2], and Daniel Veit[2]

[1] Chair in Information Systems III,
University of Mannheim,
68131 Mannheim, Germany
[2] Dieter Schwarz Chair of Business Administration,
E-Business and E-Government,
University of Mannheim,
68131 Mannheim, Germany
{nordheimer,schulze}@wifo.uni-mannheim.de

Abstract. Trust is essential for most social and business networks in the web, and determining local trust values between two unfamiliar users is an important issue. However, many existing approaches to calculating these values have limitations in various constellations or network characteristics. We therefore propose an approach that interprets trust as probability and is able to estimate local trust values on large networks using a Monte Carlo simulation method. The estimation is based on existing indirect trust statements between two unfamiliar users. This approach is then extended to the SimTrust algorithm that incorporates both trust and distrust values. It is implemented and discussed in detail with examples. Our main contribution is a new approach which incorporates all available trust and distrust information in such a way that basic trust properties are satisfied.

Keywords: Trust network, local trust values, trust properties, trust and distrust propagation, connection probability, Monte Carlo method.

1   Introduction

Today, many different networks shape the Internet and serve as platforms for various kinds of interaction between unfamiliar people and businesses. The best-known examples of such platforms include eBay, Amazon, Facebook, MySpace and LinkedIn. Due to their open nature, trust between users is essential to the successful continuation of these networks. Therefore, most of them provide their own rating systems which allow users to assign trust ratings as an expression of their direct trustworthiness to other people.

Knowing this kind of information can be very useful for aggregating, filtering, and ordering data in many domains [1]. Furthermore, the consideration of trust relationships between users is becoming a new trend for recommender systems.

M. Nishigaki et al. (Eds.): IFIPTM 2010, IFIP AICT 321, pp. 157–171, 2010.

Trust information can be used as part of the recommendation process, especially as a means to reduce the sparsity problem [2] and thus improve the quality of recommendations [3].

However, in a community with dozens of millions of users, direct trust statements are only made to a limited subset of users. For example, on Facebook with 350 million active members and with a very simple rating system, the average user has about 130 friends [4]. This may be interpreted as 130 explicit trust statements. Because of missing direct ratings among the majority of users, there is a huge lack of trust information in most online communities. Thus, the question arises whether the existing indirect trust ratings between two unacquainted people could be used to infer and predict trust between them.

In this paper, we deal with this question and present a new approach that estimates the local trust value between any two users in a network using a Monte Carlo simulation method. The contributions of our work are as follows: At first, we propose an approach, called *MoCaTrust*, for computing trust inferences mentioned above. Thereby, we consider networks with rating systems where only positive trust statements from a specific range can be made. This reflects the situation considered by many research works in this area [5,6]. However, experience with real trust systems like eBay and Epinions shows that distrust is at least as important as trust [7]. Thus, we take our approach a step further and present a new algorithm, called *SimTrust*, which incorporates distrust in the estimation process. To our knowledge, there are only a few works that consider distrust in the computation of local trust values. [7] use a different approach incorporating various matrix operations to evaluate atomic propagations of trust. [8] present the Moletrust algorithm for computing trust values between two users. It also allows distrust statements but ignores most of them in the calculation.

The remainder of the paper is organized as follows: In Section 2, we discuss issues like trust definition, trust properties, and trust elicitation. Section 3 describes our MoCaTrust approach and takes a look at some example calculations. In Section 4, we extend our approach and describe the SimTrust algorithm which incorporates distrust. Section 5 provides details for an implementation and points out opportunities for further optimization. The conclusion and opportunities for future work are presented in Section 6.

2   Background

In this paper, we consider the following situation: There is an online platform where users interact with each other with respect to specific interests. They assign trust values according to the platform-specific rating system. All assigned trust statements build a *trust network* represented as a directed weighted graph (see Figure 1). Users are shown as nodes and a directed edge between nodes indicates that one user (truster) made trust statement about another user (trustee). The corresponding trust value conveys how much this user trusts the other one. All trust statements are given about the same context and range from 0 to 1.

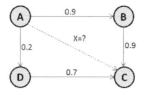

Fig. 1. A sample trust network

The prior knowledge and experiences of the truster form the basis for trusting decisions [9]. In general, many of other factors exist which influence the decision about the trustworthiness of a user - such as subjective opinions of the actions the person has taken, recommendations from friends, psychological factors, rumors, etc. Marsh [10], for example, analyzes these factors and then, based on them, formalizes and computes trust values. This issue is a complex field and is not the scope of our work. We rather take the ratings as they exist and use them to estimate trust between two people where direct trust values are not available. However, to compute with trust, it is important to be aware of its notion and properties, the rating system for assigning trust values, and their interpretation.

2.1   Notion of Trust

Considering the notion of trust, there is a variety of different understandings of its meaning in the scientific literature. Since trust is used in various ways in different disciplines, there is no standard interdisciplinary definition. In particular, social trust is a diffuse term, its properties are fuzzy, and it is not yet well understood from a computational perspective [1]. For this reason, beside the studies of trust in sociological and psychological theories [12,13,14,15,16] it has recently become an emerging research topic in computer science [2,5,7,8,17,18,19]. Here we make use of existing research results.

Sztompka, in [12], understands trust as follows: *"Trust is a bet about the future contingent actions of others"*. Golbeck, in [11], adopts this definition and sees trust in a person as *"a commitment to an action based on a belief that the future actions of that person will lead to a good outcome"*. Thus, trust seems to express the subjective expectation that the trusted person will behave in an appropriate manner.

Proceeding from that, trust has been identified with a subjective *"probability that [the trustee] will perform an action that is beneficial or at least not detrimental to [the truster]"* [20]. However, opinions diverge on the question of whether trust can be modeled as a mathematical probability. While some authors reject the notion of trust as a subjective probability [17,21], others use a probabilistic interpretation [1,6,20,22,23,24]. In our work, we also agree with [20] and assume that *"trust (or, symmetrically, distrust) is a particular level of the subjective probability with which an [user] assesses that another [user] [...] will perform a particular action, both before he can monitor such action [...] and in a context in which it affects his own action"*.

2.2   Properties of Trust

Next, we deal with properties that are important for making trust computations. Based on [5], we consider three main properties of trust that hold in trust networks. The first very simple and inherent property of trust is *asymmetry*. It means, if A trusts B at a certain level, it does not necessarily mean that B trusts A at the same level.

The next important property is *transitivity*, i.e. trust can be passed along a path of trusting users. If A trusts B and B trusts C, it can be inferred that A trusts C at a certain level. However, the transitivity of trust is not perfect in the mathematical sense [5]. Considering the relationships along the path A=>B=>C in Figure 1, we cannot follow that A trusts C exactly at 0.9. On the contrary, it is plausible to expect that A's trust in C should be less than 0.9 because of their indirect relationship. Thus, trust degrades along a path of trusting people. Measuring the rate of degradation from empirical data is an interesting topic for further research.

Composability is the third property of trust. It implies that trust information along all available paths between two unknown users must be taken into account for inferring their trust. We consider again the case in Figure 1 where A trusts B and D directly. Both of them also made some trust statements about C. It is reasonable that A should take into account the information from B and D to decide about the trustworthiness of C. Another question is how this information should be composed. An analysis of the two trust networks described in [5] showed that higher trusted neighbors tend to agree with a user more than lower trusted neighbors, and that nodes connected by shorter paths tend to agree more than nodes connected by longer paths. Thus, it is reasonable that shorter and more trusted paths should have a much greater contribution to the final trust value than longer and less trusted paths.

In Section 3 and 4 we will show that MoCaTrust and SimTrust and their computational implementation satisfy all of the properties presented above.

2.3   Rating System

Another important part of a trust network is an appropriate rating system. As mentioned above, we consider two different schemes for representing trust. The first rating system, used by MoCaTrust, allows users to assign only positive trust values from the real interval (0,1) (see Section 3). In this case, e.g. the trust value of 0.1 means very low but positive trust. An expression of distrust is not possible. In our extended approach SimTrust, users also assign trust values from the interval (0,1) with the difference that trust values close to 0 mean very strong distrust, and values close to 1 represent very strong trust (see Section 4). Here, trust is seen as a point located on a probabilistic distribution of more general expectations, which can take a number of values between 0 and 1 exclusively, and which is centered around a trust threshold point T [20]. This trust threshold of e.g. 0.5 therefore stands for a neutral evaluation, with expressed distrust below this threshold and expressed trust above the threshold.

3   Computing Trust Using the Probabilistic Interpretation of Trust

After the presentation of the background, we return to the main question of this paper: How much should one user trust another one if direct trust statements, based on the prior experience between them, are not available?

As mentioned above, we first assume that a trust network provides a very simple rating system according to which users can make only positive trust statements. Furthermore, the trust value assigned by a truster represents a subjective probability that the trusted person will behave in an expected manner. Each of these values is between 0 and 1 exclusively.

The idea of our approach is to interpret a trust value as the *connection probability* between two appropriate nodes, i.e. the probability that the start node connects to the target node in a network. The connection probability between nodes connected directly is given by the trust statement made by the truster. If there is no direct trust value between two nodes available, we can compute it as the *total connection probability*. It describes the probability that there is a path between these nodes in the network [25], i.e. that there exists an indirect connection between them. For finding this probability, we rely on the existing concepts and techniques which have proved their effectiveness in solving similar problems in the network reliability [26,27,28].

3.1   Underlying Concept

The simple way to compute the total connection probability is to use the complete enumeration of all possible states of the network [26]. Consider the trust network modeled as a directed weighted graph $G = (V, E, \bar{p})$ with K nodes and M edges. Users are represented as a node set $V = \{v_1, v_2, \ldots, v_K\}$ and trust statements as an edge set $E = \{e_1, e_2, \ldots, e_M\}$. The appropriate trust values are given as $\bar{p} = (p(e_1), p(e_2), \ldots, p(e_M))$. Let $\bar{y} = (y_1, y_2, \ldots, y_M)$ denote a state of the network where $y_i = 1$ if edge e_i operates, and $y_i = 0$ if edge e_i fails, $e_i \in E$. Let Y denote the set of all the possible states of the network and

$$P(\bar{y}, \bar{p}) = \prod_{i \in E} p_i^{y_i} (1 - p_i)^{1 - y_i} . \tag{1}$$

Then the quantity

$$Pr(v_i, v_j) = \sum_{\bar{y} \in Y} \phi(\bar{y}) P(\bar{y}, \bar{p}) . \tag{2}$$

is the probability that v_i connects v_j with $v_i, v_j \in V$. The function $\phi(\bar{y}) \to [0, 1]$ defined as

$$\phi(\bar{y}) = \begin{cases} 1 & \text{if } v_i \text{ connects } v_j \text{ when state } \bar{y} \text{ occurs} \\ 0 & \text{otherwise} \end{cases} \tag{3}$$

indicates whether the target node is reachable by the source node through an indirect path when a certain state occurs.

Let us consider Figure 1 and compute how much A should trust C applying the presented method. For the depicted network there are 2^4 possible states. A few of them are listed in Table 1, as well as the respective values of ϕ and P. The

Table 1. Complete enumeration for computing $Pr(A, C)$

Network state $\bar{y}$ (AB,BC,AD,DC)	$P(\bar{y}, \bar{p})$	$\phi(\bar{y})$
$(0,0,0,0)$	$(0.9^0 \cdot 0.1^1) \cdot (0.9^0 \cdot 0.1^1) \cdot (0.2^0 \cdot 0.8^1) \cdot (0.7^0 \cdot 0.3^1) = 0.0024$	0
$(0,0,0,1)$	$(0.9^0 \cdot 0.1^1) \cdot (0.9^0 \cdot 0.1^1) \cdot (0.2^0 \cdot 0.8^1) \cdot (0.7^1 \cdot 0.3^0) = 0.0056$	0
$\ldots$	$\ldots$	$\ldots$
$(1,1,1,0)$	$(0.9^1 \cdot 0.1^0) \cdot (0.9^1 \cdot 0.1^0) \cdot (0.2^1 \cdot 0.8^0) \cdot (0.7^0 \cdot 0.3^1) = 0.0486$	1
$(1,1,1,1)$	$(0.9^1 \cdot 0.1^0) \cdot (0.9^1 \cdot 0.1^0) \cdot (0.2^1 \cdot 0.8^0) \cdot (0.7^1 \cdot 0.3^0) = 0.1134$	1

trust value $Pr(A, C)$ calculated as in expression (2) is 0.8366. In this simple case it can also be calculated as $Pr(A, C) = 0.9 \cdot 0.9 + (1 - 0.81) \cdot 0.2 \cdot 0.7 = 0.8366$.

Now, we recall the properties of trust discussed in Section 2.2. The asymmetry of trust holds because the trust network is modeled as a directed graph. Transitivity and composability are satisfied by the calculation rules of this method. The multiplication of trust values along the path lets trust pass from the source node to the target node. Moreover, the transitivity is not perfect because all trust values range between 0 and 1. Thus, as is to be expected, the longer the path, the more trust degrades along it. Computing the total connection probability all the possible paths are aggregated and taken into account. Therefore, the local trust value captures all available information about trust between the start node and the target node. Another effect is that each additional trust path between nodes increases the overall trust value. Above all, the information from shorter and more trusted paths inherently influences the final trust value more than that from longer and less trusted paths.

Unfortunately, the computation of the local trust value between two unacquainted users by the complete enumeration method belongs to the class of #P-complete problems [26,27]. The number of all the possible network states is 2^M and it increases exponentially with the number of edges M. This method is thus not applicable for real world networks and we need a useful approximation for the trust value. Monte Carlo sampling emerges as a well-suited solution for this kind of problem. In the next section we briefly describe a Monte Carlo method [26] that approximates the trust value effectively.

3.2 Monte Carlo Approximation

The basic idea of a Monte Carlo method is to obtain the required solution by multiple repetitions of random tests and by performing some statistical analysis of the obtained results. In our case, a state of the trust network is generated randomly, and it is determined whether the start node connects to the target node in this state. An estimator for the trust value is then simply obtained by repeating this experiment independently and calculating the mean value of the function ϕ.

To create a network state $\bar{y} \in Y$, we generate a $(0, 1)$-uniform distributed random number for each of the M edges and determine whether the edge operates or fails. We compare the generated number with the respective trust value. The edge fails if the random number is greater than the trust value, and this edge is removed from the graph. If the random number is lower than the trust value, the edge remains intact. Next, for this randomly generated state of the network we evaluate the function $\phi(\bar{y})$. Finally, after N repetitions of the described simulation step the solution is estimated as follows:

$$\hat{Pr}(v_i, v_j) = \frac{1}{N} \sum_{i=1}^{N} \phi(\bar{y}_i) . \tag{4}$$

The generation of uniformly distributed random numbers and comparison of them with the connection probability of the edge ensures that after a sufficient number of simulation steps each edge operates with that probability. Thus, the obtained relative number of existing connections from the source node to the target node is the required total connection probability. The pseudo code in Figure 2 shows how to implement the described method. Note, this algorithm has long been used to solve problems in network reliability theory [26]. We call this approach of using the Monte Carlo method to trust calculation MoCaTrust.

```
1.  counter ← 0
2.  for n ← 1 to N
3.      E' ← E
4.      for all edges e ∈ E'
5.          u ← U(0, 1)
6.          if u > p(e)
7.              then remove e from E'
8.          end if
9.      end for
10.     if v₁ connects v₂
11.         then counter = counter + 1
12.     end if
13. end for
14. return P̂r(v₁, v₂) ← counter/N
```

Fig. 2. Pseudo code of the Monte Carlo simulation method

We now apply MoCaTrust on the sample trust network depicted in Figure 1 in order to estimate how much user A should trust user C. Figure 3 shows the simulation process by plotting the estimator of the trust value in each simulation step.

It is easy to see that even after a few simulation steps the estimated value converges to the real trust value of 0.8366 calculated in Section 3.1 using the complete enumeration method.

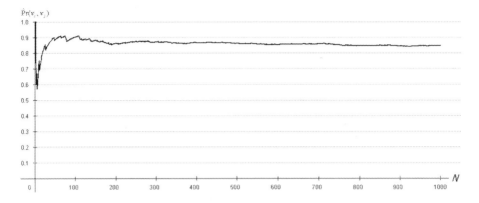

Fig. 3. Estimation of the trust value between users A and C in the sample network from Section 2 using the MoCaTrust approach

4 SimTrust: Extended Approach Incorporating Trust and Distrust

4.1 Trust and Distrust

In the previous section, we introduced the MoCaTrust approach to use connection probabilities between nodes in networks to calculate local trust values. The basic approach considers only ratings where every value is treated as trust. However, most existing rating systems also include some form of distrust like a binary rating (e.g. whether a review was helpful or not) or a star ranking with four or five increments (where one star stands for 'strongly disagree').

Many existing rating systems also use distrust for trust propagation. [7] find out that distrust has significant impact on how trust is propagated and that direct distrust propagation offers the most promising results. [29] also use distrust in their models and use a similar approach. The local trust metrics of [8] and [5] also account for distrust to a certain degree. Therefore, we introduce our algorithm SimTrust, extending the simulation approach explained in Section 3 with a 'trust threshold' and transformation rules in order to account for trust and distrust.

In order to incorporate distrust, a couple of preliminary considerations have to be taken into account. Most of the existing rating systems are not able to account for a detailed and differentiated rating of a person. It is unclear whether a positive binary rating does really mean 100% trust for this person. Consider for example eBay where a vast majority of ratings is positive, and negative or even neutral feedback is hardly given. A five star ranking could be considered as a ranking where '3' stands for indifferent or neutral and '4' and '5' are equidistant values somewhere between 0.5 and 1.0. But other interpretations are also possible which makes it difficult to work with these imprecise values for local trust values.

In this paper, we use a rating system where users assign trust values from the continuous interval (0,1). So, they have the possibility to rate each other in detail. This initial rating scale includes both trust and distrust; therefore a value close to 0 represents very strong distrust, and a value close to 1 means very strong trust. With regards to the meaning and interpretation of existing trust values, they could be transformed to this continuous scale. For example, the 5 star rating could stand for 0.1, 0.3, 0.5, 0.7 and 0.9 to work with our approach.

These continuous trust values cannot be treated as probabilities in networks directly. Intuitively, if the source user A rates the target user B with a trust value below a certain threshold, this rating should reduce the overall local trust value from user A to user B. According to [20], we call this value 'trust threshold' T. Naturally, this trust threshold would be 0.5 in most cases[1] - which is also the trust value issued to individuals where no information is available [20]. Thus, every value below 0.5 shall reduce the overall trust value, and every value above 0.5 shall increase it respectively. However, as stated earlier, when calculating trust in networks every path from the source user to the target user increases the overall trust value.

4.2   Calculating Local Trust Values Using Trust and Distrust

For calculation purposes, we therefore introduce two temporary graphs G^{trust} and $G^{distrust}$ that are calculated separately in order to account for trust and distrust. These two graphs are copies of the original graph $G = (V, E, \bar{p})$ where the values of the direct predecessors of the target node are modified. For these direct predecessors of the target node, it is intuitively clear that a low trust value of e.g. 0.1 should reduce the local trust value for this target and a high trust value of e.g. 0.9 improves the local trust value.

For the temporary trust graph, we therefore use the trust threshold T and transform the trust values above this threshold to a new scale ranging from 0 to 1 using a simple linear transformation. The incoming edges of the target node with values below the threshold $(p(e_i) < T)$ are deleted (setting the probability to zero). Hence, in the temporary trust graph $G^{trust} = (V, E', \bar{p}')$, every value $p(e_i)$ of direct predecessors of the target node is transformed according to:

$$p'(e_i) = \begin{cases} (p(e_i) - T) \cdot \frac{1}{1-T} & \text{if } p(e_i) \geq T \\ 0 & \text{otherwise} \end{cases} \tag{5}$$

For a trust threshold of $T = 0.5$ this leads to

$$p'(e_i) = \begin{cases} (p(e_i) - 0.5) \cdot 2 & \text{if } p(e_i) \geq 0.5 \\ 0 & \text{otherwise} \end{cases} \tag{6}$$

Correspondingly, in the temporary distrust graph $G^{distrust} = (V, E'', \bar{p}'')$, every value $p(e_i)$ of direct predecessors of the target node is transformed according to:

$$p''(e_i) = \begin{cases} (T - p(e_i)) \cdot \frac{1}{T} & \text{if } p(e_i) < T \\ 0 & \text{otherwise} \end{cases} \tag{7}$$

---

[1] For certain networks and with respect to real data, other values than 0.5 are possible for T, for example in networks with overall positive ratings the threshold could be set other values like 0.3, 0.7 or 0.9 in order to capture the average or median overall value.

And for $T = 0.5$:

$$p''(e_i) = \begin{cases} (0.5 - p(e_i)) \cdot 2 & \text{if } p(e_i) < 0.5 \\ 0 & \text{otherwise} \end{cases} \qquad (8)$$

We only change values of direct predecessors of the target node and do not change the values 'in the middle'. The reasons for not changing these values are given below.

There are many approaches to treat these values. [7] introduce and evaluate some of them. One extreme suggests that the "*enemy of your enemy is your friend*" [30] and these values should therefore be inverted. However, such interpretation only holds true in very special circumstances. Other approaches like Moletrust [8] suggest ignoring all values below a certain threshold completely and deleting the corresponding edges. This approach might lead to a significant reduction of edges in the graph but at the same time significant distrust information might get lost.

We, on the other hand, use the interpretation that even a strong distrust towards a node does not necessarily mean that the judgment of this node is flawed when rating others. For example, a person writing low quality reviews in a product portal might very well be able to rate other reviews. Thus, it is reasonable to consider such ratings to a certain degree. Of course, trust values issued from distrusted nodes should have a much lower effect than those issued by edges where we have a strong trust connection. This property holds for SimTrust if no modification is done to the trust values in the middle at all. You can see that a path including a value like 0.1, indicating strong distrust towards a person, has only a minor effect on the overall local trust values, especially when other trusted paths suggest strong trust or distrust.

It can also be shown that our approach calculates much better values if a trust value along a path is just slightly below the threshold value used for deleting edges in other approaches. E.g., in [8], changing one trust value just slightly can have significant changes on the overall local trust value if this change moves the value above or below the threshold and there are few paths from source to target. Our approach avoids this harsh cutoff depending on a binary segmentation in trust (which counts fully) and distrust (which is ignored).

For each of the two temporary graphs G^{trust} and $G^{distrust}$ with the transformed values of the direct predecessors of the target nodes, we now run the simulation described in Section 3. This leads to two trust values $\hat{Pr}^{trust}(v_i, v_j)$ and $\hat{Pr}^{distrust}(v_i, v_j)$. These values are now inversely transformed to get the overall trust value:

$$\hat{Pr}^{local}(v_i, v_j) = \begin{cases} D \cdot T + T & \text{if } D < 0 \\ D \cdot (1 - T) + T & \text{if } D \geq 0 \end{cases} \qquad (9)$$

where $D = \hat{Pr}^{trust}(v_i, v_j) - \hat{Pr}^{distrust}(v_i, v_j)$.

This transformation brings the two values back to the original scale where T is the trust threshold between trust and distrust. The first case is used if the trust value is higher than the distrust value. The overall trust value then lies between T and 1. In the second case, distrust outweighs trust and the overall trust value falls between 0 and T. For a threshold of $T = 0.5$ the equation is simplified to:

$$\hat{Pr}^{local}(v_i, v_j) = \frac{\hat{Pr}^{trust}(v_i, v_j) - \hat{Pr}^{distrust}(v_i, v_j)}{2} + 0.5 \ . \tag{10}$$

An implementation of the complete algorithm including procedure, evaluation and results can be found in Section 5.

5   Implementation

In order to evaluate SimTrust, we have implemented the approach in a simple program. The basic procedure of the approach (as explained in detail in Section 4) can be found in Table 2.

Table 2. Procedure of SimTrust algorithm

1	Duplicate the original graph twice into G^{trust} and $G^{distrust}$
2	Find the direct predecessors of the target node
3	Transform both graphs according to the rules in equation (5) and (7)
4	Run simulation on G^{trust} and save obtained value in $\hat{Pr}^{trust}(v_i, v_j)$
5	Run simulation on $G^{distrust}$ and save obtained value in $\hat{Pr}^{distrust}(v_i, v_j)$
6	Reverse transform the obtained values using equation (9)
7	Display the output local trust value

We use JUNG 'Java Universal Network/Graph Framework' [31] as a basis for our implementation. The implementation itself is quite straightforward using mostly methods already implemented by JUNG. We use the Dijkstra algorithm [33] in order to determine the reachability of target and source nodes during the simulation steps.

5.1   Example

We now show an example calculation of the complete SimTrust algorithm using two sample graphs. Figure 4 shows a sample graph and the two transformations to G^{trust} and $G^{distrust}$ for the trust threshold $T = 0.5$. The two simulation runs converge to $\hat{Pr}^{trust}(A, F) = 0.8416$ and $\hat{Pr}^{distrust}(A, F) = 0.2272$. Inverse transformation leads to the overall trust values of $\hat{Pr}^{local}(A, F) = 0.8072$.

Figure 5 presents another example where we have two positive and two negative ratings of the target node. The source node A rates the nodes B, C, D,

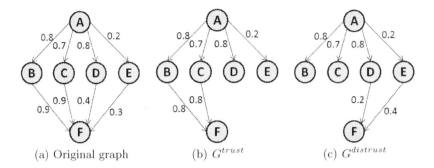

Fig. 4. A sample graph and transformations for $T = 0.5$

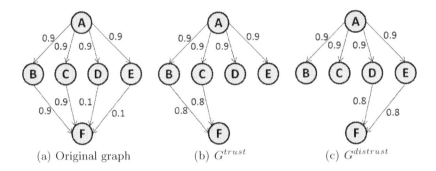

Fig. 5. A sample graph with neutral trust prediction

and E with an equal trust value of 0.9. Further, B and C rate the target node F with strong trust while D and E express strong distrust. Intuitively, based on this information neither trust nor distrust can be predicted.

In fact, the SimTrust algorithm results in a neutral trust value: The simulation runs converge to $\hat{Pr}^{trust}(A, F) = 0.9216$ and $\hat{Pr}^{distrust}(A, F) = 0.9216$. The overall trust calculated as in expression (10) is $\hat{Pr}^{local}(A, F) = 0.5$.

5.2   Evaluation

Complexity. In this section, we will evaluate the complexity of our approach using the Big-O notation; for an introduction, see e.g. [32]. According to graph theory literature, n stands for the number of nodes and m stands for the number of edges in the current graph. Duplicating the graph has a complexity of $O(1)$. Transforming the graph has a worst case complexity of $O(m)$ if all users rate the target node.

The simulation runs are the most complex parts. Here, checking the reachability (whether the source node connects the target node) is most complex. We use the Dijkstra algorithm [33] in our implementation which, using some optimization techniques, has a complexity of $O(m + n \cdot log(n))$ if all distances are positive and there are less than n^2 edges [34]. Since we do not need to find the shortest path but are only concerned with reachability, there might be more efficient ways to solve the problem. [35] introduce an algorithm with almost linear update time. Among others, [36,37] also introduce reachability algorithms that are more efficient than Dijkstra. Since all of them have specific restrictions or limitations, an optimal algorithm depends on the specifics of actual networks. The rest of the SimTrust algorithm works in constant time. Reverse transformation and output both work in $O(1)$.

In summary, the current implementation has a complexity of $O(m+n \cdot log(n))$. Note that in complexity theory, only the most complex part is used for the total complexity. A constant factor of 1000 simulation steps also does have no effect on the complexity. Approaches to improve the current implementation are given in the next section.

Optimization. As already stated above, our current implementation is only a proof of concept with a few suggestions for efficient algorithms. For an implementation in a real world scenario, there are several possibilities to improve our approach. Some of them are presented below.

First, only paths that have a certain maximum depth could be used. Due to the multiplication of trust values, it can be shown that starting from a certain path length, additional values have little to no effect. The exact depth has to be evaluated depending on real implementations.

Second, our current approach uses a fixed number of simulation steps. In order to improve the runtime, a dynamic number of simulation steps can be used. For this purpose, however, an appropriate convergence diagnostic is needed.

Finally, because of the parallel nature of the SimTrust algorithm (each simulation step does not depend on the result of the previous one), it can be implemented in a parallel environment. Furthermore, if local trust values for more than one target user shall be calculated at the same time, distributing the code between various (virtual) computers might also improve the runtime.

6   Conclusions and Future Work

In most online platforms, trust is a prerequisite for successful interaction. The a priori knowledge of how much a user should trust other unfamiliar users can considerably improve its quality. In this paper, we presented two approaches to infer local trust values between unknown users based on their indirect trust statements. We first considered the situation where only positive trust statements could be made and introduced MoCaTrust, an approach for calculating these trust values using a Monte Carlo simulation method. Next, we modified it and presented the SimTrust algorithm in order to account for trust and distrust. Implementation details and examples were given for illustration.

In the future, our intention is to improve the described approach, particularly with regard to the runtime, and evaluate it on real world networks. The latter could not be done yet because of the unavailability of suitable real trust and distrust data.

References

1. Kuter, U., Golbeck, J.: SUNNY: a new algorithm for trust inference in social networks using probabilistic confidence models. In: Proceedings of the 22nd national conference on Artificial intelligence, pp. 1377–1382. AAAI Press, Menlo Park (2007)
2. O'Donovan, J., Smyth, B.: Trust in recommender systems. In: Proceedings of the 10th International Conference on Intelligent User Interfaces, pp. 167–174. ACM, San Diego (2005)
3. Avesani, P., Massa, P., Tiella, R.: A trust-enhanced recommender system application: Moleskiing. In: Proceedings of the 2005 ACM symposium on Applied computing, pp. 1589–1593. ACM, Santa Fe (2005)
4. Facebook, http://www.facebook.com/press/info.php?statistics
5. Golbeck, J.A.: Computing and applying trust in web-based social networks, University of Maryland at College Park (2005)
6. Richardson, M., Agrawal, R., Domingos, P.: Trust Management for the Semantic Web. In: Fensel, D., Sycara, K., Mylopoulos, J. (eds.) ISWC 2003. LNCS, vol. 2870, pp. 351–368. Springer, Heidelberg (2003)
7. Guha, R., Kumar, R., Raghavan, P., Tomkins, A.: Propagation of trust and distrust. In: Proceedings of the 13th international conference on World Wide Web, pp. 403–412. ACM, New York (2004)
8. Massa, P., Avesani, P.: Controversial users demand local trust metrics: an experimental study on Epinions.com community. In: Proceedings of the 20th national conference on Artificial intelligence, pp. 121–126. AAAI Press, Pittsburgh (2005)
9. Luhmann, N.: Trust and Power. John Wiley & Sons Inc., Chichester (1979)
10. Marsh, S.P.: Formalising Trust as a Computational Concept, University of Stirling, Department of Mathematics and Computer Science (1994)
11. Golbeck, J.A.: Trust and nuanced profile similarity in online social networks. ACM Trans. Web 3, 1–33 (2009)
12. Sztompka, P.: Trust: A Sociological Theory. Cambridge University Press, Cambridge (2000)
13. Luhmann, N.: Familiarity, Confidence, Trust: Problems and Alternatives. In: Gambetta, D. (ed.) Trust: Making and Breaking Cooperative Relations, pp. 94–107. University of Oxford, Oxford (2000)
14. Coleman, J.: Foundations of Social Theory. The Belknap Press of Harvard University Press (1990)
15. Falcone, R., Castelfranchi, C.: Social trust: a cognitive approach. In: Castelfranchi, C., Tan, Y. (eds.) Trust and deception in virtual societies, pp. 55–90. Kluwer Academic Publishers, Dordrecht (2001)
16. Williamson, O.: Calculativeness, Trust, and Economic Organization. Journal of Law and Economics 36, 453–486 (1993)
17. Abdul-Rahman, A., Hailes, S.: Supporting Trust in Virtual Communities. In: Abdul-Rahman, A., Hailes, S. (eds.) HICSS 2000. Proceedings of the 33rd Hawaii International Conference on System Sciences (2000)
18. Massa, P., Bhattacharjee, B.: Using Trust in Recommender Systems: An Experimental Analysis. In: Jensen, C., Poslad, S., Dimitrakos, T. (eds.) iTrust 2004. LNCS, vol. 2995, pp. 221–235. Springer, Heidelberg (2004)
19. Golbeck, J.A. (ed.): Computing with Social Trust. Springer, Berlin (2008)
20. Gambetta, D.: Can We Trust Trust? In: Gambetta, D. (ed.) Trust: Making and Breaking Cooperative Relations, pp. 213–237. University of Oxford, Oxford (2000)

21. Castelfranchi, C., Falcone, R.: Trust Is Much More than Subjective Probability: Mental Components and Sources of Trust. In: Proceedings of the 33rd Hawaii International Conference on System Sciences. IEEE Computer Society, Los Alamitos (2000)

22. Dasgupta, P.: Trust as a Commodity. In: Gambetta, D. (ed.) Trust: Making and Breaking Cooperative Relations, pp. 49–72. University of Oxford, Oxford (2000)

23. DuBois, T., Golbeck, J., Srinivasan, A.: Rigorous Probabilistic Trust-Inference with Applications to Clustering. In: Proceedings of the 2009 IEEE/WIC/ACM International Joint Conference on Web Intelligence and Intelligent Agent Technology, pp. 655–658. IEEE Computer Society, Los Alamitos (2009)

24. Gulati, R.: Does Familiarity Breed Trust? The Implications of Repeated Ties for Contractual Choice in Alliances. The Academy of Management Journal 38, 85–112 (1995)

25. Chen, Y., Li, J., Chen, J.: A new algorithm for network probabilistic connectivity. In: Military Communications Conference Proceedings, pp. 920–923 (1999)

26. Fishman, G.: Monte Carlo: Concepts, Algorithms, and Applications. Springer, Berlin (1996)

27. Provan, J.S., Ball, M.O.: The Complexity of Counting Cuts and of Computing the Probability that a Graph is Connected. SIAM Journal on Computing 12, 777–788 (1983)

28. Agrawal, A., Satyanarayana, A.: An $O(|E|)$ Time Algorithm for Computing the Reliability of a Class of Directed Networks. Operations research 32, 493–515 (1984)

29. Ziegler, C., Lausen, G.: Propagation Models for Trust and Distrust in Social Networks. Information Systems Frontiers 7, 337–358 (2005)

30. Rosenberg, J.L.: The 1941 Mission of Frank Aiken to the United States: An American Perspective. Irish Historical Studies 22, 162–177 (1980)

31. JUNG, http://jung.sourceforge.net/index.html

32. Sipser, M.: Introduction to the Theory of Computation. International Thomson Publishing (1996)

33. Cormen, T.H., Stein, C., Leiserson, C.E., Rivest, R.L.: Introduction to Algorithms. B & T (2001)

34. Goldberg, A.V., Tarjan, R.E.: Expected Performance of Dijkstra's Shortest Path Algorithm, NEC Research Institute Report (1996)

35. Roditty, L., Zwick, U.: A fully dynamic reachability algorithm for directed graphs with an almost linear update time. In: Proceedings of the thirty-sixth annual ACM symposium on Theory of computing, pp. 184–191. ACM, Chicago (2004)

36. Khoussainov, B., Liu, J., Khaliq, I.: A Dynamic Algorithm for Reachability Games Played on Trees. In: Královič, R., Niwiński, D. (eds.) MFCS 2009. LNCS, vol. 5734, pp. 477–488. Springer, Heidelberg (2009)

37. Wang, H., He, H., Yang, J., Yu, P.S., Yu, J.X.: Dual Labeling: Answering Graph Reachability Queries in Constant Time. In: Proceedings of the 22nd International Conference on Data Engineering (ICDE 2006), pp. 75–87. IEEE Computer Society, Los Alamitos (2006)

Design of Graded Trusts by Using Dynamic Path Validation

Akira Kubo[1] and Hiroyuki Sato[2]

[1] symmetriccipher@gmail.com
[2] Information Technology Center,
The University of Tokyo, Japan
schuko@satolab.itc.u-tokyo.ac.jp

Abstract. In modern information service architectures, security is one of the most critical criteria. Almost every standard on information security is concerned with internal control of an organization, and particularly with authentication. If an RP (relying party) has valuable information assets, and requires a high level to authentication for accepting access to the valuable assets, then a strong mechanism is required. Here, we focus on a trust model of certificate authentication. Conventionally, a trust model of certificates is defined as a validation of chains of certificates. However, today, this trust model does not function well because of complexity of paths and of requirement of security levels. In this paper, we propose "dynamic path validation," together with another trust model of PKI for controlling this situation. First, we propose Policy Authority. Policy Authority assigns a level of compliance (LoC) to CAs in its domain. LoC is evaluated in terms of a common criteria of Policy Authority. Moreover, it controls the path building with considerations of LoC. Therefore, we can flexibly evaluate levels of CP/CPS's in one server. In a typical bridge model, we need as many bridge CAs as the number of required levels of CP/CPS's. In our framework, instead, we can do the same task in a single server, by which we can save the cost of maintaining lists of trust anchors of multiple levels.

1 Introduction

In modern information service architectures, security is one of the most critical criteria. Today, security is discussed in terms of computer security, network security, and information security. It is not long before information security is considered to be important. Information security is concerned with controls of behaviors of systems and humans for protecting information assets. As one of major differences of information security to others, we must consider organizations as major players of security. "Internal control" is discussed organization-wise. Security policies are also organization-wise defined and published.

Information security is closely related to the concept of information assets. An organization recognizes that information itself has and produces value, whenever it experiences information theft, leakage, and insider trading. Moreover, information security is related to legal issues such as privacy. Privacy related information

M. Nishigaki et al. (Eds.): IFIPTM 2010, IFIP AICT 321, pp. 172–183, 2010.

is often accumulated in an organization. In such a situation, the organization is required by law to protect such information that is considered to be "owned" by individuals, not by the organization. Thus, protection of information assets is demanded. By controlling systems and humans that handle information assets, information security gives some guarantee to such protection.

There are defined several standards on information security. For example, ISMS, or ISO 27001, is commonly used as a criteria of system and information security. Actually, almost every standard such as ISMS is concerned with internal control of an organization. Among several issues of internal control, authentication is the most critical. Allowing access of critical information assets is guaranteed by how assured the used authentication is. A Level of assurance associated with an authentication differs in its mechanism. For example, certificate authentication certainly provides higher level mechanism than password authentication. Even in certificate authentication, its strength differs in CPs of certificates.

If an RP (relying party) has valuable information assets, and requires a high level to authentication for accepting access of the valuable assets, then a strong mechanism is required. Although it is of course that the strength of authentication is brought by its mechanism, initial setups and lifecycle management of credentials and IDs must also be considered. In certificate authentication, they are defined and published in CP/CPS's of certificates. Matching of the strength of IdP (ID providers) and requirements by RPs are the source of trust in a federation.

In this paper, we focus on a trust model of certificate authentication. Conventionally, a trust model of certificates is defined as a chain of certificates. A certificate chain is constructed so that an issuing CA is endorsed, or given its digital signature by another CA. If the anchor of the chain is contained in a list of trusted CAs, then the target CA of the chain can be trusted. These chains are central in constructing the trust of PKI.

However, today, this trust model does not function very well. Its reasons are classified in twofold: one is that there can be constructed an arbitrary complex chain, in which chains are hard to control. Although there are defined three trust models, hierarchical, mutual, and bridge for taming this complexity, they are only partially implemented to validate complex chains. The other reason is more critical: because there are provided several levels of certificate policies, CAs of the same levels are fragmented into small groups. This means that we need as many as CAs as levels, which proliferates the number of CAs. Actually, major commercial PKI vendors operate as many CAs of different assurance as required even for the same usage such as client authentication. Although the difference of levels can be inferred by checking CP/CPS's, it must manually be done. This will cause a long negotiation in building a bridge CA. To control such fragmentation is strongly required.

This paper proposes dynamic path validation, together with another trust model of PKI for controlling this situation. First, we propose a policy management server. This server assigns a level to CP/CPS of a given CA. The assignment may mutually be done in an agreement of the policy management server with the CA. Or, some criteria approved by a group of CAs may be used. Second, we propose an extended path validation based on the levels provided by the policy evaluation server. In the path construction, levels are used together with certificate chains. The consistency of levels is also discussed.

Our framework assumes one policy management server, which plays as a pivot among policies of CAs. Instead of mutually agreeing or fighting on CP/CPS of a bridge CA, this policy management server accepts multiple levels of securities of CAs. Therefore, we can flexibly evaluate levels of CP/CPS's in one server. In a typical bridge model, we need as many bridge CAs as the number of required levels of CP/CPS's. In our framework, instead, we can do the same task in a single server.

The rest of this paper is organized as: Section 2 studies scenarios in which efficiently handling multiple levels is important. Section 3 proposes dynamic path validation as our solution. Policy Authority is introduced. Furthermore, path validation is extended in the way that levels of CP/CPS's are reflected. Section 4 surveys related work. Section 5 summarizes this paper.

2   Stratified Paths Depending on LoA

Recently, many of critical services have been implemented as Web applications. Accordingly, there are many services of various levels of significance. Today, even in a single organization, there are provided many services that have various levels of significance. The significance is evaluated in the information assets handled by the service. For example, if a service handles privacy, it must be treated with care. If a service handles medical information, it must be treated with the highest security.

Authentication is a key mechanism that implements the levels of significance. Its idea is to control the access by identifying end users with how assured the authentication can be. Generally, they are called *"level of assurance (LoA)."* There are defined some standards of LoAs such as NIST 800-63[4] for evaluating the levels. In such situations, an SP(service provider) requires an appropriate LoA to an IdP(ID provider) for accessing its information assets. In a fixed trust circle, it is common that its member IdPs and SPs are under some agreement as for keeping LoA of IdPs, which actually gives trust in the circle.

Among various authentication mechanisms, certificate authentication is usually given the highest LoA. Certificate authentication includes a process of path validation: a path between two CAs is constructed if a CA trusts the other CA. If the root of the path constructed in the validation process is in the domain of trusted CAs, then the validation, and therefore authentication succeeds. Thus, the trust of certificates is reduced to path construction whose root is trusted.

Trust brought by path validation causes a problem: the "LoA" of the trusted domains. In general, CAs are operated in various levels of CP/CPS. Some CP/CPS can be stricter than others. More strictly operated CAs can provide a higher LoA to SPs. SPs that require a higher LoA can trust only strictly operated CAs. A problem is that high level requirements result in inconvenience to users and high cost in operations. Today, a solution to such trade-offs is given in such a way that an organization operates CAs of multiple roots that correspond to multiple levels of operations. Looser certificates are used to access less important information assets, but with less cost than strictly issued certificates.

Typical examples of multiple roots can be seen in server certificates. Today, most major browsers classify server certificates as three: EV certificates[5], web trust[3], and others. In the path validation of server certificates, the three never intersect. Even in client certificates, major vendors such as Verisign provide multiple roots of different levels of trust. In a complex organization, the situation is very similar to the real world. There are many organizational units that have various levels of independence. There are many services that require various LoAs. The result would be many CAs of various LoAs to cope with the various requirements of services.

This kind of scenarios causes fragmentation and maintenance problems. In the real world, many CAs are established to provide required LoAs. In such a situation, the cost of maintenance of trust domain is high. The domain is fragmented according to LoAs. Moreover, if a requirement level of an SP changes, the list of trusted CAs must be accordingly modified, causing a problem in maintenance. Even if no change occurs to an SP, because the world of CAs continuously changes, the maintenance is still a problem.

3   Dynamic Path Validation

In this paper, we propose *"dynamic path validation."* to tame the fragmentation and maintenance problems stated above. Dynamic path validation is a kind of delegated path validation in which Policy Authority plays as a key component.

3.1   Architecture of Dynamic Path Validation

In our scenario, there are three players: end entities, RP(or SP), and Policy Authority. An end entity requests authentication for a service with his/her certificates. An RP (Replying Party) or an SP (Service Provider) is a server that authenticates a user. In this scenario, an RP requires that a certificate of an end entity has a certain level of assurance. The RP delegates the path validation to Policy Authority. The Policy Authority checks whether a path provided by an end entity is valid. Policy Authority dynamically builds the path by using levels of CP/CPS's. Specifically, it checks whether requirements of an RP given as a level of certificates is satisfied in the certificate chain. In other words, this framework checks conditions of path validation in a way not related to information statically embedded in certificates. This is the name of "dynamic" path validation We illustrate our architecture in Fig. 1.

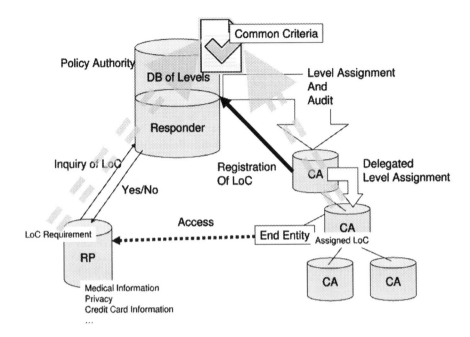

Fig. 1. Architecture of Dynamic Path Validation

Policy Authority. The key component in our framework is Policy Authority. The functions provided by Policy Authority are:

1. to decide and publish the common criteria of CP/CPS,
2. to register CAs that comply with the published criteria of CP/CPS, and
3. to validate paths on behalf of RPs.

In Fig. 1, 1. corresponds to "Common Criteria," 2. to DB of Levels, and 3. to Responder, respectively.

Policy Authority must be operated under an agreement with participating CAs. It assumes that participating CAs agree on some predefined criteria. This at least includes those on audit and delegation of assignment of levels to subordinate CAs. Today, audit is considered to be a standard way to assure the quality of operations. Therefore, we demand audit to assure the compliance with the criteria. Moreover, delegation must be operated in an appropriate way.

In general, delegation is one of major solutions of distributed system management in the case that specific tasks are hard to control or to maintain. In this case, path validation is a heavy task, and hard to maintain in a single client.

In this way, with Policy Authority as the core, CAs and RPs participate in the circle, which simulates the circle of trust in Liberty-like federations. The difference is that in the latter (Liberty), IdPs and RPs mutually evaluate the quality of their services, while in the former (ours), they refer to the criteria via Policy Authority. In this meaning, Policy Authority plays as a pivot in the circle.

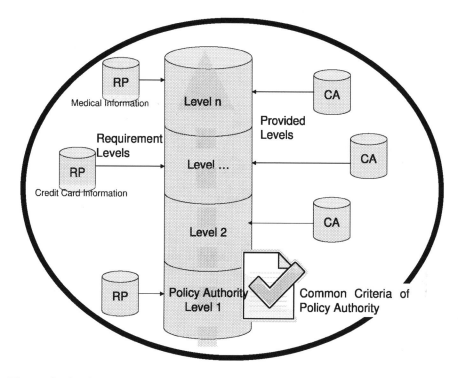

Fig. 2. Circle of Trust consisting of servers of various LoCs as Policy Authority as the Pivot

We illustrate our concept of circle in Fig. 2. Actually, building circles of trust is one of key issues in federations. by Policy Authority acting as the pivot of the circle, we can save cost of building multiple circles. This scenario resembles putting bridge CAs as a pivot in path building.

RP and CA. An RP delegates path validation to Policy Authority. In the delegation, maintaining the list of trust anchors is a task of the delegated server. In our framework, an RP maintains its requirement to levels of certificates. Policy Authority, or the delegated server receives the requirement together with a path, then validates it. This means that it can house multiple path validation methods in one server. Policy Authority controls path validation by using required levels together with trust anchors (i.e. registered CAs) as illustrated in Fig. 3

We see that in the figure, instead of having as many bridge CAs as the number of levels, we can house multiple levels of path building in one Policy Authority.

3.2 CP Certification

The relation that a CA trusts another CA is determined by some kind of evaluation of CP of the target CA. The evaluation must be based on a common criteria such as EV, Web Trust and RFC 3647.

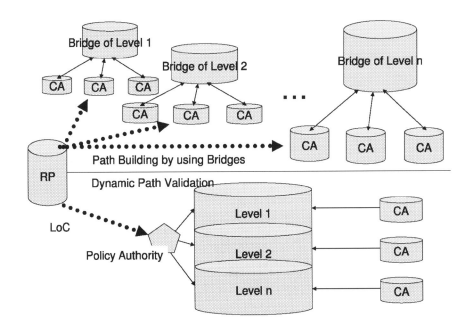

Fig. 3. Housing Multiple Path Validations in One Policy Authority

Levels of Compliance of Certificates. Conventionally, a level of assurance is given to a CA according to a specific criteria and certification based on the criteria and related audit. Typical criteria include WTCA [3], EV [5], and "Specified Certification Business" [22] in Japan. All of these criteria require audit to assure the quality of CA operations. However, the audit is done for checking compliance with CP/CPS's of given CAs. Compliance of a CP/CPS with a given criteria must be proved as another process.

In this paper, we define *"level of compliance (LoC)."*

Definition: We define a level of compliance (LoC) for a criteria as a numeric value that represents how strictly a server is operated in compliance with the given criteria.

As a criteria of LoC, we have some standard templates for CP/CPS's such as EV, WTCA, and RFC3647. Conventionally, because they define the minimum set of requirements, compliance levels are just 0/1 (yes or no). In our extended compliance, we may define optional criteria that enhances the level of security in the same template. Therefore, we have more than two levels as for compliance: enhanced compliance/minimum compliance/no. In this meaning, LoC can be considered as an extension of conventional certification.

Moreover, LoC can be defined as an extension of LoA. Usually, certificate authentication is given the highest level. In LoC, the level of operations of CA is in concern, which is the same framework as the assignment of LoA in which the level of ID providers is in concern.

In evaluating LoC, operations of a given CA are audited for a given criteria. In LoC, audit is done not only for CP/CPS, but also for a predefined criteria. The evaluation must be done by an authority for the criteria. Here, Policy Authority plays as an auditor.

Assigned Levels and Derived Levels. In our framework, in addition to Policy Authority, which assigns a level to a CA, a CA can assign derived levels to its subordinate CAs. This delegation is essential in saving cost of Policy Authority operations. It is a fundamental assumption that a CA must control its subordinate CAs in path validation. This means that a level of a given CA is inherited to its subordinate CAs. In this paper, this control is extended to derived level assignment. This assignment is done under the restriction that the derived level must not be greater than the level of the parent CA.

Evaluation Axis of Criteria. In NIST standard[4], we see four axis for evaluating authentications. In this paper, we borrow related two axes of evaluation: levels of initial identification (more generally, ID lifecycle management in [17,18]), and levels of tokens. For example, Verisign defines three levels as for the levels of assurance depending on the methods of initial identification and the coverage of assurance. In this meaning, our proposal is already implemented in the real world.

Moreover, a CA must be operated under a certain security constraint. RFC 3647 also defines security constraint in operations. [17] proposes criteria for both IdPs and SPs. Here, we propose our evaluation axes of criteria in terms of [17]:

1. ID lifecycle management,
2. levels of tokens
3. Quality of management of the server:
   (a) Management of access control
   (b) Control of physical security.
   (c) Management of privileges in operation

In addition to these axes, we require audit as the mechanism that guarantees the quality in terms of published criteria. To control the quality of operations, audit is considered to be very effective. It is mandatory that Policy Authority audits participating CAs.

3.3   Extended Path Validation by Using Dynamic Path Validation

Now we have two components: LoC and Policy Authority. We extend path validation so that a CA of a lower LoC can trust a CA of a higher LoC, even if there is no path between the two in conventional meaning. We call this extension as *"dynamic path validation (DyPV)."*

Our DyPV is processed as follows: first, all CAs registered at the given Policy Authority are considered to be in its domain. In other words, a CA in the domain is given an LoC under the common criteria. Second, the path validation is extended by using levels: if a certificate issued by CA_1 is presented at an RP that requires n_2 as LoC, and n_1 is given to CA_1, then the certificate is validated if $n_1 \geq n_2$. We extend this validation to a general certificate chain. If a path is built whose root is CA_1, and $CA_1 \cdots CA_n$, are registered, then we compare their LoCs with the required LoC.

The algorithm of DyPV is given in Fig. 4. A validating RP delegates the validation to Policy Authority. Policy Authority responds with true/false depending on whether DyPV succeeds or not. The given inputs are CC[], a certificate chain given by a validatee, and LoC, a required LoC given as a policy of the validating RP. This algorithm partially extends CC[] so that the root of the path is in the domain. Here, Policy Authority builds a path in the conventional way so that its root is in the domain. Then, Policy Authority compares the required LoC with LoCs in the domain. In other words, registered CAs play as trust anchors in a conventional sense. Instead of maintaining the list of trust anchors, an RP just makes an inquiry of LoC as its requirement, and Policy Authority returns yes/no to the inquiry.

A problem arises in the algorithm: the path extension. There can be a case that there are two or more possibilities of extension, and in one extension, the extended validation succeeds, and in another extension, it fails. Our algorithm requires that the extension must be done so that the extended certificate chain $DD[]$ satisfies the condition $DD[1] \geq LoC$. By this restriction, we can eliminate false cases. If validation fails in a path extended in this way, we restart the path building.

If we can validate a path, then we must guarantee that a validation of any extension of the path also succeeds. Therefore, we require that if there is a path from $CA_1 \longrightarrow CA_2$, meaning that CA_1 issues a certificate to CA_2, then their LoCs must satisfy $LoC(CA_1) \geq LoC(CA_2)$. This consistency must be maintained by Policy Authority.

3.4   Comparison with RFC 5280

Conventionally, path validation is defined as RFC 5280 [8]. In RFC5280, there is defined control of path building via policy extension fields in certificates. In our framework, for representing policies of CAs, we use LoC under a common criteria of Policy Authority. Our idea is that lifecycles of CAs and of their policies are not the same. Policies and operations can continuously be enhanced even in the same CA. We separate the two lifecycles, and manage policies by using Policy Authority on-line.

3.5   Control of Subordinate CAs

In our framework, Policy Authority allows registered CAs to assign levels to subordinate CAs. This delegation is a key to save the cost of operations of Policy Authority. Assignment of LoC assumes that subordinate CAs have lower or equal LoCs than those of their parents. Policy Authority must enforce this restriction on every participating CAs Audit must also be effective for this enforcement.

```
Policy Authority:

Boolean validate(cert chains CC[], int LoC)
{
start:
 if (CC[1] is in the domain of Policy Authority) {
   DD[] = CC[]; // guarantees an LoC is assigned to DD[1].
 } else {
  if (CC[1] can be extended by using information in Policy Authority) {
     select a chain CC1[] such that LoC(CC1[1]) >= LoC;
     DD = CC1 + CC;  //Extend CC[] with CC1[];
  } else
     return false;
 }

 validate DD[]; // RFC 5280 compliant path validation

 for (C = tail of DD[]; C != DD[1]; C = parent(C)) {
   if (C is in the domain of Policy Authority) {
     if (LoC(C) < LoC) goto start;
     // Validation fails for DD[]. Reset and Restart.
     if (LoC(C) is undefined) continue;
     // if undefined, LoC of C inherits its parent's.
   } else {
     continue;
   }
 }
 // check if all of LoC's of certificates in CC are
 // higher than the requirement.
 return true; // validated.
}
```

Fig. 4. Algorithm of Dynamic Path Validation

4   Related Work

Path building[7], and validation[8] have been central issues in PKI domain extensions. There have been proposed three major methods of path construction models: hierarchical, mutual, and bridge models. Although the bridge model has been considered to scale, and has been implemented on some major domains, there are found some problems other than technical ones to hinder its growth. Furthermore, delegation of tasks related to them is studied because they are too heavy for general RPs. The discussions are summarized as RFC 3379[16]. OCSP[11] and SCVP[9] are also classified as protocols partly delegating validation. Our framework is also classified as delegation. Ours considers LoCs in path validation.

It is commonly understood that operations of CAs can differ in their CPs. They include usage, profile, and security. There are some standard templates of CPs such as RFC 3647[6], and PKI lite[21].

Evaluating IdPs and assigning specific LoA is required by some security-sensitive SPs[2]. There have been proposed several systems that use LoA. As major federated identity systems, both Liberty and OpenID provide a mechanism of sending LoA of IdPs to SPs [13,15].

Moreover, in Grid, there are established policy management authorities[23] to enforce the policies of Grid on participants.

Although discussions of LoA [12] have been limited to ID and authentication, they are very fruitful in assuring security level in building federations. In particular, they are essential in the framework that ID information is provided to an SP by IdPs in multiple organizations via SSO. OMB guidance[14] and NIST standard[4] are milestones in the discussion. They are also the driving force to define LoA to large federations. Today, LoA is widely discussed in many organizations, grids, federations [10], and inter-federations [1].

LoA can be generalized to SPs. [17,18] propose a consistent assignment of LoA to SPs in terms of security policies of organizations.

Note that all of these must be done as a part of risk management. [19,20] discuss authentication in terms of risk management.

5   Concluding Remarks

In this paper, we have proposed dynamic path validation (DyPV). In DyPV, CAs in a domain are registered in Policy Authority, which plays as a pivot. Moreover, according to a common criteria, LoC is assigned to each CA. In this way, Policy Authority houses multiple levels of compliance in one server. Furthermore, path validation has been extended so that an LoC, or a level of CP/CPS's is reflected.

Our framework uses LoC instead of a list of trust anchors. CAs are not required to issue unnecessary certificates for path building, but Policy Authority checks whether the validation in terms of LoC requirement succeeds. Operations under a common criteria of Policy Authority is easier than maintaining lists of trust anchors of multiple levels in multiple bridges.

References

1. Alterman, P.: Interfederation Initiatives for Identity Authentication. Federal Demonstration Partnership, January meeting (2008)
2. Alterman, P., Keltner, J., Morgan, R.: InCommon Federation: Progress, Partnerships, Opportunities. Internet2 2007 Fall Meeting (2007)
3. American Institute of Certified Public Accountants and Canadian Institute of Chartered Accountants: Trust Services Principles, Criteria and Illustrations for Security, Availability, Processing Integrity, Confidentiality, and Privacy (2006)
4. Burr, W., Dodson, W., Polk, W.: Electronic Authentication Guidelines. NIST SP800-63 (2006)

5. CA/Browser Forum: Guidelines for the Issuance and Management of Extended Validation Certificates (2007)
6. Chokbani, S., Ford, W., Sabett, R., Merrill, C., Wu, S.: Internet X.509 Public Key Infrastructure Certificate Policy and Certification Practices Framework. RFC 3647 (2003)
7. Cooper, M., Dzambasow, Y., Joseph, S., Nicholas, R.: Internet X.509 Public Key Infrastructure: Certification Path Building. RFC 4158 (2005)
8. Cooper, D., Santesson, S., Farrell, S., Boeyen, S., Housley, R., Polk, W.: Internet X.509 Public Key Infrastructure Certificate and Certificate Revocation List (CRL) Profile. RFC 5280 (2008)
9. Freeman, T., Housley, R., Malpani, A., Cooper, D., Polk, W.: Server-Based Certificate Validation Protocol. RFC 5055 (2007)
10. InCommon Federation: Identity Assurance Profiles Bronze and Silver (2008), http://www.incommonfederation.org/docs/assurance/InC_Bronze-Silver_IAP_1.0_Final.pdf
11. Myers, M., Ankney, R., Malpani, A., Galperin, S., Adams, C.: X.509 Internet Public Key Infrastructure Online Certificate Status Protocol - OCSP. RFC 2560 (1999)
12. Nedanic, A., Zhang, N., Yao, L., Morrow, T.: Levels of Authentication Assurance: an Investigation. In: Proc. 3rd Int'l. Symposium on Information Assurance and Security, pp. 155–158 (2007)
13. OASIS: Level of Assurance Authentication Context Profiles for SAML 2.0 (2009)
14. Office of Management and Budget (U.S.): E-Authentication Guidance for Federal Agencies. M-04-04 (2003)
15. OpenID: OpenID Provider Authentication Policy Extension 1.0 (2008)
16. Pinkas, D., Housley, R.: Delegated Path Validation and Delegated Path Discovery Protocol Requirements. RFC 3379 (2002)
17. Sato, H.: A Service Framework based on Grades of IdPs and SPs. In: Proc. Securiy and Management 2009, pp. 379–385 (2009)
18. Sato, H.: $N \pm \varepsilon$: Reflecting Local Risk Assessment in LoA. In: Meersman, R., Dillon, T., Herrero, P. (eds.) OTM 2009. LNCS, vol. 5871, pp. 833–847. Springer, Heidelberg (2009)
19. Stoneburner, G., Goguen, A., Feringa, A.: Risk Management Guide for Information Technology Systems. NIST 800-30 (2002)
20. Yan, J., Blackwell, A., Anderson, R., Grant, A.: Password Memorability and Security: Empirical Results. IEEE Security and Privacy, 25–31 (September/October, 2004)
21. http://middleware.internet2.edu/hepki-tag/pki-lite/pki-lite-policy-practices-current.html
22. http://www.meti.go.jp/policy/netsecurity/digitalsign-law.htm
23. http://www.tagpma.org/

Implementation and Performance Analysis of the Role-Based Trust Management System, RT^C

Tyler L. Hobbs[1] and William H. Winsborough[2]

[1] University of Texas at Austin
thobbs@cs.utexas.edu
[2] University of Texas at San Antonio
wwinsborough@acm.org

Abstract. We present representations and algorithms for the implementation of RT^C, a role-based trust management language, and announce an open-source implementation available to the public. We also design and perform large-scale performance tests on policies closely modeled after possible applications of RT in the real world. These tests aim to determine the viability of RT as an authorization solution for large and potentially complex policies in a decentralized environment; the results of the tests are analyzed to identify what policy characteristics most strongly affect the performance of RT and develop strategies to achieve the rapid response times required in real-world authorization systems.

1 Introduction

The term "trust management" (TM) has been used in a variety of ways over the years. Today it is often taken to refer to semi-automated techniques for estimating the likely trustworthiness of individuals, organizations, and software agents. This paper focuses instead on the classical notion of TM introduced by Blaze, Feigenbaum and Lacy [1], which focuses on placing into the hands of individuals and organizations security management decisions that are appropriate to their expertise and to their exposure as stakeholders. This has the effect of decentralizing authority, which serves to place decisions in the hands of experts and interested parties.

Several TM systems have received a great deal of attention in the literature [1, 2, 3, 4, 5, 6, 7, 8]. The aim of the current work is not to advance the underlying theory of TM, but rather to analyze the adequacy of one rich TM system as an authorization framework in highly decentralized and distributed environments. We have developed a Java-based system implementing RT^C, a modern TM system. RT^C uses a variant of the classical notion of role in which roles are owned by principals that have control over how the membership of their roles are defined. These roles can be used to express any property or characteristic of principals that role membership is intended by the role owner to assert. In particular, the roles can take parameters, such as the members date of birth or the path to a subdirectory to which the member has authorized access.

M. Nishigaki et al. (Eds.): IFIPTM 2010, IFIP AICT 321, pp. 184–199, 2010.

In RT^C, extensive use of delegation of authority is used, so that, for instance, experts on one characteristic of principals are not expected to be experts on all characteristics. For instance, a university might own roles that capture the characteristic of being enrolled as a student, while an accrediting board might own roles that capture the characteristic of being an accredited university. Someone wishing to define a role of their own such that the role's members are students at an accredited university might delegate to the accrediting board authority to define which principals are universities and to those universities, authority to define which principals are students.

RT^C is a member of the RT family of languages [9, 10, 6]. These languages introduce authority management abstractions that are given precise semantics via translation to the well understood subset of first-order predicate calculus, Datalog. RT^C in particular is translated into Datalog with constraint systems that admit efficient evaluation [11]. Constraints are logical formulas that serve to specify valuations over variables appearing as parameters in RT^C roles. For instance, constraints would be helpful in our university student example if the aim is to define a role whose members graduated in the last 10 years.

The current paper introduces techniques for the implementation of RT^C, including constraint representation and sketch an algorithm that performs the most interesting operation on them, namely conjunction. We have validated these techniques by building a distributed implementation, which is available to the public under the open source BSD license; all code and related documentation is available for public use at `http://sourceforge.net/projects/rtcredential`. This represents the first of the two present contributions.

The second contribution is a comprehensive investigation of the performance of our implementation. We investigate scenarios in which large numbers of credentials must be retrieved from widely distributed repositories, as well as assess the considerable improvements that can be obtained when credential caching is exploited. We do this in a variety of scenarios that we believe are representative of environments in which RT^C would be most helpful. The thesis we aim to support is that TM languages such as RT^C represent an important component in security solutions in the ever-widening need for decentralized authorization policy management.

The remainder of the paper is organized as follows: Section 2 gives a brief summary of RT^C [9,12]. Section 3 describes the RT Credential Toolkit. Section 4 presents and analyzes performance results for RT^C on large, real world scenarios and analyzes the results, and Section 5 concludes.

2   Brief Overview of RT^C

A main feature of RT^C is its ability to use parameterized roles with constraints [12]. Parameters allow us to convey information about principals that could not be easily represented by role membership alone, such as values in a large domain. This in turn enables policy to define authorization with much finer granularity than when constraints are not supported. For instance, in the university student example, constraints easily capture the requirement that graduation must have occurred within the last 10 years. Without constraints, each of the 10 years has to be treated as a separate case. In general, constraints greatly facilitate giving concise definitions of roles that involve parameters that range over large sets of possible values.

The aim of an RT^C [12,9] policy is to assign *principals* (also called entities) to *roles*. A principal may be a user, an organization, a virtual organization (VO), or a software or hardware agent. A role takes the form $A.r(x_1, \cdots, x_k)$ in which A is an principal, $r(x_1, \cdots, x_k)$ is called a *rolename*, and $x_1, \cdots, x_k$ are sorted[1] variables. We call r a role *identifier*, and intuitively it resembles a predicate over the owner, role member, and $x_1, \cdots, x_k$. We use capital roman letters A, B, D to range over principals and r, possibly with subscripts, to range over role identifiers.

A policy in RT^C is given by a set of statements, which are described just below. We index variables x_i^j occurring in a statement so that j indicates the role the variable occurs in and i indicates the parameter position with that role. We denote vectors of variables by using bold face, so x^j denotes the vector of variables appearing as parameters to the jth role in the statement. All variables occurring in a given statement are distinct from one another.

A *valuation* is a mapping from variables to values in the carrier appropriate to their sort. In the treatment given here, *primitive constraints* are predicates applied to variables that are given an intended interpretation over the specified carriers. For instance, if two distinct variables x_i^j and x_ℓ^k are intended to assume the same value, a primitive constraint $x_i^j = x_\ell^k$ is used to express this. Different constraint systems include different carriers and different primitive constraints (*interpreted* predicates). A *constraint* is a conjunction of primitive constraints, possibly with existential quantifiers. A constraint is satisfiable if there exists a valuation that makes each primitive constraint true. A constraint is said to be *over* any set of variables that includes the variables that occur free in it.

There are four types of policy statements in RT^C, each of which includes a constraint, denoted by $\psi(x)$, in which x is the list of variables occurring in the remainder of the statement:

- *Type-1:* $A.r(x^0) \longleftarrow B; \psi(x^0)$
  This statement defines B to be a member of A's role $r(x^0)$ under all valuations that satisfy $\psi(x^0)$.
- *Type-2:* $A.r_1(x^0) \longleftarrow B.r_2(x^1); \psi(x^0, x^1)$
  This statement defines $A.r_1(x^0)$ to include all members of $B.r_2(x^1)$
- *Type-3:* $A.r(x^0) \longleftarrow A.r_1(x^1).r_2(x^2); \psi(x^0, x^1, x^2)$
  The body of this statement is referred to as a *linked role*. Under each valuation that satisfies $\psi(x^0, x^1, x^2)$, the statement says that for each B in $A.r_1(x^1)$, $B.r_2(x^2)$ is a subset of $A.r(x^0)$.

---

[1] Sorts resemble a very simple notion of variable types; each variable is assigned to exactly one sort, which defines the set of values over which it can range. This set is called the *carrier* of the sort.

- *Type-4:* $A.r(\boldsymbol{x}^0) \longleftarrow B.r_2(\boldsymbol{x}^1) \cap C.r_3(\boldsymbol{x}^2); \psi(\boldsymbol{x}^0, \boldsymbol{x}^1, \boldsymbol{x}^2)$
  The body of this statement is referred to as an *intersection*. Under each valuation that satisfies $\psi(\boldsymbol{x}^0, \boldsymbol{x}^1, \boldsymbol{x}^2)$, the statement defines $A.r(\boldsymbol{x}^0)$ to include principals that are members of both roles, $B.r_2(\boldsymbol{x}^1)$ and $C.r_3(\boldsymbol{x}^2)$.

Each of these statements is said to *define* $A.r(\boldsymbol{x}^0)$. A is called the *owner* of the role and the *issuer* of these statements, and has sole authority to define such statements in the policy. The *body* of a statement consists of the right-hand-side, to the right of the arrow. We abuse the terminology by saying that a constraint over the variables that occur in a statement (resp., role) is *a constraint over* that statement (role).

Semantics and Supported Constraint Domains. Extending work by Li *et al.* [10], Li and Mitchell [6] define the semantics of RT^C by translating policy statements into clauses in Datalog with constraints [11]. In this context, queries about role membership are given a standard semantics based on logical entailment. Li and Mitchell [11] identify some classes of constraint domains that efficiently support all the operations that are necessary for evaluating queries under Datalog with constraints. Our implementation techniques and the implementation itself support several such constraint domains. In them, all primitive constraints involve only a single variable, with the single exception of equality. (An equality $x = y$ is satisfied by a valuation only if that valuation assigns both variables the same value.) Other primitive constraints we consider require variable values to belong either to a set identified through enumeration, a numerical range, which may be unbounded on one or both ends, or to bear a hierarchical relation to a node in a tree.

In RT^C, a *query* asks about role membership. There are three kinds of queries. An *all-members* query is given by a constrained role, which takes the form $A.r(\boldsymbol{x}); \psi(\boldsymbol{x})$. A *principal solution* to an all-members query is the set of all principal/constraint pairs, $\langle D, \varphi(\boldsymbol{x}) \rangle$, such that the Datalog translation logically entails that D is in $A.r(\boldsymbol{x})$ under all valuations that satisfy $\varphi(\boldsymbol{x})$, $\varphi(\boldsymbol{x})$ is satisfiable, and $\varphi(\boldsymbol{x}) \Rightarrow \psi(\boldsymbol{x})$. An *all-roles* query is given by a principal D and determines a set of constrained roles $A.r(\boldsymbol{x}); \psi(\boldsymbol{x})$ that the Datalog semantics makes D a member of under all valuations satisfying $\psi(\boldsymbol{x})$; these constrained roles are referred to as *role solutions*. A *membership-decision* query, given a constrained role $A.r(\boldsymbol{x}); \psi(\boldsymbol{x})$ and a principal D, determines the set of constraints $\phi(\boldsymbol{x})$ under which D is a member of $A.r(\boldsymbol{x})$ for all valuations of $\boldsymbol{x}$ satisfying $\phi(\boldsymbol{x})$ and such that such that $\phi(\boldsymbol{x}) \Rightarrow \psi(\boldsymbol{x})$ [12].

2.1   The Credential Chain Discovery Algorithm

Our query evaluation engine implements the algorithm introduced by Mao *et al.* [12], which in turn is based on the algorithm for RT_0 introduced by Li *et al.* [9]. (RT_0 has no role parameters or constraints.) We now briefly summarize that algorithm.

Queries are answered by creating a portion of a directed graph called a *credential graph*. Each node in the graph represents either a role or a principal. The graph contains several types of edges, which correspond to statements in the RT^C policy. For instance, when the policy contains a statement of the form $A.r(\boldsymbol{x}^0) \longleftarrow B.r_2(\boldsymbol{x}^1); \psi_2(\boldsymbol{x}^0, \boldsymbol{x}^1)$, the credential graph contains an *implication edge* from the node representing $B.r_2(\boldsymbol{x}^1); \psi(\boldsymbol{x}^1)$ to the node representing $A.r(\boldsymbol{x}^0); \psi_1(\boldsymbol{x}^0)$, in which the constraints $\psi(\boldsymbol{x}^1)$ and $\psi_1(\boldsymbol{x}^0)$ depend on the manner (direction) in which the (partial) credential graph is constructed. To deal with Type 3 and 4 credentials (and other special cases), other types of edges are created which perform actions in concordance with their type; for example, an *intersection edge* requires principals to be members of both roles in the intersection before it may become a member of the role to which the edge leads.

Search Algorithms. The all-members query is answered through a *backward search* algorithm, which constructs the credential graph by creating a node representing the constrained role given by the query and expanding the constructed graph by traversing edges in a backward direction. Constructing and traversing edges requires the algorithm to access (possibly remote) repositories to retrieve the credentials that define those edges. Backward searches create only role nodes; principals are mentioned only in solutions and do not receive their own node. The *forward search* algorithm answers the all-roles query. It begins by creating a principal node, and expanding the graph by traversing edges in a forward direction. To handle linked roles in the forward search, principal nodes must also be used in addition to role nodes. Although the membership-decision query may be answered by either forward or backward search, a third algorithm referred to as the *bidirectional search* may also be used. A bidirectional search involves both a backward search on the query role and a forward search on the query principal simultaneously; these terminate as soon as the query principal is shown to be a member of the query role under the given constraint.

When a query is evaluated, the graph may be reused for any other queries thereafter (maintaining the graph through multiple queries is referred to as *graph caching* in later portions of this paper).

3   RT Credential Toolkit

The RT Credential Toolkit was designed to supply most of the components necessary for an authorization solution. The toolkit is composed of three main components: the credential authoring tool, the query engine, and the credential repository. Each of these components are detailed below.

3.1   Implementation Design Decisions

Representation of Constraints. The representation must support several operations: construction of internal representation from the representation given in credentials; conjunction of constraints; existential quantifier elimination; subsumption of one constraint by another; and duplication of representation. As mentioned above, the only primitive constraints we support that involve more than one variable are equalities, which leads to their having special treatment:

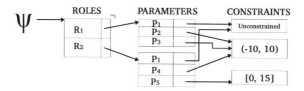

$$A.R_1(P_1, P_2, P_3) \longleftarrow B.R_2(P_1, P_4, P_5);$$
$$P_2 \in (-10, 20), \quad P_4 \in (-20, 10), \quad P_5 \in [0, 15], \quad P_2 = P_4, \quad P_3 = P_4$$

Fig. 1. Depiction of a constraint created for the credential shown

all variables that are constrained to be equal refer to a single object representing the constraint on values they can assume. Due to the simplicity of the constraint domains we consider, any consistent conjunction of non-equality primitive constraints can be reduced to a single primitive constraint. This enables a simple representation, illustrated in Figure 1. The representation of a constraint over a statement (or a role) has an entry for each role in the statement. Each role entry has an entry for each parameter of that role and each of these parameter entries is associated with an object representing a primitive constraint, which may be shared with other parameter entries. The special primitive-constraint object (PCO), *unconstrained*, indicates that all values of the corresponding carrier satisfy the constraint.

Among the operations that must be supported, providing an algorithm to implement conjunction is the least straightforward. We outline the conjunction algorithm in the next section.

Conjunction Algorithm. Our algorithm implementing conjunction needs to handle only the case in which one conjunct, ψ_1, is over some statement, and the other, ψ_2, is over a single role from that statement. The result, ψ_3, must be constructed without modifying ψ_1 or ψ_2. The algorithm begins by duplicating ψ_1. To maintain equality constraints from ψ_1, the duplication procedure uses a table that associates PCOs in ψ_1 with PCOs in the duplicate. (Note that this association is between objects, not the primitive constraints they represent.) Processing each role parameter in turn, when the PCO for that parameter in ψ_1 does not yet have an associated object in the duplicate, a new copy of that PCO is created and entered into the table as well as into the duplicate's parameter entry. When the table already contains an associated object in the duplicate, a reference to that PCO is entered in the duplicate's parameter entry. Thus, the sharing of PCOs in the duplicate is made to correspond precisely to that in ψ_1.

Next, we modify the duplicate, generating the result ψ_3, by conjoining the PCOs in ψ_2 with the corresponding PCOs in (the data structure that will become) ψ_3. Recall that ψ_2 is a constraint over some role in the statement that (the duplicate of) ψ_1 is over. The procedure considers each parameter of that role in turn, constructing a new PCO that represents the conjunction of those in ψ_2 and in the duplicate. This new PCO then replaces the old one in the duplicate. To preserve the equality constraints in the duplicate coming from ψ_1 while introducing the equality constraints from ψ_2, an association table is used to associate PCOs in ψ_2 with PCOs in ψ_3.

When processing a parameter, the table is used as follows. Let us call the PCO in the parameter's ψ_2 entry pco_2 and that in the parameter's ψ_3 entry pco_3. When the table does not contain an association for pco_2, the (simplified) conjunction of pco_3 and pco_2 is computed, entered into the table in association with pco_2, and is used to replace pco_3 in the constraint being constructed (ψ_3). (Note that when conjunctions are unsatisfiable, this is detected and handled at a higher level in the algorithm as this leads to greater efficiency.) When the table *does* contain an associated PCO, call it pco_3', we check to see whether pco_3' and pco_3 are one and the same object. If so, no further action is required. Otherwise, the (simplified) conjunction of pco_2, pco_3', and pco_3 is computed, entered into the table in association with pco_2, and used to replace pco_3 in the constraint being constructed (ψ_3).

Repository Locations and Credential Typing. An acknowledged limitation of the currently available system is that it does not support credential typing of the type described by Li *et al.* [9]. This type discipline enables credentials to be stored with either their issuers or their subjects in a manner that ensures credential chains, if they exist, can be found. However, as a means of supporting distributed sets of credentials, each credential optionally contains the location of one or more credential repositories where other credentials relevant to the issuer, defined role, and body of that credential may be found. The engine is able to use this information during proof construction to find other credentials as needed. Extending the current system to support full credential typing is a possible future activity.

3.2   Components of the Toolkit

Credential Authoring Tool. The credential authoring tool enables users to create RT credentials easily by using a special-purpose graphical user interface. Technical activities such as public key creation, credential signing, and distributing credential to repositories are easy to perform.

Credentials are stored in an XML format with elements for the defined role, body, the credential validity period, and relevant credential repositories; the credentials are cryptographically signed by the issuer of the credential. To support the use of *RT* within an organization, public keys, role names, credentials, and repository locations may be imported along with their metadata from a local or online repositories. This allows one to start with a working set of useful objects, such as public keys for company employees or commonly used role names. The metadata associated with each object allows them to be referred to by short local names instead of their globally unique identifiers and also provides a way to attach and display easy to read descriptions of each object.

The ability to import and search existing credentials allows one to view a policy set that the user may wish to modify or extend; this feature may also help to present a simple or small portion of the overall policy set to organizational members who need to write only a limited set of new policy statements. Additionally, test queries may be run from the authoring tool to ensure that new policies have the desired effect.

Engine. The engine is responsible for evaluating RT credentials to answer queries. Forward, backward, and bidirectional searches are supported. The engine has both Java API and command line interfaces which may be used to pose queries and read results. The engine automatically fetches relevant credentials from the appropriate repositories for processing.

Credential Repository. The credential repository is a relatively simple application which hosts, indexes, and serves credentials to engines. Credentials may be added to a repository remotely or locally. The repository also maintains information about what credentials have been served to an engine during the current connection to avoid sending credentials multiple times.

4   Performance Evaluation

Although other RT query evaluation programs have been developed, there has been little investigation into the costs of an RT system which is usable by the public, stores credentials in a distributed manner, or deals with policies approaching the size and complexity expected in real world scenarios.

The costs of using RT in terms of latency, throughput, network usage, and computational power required need to be assessed. It also must be determined whether RT is efficient under certain usage scenarios but performs poorly under others and what factors primarily determine this difference. If performance is poor, new strategies may be necessary to maintain the low latency required for a useful authorization system.

4.1   Policy Benchmarks

Large scale authorization policies used in practice are difficult to obtain. Instead, we base our analysis on automatically generated policies designed to have characteristics likely to arise in realistic scenarios. To this end, we have constructed a policy generator that uses pseudo-random methods to generate policies based on a collection of parameters that can be tuned to yield policies likely to be representative of policies that would be used in a variety of scenarios. We begin by describing the policy generator and its parameters. We then describe scenarios that seem appropriate candidates for application of RT^C.

Policy Set Generator. The policy set generator creates all of the credentials necessary to define a rough hierarchy of roles based on a set of input parameters described below. At a high level, the generator creates the policy set for the hierarchy one level at a time, beginning at the base, and takes the following steps to do so:

1. The generator begins by defining the *base roles*. The base roles are the roles at the bottom level of the hierarchy which directly include the main body of principals and are generally defined by Type-1 policies only.
2. A new level of roles are created above the previous level. The set of policies created in step 3 will define these new roles and will include roles from the previous level in the body. The number of roles defined at each level must be at least one fewer than the level below it.
3. For each of the roles in the previous level, we will create a statement whose type is randomly selected based on the given parameters. If we select Type-2, the role itself is used as the body of the new statement. If we select Type-4, the role appears in an intersection in the body of the statement along with another role randomly chosen from the set of already defined roles. If we select Type-1, we create two policies: a Type-1 with a randomly selected principal as the body and a Type-2 with the role as the body. For Type-3, we do the following:
   (a) Create a linked role of the form $A.r_1.r_2$ where A is a randomly selected principal and r_2 is the role name from the role we are currently working with. This linked role will appear in the body of the new statement.
   (b) Create $(i - 1)$ Type-1 policies of the form $A.r_1 \longleftarrow B$ where B is a randomly selected principal and i is the parameter described below.
   (c) Create one Type-1 statement of the form $A.r_1 \longleftarrow D$ where D is the principal from the role we are currently working with.

   For each statement statement written, we advance use the next available role from the new level as the defined role. When we reach the end of the list of new roles, we start again from the beginning.
4. Repeat from step 2 until we arrive at a level with only one defined role.

Parameters for the Policy Set Generator.

1. Number of principals, n: the number of principals that are eligible to be members of the base roles. Principles defining roles within the tree are also randomly drawn from this range.
2. Number of base roles, r: the number of base roles for the hierarchy.
3. Principal inclusion percentage, p: the probability that any given principal is a member of any given base role. This results in an approximately normal distribution of the number of principals in any base role with mean np and variance $np(1 - p)$.
4. Level-to-level reduction percentage, l: the reduction in the number of roles defined from one level to the level above it. This governs how quickly the hierarchy narrows, controlling the number of levels and correspondingly the maximum height of any credential chain.
5. Chain die-off percentage, d: the percentage of roles at each level which will not appear in the body of any credentials defining the next level of roles. This controls the variability of chain height; a value of 0.0 will result in all chains reaching the maximum height while a value of 0.5 will result in approximately half of the remaining chains ending at each level.

6. Type-1 percentage within the hierarchy, t_1: the percentage of credentials defining roles within the hierarchy that are Type-1. Note that this percentage does not include Type-1 credentials that define the base roles. This parameter can be used to account for management or other special principals who may be included directly in a mid to high level role.

7. Type-3 percentage within the hierarchy, t_3: the percentage of credentials defining roles within the hierarchy that have linked roles as their body.

8. Number of principals in the intermediate role of every linked role, i: whenever a linked role is created, this many principals are randomly picked from existing roles in the hierarchy and are added to the intermediate role of the linked role. There is no guarantee that one of these principals will define a role whose role name matches the second role name from the linked role.

9. Type-4 percentage within the hierarchy, t_4: the percentage of credentials defining roles within the hierarchy that have intersections as their body.

All credentials within the hierarchy that are not Types 1, 3, or 4 are Type-2.

Scenarios. The following scenarios are possible real world examples which might require policies that RT is well suited for describing. These policies may rely heavily on delegation of authority, which is relatively flexible and straightforward in RT. Credentials storage is likely to be distributed in two of the scenarios, which RT is designed for, while the other two may have more centralized storage.

Parameters and constraints were not used in these scenarios due to the complexity involved their generation. However, our benchmarks show that the performance impact of using parameters throughout a set of policies similar to the government department scenario described below is minimal, generally resulting in less than a 10% increase in time to complete a query, including the retrieval of credentials from remote repositories.

Grid Scenario. Several virtual organizations (VOs) collaborate to create a grid infrastructure. Each VO has a separate internal policy. A small set of policy statements is created to govern access to the various grid tools by VO members; these policies reference one or two top level roles from each VO. Additionally, some principals are members of more than one VO.

Policy sets for five VOs of different sizes were generated, with n ranging from 100 to 500, r ranging from 10 to 20, l ranging from .25 to .4, p ranging from .35 to .25, i ranging from 3 to 5, t_1 equal to .1, t_3 equal to .05, t_4 equal to .15, and d equal to .1. The sets of principals used for the different VOs were nearly disjoint, with an overlap of 20 or fewer principals.

The parameters which vary depending on the size of the VO follow these expectations: first, while the average group size will increase, the overall number of groups will not increase as quickly. Second, as the size of an organization grows, specialization is likely to occur, causing the average number of roles a single principal is a member of to grow more slowly than the total number of roles available. Third, the hierarchy is likely to increase in width more quickly than height.

Credentials representing grid authorization roles were written by hand. These defined a single top level role and three roles below it, each of which included roles from the top and middle of the hierarchies for three of the five VOs.

Government Department Scenario. A large government department creates a policy that roughly resembles a single hierarchy with many management roles. Credential storage is mostly centralized.

The following parameters were used: $n = 10000$, $p = .1$, $r = 100$, $l = .5$, $t_1 = .2$, $t_3 = .1$, $i = 10$, $t_4 = .15$, and $d = .1$. These represent a more complex policy, with a greater number of linked roles and intersections. The maximum chain height was seven.

E-Bookstore. An electronic bookstore wishes to offer discounts to students of all small accredited universities nearby. Each university maintains its own simple policy which groups students by department and describes membership for several of the larger extra-curricular roles.

Policy sets for 13 universities were generated, each with the following parameters: $n = 5000$, $p = .1$, $r = 10$, $l = .6$, $t_1 = 0$, $t_3 = .02$, $i = 3$, $t_4 = .1$, and $d = .1$. These create very simple policies with a maximum chain height of three. The top level role for each university was $University_i.student()$, where $1 \leq i \leq 13$. The following credentials were created by hand for the E-bookstore:

1. $E\text{-}Bookstore.discount() \longleftarrow AccredBoard.university().student()$
2. $AccredBoard.university() \longleftarrow University_i$

Social Network. A new social network is created. Every principal defines a set of friends, and each principal can see their extended network, which includes friends of friends, and their 2nd extended network, which includes friends of extended friends.

Policy sets for 10000 principals were created. Each principal randomly added principals to their *friends()* role from a range of 1000 principals, with each principal having a 10% chance of inclusion in the role. The range of principals that friends were selected from was occasionally shifted to give the effect that principals nearby are likely to share many friends, while principals far apart share few or no friends. Each principal, P, also created the following credentials:

1. $P.extendedFriends() \longleftarrow P.friends().friends()$
2. $P.secondExtendedFriends() \longleftarrow P.extendedFriends().friends()$

Repository Distribution. The repositories were spread between the University of Texas at Austin the University of Texas at San Antonio. The bandwidth available to the repositories was great enough to not be a significant limiting factor during performance testing.

For the grid and E-bookstore scenarios, all credentials for each VO or university were stored in a single repository, with all repositories being used. This simulates what one is likely to find in real world scenarios where credentials are

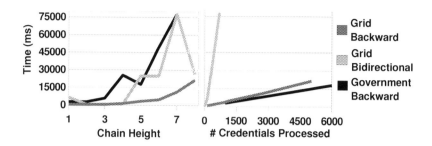

Fig. 2. Total Query Processing Time for: Backward Search in the Government Scenario; Backward and Bidirectional in the Grid Scenario

likely to be stored centrally per organization, but the organizations themselves are likely to be distributed.

For the government department and social networking scenario, all credentials were split evenly between two repositories near the engine. For these scenarios, we felt that centralized storage of the credentials was more likely in real world examples. Users of such facilities seem unlikely to avail themselves of repositories not operated by the sites in questions.

4.2   Results

The credential repositories were run on machines of varying hardware, including a 2.13GHz Core2 with 2GB of RAM, a 4-core 2.66GHz Xeon with 16GB of RAM, an 8-core 2.0GHz Xeon with 8GB of RAM, and 8-core 3.0GHz Xeon with 32GB of RAM that was also used for the engine.

All results shown below are for searches with no portion of the graph cached unless stated otherwise. With a fully cached graph (meaning all nodes have been processed), the time to execute any query, regardless of query type or which roles and principals the query was performed on, was less than 10ms.

Grid Scenario. As seen in Fig. 2, the total time required to evaluate a query by using backward search in the Grid Scenario was linearly proportional to the number of credentials processed. Because of the hierarchical nature of the policies used in this scenario, the number of credentials processed increased exponentially with respect to the maximum chain height of the query role. The average time required per credential processed was 4.25ms. The time required to perform a forward search was also approximately linearly proportional to the number of credentials processed, but the average time required per credential processed was much higher, at 250ms.

Like the backward and forward search, bidirectional search exhibited a linear increase in time proportional to the number of credentials processed. The number of credentials processed with respect to the length of the chain between the query role and principal was far fewer than backward search: anywhere from .2 to .06 the number of credentials processed during a backward search of the same

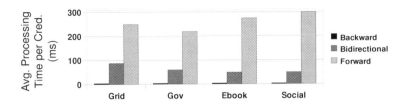

Fig. 3. Average processing time per credential among the three query types

height. The average time required per credential processed was in between that of backward and forward search, at 88ms.

Backward search in the grid scenario generated a maximum of 400 KB/s of download traffic and 200 KB/s of upload traffic for the engine, while forward search generated only 45 KB/s down and 80 KB/s up. Bidirectional search generated 80 KB/s of download traffic and 80 KB/s up.

CPU utilization on the engine remained at or above 90% during backward search. During forward search it was much lower: usually less than 10%; CPU utilization during forward search also had a downward trend as a search progressed. Although bidirectional searches initially showed greater CPU utilization than forward searches, they progressed more slowly as the search continued and CPU utilization became only slightly better than that of forward search.

Government Department Scenario. As seen in Fig. 2, backward search performance in the Government Department Scenario was similar to that of the Grid Scenario, but with a slightly lower time required per credential processed at 4ms. CPU utilization and network traffic was similar to that of the Grid Scenario. Bidirectional searches took an extremely long time to complete. In the case that the query principal was not a member of the query role, a single search took about 90 minutes and processed about 90000 credentials, averaging about 60ms per credential processed.

E-Bookstore Scenario. Backward searches in the E-Bookstore scenario completed in 9 seconds on average when performed on *University.student()* roles with an average of 3ms required per credential processed; when the query role was *E-Bookstore.discount()*, the time required per credential increased to 6ms. Forward and search performed more poorly than in the grid and government department scenarios, requiring 275ms per credential processed. Bidirectional search was slightly better than the government dept. scenario, at 50ms per credential processed.

Social Networking Scenario. For backward search, queries on *friend()*, *extendedFriend()*, and *secondExtendedFriend()* queries took .5, 28, and 490 seconds on average, and average time per credential processed was was 5.6, 3.5, and 2.8ms, respectively. CPU and network utilization remained extremely high, similar to the other scenarios.

Forward search performed extremely slowly, with low CPU utilization and network usage. The completion time for a single query was roughly two hours.

After extended periods of time, the forward search slowed to a rate of three credentials processed per second.

Bidirectional search performed moderately in the case that the query principal was a member of the query role; for *friend()* and *extendedFriend()* roles, queries completed in about 10 seconds, while *secondExtendedFriends()* queries completed in about 20. When the query principal was not a member of the query role, bidirectional searches initially had moderate CPU utilization and network traffic before degenerating into performance slightly better than forward search.

4.3   Analysis

As the results from the performance tests show, the difference in response times for queries with and without graph caching is staggering. At the scale of these tests, it is clear that caching all or most of the credential graph makes an enormous difference to the expected query response time. When the graph is fully cached, query response times are consistently extremely low. We suggest techniques for maintaining such a cache in the next section.

The amount of time required to complete a query increased nearly linearly with respect to the number of credentials processed for all three types of queries across all scenarios. The average processing time per credential did decrease slowly for backward search as the number of credentials grew, while the average time per credential increased slowly for forward and bidirectional searches.

Backward search performed very similarly regardless of the scenario. Its performance appears to be almost entirely CPU bound, although network traffic could become a limiting factor in some cases. The primary factor which affected backward search performance was the number of roles overall; the percentage of Type-3 and Type-4 credentials also impacted performance to a lesser degree.

The differences in performance between forward and backward search were unexpected and quite large. There are two primary differences which may account for the disparity:

First, backward searches create only role nodes, while forward searches create both principal nodes and role nodes. In these scenarios, the number of principals greatly exceeds the number of roles. The large increase in the number of nodes requires much more memory and substantially increases the rate of cache misses, which results in the extremely low CPU utilization seen during forward searches.

Second, backward searches need to perform extra work only to deal with linked roles and intersections when a Type-3 or Type-4 credential is encountered while processing a role node. By contrast, to handle linked roles a forward search must create new nodes and perform several actions for each node processed.

For these reasons, forward search is unable to effectively utilize the CPU or generate network traffic; memory access time is the limiting factor.

Because bidirectional search runs both a forward and a backward search, it suffers from the same performance problems as forward search. Although the number of credentials processed are often low when the query is a success, the average time per credential processed is still high. Therefore, it cannot be depended upon as a means of graph creation.

The average processing time per credential grows faster with the number of credentials in the forward search than in the backward search. This is because Type-1 credentials tend to constitute above 90% of the number of credentials in a policy, processing a greater number credentials in a forward search generally results in the creation of many additional principal nodes, and consequently, poorer performance. On the other hand, an increase in the number of credentials processed in a backward search results in the creation of relatively few role nodes whose performance impact does not outweigh the loss of performance overhead during earlier portions of graph construction.

4.4   Optimizations

Because the performance of an RT system is largely dependent on fully caching the graph, optimizations should concentrate on caching the graph quickly and efficiently. Due to the performance differences between forward, backward, and bidirectional search, the quickest way to build a complete graph is through backward searches on all roles that are used for authorization purposes. By avoiding forward and bidirectional searches entirely, performance is significantly enhanced. However, for this strategy to work, all credentials chains must be backward-traversable [9]. This requirement is not particularly onerous, but may be difficult to maintain in loosely organized, widely distributed scenarios. Without this guarantee, designing an efficient caching strategy is more complex.

Additionally, because backward search is primarily CPU bound, converting the currently single-threaded engine to a multi-threaded model is expected to improve performance significantly.

Multiple Engines. Because revocation and expiration become frequent for large policies, their effect on query response times must be minimized. Currently, when a credential expires or is revoked, our only available strategy is to rebuild the entire graph without that credential. An engine that is busy constantly rebuilding the graph will have no way to respond to queries in a timely manner. Although one possible solution to this problem is to devise a way to alter the graph so that the work required to handle credential invalidation is lessened, the frequency of these events and the expected time to deal with them still prevents the engine from responding to queries quickly.

An alternative strategy runs multiple engines simultaneously. One engine is dedicated to answering all queries with the latest complete version of the graph. For each credential invalidation, a separate engine constructs a new version of the graph in the background; when the new graph is complete, that engine assumes the role of servicing queries while the engine it replaces waits to build a new version of the graph after the next credential invalidation. The number of engines running concurrently could grow to accommodate increased workloads.

5   Conclusion

In this paper, we announced the availability of an open source implementation of RT^C and used it to test and analyze the performance of RT^C systems in a large, distributed environment. The results of these tests show that low response times for role membership queries may only be achieved through thorough caching of the graph. Furthermore, the characteristics of the backward search algorithm make it a much better candidate for graph creation than either forward or bidirectional search due to more efficient memory usage. Utilizing this knowledge, we have proposed strategies for cached-graph management that will allow RT^C to achieve the query evaluation-response times necessary to make it a viable authorization solution in distributed environments that benefit from easy delegation of authority.

References

1. Blaze, M., Feigenbaum, J., Lacy, J.: Decentralized trust management. In: Proceedings of the 1996 IEEE Symposium on Security and Privacy, pp. 164–173. IEEE Computer Society Press, Los Alamitos (1996)
2. Blaze, M., Feigenbaum, J., Ioannidis, J., Keromytis, A.D.: The KeyNote trust-management system, version 2. IETF RFC 2704 (1999)
3. Clarke, D., Elien, J.E., Ellison, C., Fredette, M., Morcos, A., Rivest, R.L.: Certificate chain discovery in SPKI/SDSI. Journal of Computer Security 9(4), 285–322 (2001)
4. Gunter, C.A., Jim, T.: Policy-directed certificate retrieval. Software: Practice & Experience 30(15), 1609–1640 (2000)
5. Jim, T.: SD3: A trust management system with certified evaluation. In: Proceedings of the 2001 IEEE Symposium on Security and Privacy, pp. 106–115. IEEE Computer Society Press, Los Alamitos (2001)
6. Li, N., Mitchell, J.C.: RT: A role-based trust-management framework. In: The Third DARPA Information Survivability Conference and Exposition (DISCEX III). IEEE Computer Society Press, Los Alamitos (2003)
7. Becker, M.Y., Sewell, P.: Cassandra: Distributed access control policies with tunable expressiveness. In: POLICY 2004: Proceedings of the Fifth IEEE International Workshop on Policies for Distributed Systems and Networks (POLICY 2004), Washington, DC, USA, p. 159. IEEE Computer Society, Los Alamitos (2004)
8. Czenko, M., Tran, H., Doumen, J., Etalle, S., Hartel, P.H., den Hartog, J.: Non-monotonic trust management for p2p applications. CoRR abs/cs/0510061 (2005)
9. Li, N., Winsborough, W.H., Mitchell, J.C.: Distributed credential chain discovery in trust management. Journal of Computer Security 11(1), 35–86 (2003)
10. Li, N., Mitchell, J.C., Winsborough, W.H.: Design of a role-based trust management framework. In: Proceedings of the 2002 IEEE Symposium on Security and Privacy, pp. 114–130. IEEE Computer Society Press, Los Alamitos (2002)
11. Li, N., Mitchell, J.C.: Datalog with constraints: A foundation for trust management languages. In: Dahl, V., Wadler, P. (eds.) PADL 2003. LNCS, vol. 2562, pp. 58–73. Springer, Heidelberg (2002)
12. Mao, Z., Li, N., Winsborough, W.H.: Distributed credential chain discovery in trust management with parameterized roles and constraints (short paper). In: Ning, P., Qing, S., Li, N. (eds.) ICICS 2006. LNCS, vol. 4307, pp. 159–173. Springer, Heidelberg (2006)

A Formal Notion of Trust – Enabling Reasoning about Security Properties

Andreas Fuchs, Sigrid Gürgens, and Carsten Rudolph*

Fraunhofer Institute for Secure Information Technology SIT,
Rheinstrasse 75, 64295 Darmstadt, Germany
{andreas.fuchs,sigrid.guergens,carsten.rudolph}@sit.fraunhofer.de

Abstract. Historically, various different notions of trust can be found, each addressing particular aspects of ICT systems, e.g. trust in electronic commerce systems based on reputation and recommendation, or trust in public key infrastructures. While these notions support the understanding of trust establishment and degrees of trustworthiness in their respective application domains, they are insufficient for the more general notion of trust needed when reasoning about security in ICT systems. In this paper we present a formal definition of trust to be able to exactly express trust requirements from the view of different entities involved in the system and to support formal reasoning such that security requirements, security and trust mechanisms and underlying trust assumptions can be formally linked and made explicit. Integrated in our Security Modeling Framework this formal definition of trust can support security engineering processes and formal validation and verification by enabling reasoning about security properties w.r.t. trust.

1   Introduction

The meaning of the term *trust* in the context of information and communication technology (ICT) systems differs from the concept of trust between people. In particular trust as seen in the notion of *trusted computing* (e.g. as defined by the Trusted Computing Group TCG) refers to particular properties of a technical system. This notion of trust stands in contrast to some more intuitive notions of trust expressing that someone behaves in a particular well-behaved way. Trust in a technical system always has to be seen as trust in a property of the system. A more meta-level generic trust as it is possible for people ("I trust you") is not useful for computers or technical entities as parts of communication networks. A variety of existing notions of trust in the context of ICT systems addresses particular aspects, e.g. trust in electronic commerce systems based on reputation and recommendation, or trust in public key infrastructures (see Section 3 for a survey). While these notions are useful to understand trust establishment and degrees of trustworthiness in these application domains, they cannot be used for

---
* Part of this work was accomplished within the project EVITA 224275 funded by the European Commission.

M. Nishigaki et al. (Eds.): IFIPTM 2010, IFIP AICT 321, pp. 200–215, 2010.

a more general notion of trust needed to reason about trust in ICT systems. In addition to the restricted applicability there is also a lack of formal semantics for the properties expressed by these different notions of trust. However, when used in a security engineering process, formal semantics are essential for traceability of trust and security requirements through the different steps of the process. This traceability is necessary to show relations between high-level requirements and underlying security mechanisms (e.g. particular cryptographic algorithms) and trust assumptions (e.g. trust in hardware security or trust in a particular behaviour of people using the system).

The goal of the formal notion of trust presented in this paper is to be able to exactly express trust requirements for ICT systems from the view of the different entities involved in the system, and to support formal reasoning such that finally security requirements, security and trust mechanisms and underlying trust assumptions can be formally linked and made explicit. Such a formal notion of trust can support security engineering processes as well as formal validation and verification. Previously established notions for security properties with formal semantics can provide traceability in a security engineering process as well and are used for validation and verification. However, trust adds another layer of information. While security properties may or may not be global properties of the system, trust always expresses the view of a particular entity or agent of the system. Trust depends on the individual perception of the agents. Therefore, different agents can have trust in contradictory properties. Furthermore, it must also be possible to express that one agent trusts that another agent has trust in a particular property (e.g. for expressing trust in certification authorities).

The notion of trust presented here extends the existing security modelling framework SeMF [1]. This framework uses formal languages and is independent of specific representations of the system. The example used throughout the paper discusses trust of an agent in that a specific authenticity property holds in a system. This example is used to explain our new notion of trust and to show how reasoning can lead to refined trust properties that express underlying trust assumptions and assumptions on security mechanisms that are not further refined within the model.

The following two sections first provide some terminology and then briefly discuss its relation to existing notions of trust. In Section 4 we introduce an example that will be used throughout the rest of the paper and that imposes some interesting questions related to trust. Section 5 then gives a brief summary of our Security Modeling Framework SeMF. Based on this, we present our formal notion of trust in Section 6 and use it to formally prove some security properties of our example in Section 7. Finally we present our conclusions in Section 8.

2   Terminology

The meaning of the word *trust* has been subject to many (more or less philosophical) discussions, many different interpretations with subtle differences exist. Achieving a common understanding of the term trust is further complicated by mixing it with the related notions of *trustworthiness* or *reputation*. The formal notion of trust introduced in this paper is supposed to be useful mainly for reasoning about trust in the context of technical systems in the area of ICT. The work was motivated by concepts such as trusted computing using the so-called Trusted Platform Module (TPM) [2]. Therefore, we do not intend to contribute to the philosophical discussions on trust or the relation between trust and reputation.

Within our formal framework we will use the following terminologies:

The term **trust** refers to a relation from one agent in the system to another agent with respect to a property, or from an agent directly to a property in the system. Thus, agents can have three slightly different types of trust:

1. Agents can trust that some (global) property holds in a system.
2. Agents can trust that another agent behaves in a certain way, i.e. that a property concerning the behaviour of this other agent is satisfied.
3. Agents can trust that another agent has a particular trust.

Being a relation, this notion of trust cannot be used to express different degrees of trust. Agents can either trust or not trust. In a refinement process the notion of trust can be broken down into more detailed trust assumptions. These are expressed using the same formal notion of trust. However, as input for a subsequent security evaluation or risk assessment it is necessary to express to which degree this trust can be substantiated, i.e. what is the *trustworthiness*. Thus, we clearly distinguish between trust and trustworthiness. This motivates the following notion of trustworthiness.

The term **trustworthiness** expresses the degree to which a particular trust assumption can be made. Trustworthiness can be expressed as a probability or can simply have fixed values (e.g. high, medium, low). Depending on the particular representation of trustworthiness, agents within the system can reason about the *trustworthiness* of other agents, or reasoning mechanisms can be used for risk analysis and risk assessment.

3   Related Work

A huge part of the approaches that use a notion of trust is concerned with reputation systems. In this area, trust is understood in the sense of trustworthiness as explained in Section 2 and e.g. defined by the research project Trust4All [3]:

> "Trust is the degree to which a trustor has a justifiable belief that the trustee will provide the expected function or service."

Jøsang et al. [4] present two different notions of trust that capture main aspects in the context of reputation systems:

- **Reliability Trust**: "Trust is the subjective probability by which an individual, A, expects that another individual, B, performs a given action on which its welfare depends."

This definition captures both the concept of dependence on the trusted party and the non-binary nature of trust in the context of reputation systems.

- **Decision Trust**: "Trust is the extent to which one party is willing to depend on something or somebody in a given situation with a feeling of relative security, even though negative consequences are possible. (inspired by [5])"

Hence the concept of Decision Trust is useful in the context of risk assessment.

This or similar characterizations of "trust" can be found in many of the approaches in this area. A very good overview of approaches regarding trust in reputation systems along with a clarification and classification of the main concepts is given by Jøsang et al. [4]. They explain these concepts further by means of temporary reputation based systems such as eBay. Another survey that focusses particularly on trust management systems is given by Grandison and Sloman [6].

A second branch of research focusses on formal models that capture certain aspects of trust. In [7] Carbone et al. introduce a formal model of trust that focusses on the formation, evolution and propagation of trust. Trust in their model is viewed as a function that assigns values to pairs of principles. The model can be used to formulate trust policies, however these seem to be restricted to access control. Further, their approach is not aimed at reasoning about security properties holding or not holding in a system. Delombe [8] provides a formal definition for trust that distinguishes between different properties an agent may have trust in. Axioms related to these properties are defined, and the resulting axiomatic structure can then be used to reason about conditional trust between agents with respect to ratings regarding aspects such as cooperativity and credibility.

Another branch of research that takes a similar axiomatic approach are the so-called authentication logics. These logics use a specific notion of trust and aim at reasoning about security properties of a system. In particular, these logics are useful for the security verification of cryptographic protocols. The first such logic was the BAN Logic [9] by Burrows et al. Here the concept of *jurisdiction* models trust of agents in statements of specific other agents about for example the trustworthiness of a key. The BAN logic inspired a large number of similar logics (see for example [10,11,12,13]). Each of these logics constitutes an axiomatic system, i.e. formulates axioms and inference rules that capture the nature of security mechanisms and proves that certain security properties are provided given that certain assumptions on the system hold.

Although these approaches seem to be closely related to the one introduced in this paper, there is a fundamental difference: Our formalization of trust and the thereby enabled reasoning about security properties does not use *axioms* but is *based on a formal semantics* that uses only formal language theory. Further, our notion of trust applies to any security property and is independent of any security mechanism that might be employed to achieve a security property, while the security properties handled by authentication logics are directly derived from specific aspects of security mechanisms.

As already explained in Section 1, we do not address trust in the context of reputation systems. Our notion of trust is motivated by the work in the area of trusted computing [2] where trust refers to particular properties of a technical system. Our work aims at providing means to support formal reasoning such that security requirements, security and trust mechanisms, and underlying trust assumptions can be formally linked and made explicit. However, reputation systems can be seen as complementary to our approach. Results achieved by our reasoning can be used as input for a subsequent security evaluation or risk assessment where it is necessary to express to which degree trust can be substantiated. On the other hand, reputation systems can be used for substantiating trust assumptions being input for our reasoning.

4   An Example

In this section we introduce a very simple use case that includes a security requirement involving specific trust requirements. Similar situations typically arise in many scenarios from different domains, such as car-to-car, distributed sensor networks or email. This use case serves both as a motivation for our concept of trust and as an example of how to use this concept in order to prove that specific security mechanisms together with certain trust assumptions result in the satisfaction of specific security properties.

However, we discuss the security properties and resulting trust requirements only informally in this section in order to give an understanding of the practical implication of our notion of trust. In the subsequent sections we will provide a brief introduction to our formal Security Modeling Framework (SeMF), will introduce the formal definition of trust, some resulting theorems, and will revisit the example formally.

In order to explain our approach we will use the scenario illustrated in Figure 1.

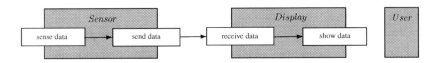

Fig. 1. Example System

Our example system consists of two active nodes and an end user. *Sensor* is a node deployed somewhere in the system that performs measurements (e.g. measures the temperature outside a house) and sends the resulting data over the network. *Display* is the second node of the system. It receives data from the network and displays them to the end user *User* (e.g. the owner of the house).

An obvious requirement of the above use case is that the user, when being shown some data, wants this data to be indeed measured by the Sensor. This requirement is usually denoted by *data origin authenticity* and can be informally stated as follows:

P0 *It must be authentic for the end user that the data he/she is shown on the display is the data that was measured by the Sensor.*

There exist several schemes that can be used to secure a communication channel and provide data origin authenticity for a message during transfer over the network, such as digital signature schemes or message authentication codes (MACs). However, whatever mechanism is used, the user, a human being, cannot validate a digital signature or MAC, this has to be done by the Display node. Therefore it is the Display node that can be assured of the authenticity and not the user. Further what can actually be provided when applying these mechanisms to our use case is that each time the Display node receives some data and verifies the signature or MAC, it can be sure that the signature or MAC was generated by the Sensor. Yet, this assurance does not extend to the action of measuring the data, the Sensor can very well sign data different to the one that it has measured. Also, it is the action of showing the data that is relevant for the user, not the action in which the Display node receives and verifies it (the Display might show data different to the one received).

In order to capture this situation and simplify the example, we abstract the Sensor actions of signing and sending the data to a sending action, the Display actions of receiving and verifying the data to a receiving action, but keep the measuring and displaying actions, respectively, separate. The property provided by a digital signature or MAC can then be expressed as follows:

P1 *It is authentic for the Display node that the data received is the data that was sent by the Sensor.*

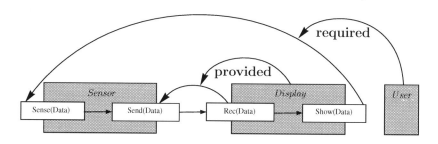

Fig. 2. Discrepancy between required and provided property

The discrepancy between property P0 we want the system to provide and property P1 that is actually provided by a digital signature or MAC is illustrated in Figure 2. For achieving P0 we need the system to provide more properties: In order for the Display to "extend" the authenticity of the send action by the Sensor node to the actual measuring action, the Display must trust the Sensor that it only sends data it has measured. Further, the user must trust the Display to show only what it has received and verified. Hence we need a concept of trust that allows to relate agents to the system properties they trust in and that enables formal reasoning about these properties.

An agent trusts in a property to hold in a system if in *its conception* of the system this property is fulfilled.

In the next section we give a brief introduction of those parts of the Security Modelling Framework SeMF that are the basis for the notion of trust presented in this paper. We then explain the concept of a property being fulfilled in an agent's conception of a system, the basis for our definition of trust.

5   The Security Modeling Framework SeMF

The behaviour B of a discrete system S can be formally described by the set of its possible sequences of actions (traces). Therefore $B \subseteq \Sigma^*$ holds, here Σ (called the alphabet) is the set of all actions of the system, Σ^* is the set of all finite sequences (called words) of elements of Σ, including the empty sequence denoted by ε, and subsets of Σ^* are called formal languages. Words can be composed: if u and v are words, then uv is also a word. For a word $x \in \Sigma^*$, we denote the set of actions of x by $alph(x)$. For more details on the theory of formal languages we refer the reader to [14].

We further extend the system specification by two components: *agents' initial knowledges* about the global system behaviour and *agents' local views*. The initial knowledge $W_P \subseteq \Sigma^*$ of agent P about the system consists of all traces P initially considers possible, i.e. all traces that do not violate any of P's assumptions about the system. Every trace that is not explicitly forbidden can happen in the system. An agent P may assume for example that a message that was received must have been sent before. Thus the agent's W_P will contain only those sequences of actions in which a message is first sent and then received. Further we can assume $B \subseteq W_P$, as reasoning within SeMF primarily targets the validation and verification of security properties in terms of positive formulations, i.e. assurances the agents of the system may have. Other approaches that deal with malfunction, misassumptions and attacker models could not rely on this assumption.

In a running system P can learn from actions that have occurred. Satisfaction of security properties obviously also depends on what agents are able to learn. After a sequence of actions $\omega \in B$ has happened, every agent P can use its *local view* λ_P of ω to determine the sequences of actions it considers to have possibly happened. Examples of an agent's local view are that an agent can see only its own actions, or that an agent P can see that an action $send(sender, message)$ occurred but cannot see the message, in which case $\lambda_P(send(sender, message))$ $= send(sender)$.

For a sequence of actions $\omega \in B$ and agent $P \in \mathbb{P}$ ($\mathbb{P}$ denoting the set of all agents), $\lambda_P^{-1}(\lambda_P(\omega)) \subseteq \Sigma^*$ is the set of all sequences that look exactly the same from P's local view after ω has happened. Depending on its knowledge about the system S, underlying security mechanisms and system assumptions, P does not consider all sequences in $\lambda_P^{-1}(\lambda_P(\omega))$ possible. Thus it can use its initial knowledge to reduce this set: $\lambda_P^{-1}(\lambda_P(\omega)) \cap W_P$ describes all sequences of actions P considers to have possibly happened when ω has happened.

Security properties can now be defined in terms of the agents' initial knowledges and local views. In [1] we have introduced a variety of definitions of security properties (e.g. authenticity, proof of authenticity, confidentiality). Our concept of trust introduced in the next section applies to all of them, however, we will use our notion of authenticity as a demonstrating example.

We call a particular action a authentic for an agent P if in all sequences that P considers to have possibly happened after a sequence of actions ω has happened, some time in the past a must have happened. By extending this definition to a set of actions Γ being authentic for P if one of the actions in Γ is authentic for P we gain the flexibility that P does not necessarily need to know all parameters of the authentic action. For example, a message may consist of one part protected by a digital signature and another irrelevant part without protection. Then, the recipient can know that the signer has authentically sent a message containing the signature, but the rest of the message is not authentic. Therefore, in this case, Γ comprises all messages containing the relevant signature and arbitrary other message parts.

Definition 1. *A set of actions $\Gamma \subseteq \Sigma$ is authentic for $P \in \mathbb{P}$ after a sequence of actions $\omega \in B$ with respect to W_P if $alph(x) \cap \Gamma \neq \emptyset$ for all $x \in \lambda_P^{-1}(\lambda_P(\omega)) \cap W_P$.*

We define the following instantiation of this property that states that whenever an action b has happened in a sequence of actions ω, it must be authentic for agent P that action a has happened as well. Note that in most cases, action b is in P's local view.

Definition 2. *For a system S with behaviour $B \subseteq \Sigma^*$, agent $P \subseteq \mathbb{P}$, and actions $a, b \in \Sigma$, $auth(a, b, P)$ holds in B if for all $\omega \in B$, whenever $b \in alph(\omega)$, the action a is authentic for P.*

The precedence of actions is a weaker property:

Definition 3. *For a system S with behaviour $B \subseteq \Sigma^*$ and actions $a, b \in \Sigma$, $precede(a, b)$ holds in S if for all $\omega \in B$ with $b \in alph(\omega)$ it follows that $a \in alph(\omega)$.*

6   A Formal Definition of Trust

In the previous section we have presented several factors that are important regarding security properties holding or not holding in a system. Accordingly we include these in the formal definition of a system as follows:

Definition 4 (System). *A system $S = (\Sigma, \mathbb{P}, B, \mathbb{W}, \mathbb{V})$ consists of a set $\mathbb{P}$ of agents acting in the system, a language $B \subseteq \Sigma^*$ over an alphabet of actions Σ describing the system behaviour in terms of sequences of actions, a set $\mathbb{V} = \{\lambda_X : \Sigma^* \to (\Sigma_X)^* | X \in \mathbb{P}\}$ of agents' local views, and a set $\mathbb{W} = \{W_X \subseteq \Sigma^* | X \in \mathbb{P}\}$ of agents' initial knowledges.*

Here $(\Sigma_X)^*$ denotes the image of the homomorphism λ_X which has to be individually specified for each system. Which part of an action an agent can see depends on the specific system to specify and can contain any part of it, as indicated in the previous section.

An agent P's conception and understanding of a system S, denoted by S_P, may defer from the actual system. P may not know all about the system's behaviour, thus from P's point of view the system's behaviour consists of P's initial knowledge W_P. Further, P may not have all information with respect to the other agents' initial knowledges and local views, so P's conception of agents' initial knowledges (W_{XP}) and local views (λ_{XP}) may defer from the actual initial knowledges and local views of the system S. This motivates the following definition.

Definition 5 (Trusted System). *Agent P's conception of system S is defined by $S_P = (\Sigma, \mathbb{P}, W_P, \mathbb{W}_P, \mathbb{V}_P)$. Σ and $\mathbb{P}$ are the alphabet and set of agents, respectively, of both S and S_P, whereas P's initial knowledge (conception) $W_P \subseteq \Sigma^*$ of system behaviour B constitutes the behaviour of S_P. It further contains a set $\mathbb{V}_P = \{\lambda_{XP} : \Sigma^* \to (\Sigma_{XP})^* | X \in \mathbb{P}\}$ of agent P's conception of agents' local views of S, and a set $\mathbb{W}_P = \{W_{XP} \subseteq \Sigma^* | X \in \mathbb{P}\}$ of agent P's conception of agents' initial knowledges in S. We say that P trusts in system S_P (since it represents P's knowledge about system S).*

The definition of an agent's trusted system gives rise now to the definition of an agent's *trust in a property* holding in a system:

Definition 6 (Trusted Property). *Let* prop *be any property that refers to a system as defined in Definition 4. An agent $P \in \mathbb{P}$ trusts in* prop *to hold in a system S, denoted by* trust(P, prop), *iff* prop *is fulfilled in S_P.*

This notion of trust follows naturally from the different aspects that constitute the model of a system. If a property holds in the system as P perceives it (i.e. in S_P), then from P's point of view the property holds, i.e. P trusts in the property to hold in S. Further our notion of trust allows to specify precisely what it is an agent trusts in. An agent may have trust in one property but not in another. Of course, trust itself is a property of a system as well. Therefore the trust concept allows to model arbitrarily long trust chains such that e.g. the trust of an agent in another agent's trust in a property can be expressed.

6.1   Implications between Properties

In this section we present and prove specific implications of security and trust properties of SeMF that will then be used to reason about properties provided by the example system when introducing certain security mechanisms.

We use the following Assumption 1 to model that agents do not falsely exclude behaviour that can actually happen in the system. The correctness of this assumption must be verified during the formalization of a real system as a SeMF system model, violations identify flaws of the real system's design. Assumption 1 further models the fact that an agent P cannot assign an agent Q more knowledge about a system's behaviour than P itself knows about it. Note that the more an agent knows the smaller its initial knowledge.

Assumption 1 *In general the behaviour of a system is included in all agents' initial knowledge (see Section 5). Hence $B \subseteq W_P$, $W_P \subseteq W_{QP}$, etc.*

It is easy to show that Assumption 1 implies the following Lemma:

Lemma 1. *Let S be a system as defined in Definition 4 with behaviour B, $P \in \mathbb{P}$ an agent, λ_P this agent's local view, and $W_P \supseteq B$ this agent's initial knowledge. Then for all $\omega \in B$ holds $\omega \in \lambda_P^{-1}(\lambda_P(\omega)) \cap W_P$.*

The next Theorem explains that authenticity is a stronger property than precede. This is due to the fact that *precede* is defined on the system behaviour B, while *auth* is defined taking into account an agent's local view and initial knowledge of a system which can result in a bigger set of sequences of actions.

Theorem 1. *For a system S as defined in Definition 4, actions $a, b \in \Sigma$, and agent $P \in \mathbb{P}$, $auth(a, b, P)$ holding in S implies that $precede(a, b)$ holds in S.*

Proof. *Let S be a system as defined in Definition 4 with behaviour B, $a, b \in \Sigma$, $P \in \mathbb{P}$, and let $auth(a, b, P)$ hold in S. Let us assume that $precede(a, b)$ does not hold in S. Then there is $\omega \in B$ with $b \in alph(\omega)$ and $a \notin alph(\omega)$. $b \in alph(\omega)$ and $auth(a, b, P)$ holding in S imply that $a \in alph(x)$ for all $x \in \lambda_P^{-1}(\lambda_P(\omega)) \cap W_P$. Since by Lemma 1 ω is one of the elements of $\lambda_P^{-1}(\lambda_P(\omega)) \cap W_P$, it immediately follows that $a \in alph(\omega)$, a contradiction to the assumption. Hence $precede(a, b)$ holds in S.*

Corollary 1. *For a system S, actions $a, b \in \Sigma$ and agents $P, Q \in \mathbb{P}$, $trust(P, auth(a, b, Q))$ holding in S implies that $trust(P, precede(a, b))$ holds in S.*

Proof. *The assertion follows immediately from Theorem 1. Since $auth(a, b, P)$ implies $precede(a, b)$ in all systems, this implication holds in particular in the system S_P.*

The next Theorem shows that the authenticity of an action for an agent can be extended to a preceding action if the agent trusts in the precedence.

Theorem 2. *For a system S as defined in Definition 4, actions $a, b, c \in \Sigma$ and an agent $P \in \mathbb{P}$, $auth(b, c, P)$ and $trust(P, precede(a, b))$ holding in S implies that $auth(a, c, P)$ holds in S.*

Proof. *Let S be a system as defined in Definition 4, $a, b, c \in \Sigma$, $P \in \mathbb{P}$, and let $auth(b, c, P)$ hold in S. Then for all $\omega \in B$, if $c \in alph(\omega)$ then $b \in alph(x)$ for all $x \in \lambda_P^{-1}(\lambda_P(\omega)) \cap W_P$. Further, $trust(P, precede(a, b))$ holding in S means that for all $y \in W_P$, if $b \in alph(y)$ then $a \in alph(y)$. As $\lambda_P^{-1}(\lambda_P(\omega)) \cap W_P \subseteq W_P$, $a \in alph(x)$ in particular for all $x \in \lambda_P^{-1}(\lambda_P(\omega)) \cap W_P$. Hence $auth(a, c, P)$ holds in S.*

Corollary 2. *For a system S, actions $a, b, c \in \Sigma$, and agents $P, Q \in \mathbb{P}$, $trust(Q, auth(b, c, P)) \wedge trust(Q, trust(P, precede(a, b)))$ holding in S implies that $trust(Q, auth(a, c, P))$ holds in S.*

Proof. *Analogously to the proof of Corollary 1, we use the fact that Theorem 2 applies to all systems, hence in particular to S_Q.*

Lemma 2. *For a system S as defined in Definition 4 and actions $a, b, c \in \Sigma$, $precede(a, b)$ and $precede(b, c)$ implies that $precede(a, c)$ holds in S.*

Proof. *Let S be a system as defined in Definition 4, $a, b, c \in \Sigma$. $precede(b, c)$ holding in S means that for all $\omega \in B$, if $c \in alph(\omega)$ then $b \in alph(\omega)$. Further, $precede(a, b)$ holding in S means that for all $\omega \in B$, if $b \in alph(\omega)$ then $a \in alph(\omega)$. This concludes that if $c \in alph(\omega)$ then $a \in alph(\omega)$ for all $\omega \in B$.*

Theorem 3. *For a system S and an agent $P \in \mathbb{P}$, $trust(P, precede(a, b) \wedge precede(b, c))$ holding in S implies that $trust(P, precede(a, c))$ holds in S.*

Proof. *Analogously to the proof of Corollary 1, we apply Lemma 2 to the system S_P.*

In the next section we will apply the notion of trust and the above theorems to the example introduced in Section 4, and, by doing so, identify trust assumptions that need to hold in order for the system to provide certain security properties.

7   The Example Formally

We now specify our example system formally. It has three agents, so $\mathbb{P} = \{Sensor, Display, User\}$. The set Σ of actions consists of $Sensor\text{-}sense(data)$, $Sensor\text{-}send(data)$, $Display\text{-}rec(data)$, $Display\text{-}show(data)$ and we assume that the parameter $data$ can have different values, e.g. $warm$ and $cold$. This is a very abstract formalization of the system's actions chosen simply to facilitate understanding. Our formalism works equally well with other notational conventions, e.g. $(actionname, par_1, \ldots, par_k)$. Our formal model of the system needs to satisfy Assumption 1, in particular W_{User} must be a subset of $W_{User\,Display}$. As for our abstract system we simply assume equality. Further, agents' initial knowledges and local views must comply with the mechanisms and resulting properties discussed below. However, for our purposes we do not need to specify concrete initial knowledges of agents, and regarding the agents' local views it is sufficient to specify that the user's local view keeps the action $Display\text{-}show(data)$ and maps all other actions onto the empty word, that is, the user can only see the data that is displayed to him/her. As to the other agents we simply assume them to be able to see only their own actions.

Figure 3 illustrates the requirement we have for the example system.

Using Definition 2, this requirement informally derived in Section 4 can be formally stated as follows:

$$auth(Sensor\text{-}sense(data), Display\text{-}show(data), User) \qquad \text{(P0)}$$

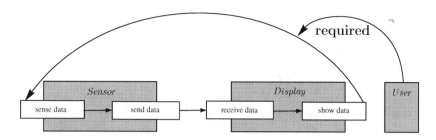

Fig. 3. Security Requirement

Note that we do not discuss here the quality of the data sensed by the Sensor, i.e. the question of how near it represents reality (although our framework allows to model this as well).

As explained in Section 4, a digital signature scheme (Sig) or message authentication code (MAC) can only establish a relation between signing/sending and receiving/verifying the data. Hence the property P1 informally stated in Section 4 can be formalized as follows:

$$auth(Sensor\text{-}send(data), Display\text{-}rec(data), Display) \tag{1}$$

As stated before, in order for the Display node to extend the authenticity of the sending action to the actual measuring action of the Sensor, the Display must trust the Sensor that it works correctly and only sends data that it has measured. As explained in Section 1, this type of trust in the correct functioning of a device can e.g. be achieved by trusted computing functionality. This involves a Trusted Platform Module (TPM) to be integrated in the Sensor that measures and signs the configuration of the Sensor, using a signature key certified by a trusted authority. The details of the very complex behaviour of a TPM are not the topic of this paper, thus we refer the reader to [15]. Using trusted computing functionality, the resulting property can be formally stated as follows:

$$trust(Display, precede(Sensor\text{-}sense(data), Sensor\text{-}send(data))) \tag{2}$$

The resulting security properties are illustrated in Figure 4.

However, as already explained, the stakeholder that requires the information to be authentic is the user rather than the Display. Thus the user has to trust in the correct functioning of the Display node. This means on the one hand that the user has to trust in that the Display node establishes its own trust into the correct functioning of the Sensor and verifies the Sensor's signature when receiving the message. This can be formalized as follows:

$$trust\big(User, trust(Display, precede(Sensor\text{-}sense(data), Sensor\text{-}send(data)))$$
$$\wedge auth(Sensor\text{-}send(data), Display\text{-}rec(data), Display)\big) \tag{3}$$

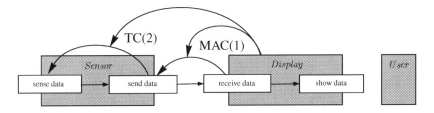

Fig. 4. Security Properties regarding the Display

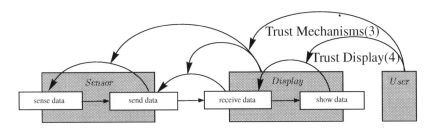

Fig. 5. Security Properties regarding the user

On the other hand, the user's trust in the correct functioning of the Display includes trust in the Display only showing data it has received. This can be captured with the following formalization:

$$trust(User, precede(Display\text{-}rec(data), Display\text{-}show(data)))$$ (4)

We do not discuss here possible mechanisms that can ensure that properties 3 and 4 hold. However, in a concrete security engineering process all properties that are assumed to hold must be substantiated and evaluated e.g. by risk analysis techniques. The above two properties are illustrated in Figure 5.

Finally, as explained at the beginning of this section, the User's local view keeps the action *Display-show*, i.e. the data being shown on the Display is visible to the user. This results in the following property:

$$auth(Display\text{-}show(data), Display\text{-}show(data), User)$$ (5)

7.1   Reasoning with Trust

In the previous section we have discussed various mechanisms and introduced the security properties provided by these mechanisms. In this section we will use the Theorems introduced in Section 6 to prove that these properties result in property P0 required to hold for our example system.

Starting from Property (3) that describes the user's trust into the trusted computing and MAC mechanisms, we can apply Corollary 2 and derive the following property:

$$trust(User, auth(Sensor\text{-}sense(data), Display\text{-}rec(data), Display)) \qquad (6)$$

Applying Corollary 1 we can conclude:

$$trust(User, precede(Sensor\text{-}sense(data), Display\text{-}rec(data))) \qquad (7)$$

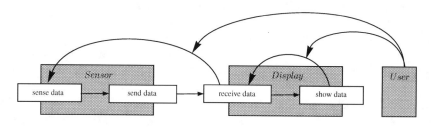

Fig. 6. Intermediate Proof Step

This intermediate step (7) together with Property 4 is illustrated in Figure 6. Theorem 3 allows to combine these to:

$$trust(User, precede(Sensor\text{-}sense(data), Display\text{-}show(data))) \qquad (8)$$

Finally the application of Theorem 2 to Properties (5) and (8) implies

$$auth(Sensor\text{-}sense(data), Display\text{-}show(data), User) \qquad (9)$$

The resulting security property is illustrated in Figure 7.

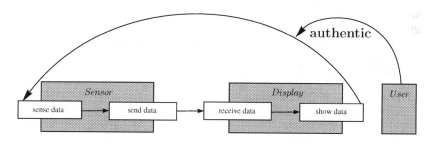

Fig. 7. Result

This proves that the User can be assured that the data displayed is the same that was measured by the Sensor before. Our proof is based on two important aspects: the properties we assume the system to provide, substantiated by security mechanisms we assume the system to use, and the relations between these properties that we have proven to hold. This proof constitutes only one way to achieve this result, there are other ways that use different relations between properties which will be introduced in forthcoming papers.

8   Conclusions and Future Work

In this paper we have presented a formal definition of trust which reflects a simple understanding of the concept: An agent trusts in a specific property to hold in a system if it holds in its conception of the system. By integrating this formal trust concept into the SeMF Security Modeling Framework we have proven some relations between trust and specific authenticity properties. Using these we have exemplarily proven that an agent's wide-spanning authenticity property that can not be provided by current security mechanisms can be refined towards security properties that are provided by applicable security mechanisms. The refinement introduces other agents and makes use of trust relations between them. This process can be continued by substantiating certain trust assumptions through introducing further security mechanisms. Our approach has several advantages: It allows to formally prove certain security properties to hold in a system, and it extracts those trust assumptions that need to be substantiated by means beyond our formal framework (such as legal contracts). It further supports traceability: It allows to precisely identify the security properties that may be violated if a specific security mechanism is removed from the system (e.g. if the generation of a digital signature is removed because it turns out to be too slow) or if a trust assumption regarding an agent's behaviour is violated. The notion of trust is irrespective of underlying trust and security mechanisms. This makes it useful for risk analysis and management with respect to the comparison of different implementations.

We are still at the beginning of our work. Transitivity of trust for example can not be assumed to hold in general, sufficient conditions have to be found. More theorems relating trust in e.g. confidentiality, authenticity, and non-repudiation will allow to capture a wider variety of security mechanisms substantiating trust. A further interesting topic is to find conditions under which abstractions preserve certain trust properties. The aim of our work is to enable a security engineering process that takes as input a high level security property and provides as result a set of conditions to implement this property and the identification of the assumptions that need to hold.

References

1. Gürgens, S., Ochsenschläger, P., Rudolph, C.: On a formal framework for security properties. International Computer Standards & Interface Journal (CSI), Special issue on formal methods, techniques and tools for secure and reliable applications 27(5), 457–466 (2005)
2. Trusted Computing Group: TCG TPM Specification 1.2 revision 103 (2006), http://www.trustedcomputing.org
3. Muskens, J., Alonso, R., Yhang, Z., Egelink, K., Larranaga, A., Gouder, A.: Trust4All Trust Framework and Mechanisms. ITEA Trust4All (2005)
4. Jøsang, A., Ismail, R., Boyd, C.: A survey of trust and reputation systems for online service provision. Decision Support Systems 43(2), 618–644 (2007)
5. McKnight, D., Chervany, N.: The Meanings of Trust. Technical report, University of Minnesota, Management Information Systems Reseach Center (1996)

6. Grandison, T., Sloman, M.: A survey of trust in internet applications. IEEE Communications Surveys and Tutorials 3(4), 2–16 (2000)
7. Carbone, M., Nielsen, M., Sassone, V.: A formal model for trust in dynamic networks, pp. 54–61 (2003) RS-03-4
8. Demolombe, R.: Reasoning about trust: A formal logical framework. In: Jensen, C., Poslad, S., Dimitrakos, T. (eds.) iTrust 2004. LNCS, vol. 2995, pp. 291–303. Springer, Heidelberg (2004)
9. Burrows, M., Abadi, M., Needham, R.: A Logic of Authentication. ACM Transactions on Computer Systems 8 (1990)
10. Syverson, P., van Oorschot, P.: On unifying some cryptographic protocol logics. In: IEEE Symposium on Security and Privacy, May 1994, pp. 14–28 (1994)
11. Abadi, M., Tuttle, M.: A Semantics for a Logic of Authentication. In: Tenth Annual ACM Symposium on Principles of Distributed Computing, Montreal, Canada, August 1991, pp. 201–216 (1991)
12. Gong, L., Needham, R., Yahalom, R.: Reasoning about Belief in Cryptographic Protocols. In: Proceedings of the 1990 IEEE Symposium on Research in Security and Privacy, pp. 234–248. IEEE Press, Los Alamitos (1990)
13. Gürgens, S.: SG Logic – A formal analysis technique for authentication protocols. In: Li, M. (ed.) ALT 1997. LNCS, vol. 1316, pp. 159–176. Springer, Heidelberg (1997)
14. Eilenberg, S.: Automata, Languages and Machines. Academic Press, New York (1974)
15. Mitchell, C., et al.: Trusted Computing. Institution of Engineering and Technology (2005)

Leveraging a Social Network of Trust for Promoting Honesty in E-Marketplaces

Jie Zhang[1], Robin Cohen[2], and Kate Larson[2]

[1] School of Computer Engineering, Nanyang Technological University, Singapore
[2] School of Computer Science, University of Waterloo, Canada
zhangj@ntu.edu.sg

Abstract. In this paper, we examine a trust-based framework for promoting honesty in e-marketplaces that relies on buyers forming social networks to share reputation ratings of sellers and sellers rewarding the buyers that are most respected within their social networks. We explore how sellers reason about expected future profit when offering particular rewards for buyers. We theoretically prove that in a marketplace operating with our mechanism: i) buyers will be better off honestly reporting seller ratings and ii) sellers are better off being honest, to earn better profit. Experiments confirm the robustness of the approach, in dynamically changing environments. With rational agents preferring to be honest, the buyer and seller strategies as specified constitute an effective approach for the design of e-marketplaces.

1 Introduction

Artificial intelligence researchers have proposed the use of intelligent agents to act on behalf of buyers and of sellers, in electronic marketplaces. These agents are capable of learning over time the behavior of their business partners, to enable each party to make effective decisions about which parties they wish to do business with, in the future. One approach that has received much attention is to have buying agents model the trustworthiness of selling agents, making use of ratings of sellers provided by other buyers in the marketplace; this is of particular benefit when buyers do not have much personal experience with the sellers. However, the important problem where buyers may provide unfair ratings to bad-mouth some sellers or promote some other sellers has to be addressed [1].

In our previous work [2], trust modeling was promoted as an important avenue for creating incentives for buyer and seller honesty in the marketplace. In this approach, buying agents make use of a neighborhood of other buying agents (known as advisors) to provide seller ratings and sellers are inclined to act honestly, because they are being modeled. But sellers also offer better rewards to buyers that belong to many neighborhoods in the marketplace, a feature motivated by the work of Gintis et al. [3] which argues that altruism in one context signals "quality" that is rewarded by increased opportunities in other contexts. Experimental evidence was presented to demonstrate that a framework like this

M. Nishigaki et al. (Eds.): IFIPTM 2010, IFIP AICT 321, pp. 216–231, 2010.

promotes honesty in reporting seller ratings, from buyers, and honesty in delivering goods as promised, by sellers.

In this paper, we begin with the model of [2], where buyers use a social network to model sellers and sellers model buyers to offer varying rewards. We then explore how sellers can reason about expected future profit, starting from refined formulae for reasoning about immediate profit. As a result, we are able to provide a specification for seller bidding behavior and for offering rewards to buyers based on their reputation. We also emphasize the importance for buyers to adopt a strategy to limit the number of sellers that are considered for each good to be purchased. Most importantly, we theoretically prove that both rational buyers and rational sellers are incentivized to behave honestly in our mechanism, in so doing providing definitive validation of the effectiveness of our proposal.

We then present a series of experimental results to provide additional detail on marketplace trends that demonstrate the value of our newly designed incentive mechanism, conducted in a simulated environment where buyers and sellers may be deceptive and they may be arriving and departing. This provides a stronger endorsement of the mechanism as one that is robust to important conditions in the marketplace. In addition, we validate the benefit of our specific proposal for the seller bidding strategy and for the buyer strategy of limiting the sellers being considered, clearly showing the gains in profit enjoyed by both sellers and buyers when our mechanism is introduced and our proposed strategies are followed.

2   System Overview

The electronic marketplace environment we are modeling is populated with self-interested buying and selling agents. Our incentive mechanism is generally applicable to any marketplace where sellers may alter quality and price of their products to satisfy buyers. For the remainder of this paper, we discuss the scenario where the buyers and sellers are brought together by a procurement (reverse) auction, where the auctioneer is a buyer and bidders are sellers. There is a central server that runs the auction.

In our system, a buyer that wants to purchase a product sends a request to the central server. This request indicates not only the product but also the buyer's evaluation criteria for the product (discussed in more detail in the following section). Sellers interested in selling the product to the buyer will register to participate in the auction.

The buyer will first limit the sellers it will consider for the auction, by modeling their trustworthiness. This is achieved by having the central server retain for each buyer a neighborhood of trusted other buyers, which will be asked to provide ratings of the sellers under consideration. The buyer will then convey to the central server which sellers it is willing to consider, and the pool of possible sellers is thus reduced.

Sellers allowed to participate in the auction will submit their bids and the buyer will select the winner of the auction as the seller whose product (described in its bid) gives the largest profit, based on the buyer's evaluation criteria.

In order to formulate their bids, sellers model the reputation of buyers and make more attractive offers to more reputable buyers. A buyer's reputation is based on the number of other buyers considering this buyer as their neighbor (as well as the trust these other buyers place on this buyer, and the reputation of these other buyers). The reputation of each buyer is maintained by the central server and released to the sellers.

Once a buyer has selected the winning seller, it pays that seller the amount indicated in the bid. The winning seller is supposed to deliver the product to the buyer. However, it may decide to alter the quality of the product or to not deliver the product at all. The buyer will report the result of conducting business with the seller to the central server, registering a rating for the seller. It is precisely these ratings of the seller that can then be shared with those buyers that consider this buyer as their neighbor.

In summary: the central server runs the auction and maintains information that is shared with sellers and buyers; buyers announce their intention to purchase products, consult with neighbors, choose a winning seller and report a final rating for the seller; sellers bid to win the sale to the buyer, consider buyer reputation in formulating their bids and then decide what product to deliver to the buyer (if at all).

3   Strategic Behavior Analysis

In this section, we propose and analyze the strategies that buyers and sellers in our mechanism should use. We also theoretically prove that these strategies will promote buyer and seller honesty.

3.1   Seller Strategy to Promote Buyer Honesty

We first present a seller's optimal strategy when sellers only take into account their instant profit. We then derive an equilibrium bidding strategy for sellers when they also take into account their expected future gain, in a simplified scenario where all sellers have the same productivity. We then remove the simplifying assumption and show that with this bidding structure, sellers are better off providing rewards to more reputable buyers and that buyers are better off participating in the social network and providing honest ratings of sellers.

Seller Strategy. We discuss our mechanism in the context of the Request For Quote (RFQ) system [4]. Building on the incentive mechanism outlined in [2], we consider a scenario where a buyer b wants to buy a product p. The buyer specifies its evaluation criteria for a set of non-price features $\{f_1, f_2, ..., f_n\}$, as well as a set of weights $\{w_1, w_2, ..., w_n\}$ that correspond to each non-price feature. Each weight represents how much its corresponding non-price feature is worth. A higher weight for a non-price feature implies that the buyer cares more about the feature. The buyer also provides information in its evaluation criteria about the conversion from descriptive non-price feature values to numeric values (for example, a 3-year warranty is converted to the numeric value of 10 on a scale of 1 to 10)[1]. We define the function $\tau()$ to denote such a conversion. Sellers $\{s_1, s_2, ..., s_m\}$ ($m \geq 1$) allowed to join the auction are able to know the buyer's values of their products, formalized as follows:

$$V_b = \sum_{j=1}^{n} w_j \tau(f_j) \tag{1}$$

Sellers will then need to formulate their bids, reflecting what they promise to deliver (e.g. a delivery time of 1 week). An honest seller is one that honors its promise.

As in the mechanism of [2], a seller s_i ($1 \leq i \leq m$) sets the price and values for the non-price features of the product p, depending on how much instant profit it can earn from selling p to the buyer b. The instant profit is the profit earned by the seller from the current transaction if it wins the auction. The seller's instant profit is defined as follows:

$$U_{s_i} = P_{s_i} - C_{s_i} \tag{2}$$

where P_{s_i} is the price of the product set by the seller s_i and C_{s_i} is the cost for the seller to produce the product p with certain values for the non-price features in its bid. The seller s_i will try to gain profit from the transaction. It is reasonable to assume that $P_{s_i} \geq C_{s_i}$.

The elements above are introduced in the mechanism of [2]. We now extend the treatment, to express more precisely the profit to be gained by the buyer and the seller, to then discuss the kind of gains that sellers can reason about and the kind of bids they should offer to buyers (and to demonstrate how honesty is thus promoted in the marketplace).

The profit gained by the buyer if it chooses to do business with the seller s_i can be formalized as follows:

$$U_b = V_b - P_{s_i} \tag{3}$$

The buyer's profit is also called the seller's "surplus offer", denoted as O_{s_i}. The seller's "realized surplus" is typically calculated as the sum of the buyer's and the seller's profit:

$$S_{s_i} = V_b - C_{s_i} \tag{4}$$

Note that the seller's realized surplus is higher when its cost C_{s_i} is lower. We also define the cumulative distribution function for S_{s_i} (over all sellers) as $F()$ and the support of $F()$ is $[S_L, S_H]$. We assume $S_L \geq 0$ to ensure that the value of a seller's product always exceeds its cost.

The seller whose surplus offer is the highest will win the auction. The RFQ auction then becomes a first-price sealed auction where a bidder's bids are not seen by others and the bidder with the highest bid (surplus offer) wins the

---

[1] In this paper, we focus on non-price features that are still objective - e.g. delivery time. Handling subjective features is left for future work.

auction. As argued in [4], a symmetric Bayes-Nash equilibrium surplus offer function can be derived as follows:

$$O_{s_i}^* = S_{s_i} - \frac{\int_{S_L}^{S_{s_i}} [F(x)]^{m-1} dx}{[F(S_{s_i})]^{m-1}} \tag{5}$$

where m is the number of bidders. Recall that O_{s_i} is the same as U_b. From Equations 3, 4 and 5, the equilibrium bidding function for the seller can then be derived as follows:

$$P_{s_i}^* = C_{s_i} + \frac{\int_{S_L}^{S_{s_i}} [F(x)]^{m-1} dx}{[F(S_{s_i})]^{m-1}} \tag{6}$$

The seller in our mechanism also reasons about the expected future gain from winning the current auction. It takes into account the reputation of buyer b. In our mechanism, each buyer in the marketplace has a fixed number of neighbors that the buyer trusts and from which it can ask advice about sellers. This forms a social network of buyers where there is a directed link (edge) from a buyer to its neighbors. The edges are assigned weights $\in (0, 1]$ representing how much a buyer trusts its neighbors modeled using the approach that will be described in Section 3.2. A buyer becomes reputable if based on its reports about sellers it is accepted into the neighborhood of many other buyers. Cooperating with reputable buyers will allow the seller to build its own reputation and to be known as a trustworthy seller by many buyers in the marketplace. It will then be able to obtain more opportunities for doing business with buyers and to gain more profit in the future. We next provide formulae for the seller's reasoning about its expected future gain and prove that the expected future gain the seller s_i can earn after doing good business increases with the reputation of buyer b.

We define the global reputation of buyer b (denoted as $R_b \in (0, 1]$) on the social network to be the network effect of the buyer, which represents how much this buyer influences other buyers' decisions on the entire network. According to [5], reputation should be calculated as the effect that this buyer has on other buyers it influences, multiplied by these other buyers' effect on the network. This is a recursive and fixed-point computation. We use the following formula to compute the reputation of the buyer:

$$\overline{R} = \overline{L}^T \cdot \overline{R} \tag{7}$$

where $\overline{R}$ is a vector containing each buyer's reputation. $\overline{L}$ is an asymmetric matrix of the normalized weights of edges between all two-buyer pairs. The weight between two buyers is 0 if there is no link between them. Therefore, $\overline{R}$ can be computed as the dominant eigenvector of $\overline{L}^2$.

If the seller cooperates with the buyer, the new satisfied encounter between the buyer and the seller will then increase the seller's trustworthiness. The seller's probability of being allowed to join the buyer's auctions in the future will be increased by some amount, $\triangle P_b$, where $\triangle P_b > 0$. Since this increment in probability is fairly small and relatively stable, we can assume that the probability

---

^{2} $\overline{R}$ can be recorded by the central server and shared with sellers.

of the seller being involved in auctions of other neighboring buyers increases linearly with how much these other buyers trust the current buyer b. The increase in probability of a seller being involved in every buyer's auctions across the network is $\triangle P_b R_b$.

If the seller is involved in a buyer's auction, the average probability of winning the auction is $\frac{1}{m}$, given that the number of bidders in the buyer's auction is m. The seller's average profit of being involved in a buyer's auction will then be $\frac{S_{s_i}}{m^2}$, which is the average probability of winning the auction multiplied by the average instant profit gained from winning the auction[3]. We use $E_{s_i}(R_b)$ to denote the amount of the seller's expected future gain and $n' > 0$ the number of expected purchases from buyers. The expected future profit $E_{s_i}(R_b)$ is then

$$E_{s_i}(R_b) = n'\frac{S_{s_i}}{m^2}\triangle P_b R_b \tag{8}$$

From Equation 8, we have the following inequality:

$$\frac{\partial[E_{s_i}(R_b)]}{\partial R_b} = \frac{\partial[n'\frac{S_{s_i}}{m^2}\triangle P_b R_b]}{\partial R_b} = n'\frac{S_{s_i}}{m^2}\triangle P_b \geq 0 \tag{9}$$

The expected future gain the seller s_i can earn increases with the reputation of the buyer b.

Let us first consider a simplified scenario where sellers $\{s_1, s_2, ..., s_m\}$ have the same productivity. They have the same cost for producing the products that are valued equally by the buyer. In other words, we make the following assumption that the distribution of S_{s_i}, $F()$ is a uniform distribution. Let us also assume that the seller's lowest realized surplus S_L for a transaction is 0. Equation 6 can then be simplified as follows:

$$P_{s_i}^* = C_{s_i} + \frac{\int_{S_L}^{S_{s_i}}[F(x)]^{m-1}dx}{[F(S_{s_i})]^{m-1}} = C_{s_i} + \frac{\int_0^{S_{s_i}}(\frac{x}{S_H})^{m-1}dx}{(\frac{S_{s_i}}{S_H})^{m-1}} = C_{s_i} + \frac{S_{s_i}}{m} \tag{10}$$

Since the seller's realized surplus is equal to the sum of the buyer and the seller's profit and the seller has expected future gain from winning the current auction, the seller's realized surplus S_{s_i} can then be changed as follows:

$$S_{s_i}' = U_b + U_{s_i} + \lambda E_{s_i}(R_b) = V_b - C_{s_i} + \lambda E_{s_i}(R_b) = S_{s_i} + \lambda E_{s_i}(R_b) \tag{11}$$

where $\lambda \in [0,1]$ is a discounting factor[4]. The lowest S_{s_i}' becomes $\lambda E_{s_i}(R_b)$ instead of zero and the upper bound of S_{s_i}' becomes $S_H + \lambda E_{s_i}(R_b)$. Accordingly, the symmetric Bayes-Nash equilibrium surplus offer function formalized in Equation 5 should be changed as follows[5]:

---

[3] The average instant profit is $\frac{S_{s_i}}{m}$, as shown in Equation 10.

[4] We suggest the inclusion of a discounting factor to allow sellers to learn over time the likelihood of receiving their expected future gain. The proofs that follow do not depend on its inclusion.

[5] We replace $E_{s_i}(R_b)$ by E_{s_i} for a more concise formulation.

$$O^*_{s_i} = S_{s_i} + \lambda E_{s_i} - \frac{\int_{\lambda E_{s_i}}^{S'_{s_i}} [F(x)]^{m-1} dx}{[F(S'_{s_i})]^{m-1}} \tag{12}$$

From Equations 3, 4 and 12, we then can derive the modified equilibrium bidding function for the seller as follows:

$$P^*_{s_i} = C_{s_i} - \lambda E_{s_i} + \frac{\int_{\lambda E_{s_i}}^{S'_{s_i}} [F(x)]^{m-1} dx}{[F(S'_{s_i})]^{m-1}} \tag{13}$$

$$= C_{s_i} - \lambda E_{s_i} + \frac{\int_{\lambda E_{s_i}}^{S_{s_i}+\lambda E_{s_i}} (\frac{x}{S_H})^{m-1} dx}{(\frac{S_{s_i}+\lambda E_{s_i}}{S_H})^{m-1}}$$

$$= C_{s_i} + \frac{S_{s_i}}{m} - \frac{1}{m}[\frac{(\lambda E_{s_i})^m}{(S_{s_i} + \lambda E_{s_i})^{m-1}} + (m-1)\lambda E_{s_i}]$$

Comparing Equation 10 with Equation 13, we can see that the seller should offer the buyer reward $D_{s_i}(R_b)$ as follows:

$$D_{s_i}(R_b) = \frac{1}{m}[\frac{(\lambda E_{s_i})^m}{(S_{s_i} + \lambda E_{s_i})^{m-1}} + (m-1)\lambda E_{s_i}] \tag{14}$$

The reward can be the decreased price of the product[6]. According to Equation 9, the seller's expected future gain $E_{s_i}(R_b)$ is a monotonically increasing function of R_b, the reputation of buyer b. We can then prove that the reward $D_{s_i}(R_b)$ offered to the buyer is also a monotonically increasing function of R_b, shown as follows:

$$\frac{\partial D_{s_i}}{\partial R_b} = \frac{\partial\{\frac{1}{m}[\frac{(\lambda E_{s_i})^m}{(S_{s_i}+\lambda E_{s_i})^{m-1}} + (m-1)\lambda E_{s_i}]\}}{\partial R_b} \tag{15}$$

$$= \frac{1}{m}[\frac{\partial \frac{(\lambda E_{s_i})^m}{(S_{s_i}+\lambda E_{s_i})^{m-1}}}{\partial(\lambda E_{s_i})} \lambda\frac{\partial E_{s_i}}{\partial R_b} + (m-1)\lambda\frac{\partial E_{s_i}}{\partial R_b}]$$

$$= \frac{\lambda}{m}[\frac{m(\lambda E_{s_i})^{m-1}}{(S_{s_i} + \lambda E_{s_i})^{m-1}} - \frac{(m-1)(\lambda E_{s_i})^m}{(S_{s_i} + \lambda E_{s_i})^m} + m - 1]\frac{\partial E_{s_i}}{\partial R_b}$$

$$\approx \{\frac{m(\lambda E_{s_i})^{m-1}}{(S_{s_i} + \lambda E_{s_i})^{m-1}} + (m-1)[1 - (\frac{\lambda E_{s_i}}{S_{s_i} + \lambda E_{s_i}})^m]\}\frac{\partial E_{s_i}}{\partial R_b} > 0$$

We have now proved the following proposition:

Proposition 1. *Sellers are better off providing better rewards to reputable buyers in the case where all sellers have the same productivity.*

The above analysis depends on the simplified assumption that sellers have the same productivity. We can generalize this result by removing this assumption.

---

[6] According to Equation 3, if the bidding price is fixed, the reward can also be the increased values of the product offered to the buyer.

In this case, sellers may have different costs for producing the product with the same value of V_b. We first modify the seller's original equilibrium bidding function formalized in Equation 6 based on Equation 4, shown as follows:

$$P^*_{s_i} = V_b - S_{s_i} + \frac{\int_{S_L}^{S_{s_i}} [F(x)]^{m-1} dx}{[F(S_{s_i})]^{m-1}} \tag{16}$$

We then prove that the seller's original equilibrium bidding function is a monotonically decreasing function of S_{s_i}:

$$\frac{\partial P^*_{s_i}}{\partial S_{s_i}} = \frac{\partial \{ V_b - S_{s_i} + \frac{\int_{S_L}^{S_{s_i}} [F(x)]^{m-1} dx}{[F(S_{s_i})]^{m-1}} \}}{\partial S_{s_i}} \tag{17}$$

$$= \frac{\partial [\int_0^{S_{s_i}} F(x)^{m-1} dx]}{\partial S_{s_i}} \cdot \frac{1}{[F(S_{s_i})]^{m-1}} - \frac{\frac{\partial [F(S_{s_i})]^{m-1}}{\partial S_{s_i}} \int_0^{S_{s_i}} [F(x)]^{m-1} dx}{[F(S_{s_i})]^{2m-2}} - 1$$

$$= 1 - \frac{(m-1)\frac{\partial F(S_{s_i})}{\partial S_{s_i}} [F(S_{s_i})]^{m-2} \int_0^{S_{s_i}} [F(x)]^{m-1} dx}{[F(S_{s_i})]^{2m-2}} - 1$$

$$= -\frac{(m-1)\frac{\partial F(S_{s_i})}{\partial S_{s_i}}}{[F(S_{s_i})]^m} \int_0^{S_{s_i}} [F(x)]^{m-1} dx < 0$$

Based on Equation 9, we can see that the seller's modified realized surplus S'_{s_i} formalized in Equation 11 will also increase as R_b increases:

$$\frac{\partial S'_{s_i}}{\partial R_b} = \frac{\partial [S_{s_i} + \lambda E_{s_i}(R_b)]}{\partial R_b} = \lambda \frac{\partial [E_{s_i}(R_b)]}{\partial R_b} > 0 \tag{18}$$

Therefore, the following proposition holds:

Proposition 2. *The seller's equilibrium bidding function is a monotonically decreasing function of R_b, which indicates that the seller will give more reward $D_{s_i}(R_b)$ to the buyers that are considered as more reputable in the marketplace.*

Buyer Honesty. Here we prove the following proposition:

Proposition 3. *The seller strategy creates incentives for buyers to truthfully report the results of their business with sellers in order to become more reputable in the marketplace.*

From Equation 3, we first formalize the total profit gained by the buyer b from l times of doing business with sellers, shown as follows:

$$T_b = \sum_{k=1}^{l} U_{b,k} = \sum_{k=1}^{l} (V_{b,k} - P^*_{s_k}) \tag{19}$$

Based on Proposition 2 that a seller's equilibrium bidding function $P^*_{s_k}$ is a monotonically decreasing function of R_b, we then can prove that the buyer's total profit T_b will increase with the increase of its reputation R_b, as follows:

$$\frac{\partial T_b}{\partial R_b} = \frac{\partial[\sum^l_{k=1}(V_{b,k} - P^*_{s_k})]}{\partial R_b} = \sum^l_{k=1}\frac{\partial V_{b,k}}{\partial R_b} - \sum^l_{k=1}\frac{\partial P^*_{s_k}}{\partial R_b} = -\sum^l_{k=1}\frac{\partial P^*_{s_k}}{\partial R_b} > 0 \quad (20)$$

since $\frac{\partial P^*_{s_k}}{\partial R_b}$ is negative (and considering $V_{b,k}$ as independent of R_b). Therefore, in order to gain more total profit, it is better off for the buyer to maintain high reputation. This can be achieved by participating in the social network and honestly reporting the results of its business with sellers. The value of honest reporting is demonstrated as well in the experiments of Figures 1(a) and 4(a) in Section 4.

3.2   Buyer Strategy to Promote Seller Honesty

In this section, we present an effective strategy for buyers to choose their business partners. Buyers using this strategy are able to gain more profit, which is further validated by experimental results presented in Section 3.2. We also discuss how this strategy creates incentives for sellers to deliver what they promised in bids.

Buyer Strategy. To avoid doing business with possibly dishonest sellers, the buyer b in our mechanism first models the trustworthiness of sellers. Different existing approaches for modeling sellers' trustworthiness can be used here, for example the approach advocated by Zhang and Cohen [6] and the TRAVOS model proposed by Teacy et al. [7]. Both approaches propose to take into account the buyer's personal experience with the sellers as well as ratings of the sellers provided by other buyers. The buyer in our mechanism will allow only a number of the most trustworthy sellers to join the auction. Sellers about which the buyer b does not have information will also be allowed to join the auction with a small probability.

However, buyers may provide unfair ratings of sellers. Our mechanism allows the central server to maintain a fixed number of neighbors for each buyer: a list of the most trustworthy other buyers to this buyer, used to provide advice about sellers, in order to form a social network of buyers[7]. The trustworthiness of these other buyers then also needs to be modeled for periodically updating the buyer's neighbor list. In the experiments presented in Section 4, the approach of Zhang and Cohen [6] is used for this purpose. This approach allows the central server to model how trustworthy a buyer privately feels another buyer (advisor) to be based on their ratings (0 or 1) for commonly rated sellers (where, briefly, an advisor is trustworthy if its ratings of sellers within limited time windows agree with those of the buyer). When the buyer has limited private knowledge of the advisor, the public reputation of the advisor will also be considered, based

---

[7] Note for a new buyer, the central server randomly assigns to it some other buyers as its neighbors.

on all ratings for the sellers ever rated by the advisor held in the central server (where, briefly, an advisor is trustworthy if it consistently agrees with the ratings provided for sellers by others). Finally, the trustworthiness of the advisor will be modeled by combining the private and public values. The ones with the highest trustworthiness will be chosen by the central server to be the buyer's neighborhood; untrustworthy ones will therefore decrease their opportunities for rewards from sellers.

Seller Honesty. Our idea of allowing the buyer to limit the number of selected bidders in its auctions is supported by Kim's results demonstrated in [8]. Kim claims that public tendering could lead to quality reduction by bidders; in contrast, selective tendering depending on bidders' trustworthiness may avoid such difficulties. More specifically, Kim proves that by using a buyer strategy as described above (modeling the trustworthiness of sellers and limiting the number of sellers that are considered), dishonest sellers will not be able to gain more total profit than that gained by honest sellers. Suppose that a dishonest winning seller s decides not to deliver its promise in its bid submitted to the buyer b in the current auction. Also suppose that the seller's equilibrium bidding price is P_s and C_s is the cost for s to produce the delivered product. By assuming that a dishonest seller will lose the chance to do business with the buyer in the future, the total profit gained by the seller s can then be formalized based on Equation 2:

$$T_s = U_s = P_s - C_s \tag{21}$$

The study of [8] does not consider the case where buyers form a social network. The seller therefore does not take into account the future profit gained by doing business with other buyers influenced by the feedback about the seller provided by the buyer b. In our case, the seller bids to sell the product to the buyer by also taking into account the future gain obtained by doing business with other buyers that consider b as their neighbor. The seller's expected gain is then greater than or equal to that in their case. Greater expected future gain leads to a larger realized surplus (see Equation 11). Based on the argument supported by Equation 17 that the seller's equilibrium bidding function is a monotonically decreasing function of its realized surplus, the seller's equilibrium bidding price P'_s should then be less than or equal to P_s. The profit that the seller s is able to earn will be less than or equal to the profit that it can earn in the case where sellers do not take into account the expected future gain obtained from other buyers in the marketplace:

$$T'_s = U'_s = P'_s - C_s \leq P_s - C_s = T_s \tag{22}$$

Honest sellers in both cases (taking future gain into account, or not) instead are able to gain the same amount of profit. The sellers in our mechanism decrease their instant profit, which will be complemented by their expected future gain. Based on the above analysis, honest sellers in our mechanism therefore will be able to gain more total profit than that gained by dishonest sellers. Rational sellers desire profit and therefore will be honest. In conclusion, we have now proved the following:

Proposition 4. *The buyer strategy is able to promote seller honesty.*

4   Experimental Results

This section presents experimental results to confirm the value of our proposed incentive mechanism, showing that: honesty is more profitable, for both buyers and sellers; sellers are more profitable when modeling the reputation of buyers; buyers are more profitable when they participate, by providing ratings to others; limiting the number of bidders by buyers promotes seller honesty; buyers derive better profit when they use the ratings of sellers provided by neighbors.

We simulate a marketplace operating with our mechanism for a period of 30 days. The marketplace involves 90 buyers. These buyers are grouped into three groups. They have different numbers of requests. Every 10 of the buyers in each group has a different number (10, 20 and 30) of requests. In our experiments, we assume that there is only one product in each request and each buyer has a maximum of one request each day. For the purpose of simplicity, we also assume that the products requested by buyers have the same non-price features. After they finish business with sellers, buyers rate sellers. Some buyers will provide unfair ratings. Each group of buyers provides different percentages (0%, 20% and 40%) of unfair ratings. We allow 2 buyers from each group to leave the marketplace at the end of each day. Accordingly, we also allow 6 buyers to join the marketplace at the end of each day. These buyers will also provide different percentage (0%, 20% and 40%) of unfair ratings, to keep the number of buyers in each group the same. Initially, we randomly assign 5 buyers to each buyer as its neighbors. As discussed in Section 3.2, buyers' neighbor lists will be updated.

There are also 9 sellers in total in the marketplace. Each 3 sellers acts dishonestly in different percentages (0%, 25% and 75%) of their business with buyers. We assume that all sellers have the same cost for producing the products because all products have the same non-price features.

4.1   The Value of Honesty

Here, we provide some general results to show that our mechanism promotes buyer and seller honesty. We first measure the reputation of buyers that provide different percentages of unfair ratings. In our experiments, a buyer's reputation is computed using Equation 7. The results[8] are shown in Figure 1(a). From this figure, we can see that the buyers providing the smaller percentages of unfair ratings have the larger reputation values. Due to the randomness of the initial setting for our experiments, buyers' reputation values change stochastically at the beginning. After approximately 10 days when our marketplace converges, the changes of buyers' reputation clearly follow a trend. After each day, we measure

---

[8] All experimental results in Section 4 are averaged over 500 rounds of the simulation.

total profit gained by buyers that provide different percentages of unfair ratings. The profit gained by a buyer from buying a product is formalized in Equation 3. From Figure 1(b), we can see that buyers providing fewer unfair ratings gain more total profit. Our mechanism promotes buyer honesty (Proposition 3). Note that the profit difference of different types of buyers is fairly small. This is because buyers have at most 30 requests in total.

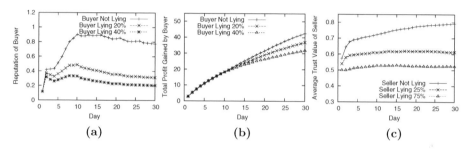

Fig. 1. (a) Reputation of Buyers being Honest vs. Dishonest; (b) Profit of Buyers being Honest vs. Dishonest; (c) Average Trust of Sellers being Honest vs. Dishonest

We compare the average trust values of different sellers. The average trust value of a seller is calculated as the sum of the trust value each buyer has of the seller divided by the total number of buyers in the marketplace (90 in our experiments). As shown in Figure 1(c), results indicate that sellers being dishonest more often have smaller average trust values. From this figure, we can see that the average trust values of the sellers being dishonest in 75% of their business are nearly 0.5. This is because they do not have much chance to do business with buyers and do not have many ratings. A seller without any ratings will have a default trust value of 0.5. We also record the total profit gained by different sellers using our new incentive mechanism. Results are shown in Figure 2(a). From this figure, we can see that sellers being honest more often gain more profit. Therefore, our mechanism promotes seller honesty (Proposition 4). We can also see that the profit difference between the honest sellers and the sellers lying 25% is much larger than that between the sellers lying 25% and the sellers lying 75%. The reason is that we set the threshold for sellers to be considered trustworthy to be very high. The sellers lying 25% are not considered as trustworthy sellers, therefore have few occasions to be selected as business partners by buyers.

4.2   Seller Strategy

This experiment is to examine the average trustworthiness of and the total profit gained by sellers using different strategies. We have two groups of sellers. One group of sellers model reputation of buyers and offer better rewards to reputable buyers. Another group of sellers do not model reputation of buyers and ask for the same price from different buyers. Sellers in each group lie in different percentages (0%, 25% and 75%) of their business with buyers. We measure the average trust values of sellers from each group. Results shown in Figure 2(b) indicate that sellers modeling reputation of buyers have higher average trust values. We also measure the total profit gained by different sellers. Results in Figure 2(c) indicate that sellers are better off to model reputation of buyers and adjust prices of products according to buyers' reputation. By satisfying reputable buyers, these sellers are able to attract more buyers to do business with, in order to gain more profit.

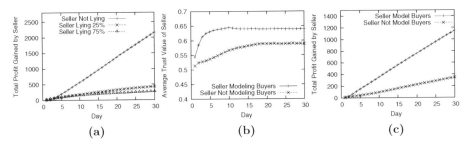

Fig. 2. (a) Total Profit Gained by Sellers being Honest vs. Dishonest; (b) Average Trust of Sellers Modeling vs. not Modeling Reputation of Buyers; (c) Total Profit Gained by Sellers Modeling vs. not Modeling Reputation of Buyers

4.3   Buyer Strategy

Buyers in the marketplace may also have different strategies. They may allow a lot of sellers to join their auctions. They may not always provide ratings for sellers. They may use different methods to model sellers, or may not model sellers at all. In this section, we carry out experiments to show the value of limiting the number of bidders and compare reputation values and total profit of buyers using different strategies. Results show that limiting the number of bidders promotes seller honesty, our mechanism provides incentives for buyers to provide ratings of sellers, and the modeling methods we propose provide buyers with more profit.

Limiting Number of Bidders. In this experiment, we have 90 sellers. Every 30 sellers acts dishonestly in different percentages (0%, 25% and 75%) of their business with buyers. In the first experiment, we allow 30 sellers to join each buyer's auctions. Figure 3(a) shows the amount of business (number of transactions) done by different sellers. Sellers being honest more often are still able to gain more opportunities to do business with buyers. We also compare total profit gained by different sellers in this setting. However, from the results shown in Figure 3(b), we can see that sellers being dishonest more often gain more total profit. In this case, because more sellers are allowed to join buyers' auctions, each seller's equilibrium bidding price should be lower in order to win the auctions. Sellers being honest gain very little profit from each business with a buyer; therefore, dishonesty is promoted.

In the second experiment, we limit the number of bidders allowed in each of the buyers' auctions to be 6. As shown in Figure 3(c), sellers being honest

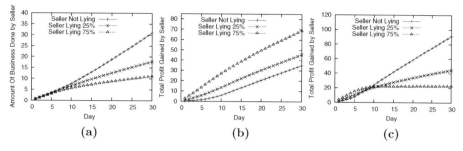

Fig. 3. (a) Sellers' Amount of Business When Allowing Many Sellers to Bid; (b) Total Profit Gained by Sellers When Allowing Many Sellers to Bid; (c) Total Profit Gained by Sellers When Limiting Seller Bids

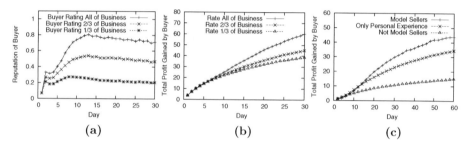

Fig. 4. (a) Reputation of Buyers Sharing Different Number of Ratings; (b) Total Profit Gained by Buyers Sharing Different Number of Ratings; (c) Total Profit Gained by Buyers Modeling vs. not Modeling Sellers

more often are able to gain more total profit. Honest sellers in this case are more likely to win the future auctions of buyers. They are offered sufficient future gain because limiting the number of bidders increases each seller's equilibrium bidding price. Therefore, limiting the number of bidders promotes seller honesty.

Incentives for Providing Ratings. We examine how our mechanism provides incentives for buyers to provide ratings. We compare reputation values and total profit of buyers providing different number of ratings. In this experiment, all buyers are honest. They have the same number of requests. However, they rate different percentages (1/3, 2/3 and 3/3) of their business with sellers.

We first measure the reputation of the buyers. Results are shown in Figure 4(a). Buyers that provide more ratings have larger reputation values. We also measure total profit of these buyers. Results shown in Figure 4(b) indicate that buyers that have provided more ratings are able to gain more total profit. Therefore, it is better off for buyers to provide ratings of sellers. These ratings can then be shared with other buyers that consider these buyers as their neighbors, when modeling the trustworthiness of sellers.

Buyer Modeling Sellers. In this experiment, one third of the buyers models the trustworthiness of sellers based on their personal experience with the sellers and advice about the sellers provided by their neighbors. Another third of the buyers uses only personal experience to model the trustworthiness of sellers. These buyers allow only a number of the most trustworthy sellers to join their auctions. The rest of the buyers do not model sellers. They allow every seller to submit a bid. We compare the total profit gained by these three types of buyers. We can see from Figure 4(c) that buyers modeling the trustworthiness of sellers and limiting their participation are able to gain more total profit. It is also clear that buyers modeling sellers by taking into account as well the advice provided by other buyers (an important element of our incentive mechanism) are able to gain more profit. In summary, it is better off for buyers to selectively choose sellers to participate in their auctions and to take into account the advice provided by other buyers when buyers lack personal experience with sellers.

5   Related Work

Side payment mechanisms [1,9] have also been developed for promoting honesty in e-marketplaces. These mechanisms offer payment to buyers that fairly rate results of business with sellers. One facet of the side payment mechanisms in these papers is the requirement of a center to control monetary payments, so that budget balance is a concern. In contrast, in our mechanism the central server does not handle payments; rewards are directed from sellers to buyers. Brynov and Sandholm [10] design a mechanism that provides incentives for sellers to truthfully reveal their trustworthiness at the beginning of their business with buyers. Their mechanism has the limitation that the number of goods the buyers will purchase may not depend on their actual needs but has to be dependent on the trustworthiness of the seller.

The problem that strategic agents may collude with each other has been acknowledged as an important consideration by several researchers in the field (e.g [1]). Side payment mechanisms based simply on the similarity of buyers' ratings may therefore have difficulty with the situation where buyers collude in giving unfair ratings. Jurca and Faltings [11] investigate side payment mechanisms that can cope with collusion. However, they do not consider the case where a seller may collude with a group of buyers in promoting the seller itself or bad-mouthing another seller. In contrast, our mechanism's use of neighborhoods provides an avenue for excluding colluding buyers. Assuming that some honest buyers exist in the marketplace, they will use that honesty to gain rewards and will also serve to exclude the differing, colluding buyers from their neighborhoods. The use of neighborhoods also helps to detect and avoid dishonest, colluding sellers (those that differ from the predominant opinion).

6   Conclusions and Future Work

In this paper, we presented a detailed incentive mechanism to encourage honesty, intended for use in designing e-marketplaces. We provided theoretical proofs to show that buyers have incentives to be honest in reporting about sellers, when sharing ratings with the buyers in their neighborhoods, under our particular framework. This occurs as a result of sellers offering better rewards to more reputable buyers, as part of their reasoning about how to obtain profit. We are also able to show that seller honesty is promoted, within our proposed framework, in order for sellers to receive higher profit. We further validated our mechanism through a set of experiments carried out using a simulated dynamic e-marketplace. As a result, our research emphasizes the value of using trust modeling and the sharing of reputation ratings in social networks in the design of an effective incentive mechanism.

In future work, we will carry out more extensive experimentation to continue to validate our model by comparing with others' models. In our future experiments, we will examine the situation where agents may vary their behavior widely to exploit the marketplace. In addition, we are particularly interested in empirically demonstrating how our framework is able to handle marketplaces where strategic agents collude with each other, more effectively than competing incentive-based trust models.

References

1. Jurca, R., Faltings, B.: An incentive compatible reputation mechanism. In: Proceedings of the IEEE Conference on E-Commerce (2003)
2. Zhang, J., Cohen, R.: Design of a mechanism for promoting honesty in e-marketplaces. In: Proceedings of AAAI (2007)
3. Gintis, H., Smith, E.A., Bowles, S.: Costly signaling and cooperation. Journal of Theoretical Biology 213, 103–119 (2001)
4. Shachat, J., Swarthout, J.T.: Procurement auctions for differentiated goods. Experimental Economics Center Working Paper Series. Georgia State University (2006)
5. Richardson, M., Domingos, P.: Mining knowledge-sharing sites for viral marketing. In: Proceedings of KDD, pp. 61–70 (2002)
6. Zhang, J., Cohen, R.: A personalized approach to address unfair ratings in multi-agent reputation systems. In: Proceedings of the AAMAS Workshop on Trust in Agent Societies (2006)
7. Teacy, W.T.L., Patel, J., Jennings, N.R., Luck, M.: Coping with inaccurate reputation sources: Experimental analysis of a probabilistic trust model. In: Proceedings of Fourth International Autonomous Agents and Multiagent Systems (2005)
8. Kim, I.G.: A model of selective tendering: Does bidding competition deter opportunism by contractors? The Quarterly Review of Economics and Finance 38(4), 907–925 (1998)
9. Miller, N., Resnick, P., Zeckhauser, R.: Eliciting informative feedback: The peer-prediction method. Management Science 51(9), 1359–1373 (2005)
10. Braynov, S., Sandholm, T.: Trust revelation in multiagent interaction. In: Proceedings of CHI 2002 Workshop on the Philosophy and Design of Socially Adept Technologies, pp. 57–60 (2002)
11. Jurca, R., Faltings, B.: Collusion-resistant, incentive-compatible feedback payments. In: Proceedings of the Eighth ACM EC, pp. 200–209 (2007)

Does Trust Matter for User Preferences?
A Study on Epinions Ratings

Georgios Pitsilis[*] and Pern Hui Chia

Q2S[**] NTNU
O. S. Bragstads plass 2E
Trondheim 7491 Norway
{pitsilis,chia}@q2s.ntnu.no

Abstract. Recommender systems have evolved during the last few years into useful online tools for assisting the daily e-commerce activities. The majority of recommender systems predict user preferences relating users with similar taste. Prior research has shown that trust networks improve the performance of recommender systems, predominantly using algorithms devised by individual researchers. In this work, omitting any specific trust inference algorithm, we investigate how useful it might be if explicit trust relationships (expressed by users for others) are used to select the best neighbours (or predictors), for the provision of accurate recommendations. We conducted our experiments using data from *Epinions.com*[1], a popular recommender system. Our analysis indicates that trust information can be helpful to provide a slight performance gain in a few cases especially when it comes to the less active users.

Keywords: Trust, Epinions, Recommender system.

1 Introduction

Reputation systems compute global scores about products (people, companies, etc) based on opinions that users hold about them and assist prospective users in deciding whether to buy these products. Different from reputation systems that provide global scores, *recommender systems* provide personalized (local) recommendations based on correlations of ratings (browsing history, search keywords or other actions) made by likeminded users. Recommendations are generated automatically to assist users to choose from multiple options available on the Internet. Amazon.com and You-tube.com, for example, correlate the users' browsing history to determine the similarity between users. In order to learn from similar users, recommender systems employ filtering techniques such as *Collaborative filtering* to identify influential users with similar behaviour and label them as "neighbours" or "predictors".

---

* The first author carried out this work during the tenure of an ERCIM "Alain Bensoussan" Fellowship program.

** Centre of Quantifiable Quality of Service in Communication Systems (Q2S), Centre of Excellence, appointed by The Research Council of Norway, is funded by the Research Council, Norwegian University of Science and Technology (NTNU) and UNINETT. http://www.q2s.ntnu.no

[1] Epinions.com – an online consumer review site: http://www.epinions.com

M. Nishigaki et al. (Eds.): IFIPTM 2010, IFIP AICT 321, pp. 232–247, 2010.
© IFIP International Federation for Information Processing 2010

Although involving more predictors (users whose ratings are taken into account in predictions) may help in improving the prediction accuracy, the number of predictors should be kept low to avoid expensive computation. Herlocker et.al. reported that having too many predictors will conversely reduce the accuracy of predicted recommendation [3]. Rather than trying to guess the magical number of predictors, we believe that much focus could be placed in determining (a small set of) the most suitable predictors.

In classic recommender systems the criteria used for selecting suitable neighbours regard only users' past behaviour and liking (ratings) towards products that are common with other users to compute a similarity value for each user-pair. There are then several strategies to pick the most suitable predictors. These include clustering, correlation thresholding and best-k-neighbours. Clustering organizes the whole user population into groups of similar tastes but in general it is done statically in such a way that predictions are always made using the same set of predictors (or neighbourhood). Correlation thresholding considers only neighbours that are correlated with a particular user over a certain threshold. Meanwhile, the best-k-neighbours technique selects some k best (most similar) neighbours to be considered in the prediction algorithm. The best-k-neighbours technique is also widely known as the k-Nearest Neighbourhood (kNN) approach, and it has been found that kNN outperforms the correlation thresholding approach (in both accuracy and coverage) with reasonable k values [3]. Various kNN-based algorithms have been proposed for selecting the best predictors [7][8].

In real life, users consult opinions of people whom they trust for forming their own decisions. Such trust relationship is being collected by advanced recommender services. The network of explicitly formed trust relationships is known as web-of-trust [22]. A trust-based recommender system incorporates the web-of-trust into its recommendation algorithm, mimicking the way that people get good advices from trusted sources in real life. A trivial case is to consider only reviews and ratings from sources that have been explicitly indicated as 'trusted' by individual users. Explicit-trust is hence binary. On the other hand, sophisticated systems propagate trust relationship across the user network in order to infer (non-binary) trust values. Several approaches have been proposed to compute implicit-trust values, including Advogato [15], Mole-trust [21] and Subjective logic [14]. Implicit-trust values are particularly helpful when explicit trust information is scarce. For example, if there is a consistent trend that user a could provide user b with good advices, even though user a has not explicitly indicated that she trusts user b, it is likely that user b's suggestion would be useful in the future (or considered with a higher weight) and should be implicitly trusted.

Our intuition is that explicit trust information can be exploited to improve the traditional recommender systems in the selection of the most suitable predictors needed in the collaborative filtering. In this work, we investigate whether it is beneficial in the form of improved prediction accuracy when (a small set of) the most suitable predictors are selected with and without explicit trust. If trust helps to select better predictors, combining the classical collaborative filtering with users' personal assessments (i.e. trust) towards the usefulness of others' recommendations might be of much benefit to improve prediction quality. To enhance comparison, we also present a trust-experience-selection strategy with the intuition that users will be more likely to take into account opinions from trusted users that are more experienced, in real life.

The research contribution and purpose of this work is two fold. First, we investigate the potential benefits of using trust in selecting better predictors with the objective to improve the collaborative filtering scheme in classical recommender system. Second, we investigate the possibility of using usage experience along with trust as a criterion to help selecting suitable predictors.

The rest of the paper is organized as follows. In section 2 we discuss the related work in the field of recommender systems, social networks and trust. Next in section 3, we elaborate on how explicit trust and usage experience could be incorporated to potentially improve the selection of suitable predictors. We describe our experimental setting in section 4 and present the evaluation results in section 5. Finally, in section 6 we discuss our findings before concluding.

2   Related Work

Research related to the *Epinions* dataset includes that of conducted by Massa et. al. [21] that reports interesting findings on "controversial" users who are simultaneously trusted and distrusted by many. They argue that personalized trust metrics are needed given the fact that the controversial users take up to a fraction of 20%. The same authors in [2] address the problem of information overload by exploiting the trust information that users provide explicitly. Even though their concept of making use of the trust graph is quite similar with ours, in their work they used different mechanism/formulae for working out predictions for user items. In our approach we tested various strategies for deciding the best-k neighbours while keeping the similarity-based methodology.

Liu et.al. [6] propose a classification approach for predicting the trust between users from reputation in the absence of first-hand knowledge. Their solution addresses the problem of sparse webs-of-trust by using pre-trained classifiers, but some minimum information, such as user attributes, is required to exist. There is also much research done concerning the topological properties of social networks. We mention that of Wilson et.al. [4] as one of the most recent and complete piece of work.

As for approaches that cluster users into groups of similar tastes, there is a wealth of literature that essentially focused on overcoming the poor prediction quality (e.g. in [9]). Geng et.al. [19] explores the idea of clustering users by imitating the way that people of common interests can be grouped together. Other clustering-based proposals include that by Truong et.al. [17] which uses the common knowledge that exists about the rating behaviour of people for allocating them into clusters of interests. Kwon [7] proposes a technique for selecting the best neighbours as improvement to the *k*-nearest neighbour approach. As opposed to our approach he uses the variance of predictions in a user-specific metric that describes the deviation of the examined user. Other work related to finding best neighbours is that of Lathia et.al. [16] in which a policy based on trustworthiness is proposed. Contrary to our approach they use implicit trust for finding the best k-trusted neighbours to forming groups of collaborative users. In their idea the trust for some user is derived from the knowledge about her particular ratings. The work in [20] introduced a hybrid Collaborative Filtering System which differs from the standard similarity-based approaches by using weighted similarities computed from the number of common experiences with the predictor.

Sparsity is also recognized as a problem that affects the quality of predictions, and in the past it has been investigated from two different directions. Latent factor analysis, known as *Dimensionality Reduction*, has shown very promising results [18]. However, the simplicity and intuitiveness of *Neighbourhood-based* methods have made themselves more applicable and suitable for social-networking-based models. Trust has also been the subject of investigation by many researchers in the past as a solution for alleviating issues concerning sparsity and security of recommender systems. O'Donovan and Smyth [23] proposed to use implicit trust derived from the reliability of partners as another factor to influence predictions in conjunction with similarity.

To our knowledge, the concepts to use both users' usage experience and explicit trust for building dynamic clusters of suitable predictors have not been explored adequately so far. In the existing solutions no emphasis has been given on the phenomenon of social connectivity in online communities neither on how this could benefit the provision of electronic recommendation services.

3 Neighbourhood Selection Schemes

3.1 Conventional Similarity-Based Neighbourhood (S)

Central to most recommender systems that employ collaborative filtering is the computation of similarity between users. Pearson's similarity is the best known formula for user-based recommender systems. It measures the proximity between two users and is computed along the rows (or columns) in the Users by Items matrix. Formula (1) computes the Pearson's similarity $w_{a,b}$ between users a and b using the set of common items between the two users. The outcome is in the range of [-1,1].

$$w_{a,b} = \frac{\sum_k (r_{a,k} - \bar{r}_a)(r_{b,k} - \bar{r}_b)}{\sqrt{\sum_k (r_{a,k} - \bar{r}_a)^2 \sum_k (r_{b,k} - \bar{r}_b)^2}} \tag{1}$$

$\bar{r}_a$ and $\bar{r}_b$ are the average of all ratings by user a and b while $r_{a,k}$ and $r_{b,k}$ are the ratings given by users a and b respectively for item k.

Pearson's similarity is then used in conjunction with Resnick's formula to work out the predicted recommendation [13]. Formula (2) computes the predicted rating $\hat{p}_{a,i}$ of item i for user a using the set of existing ratings $r_{j,i}$ given to this item i by predictor j.

$$\hat{p}_{a,i} = \bar{r}_a + \frac{\sum_j \{w_{a,j} \cdot (r_{j,i} - \bar{r}_j)\}}{\sum_j |w_{a,j}|} \tag{2}$$

Resnick's formula (as it is highly sensitive to the number of predictors) does not provide accurate prediction in sparse datasets [3]. The selection of the most suitable predictors is hence of major significance when it comes to the performance of collaborative filtering [3]. Previous research [12] highlighted the importance of selecting the most suitable predictors (for achieving good prediction accuracy) and suggested that only those who are most similar in terms of product ratings should be chosen. We refer this selection scheme as Similarity-based neighbourhood (S), as shown in Figure 1a.

We provide a formal description of the Similarity-based neighbourhood. Let U be the set of all users and I is the set of all items that have been rated in the system. Let $r_a(i) \neq \perp$ denote that user a has given a rating for an item i (i.e. not null), the set of ratings $I_a \subset I$ given by a user a can then be written as:

$$I_a = \left\{ \forall i \in I : r_a(i) \neq \perp \right\} \qquad (3)$$

We require that only those who have similar rating behaviour with some user a and have experienced the item i (that user a is interested in) be considered. The set of these similar neighbours can be expressed as:

$$S_{a,i} = \left\{ \forall b \in U : b \neq a \wedge |\, I_b \cap I_a\, | \geq q \wedge r_b(i) \neq \perp \right\} \qquad (4)$$

with q denoting the minimum number of common items that have been rated by both user a and her neighbour. Setting such as minimum count is necessary as correlation coefficient (Pearson's similarity value) would not be computable (or not meaningful) unless both users have rated at least some common set of items. From equation (4), one can realize that the top-k neighbourhood is not static, depending also on the item of interest.

In addition, to require that Pearson's similarity to be computable, we introduce two neighbourhood formation schemes with additional criteria based on explicit trust and rating experience. We elaborate on these schemes in subsections 3.2 and 3.3.

3.2 Trust-Based Neighbourhood (T)

In our first extension to the neighbourhood selection scheme, we consider only neighbours who have been explicitly indicated as trusted by a user, on top of the requirement that Pearson's similarity value is computable. Note that we only consider binary explicit trust; we do not infer or compute implicit trust values between users. Let $t(a,b) = 1$ denotes the existence of an explicit directional trust relationship from user a to user b, the set of neighbours fulfilling the criterion of being trusted and have also rated item i (that user a is interested in) can be expressed as:

$$T_{a,i} = \left\{ \forall b \in U : b \neq a \wedge |\, I_b \cap I_a\, | \geq q \wedge t(a,b) = 1 \wedge r_b(i) \neq \perp \right\} \qquad (5)$$

These neighbours are then ordered by their respective trustworthiness index, which is simply the count of in-degree trust links. Finally, the top-k neighbours (predictors) are selected to predict recommendations for this user using the Resnick's formula. We refer this selection scheme as Trust-based neighbourhood (T), as shown in Figure 1b.

3.3 Trust-Experience-Based Neighbourhood (T-E)

We further explore if user experience could be taken into account to help selecting better predictors. The intuition is that users are more likely to seek advice from people who are more (or equally) experienced than those who are less experienced. For that reason our objective is to examine whether users who have given more product ratings should be considered better candidates. Considering this as an opinion flow, we impose that the direction is from the more experienced to the less experienced ones.

The experience level of a user (can also be thought as the amount of knowledge) is quantified according to number of recommendations that have been submitted by the user. We order users according to rating count such that:

$$\forall a, b \in U \ \text{ if } |I_a| \ge |I_b| \text{ then } e_a \ge e_b$$

where e_a denotes the experience level of user a and $|I_a|$ is the number of items that have been rated by user a. In this work, we categorize all users U into five experience levels, each consisting of $\frac{1}{5}|U|$ users. In this way, the set of neighbours that have

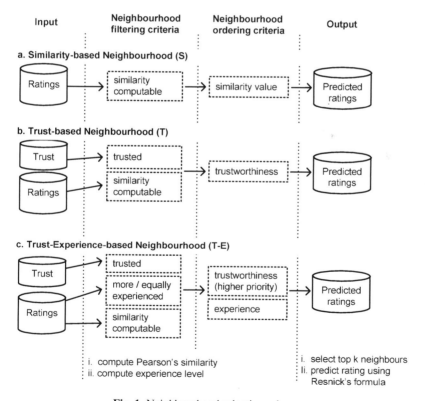

Fig. 1. Neighbourhood selection schemes

rated some item i (that user a is interested in) and have a higher (or equal) experience level than user a, can be expressed as:

$$E_{a,i} = \left\{ \forall b \in U : b \neq a \wedge e_b \geq e_a \wedge r_b(i) \neq \perp \right\} \tag{6}$$

Combining the computable similarity, trust and experience criteria in (4), (5) and (6), the set of neighbours that can potentially become the top-k predictors can be expressed as:

$$TE_{a,i} = \left\{ \forall b \in U : b \neq a \wedge |I_b \cap I_a| \geq q \wedge t(a,b) = 1 \wedge e_b \geq e_a \wedge r_b(i) \neq \perp \right\} \tag{7}$$

We refer to this selection scheme as Trust-Experience-based neighbourhood (T-E), as depicted in Figure 1c. When selecting the top-k neighbours, the trustworthiness index has a higher priority over the experience.

4 Experimental Setting

To evaluate our central question of whether trust helps to select better predictors we performed a series of simulations and compared the performance of the neighbourhood selection schemes as described in section 3.

4.1 Data

We used data from a popular recommender system, *Epinions.com* for the reason that it contains both product ratings and trust information we needed for our experiments. *Epinions.com* allows member users to write reviews about products consisting of a text and a quantitative rating from 1 to 5 stars. *Epinions.com* allows also users to build their web-of-trust by indicating other users whom they find have given consistently valuable reviews as trusted. In the current form of the system assistance is limited to the provision of textual and rating information from trusted users about the products of interest; input from trusted sources have to be digested by users manually.

The dataset was collected by Paolo Massa [11] by crawling the *Epinions.com* website during Nov-Dec 2003. In total, there are over 664K ratings given by 49K users on 139K products. Also included are 487K outward trust statements from users. Shown in Figure 2, both the distribution of rates and trust relationship in *Epinions.com* seem to follow power-law distribution, which is a feature of most social networks [4]. The figures are plotted in log scale showing the number of outward trust links per user (Fig. 2a) and the number of ratings given by individual users (Fig. 2b). The number of outward trust links and products rating count per user decrease sharply going from the very active users to the non-actives ones. This further suggests that the ratings on common products and the trust towards same users are sparsely distributed. As such, we used only a subset of Paolo Massa's dataset consisting of 1500 active users selected on the basis of number of ratings given by each user (no matter how many inward or outward trust links they have). This was also done to ensure that the Pearson's similarity value between users is computable with an adequate number of commonly rated products.

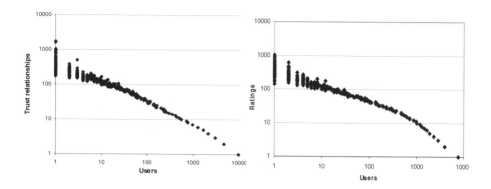

Fig. 2a. Outward trust links vs. trustors. There are 487K outward trust links in total.

Fig. 2b. Individual rating count vs. raters. There are 664K item ratings in total.

The 1500 users were then divided into three communities referred to as "most active", "medium active" and "least active" of 500 users each (again based on the number of ratings that have been given by each user). Table 1 shows the average outward trust links and average number of ratings of the different communities.

Table 1. Trust links and average rating count of different communities

Community	Average outward trust links	Average number of ratings
Most active	40.33	260.91
Medium active	9.02	114.09
Least active	4.32	83.02

4.2 Evaluation Metrics

We considered both Predictive and Classification accuracy as being equally important to be measured. The former is demonstrative of the efficiency of the system in making accurate predictions for users. The latter as suggested by many researchers in *Information Retrieval* [1][10] is useful for measuring the frequency at which the system decides correctly or incorrectly about if an item is potentially liking for a particular user. Its usefulness in recommender systems is found in the creation of lists of products that are of high interest to users.

Predictive accuracy means the ability of the algorithm in producing accurate predictions for individual products. To demonstrate this we used the metrics *Mean Average Error (MAE)* and *Root Mean Square Error (RMSE)*. The latter is especially useful for identifying undesirably large errors. MAE and RMSE are both computed by comparing the real ratings (given by users) and the predicted ones. In our experiment the predicted values were rounded to the closest integer. We also applied correction on any predicted values that were out of range. Specifically, predicted values lower than 1 or higher than 5 were corrected to 1 and 5 respectively.

For evaluating the Classification accuracy we used the rating of 4 as the threshold for indicating a product that is of user's interest, meaning that a predicted value of 4 or 5 would be considered successful. *Recall (R)* is a metric to express the relative success in retrieving items of interest (either highly rated or lowly rated) in relation to the number of all items claimed to be of interest. *Precision (P)* is the relative success in retrieving items that are of user's interest. Both metrics can then be combined to express the effectiveness of retrieval with respect to the cost of retrieval to give the *F-Score*. *F-Score* is also known as *Harmonic Mean* [10] and it describes the trade-off between true positive (TP) and false positive (FP). *Precision (P)* and *Recall (R)* and *F-score* can be computed as follows:

$$P = \frac{TP}{TP + FP} \qquad R = \frac{TP}{TP + FN} \qquad F = \frac{2PR}{P + R}$$

We used *Precision (P)* to measure the improvement in the relative success that the T and T-E schemes can possibly provide for identifying products that are of user's interest. We called a *hit* (or True Positive) for the case where some product that is of user's interest (i.e. has been rated as 4 or 5 by the user) and at the same time, using the algorithm, a high rating (4 or 5) has been predicted for it. We did not measure *Recall (R)* as is often impractical to do so in a recommender system [10]. The true positive (TP), false positive (FP) and false negative (FN) instances for our analysis are as defined in the confusion matrix in Table 2.

Table 2. The confusion matrix for classification test

	Predicted Value ≥ 4	Predicted Value < 4
Actual Rating ≥ 4	TP	FN
Actual Rating < 4	FP	TN

Since the application of filters (selection criteria) has implications to the number of items that can be actually predicted it is necessary that the level of this is also captured as well for every testing scenario. *Coverage* is a suitable metric for capturing this implication. It is defined as the ratio of recommendations for products that are of interest to the querying user and which the selected top-k neighbours can recommend, divided by the total number of items (that the querying user is interested in). The coverage of some particular user a can be computed using formula (8) where K denotes the set of top-k neighbours of user a, I being the set of all items in the system and I_a is the set of items that have been rated by user a .

$$C_a = \frac{1}{|I_a|} \cdot \left| I_a \cap \left\{ \bigcup_{b \in K} I_b \right\} \right| \tag{8}$$

4.3   Test Scenarios

The Similarity-based (S), Trust-based (T) and Trust-Experience-based (T-E) neighbourhood selection schemes formed the three main testing scenarios in our experiments. For each of the neighbourhood schemes, we studied the impact of the number of predictors on the performance by repeating kNN computation for different k values ranging from 3 to 13. When comparing the performance of neighbourhood schemes (e.g. T against S), we considered only predicted recommendations where the exact number of predictors (k) could be found.

As the ratings of common products and trust relationship are sparsely distributed, our experiments involved only a subset of 1500 active users from Paolo Massa's dataset. The 1500 users were divided into three communities referred to as "most active", "medium active" and "least active" (each with 500 users). We ran our experiments starting with the "most active" community.

When running a test scenario on a community of particular activity-level (i.e. most active, medium active and least active), we used the five-fold cross-validation method to further divide the community (500 users) into five fifths from where one fifth would be regarded as test set while the other four were used as training sets. This was repeated five times with a different fifth being used as the test set each time and the results were finally averaged.

5   Results - Discussion

We report the most interesting results from our experiments. First, in Table 3, we present the effects of trust criteria (both T and T-E schemes) on prediction accuracy for the "most-active" community with k denoting the number of predictors used in each experiment. Due to the use of sparse dataset not all predictions can be made with the T and T-E neighbourhood schemes. When comparing the predictive accuracy (MAE, RMSE), we considered only user items that could be both predicted using the S neighbourhood scheme and the alternative scheme (T or T-E), in a pairwise manner. Thus, Table 3 and Table 4 show, for each of the experiment (using T or T-E scheme), the corresponding MAE and RMSE values measured using the S neighbourhood.

Table 3. Predictive accuracy and Coverage for the "most active" community

k	MAE (%)				RMSE				Coverage (%)		
	S	T	S	T-E	S	T	S	T-E	S	T	T-E
3	12.40	14.68	12.28	14.84	0.91	1.05	0.90	1.06	37.58	8.07	5.94
4	12.01	14.29	11.86	14.56	0.88	1.02	0.87	1.03	32.22	5.02	3.42
5	12.11	14.19	11.78	14.67	0.88	0.99	0.86	1.03	28.20	3.28	2.00
6	12.04	13.93	11.61	14.32	0.87	0.98	0.86	1.01	25.04	2.20	1.22
7	12.22	13.97	11.58	14.14	0.88	0.98	0.86	1.00	22.57	1.53	0.78
8	11.93	13.90	11.81	14.29	0.85	0.97	0.87	1.02	20.36	1.11	0.49
9	11.79	13.75	11.44	14.14	0.84	0.96	0.87	1.03	18.65	0.82	0.35
10	11.55	13.82	10.30	13.33	0.84	0.97	0.82	0.97	17.10	0.59	0.23
11	11.75	13.89	10.70	12.30	0.85	0.97	0.81	0.94	15.76	0.44	0.16
12	11.82	13.95	10.29	12.90	0.86	0.98	0.79	0.99	14.61	0.33	0.10
13	11.50	13.65	10.89	12.27	0.84	0.96	0.81	0.93	13.58	0.25	0.07

From the results it can be seen that trust does not help in choosing better neighbours to improve prediction accuracy as both the MAE and RMSE are lower for similarity-based selection scheme (compared to T and T-E schemes) for all k number of predictors. This suggests using explicit trust for selecting better predictors does not help to improve predictive accuracy for the "most active" community. Experienced users may be characterized by having stronger personal opinions; they may not rely on or be influenced easily by even those whom they trust.

Using the MovieLens dataset, Herlocker et.al. [3] show that an increasing neighbourhood size (using the S scheme) will improve the predictive accuracy until a certain threshold (about 15) where performance starts to deteriorate with more neighbours. Our results show a similar trend using the Epinions dataset; predictive accuracy improves following an increasing number of predictors, for all neighbourhood schemes (S, T, and T-E). However, due to the sparse distribution of commonly rated products and trust links with the Epinions dataset, we did not investigate further on larger neighbourhood; we stopped with 13 predictors.

As for classification accuracy, the performance of *Precision (P)* for the "most active" community improves in the T-E scheme, when a sufficiently large number of trusted and more experienced predictors are employed. This is shown in Figure 3 and can be interpreted as: user intuition, in choosing neighbours (by indicating explicit trust, when assisted by the system to filter out the less experienced ones), can work better than a system-determined similarity-based neighbourhood. Another observation is the increasing trend of P in both the T and T-E schemes, which starts low but catches up with (or overtakes) the S scheme with an increasing number of predictors . This suggests that user intuitions on trusting others to give good recommendations may not be individually reliable but can be helpful when aggregated.

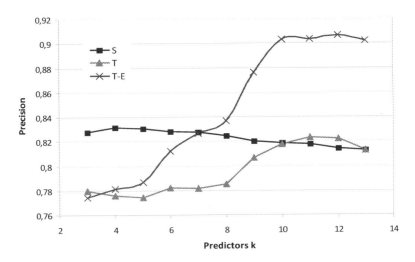

Fig. 3. Classification accuracy *(Precision)* for the "most active" community with different neighbourhood selection schemes

Finally we observed serious implications on coverage value for all test cases when involving large numbers of predictors. Trust-based filters (T and T-E) affect the coverage even worse. The results are shown in Table 3.

So far, with the only exception of *Precision*, the use of explicit trust to select predictors has not been found very helpful. Coverage is strongly affected due to the limited trust information. Deriving trust from existing relationships (e.g. inferred from propagated trust) might be helpful for, at least, overcoming the coverage problem.

We should note that in other research works the use of propagative trust has been found quite successful for improving the predictive accuracy in user communities (e.g. in [2]). However, the distinctive difference here is that we examine the suitability of using explicit trust to select better predictors. Trying propagation trust frameworks (e.g. in [14]) to infer implicit trust values is outside the scope of this paper; we have deferred this to future investigation.

For the reason that trust is known to improve the predictive accuracy for cold-start users [21] we continued our experiments with the "medium active" and "least active" communities. Cold-start users are those who have not provided a sufficiently large number of ratings; as a consequence they often receive poor recommendations. The MAE and RMSE values for these communities are shown in Table 4a and 4b. *Diff* denotes the improvement of T or T-E scheme over the baseline S scheme. We show only results for some small k predictors as the trust links within the "medium active" and "least active" communities are scarce, causing it infeasible to investigate further.

In Table 4b, it can be seen that with $k=3,4$ predictors, contrary to the "most active" community, predictive accuracy is better with both the T and T-E criteria compared to the baseline S scheme. This suggests that in the "least active" community, as users are less experienced, opinions from explicitly trusted sources can be very useful.

Table 4a. Predictive accuracy for the "medium active" community

k	MAE (%)						RMSE					
	S	T	Diff	S	T-E	Diff	S	T	Diff	S	T-E	Diff
3	12.26	14.54	-2.29	13.44	15.87	-2.43	0.94	1.09	-0.15	1.00	1.17	-0.17
4	13.10	14.71	-1.61	15.34	15.34	0.00	0.97	1.07	-0.10	1.05	1.12	-0.07
5	13.72	15.58	-1.86	15.68	18.38	-2.70	0.96	1.08	-0.12	1.05	1.29	-0.24
avg			-1.92			-1.72			-0.12			-0.16

Table 4b. Predictive accuracy for the "least active" community

k	MAE (%)						RMSE					
	S	T	Diff	S	T-E	Diff	S	T	Diff	S	T-E	Diff
3	13.44	12.79	0.66	17.27	12.72	4.54	1.00	0.97	0.03	1.11	0.90	0.20
4	16.92	07.69	9.23	-	-	-	1.14	0.62	0.52	1.00	1.00	0.00
avg			4.61			4.54			0.19			0.10

(- denotes absence of data due to scarcity of trust links).

The average MAE *Diff* values (i.e. average improvement over the baseline S scheme) for the "most active" community are -2.22 and -2.72, for T and T-E schemes respectively. The corresponding value pairs for the "medium active" community and "least active" community are (-1.92, -1.72) and (4.61, 4.54) respectively. These average *Diff* values follow an increasing trend going from "most active" to "medium active" and to the "least active" communities. In other words, using trust to select better predictors can be more helpful to the less experienced users than the more experienced ones. Similar result, but more generalized as far as the number of predictors k, has also been found by Massa et.al. in [21].

We could not read much into the trend of predictive accuracy for the "medium active" and "least active" communities as the number of predictors available using the T and T-E schemes is very limited.

Table 5 presents the classification accuracy for the "medium active" community. *Precision* performs better in the T and T-E schemes for the "medium active" community even with small neighbourhood size. This conforms to the result on better predictive accuracy (as shown in Table 4a) as trust information is helpful for less experienced users. However, the combined trust-experience (T-E) criterion does not help as much as than the trust (T) criterion alone, different from the case with the "most active" community. On average, the *Precision* value has an improvement of 2.6% for T and just over 0.22% for T-E, compared to S.

Table 5. Classification accuracy for the "medium active" community

	Precision			F-score		
k	S	T	T-E	S	T	T-E
3	0.880	0.901	0.867	0.863	0.864	0.835
4	0.884	0.919	0.894	0.864	0.850	0.849
5	0.887	0.898	0.895	0.867	0.822	0.756
avg	**0.883**	**0.906**	**0.885**	**0.865**	**0.845**	**0.813**

In short, trust is more helpful for the less active users. Nevertheless that requires that users have provided adequate trust inferences for people they can rely on, which is not always the case. When new users have little incentive or have not indicated their trusted counterparts, a recommender system could consider inferring the implicit trust values based on product ratings.

6   Further Analysis - Discussion

We further investigated the performance based on individual ratings. As we have found that trust is more useful for less active users, we excluded the "most active" community from the analysis. The accuracy gain against the Similarity-based neighbourhood selection (S) for the "medium active" community is shown in Figure 4a. As can be seen, the application of trust-based criteria has helped to improve the predictive accuracy for items that users have given a real rating of 3 or 4. Note that also the combination of trust and experience (T-E) gives, for both cases when users have rated with 3 or 4, better predictive accuracy over using trust criterion alone.

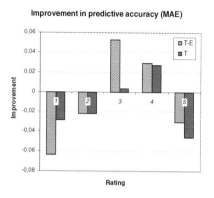

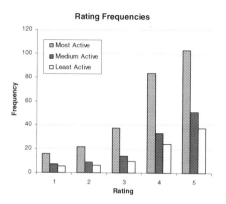

Fig. 4a. Improvement in prediction accuracy for individual ratings

Fig. 4b. The Ratings distribution for different communities

We further investigated whether the better predictive accuracy in rating 3 and 4 is related to rating distribution itself. Figure 4b showed that the (uneven) rating distribution is characterized with an increasing frequency going from rating 1 to 5. However, unlike those with a rating of 3 or 4, trust criteria do not help for items that have been rated with 5. This allows us to believe that there are other factors in effect (not due to rating distribution).

An attempt to explain the observation is that it is more likely that (Epinions) users would believe in non-extreme ratings (compared to ratings of 1 and 5) and therefore indicate their trust on these reviewers. When there are more non-extreme reviewers being trusted, it is likely that the predictive accuracy for non-extreme ratings will work out better. It would be interesting to further explore this matter from the perspectives of behavioral and cognitive sciences in the future.

7 Conclusions

We have performed a series of experiments in the context of recommender systems with the purpose to investigate our central question of whether explicit trust information can be useful in predicting user preferences. We presented two neighbourhood selection schemes involving trust criteria (Trust-based and Trust-Experience-based schemes) and compared their performances relative to the conventional Similarity-based kNN approach.

Our results show that trust criteria can help to improve the performance of recommender systems in a few cases. Specifically, trust information helps to improve the *Precision* in our classification test to provide good recommendations on items that are of users' interest.

Trust criteria are shown to be more helpful to the less experienced users judging from the increasing trend of better predictive accuracy (compared to the similarity-based scheme) going from the "most active" to the "least active" communities. Although trust-based schemes do not seem to help for active users in this work, we believe there might be other prediction algorithms where trust information can contribute. An interesting future work would be to explore if 'distrust' can be helpful for these active users.

Meanwhile, other than the *Precision* value for the "most active" community, the combined trust and experience criteria does not perform better than trust criterion alone. Although it is intuitive to filter out neighbours that are less experienced, strict selection criteria proves not to be very helpful in the Epinions dataset, where trust links and commonly rated products are scarce.

Using only explicit trust (without inference of implicit trust values) as what we have done for the purpose of our experimental setup incurs a heavy loss in terms of coverage. The performance is also restricted to the lack of trust information especially when it comes to the less active users. For these reasons, we render our support to the ongoing research in the computation of implicit trust values and building more sophisticated trust-aware recommender systems. There are also much to learn from other related disciplines including psychology and behavioural science.

References

1. McNee, M.S., Riedl, J., Konstan, J.A.: Accurate is not always good. How Accuracy Metrics have hurt. Recommender Systems. In: Proc. ACM, CHI 2006, Montreal, Canada, April 22-27 (2006)
2. Massa, P., Avesani, P.: Trust-aware recommender systems. In: Proc. RecSys 2007, pp. 17–24 (2007)
3. Herlocker, J.L., Konstan, J.A., Borchers, A., Riedl, J.: An algorithmic framework for performing collaborative filtering. In: Proc. 22nd ACM SIGIR 1999 Conference on Research and Development in Information Retrieval, Berkeley, United States, August 15-19, pp. 230–237 (1999)
4. Wilson, C., Boe, B., Sala, A., Puttaswamy, K.P., Zhao, B.Y.: User interactions in Social Networks and their Implications. In: Proc. of 4th ACM European Conference on Computer Systems, EuroSys 2009, Nuremberg, Germany, April 01-03, pp. 205–218 (2009)
5. Pitsilis, G., Marshall, L.F.: Modeling Trust for Recommender Systems Using Similarity Metrics. In: Proc. IFIPTM, Trondheim, Norway, vol. 263, pp. 103–118. Springer, Heidelberg (2008)
6. Liu, H., Lim, E., Lauw, H.W., Le, M., Sun, A., Srivastava, J., Kim, Y.: Predicting Trusts among Users of Online Communities: An epinions case study. In: Proc. of 9th ACM Conference on Electronic Commerce, Chicago, Il, USA, July 08 - 12, pp. 310–319 (2008)
7. Kwon, Y.O.: Improving Top-N Recommendation Techniques Using Rating Variance. In: Proc. RecSys 2008, Lausanne, Switzerland, October 23-25. ACM, New York (2008)
8. Kim, T.-H., Yang, S.-B.: Using Attributes to Improve Prediction Quality in Collaborative Filtering. In: Bauknecht, K., Bichler, M., Pröll, B. (eds.) EC-Web 2004. LNCS, vol. 3182, pp. 1–10. Springer, Heidelberg (2004)
9. Truong, K., Ishukawa, F., Hodinen, S.: Improving the Accuracy of Recommender System by Item Clustering. IECE Trans. Inf. & Syst. E90-D(9) (2007)
10. Herlocker, J.L.: Evaluating Collaborative Filtering Recommender Systems. ACM Transactions on Information Systems 22(1), 5–53 (2004)
11. A cooperative environment for the scientific research of trust metrics on social networks, http://www.trustlet.org/ (last accessed October 1, 2009)

12. Shardanand, ႘., Maes, P.: Social Information Filtering: Algorithms for automating "word of mouth". In: Proc. ACM CHI'95 Conference on Human Factors in Computing Systems, pp. 210–217 (1995)
13. Melville, P., Mooney, R.L., Nagarajan, R.: Content-Boosted Collaborative Filtering for Improved Recommendations. In: Proc. of 18th National conf. of Artificial Intelligence, pp. 187–192 (2002)
14. Jøsang, A.: A Logic for Uncertain probabilities. International Journal of Uncertainty, Fuzziness & Knowledge Based Systems 9(3) (2001)
15. Levien, R.: Advogato's trust metric, White Paper (2009), http://www.advogato.org/trust-metric.html
16. Lathia, N., Hailes, S., Capra, L.: Trust-Based Collaborative Filtering. In: Karabulut, Y., Mitchell, J., Herman, P., Jensen, C.D. (eds.) IFIP, Trust Management II, Trondheim, Norway, vol. 263, pp. 87–102 (2008)
17. Truong, K., Ishukawa, F., Hodinen, S.: Improving the Accuracy of Recommender System by Item Clustering. IECE Trans. Inf. & Syst. E(90)-D.N(O9) (2007)
18. Sarwar, B.M., Karypis, G., Konstan, J.A., Riedl, J.T.: Application of Dimensionality Reduction in Recommender Systems–a case study. In: ACM WebKDD Workshop, Boston, USA (2000)
19. Geng, H., Deng, X., Ali, H.: A new Clustering Algorithm using Message Passing and its applications in Analyzing Microarray Data. In: Proc. of 4th ICMLA, December 15-17, pp. 145–150. IEEE, Washington (2005)
20. Melville, P., Mooney, R.J., Nagarajan, R.: Content-Boosted Collaborative Filtering for Improved Recommendations. In: Proc. of 18th National ACM Conf. of Artificial Intelligence, Alberta, Canada, July 28-August 01, pp. 187–192 (2002)
21. Massa, P., Avesani, P.: Controversial Users demand Local Trust Metrics: an Experimental Study on Epinions.com Community. In: Proc. of 20th National conf. AAAI 2005, pp. 121–126 (2005)
22. Boyd, D., Ellison, N.B.: Social network sites: Definition, History, and Scholarship. Journal of Computer-Mediated Communication 13(1) (2007)
23. O'Donovan, J., Smyth, B.: Trust No One: Evaluating Trust-based Filtering for Recommenders. In: Proc. of the 19th International Joint Conference on Artificial Intelligence IJCAI, Edinburgh, Scotland, pp. 1663–1665. Morgan Kaufmann Publishers, San Francisco (2005)

Bringing the Virtual to the Farmers' Market: Designing for Trust in Pervasive Computing Systems

Ian Wakeman[1], Ann Light[2], Jon Robinson[1],
Dan Chalmers[1], and Anirban Basu[1]

[1] School of Informatics, University of Sussex, Brighton, UK
[2] Communication and Computing Research Centre, Sheffield Hallam University, Sheffield, UK

Abstract. Since pervasive computing applications are mostly designed to enhance existing social situations, such applications should take account of the trust relationships within the situation in their design. In this paper we describe the ethnographic approach we used to explore how trust is formed and maintained within a farmers' market, and how this understanding can be applied in the design of supporting applications. We then evaluate the applications using the same ethnographic approach, uncovering problems which would not have been visible with other evaluation techniques.

1 Introduction

In previous work we have developed computing support for a located shopping guide [9], and an augmented reality system for commenting on poster presentations [10]. The consequent research question that emerged was whether such technologies could be used to support located shopping areas, and in particular, whether such systems could be deployed with a limited fixed infra-structure such as a street market.

Street markets are commonplace all over the world. They are characterised by the temporary nature of the stalls, although particular stalls are regular attendees, and used by a diverse range of customers. Farmers' Markets are a particular form of street market, emerging from the movement to encourage local produce and connect food producers directly to their customers. The eponymous farmers run stalls providing vegetables, poultry, meat and other produce. Such markets are typically not restricted to farmers, but do emphasise local artisan producers such as chutney makers and pie bakers.

Whilst they have a long history within the US, and arguably most French markets are already farmers' markets, the first Farmers' Market in the UK started in 1997 in Bath. The Lewes Farmers' Market was started in 1998 by the Common Cause Co-operative[1], and has continued successfully to the present day. Common Cause now also run a smaller farmers' market in Hove once a month and

---

[1] http://www.commoncause.org.uk/

M. Nishigaki et al. (Eds.): IFIPTM 2010, IFIP AICT 321, pp. 248–262, 2010.

were enthusiastic when we contacted them about the potential for deployment of support systems for markets.

When we deploy ubiquitous computing systems, we are often deploying in situations which already function well. In such cases, we must ensure that the existing processes and interactions are supported and enhanced rather than interrupted and disturbed. The approach often promoted in the literature is to take an ethnographic approach, where the existing sets of interactions are observed, analysed and used as input to the design process. In developing our application we have taken a pragmatic approach to capturing qualitative data, utilising accompanied shopping trips with a researcher acting as participant/observer to gain an understanding of how the market functions, analysing this data to inform the design process, and then using more accompanied shopping to evaluate the effectiveness of our deployed applications.

From our observations, it emerged that *trust* was the fundamental concept underpinning the interactions between the consumers and the stall holders, and any applications would have to build and support trust at a number of different levels. In the rest of this paper, we will first provide a brief overview of the various theoretical approaches to describing trust. We will then discuss how trust relationships are manifested and developed within the farmers' market, based on the evidence from our observations. We will then describe the technologies we deployed within the market, and discuss the effectiveness of our deployments.

2   Theoretical Approaches to Trust

In general trust is required within a transaction when there is the possibility of consequent loss or harm and the other party can influence whether the loss or harm is suffered. If the transaction proceeds, then the party at risk is *trusting* the other party will not intentionally cause harm or loss. Of course, within a farmer's market, the loss or harm is either a perceived monetary loss in feeling that the purchased item has been oversold - the same item is found significantly cheaper in a local shop - or the damage done to the fabric of everyday life when an item is found to be unfit for purpose - the special joint of meat bought for dinner turns out to be rotten.

Following the model of McKnight et al [7], trust can be examined across a range of constructs: Dispositional Trust; Trusting Beliefs; System Trust; Situation Decision to Trust; Trusting Intention and Trusting Behaviour. Dispositional Trust refers to the intrinsic traits of an individual that predispose them to trust. Over the course of their experience, people develop expectations about how people behave in any given situation, and these expectations will be carried through into similar new situations, forming the basis for initial beliefs. As a particular situation unfolds, a person will develop from these initial beliefs into Trusting Beliefs about the other individuals. These trusting beliefs are themselves likely to be formed of judgments about the others' *ability* and competence to perform, the others' *benevolence* and good will to the believer's well-being, the others' *integrity* and principles on which the other acts, and the *predictability* and consistency of action in the given situation.

As well as the generation of trusting beliefs, an individual will be influenced by their beliefs about the systems and societal structures in place to support interactions. As long as the situation appears normal (as in Garfinkel's definition of "normality" [2]) and subject to such structures as the legal system, and local assurance criteria such as membership of trade associations, then the individual will also have *system trust* to support their trusting intentions. Further, if they have become accustomed to a particular sort of situation, and a particular trusting decision has become habitual, their intention will become affected by a situational decision to trust.

The combination of the above cognitive and affective states will influence the individual to decide whether to trust the other, and their intention to behave in a trusting manner. A trusting intention requires that the individual is willing to depend on the others with confidence, even though negative outcomes are possible, whilst the trusting behaviour is the actual act of committing to the transaction.

3   Methodology

We first approached the market organisers explaining that we had a toolkit that could support customers and stallholders in communicating to each other, and that we wished to experiment within the market. The market is held monthly, so our timetable was as laid out in Table 1. Our approach is grounded in ethnographic study. Our initial visit consisted of conversations with all the stallholders and with the market organisers. In our second visit, an experienced ethnographic investigator accompanied two separate shoppers whilst they spent £25 in the market, followed by a debriefing interview. All the conversations were recorded, and interactions recorded through photos. In subsequent visits, the applications were deployed as described below, and our ethnographer again accompanied two separate shoppers. The shoppers were drawn from a pool of female volunteers (I 44 years old, W 41 years old, K 39 years old, H 22 years old), half of whom had familial responsibilities, and all of whom had attended other farmers' markets. H had previously worked on a food stall in a market.

Table 1. Deployment Timetable

February 2009	Initial visit; discussions with stallholders and market organisers
March 2009	Accompanied Shopping; Ethnographic study of two separate shoppers
April 2009	Shopping Lense Deployment; Accompanied shopping whilst using the Shopping Lense
May 2009	QR Code Deployment; Accompanied shopping utilising a QR Code reader on a mobile phone

Fig. 1. Farmers' market view

The market is laid out as in Figure 1, with a mixture of stalls, ranging from simple tables (Figure 2) through to refrigerated vans (Figure 3).

4   The Creation and Maintenance of Trust in the Farmers' Market

In this section, we have studied the recordings, photos and notes from our accompanied shopping expeditions to understand how trust is formed and utilised within the market, using the theory of trust described in Section 2. Quotes from our shoppers come from the first accompanied shopping trips except where noted.

Farmers' markets emphasise the *local* nature of the products, and for the majority of the customers, this is the key attraction. As one of our participants claimed

> Real people who have put together their own stuff from farms, or stuff they've made. Authenticity is really important. (I)

We have defined dispositional trust as the intrinsic likelihood that someone will trust in a particular situation. Given that an individual has to make an effort to actually attend a farmers' market, it would seem likely that they believe

Fig. 2. Simple Stall

that local produce is worth the effort, and thus they are predisposed to trust the stalls within the market, unless stallholders provide counter-evidence. This follows similar arguments put forward by the studies on initial trust formation, such as those summarised by McKnight et al [8].

Our participants provided many insights into how the market and stall holders provide many different signifiers upon which to activate and build trust. Most significant was the development of conversations between the stallholder and their customers, both whilst negotiating at the point of sale, and from joining existing customers' conversations with the stallholder.

In one case, the stallholder of the pie stall invited other customers to join the negotiations of sale to provide *bona fides* of the quality of the product, and to discuss whether the product can be frozen. In consideration afterwards, the participant showed how these conversations can help induce trusting beliefs: "*So if French people think its good food then it really must be a recommendation*" (I). The other participant started a conversation with one of the couple currently being served by the butcher, exchanging tips about how to store roast beef. Such reassuring conversations help to generate trusting intentions about purchase decisions, developing trust that the decision will be well founded.

In Kirwan [6] there is an analysis of how markets are distinct from conventional shopping arenas in that they provide a temporary space for consumption. Indeed, they are often as much about theatre and participatory entertainment as about

Fig. 3. Butcher's van

locating necessary items of consumption [4]. In Gregson's analysis of car boot sales [3], the market space is described as:

> one where people come to play, where the conventions of retailing are suspended and where the participants come to engage in and produce theatre, performance spectacle and laughter.

Whilst the farmers' market is not quite so anarchic as a car boot sale, the interactions between stall-holder and customers can be viewed as creating a spectacle. For instance, as part of a conversation with four other customers, the stallholder selling pies started singing loudly to the tune of Don McLean's American Pie

> Bye, bye, my lovely steak pies.
> Have a pastie, have a pork pie, give my game pie a try
> They're really good and they're lovely to buy...

Whilst this obviously entertained the immediate customers, it also generated interest from other passers-by, and thus attracted custom.

Overall, we found there were a number of subjects around which conversation formed. The most significant of these was the provenance of the produce, when customers would ask about the place and means of production. For instance, at a stall selling goats' cheese, we had the following exchange:

Do you have your own goats? (W)

Yes, its a full time goat dairy farm... with about 400-450 on the farm

The stallholders understand that the key attraction of the farmers' market is that it's local. As one of our participant's commented, the farmer's market consists of *"Real people who have put together their own stuff from farms, or stuff they've made. Authenticity is really important."*. To that end, the stallholders not only discuss the provenance of the produce, but provide the history of how the company came to be. One stallholder proudly talked of this year being the *"30th anniversary this year, and its our 8th year of doing farmers' markets"*, whilst another stallholder told a vignette of they came to be selling on the stall:

> I'll tell you a little story about how I came to work for them. I went to a charity event and bid £27 for three pies. I bought them, put them in the fridge, ate them, they were so nice, and phoned him up went up to the farm, buying off them ever since, and eventually he says what do you do at weekends ... and now you know and I'm here and that's how it all started.

Besides contributing to the social nature of the market, such exchanges help to develop trusting beliefs in the customer, reassuring them that the products are local, and are produced in line with their expectations.

Another key set of topics for conversation is advice on what produce to choose, and how to prepare the produce for eating. At all of the stalls our participants visited, there was discussion about what they were looking for, whether the produce was for a special meal, and advice on cooking or how to present, whether the produce was venison, pork, chutneys or goats' cheese. Such conversations promote trusting intentions prior to purchase by showing that the stallholders are both interested in making sure the purchase decision is correct, and that they are knowledgeable about their products. As one of our participants reflected, *"I trust them because they have investment in their produce"* (W). However, there are differences in motivation across shoppers - our other participant reflected on how trust was engendered with a greater emphasis on the product:

> [There's a] ...genuine sense of enthusiasm from stallholders, enables trust in the stallholder and by proxy to the product. But products come first - they look yummy and good and homegrown. The stallholders then back that up. (I)

Such conversations have other positive effects. One participant noted that *"My self-esteem has has gone up through having a conversation that we're both interested in"* (W).

Determining the *Quality* of a product in food consumption is a subject studied by consumer behaviourists and others. Products from supermarkets rely upon the *uniform standards* of quality generated by marketing and the other trappings of a consumer society. However, within a farmers' market, these uniform standards don't apply, since the necessary signage is absent in packaging and other shop displays. Instead, as Kirwan describes [6], the quality of products in farmers' markets is negotiated contingent upon conversation and place:

In the case of FMs, the producers and consumers concerned are engaging in face-to-face interaction in order to create conventions of exchange which incorporate spatial and social relations that can replace 'uniform standards'.

The display of materials is set up to differentiate between the farmers' market produce and that available at conventional shops and supermarkets. Packaging is less sophisticated, emphasising the artisan nature of the product and the small scale production, in contrast to the slick packaging of supermarket produce. Produce such as cheeses and chutneys are all available to try, rather than solely those on special offer, encouraging the belief that the producer is confident you'll find something to like. Our shoppers found this to help in forming trusting beliefs - "*You can try stuff out - its just all ere for you to have a go at*" (I) - and indeed found the unsophisticated presentation a key piece of evidence for the products' quality.

A monthly street market is by definition a transient opportunity for consumers. The very appearance and presentation of the stalls signify the temporary nature of the stall. Stalls typically use a lightweight awning, and a covered table. Signage is attached to the awnings using market clips. Even the vans used by the meat suppliers, enabling the use of refrigeration equipment show the consumer that there is a time limited opportunity to get access to the stall. This can be seen as part of the "charm" of the market. Our accompanied shoppers displayed the same positions:

> You can get that feeling that its real people selling their produce, actually because it quite thin, the displays are relatively thin. Its not absolutely piled up like a commercial thing

and that there are "*Banners hanging behind stalls, there's a sense of homemade quality, the higgledy piggledy look.*" (I).

Kirwan also notes that the perception of quality is based upon "the build up of trust over time, which is facilitated by consumers being able to make direct connections with the place and nature of the good they are purchasing" [6]. In our observations, we found that customer I on her second visit to the stall was recognised and asked about how they had found the chutney they had bought previously, which was followed by the descriptions of similar chutneys.

Finally, there is an element of system trust. The norms of the farmers' market are primarily created by the organisers of the market. Producers who apply to run a stall within the market are required to fill out a form explaining their provenance chain, showing that their produce is primarily local[2] and are subject to inspections by the market organisers. The organisers also work closely with the local agricultural college to promote organic and ethical production. Producers admitted to the market are therefore aware that they are in the market because of the origin of their produce and production ethics. Although the organisers

---

[2] The emphasis is on locality of produce but obviously producers of chutney can make use of ingredients sourced outside of the locality.

conscientiously place small flyers describing the organisation and ethos behind the market, these are almost always ignored. However, in our observations, one stallholder described how stalls had to be certified to be in farmers' markets to one of our participants. Such system trust is reinforced as shoppers become more aware of the origins of the stalls and the market.

5   Integrating Trust and Technology

As described in [10], we have produced a toolkit for developing located applications for shopping environments. At the heart of our toolkit are the concepts of *pseudonyms*, *groups*, *patterns* and a *pattern registry*. A mobile phone is able to recognise a pattern such as a QRCode or a fiducial marker for augmented reality. The phone is then able to look up the pattern within the pattern registry, and retrieve data directly attached to the pattern and a list of associated *comments*. Each pattern or comment is owned by a pseudonym, allowing users to specify trust ratings on pseudonyms. Further, pseudonyms can belong to groups, allowing indirect policies to be specified based on group membership, using concepts from [12]. The system is designed so that authorisation of group membership happens offline and is subject to whatever checks are deemed necessary for the group's aims. Our system is designed to allow choice of a number of different approaches to order the list of comments returned for a pattern, based on whatever policy module is used for the application. The back end system is implemented within the Java EE framework, and is accessible over standard web services.

Given that the transient nature of the market stalls is integral to the perception of the farmers' market as local, we have adopted a low-tech approach to enabling the market for located computing applications by simply attaching A4 laminates of the patterns to the stalls by market pegs or Blu-Tack[3], as show in Figure 4. From Section 4, it can be seen that the formation of trusting beliefs comes primarily from conversations between the stallholders and the customers. To this end, we have formulated an *"AskUsAbout"* application for use whilst people are queuing for their turn with the stallholder. For each stall we create a pattern, a group and an initial pseudonym as group member. The stallholder then can add whatever information they wish to the pattern, and add comments designed to act as primers for conversation when the user takes their turn with the stallholder. The policies of the users were primed so as to maximise trust in the stallholder's group comments, and minimise trust in other comments. The comments came from interviews with the stallholders, such as:

> We have pet mince and free bones available. These are excellent value and really loved by dogs. Just £1.50, with reduced prices for regulars.

We also introduced a *Visitors' Book* application, allowing customers to add their comments about the stall. In this application, the policies were more flexible, only ordering comments based on whether the user was in the same group as the comment owner. An example of a comment left by our users was:

---

[3] Wikipedia describes Blu-Tack as " a versatile, reusable putty-like pressure-sensitive adhesive".

Fig. 4. A participant using the ARToolkit browser

> We had some pork chops from David back in February, and they were delicious. Not only did they have the porkiest taste since we had Dotty down in Devon, they were cut so large that they were almost a roasting joint in their own right.

This application was motivated by the way that customers interact, asking each for advice and building trust about the stalls based on their prior experience.

We take advantage of the dispositional trust within the participants that everything and *everybody* within the market are local, and are thus all part of a shared community to reduce the level of authentication needed to use the system. Pseudonym registration requires nothing more than the creation of a unique identifier. The system is thus open to a number of sybil and denial of service attacks. However, since our trust policies are based on group membership, and group membership does require authentication, these attacks should not be very damaging. We also believe that the located nature of the application reduces the likelihood that such attacks would be mounted.

We implemented two possible front ends, using augmented reality to build a customised Shopping Lense, and using QR Codes [5] to encode the relevant URL to the back-end application, which utilises a normal web browser to display the interface rendered in HTML.

The Shopping Lense is built on the AR Toolkit [1], a mature toolkit for overlaying graphics upon a stream of video. The toolkit uses fiducial patterns, which are pre-compiled into recognisable patterns that the ARToolkit can recognise within frames of video. The Shopping Lense interface is based around a video view, highlighting patterns that are recognised, and annotating the pattern with the name that was attached to the pattern by its owner. We then display the most trusted anchors according to the user's policy around the pattern. By trial and error, given the expected viewing distance of up to ten meters, we decided to limit the number of anchors displayed around a pattern to four.

When an anchor is selected, the mode of the viewer is changed to that of a standard list box, displaying the text or URL associated with the anchor. All the other anchors linked to the pattern are displayed in a list, ordered by the trust rating generated in the back end. The level of trust in an anchor is indicated through colour coding (green being most trusted, orange neutral and red least trusted), the font weight of the text, and the size of the text. For this experiment, the Shopping Lense ran on an ultra mobile PC, as shown in Figure 4.

Whilst our initial aim was to port the Shopping Lense to a mobile phone platform, this proved impossible with the state of the art phone of last year, so we also built the QR Code version. The QR Code interface displays the anchors directly in HTML designed for the limitations of mobile phone browsers, but is otherwise functionally equivalent to the Shopping Lense. It should be noted that QR Codes were still rare in the UK in the first half of 2009, but we expect them to become more widespread and thus allows the software to be used by a wider population base in the future.

To populate the application databases, we gathered comments for the Visitors' Books from an emailed survey to members of our university and from our own experiences, whilst the information supplied within the AskUsAbout survey came from directly talking to the stallholders and from their websites.

6   Evaluation

Our evaluation comes from observing two of our participant shoppers (I and K) using the Shopping Lense, and then one month later observing another two using the a mobile phone using a QR Code reader. Since we have no participants who used both the Shopping Lense and the QR Code reader, we will not make any direct comparison between the two interface approaches.

It appeared both applications worked. Across all four participants, conversations were cued from reading the AskUsAbout information. The pattern would typically be that the shopper would read out the information to their accompanying shopper, when the stallholder would overhear and confirm the information. Discussion would then ensue. One shopper believed that the information helped increase her confidence in talking to the stall by providing her with background - its the *"Kind of thing that's useful when you don't really know [the stall] at all."* (H).

For the Visitors' Book, both K and H were prompted to buy products they wouldn't otherwise have purchased:

> And I would, as I said earlier I think, have probably bought chicken or sausages because thats what my son likes to eat, but the fact that the

kit mentioned pork chops made me think he really likes pork chops and I dont very often buy pork chops, so, yeah, just raised that possibility like you say (K)

and similarly

Its good, if I go to that [the application] first before looking at this [stall], then I'm immediately drawn to the pork chops, which is something I wouldn't normally buy... I suppose this is really good marketing (H)

H then reasoned that that the application worked because it was *"A review at point of use which you wouldn't normally get in y other way.".* Given that a trusting belief is generated from the comment that is converted to a trusting intention of the purchase, it can be argued that the applications directly influenced the cognitive trust of the shoppers.

There were usability issues with both the Shopping Lense and the QR Codes. Although the UMPC is small, it still requires both hands to manipulate. Once the shopper was encumbered with bags, using the UMPC or paying became a struggle to coordinate all the necessary placing of bags. Although this became easier as the shoppers became accustomed to the kit,

But it didnt feel like a difficulty at that stall. I mean, I guess that was the third stall that Id bought something at and I think Id kind of.. I dont know why it was easier there, I cant remember now. Because that was the, the one stall where I didnt need to, I didnt think about it. (K)

it was noticeable that the phone was easier to use - *"This is really intuitive - I don't know this phone, but taking a photograph is really good"* (H). Underhill noted in [11] that when the hands are too full, the shopping spree is over. If we expect the shopper to then manipulate gadgets whilst holding bags, we will encounter problems. Indeed, the ballet of placing bags and kit on the stall to dive for the money to pay almost resulted in the UMPC being left behind.

We had problems with sunshine producing glare on the screen making it difficult to angle the UMPC so as to see the display - *"I cant see anything here. Hmm, Im really struggling because of the sunlight to make it work."* (K), with the shopper later referring to the need to move backwards and forwards to find a visible angle as "the dance". This may prove a major hurdle for the deployment of augmented reality in outdoors settings, since the UMPC has to be continuously pointed at the pattern to be viewed in real time. The QR Code deployment didn't suffer from these problems, since once the picture was taken, the returned HTML pages could be viewed in the shade of the stall, or by turning to position the body correctly.

Internet connectivity for our phones was occasionally problematic, and we were at the mercy of the idiosyncrasies of particular browser implementations. During the shop, one phone stopped getting 3G connectivity, so we had to switch to an alternative phone, with a different browser, and thus different approaches to scrolling the screen.

Whilst our focus has been on delivering the technical solution to facilitate communication between stallholders and queuing customers, it became obvious from our deployment that the content of the comments is all important.

Wasnt the [information] the cue for you to have a conversation with the stall holders? (interviewer)
No, it wasnt... it felt like the information from the stall holder was, em, telling me something to persuade me to buy something, whereas I feel as though my conversations with stall holders usually are about, em, getting information that I want rather than information that they want to impart. (K)

The most successful comments contained the copy that was most informal, aligning itself with the authenticity of the market.

Positioning of the patterns could also present problems. The patterns had to be placed so that they were easily visible to the queuing customers, which could be difficult when queues would form irregularly.

One shopper raised a problem about whether the Visitors' Book was intended for comments about the experience of shopping and interacting with the stall, or about the experience of consumption. Our naive answer was that it was for both, but we plan to investigate in future work how to capture and provide comments at the appropriate time.

Finally, we saw several examples of the problems of combining the virtual world with a located market. Our shoppers wanted to talk to the stallholders and found the applications to be a hindrance, especially when they weren't accustomed to the gadget:

Hmm, I guess it kind of it feels more awkward for me, yeah, em, normally I would, my focus would be to try something and then probably talk to the stall holder and em, be more interpersonally focused than elsewhere which I feel focused elsewhere today

We saw suggestions that this may be a digital divide between how the younger and older shoppers would use the kit, where the younger shoppers would naturally explore the virtual world before conversation - "*I don't know what they sell - I'm going to check out the bar code thing to see if that's any help*" (H) - whereas the older shoppers all expressed a preference for conversation if possible - "*My attention split between stallholder and and the kit*".

7   Conclusion

Trust between people is fundamentally contingent on context and continually negotiated between people. The ways in which trust is signified and maintained are often implicit in a particular situation, and are not always obvious. If we build pervasive computing applications without regard for the subtleties of how peoples' relationships are supported, we run the risk of providing computing support that is at best ignored and may possibly break the existing trust relationships. In our investigation, we showed that conversations were the essential support for trust within the market. If our applications had attempted to replace conversation, we would have broken the social context of the market. A key lesson of this work is that the requirements for located computing require a deeper investigation of the social relationships, and that ethnographic investigation of some form is needed to explicate the context for design.

Further, evaluation of the effectiveness of the solution requires use of ethnographic techniques. Whilst our applications did work mostly as we expected, there were unforeseen problems that only emerged from the ethnographic analysis. The distinction between purchase and consumption experience was not clear from our first study, and would require further work to make the application work effectively. Whilst the AskUsAbout application provoked conversations with the stall holders, it only became apparent that some of the copy was alienating our participants through reflection with our ethnographer after the event.

Technically we found that adapting the toolkit to provide applications was relatively painless, and that it was essential to provide varying levels of technological sophistication for accessing the applications. Whilst augmented reality may become widespread in the coming years, the QR Code interface will remain much more accessible for the majority of the population without high powered mobile telephones.

In future work we are deploying the system as a communication channel for our university's catering service, where we hope to explore how a more digitally aware population will make use of a located application.

References

1. Billinghurst, M., Kato, H.: Collaborative augmented reality. Communications of the ACM 45(7), 64–70 (2002)
2. Garfinkel, H.: Studies in Ethnomethodology. Prentice Hall, Englewood Cliffs (1967)
3. Gregson, N., Crewe, L.: The bargain, the knowledge, and the spectacle: making sense of consumption in the space of the car-boot sale. Environment and Planning D 15(1), 87–112 (1997)
4. Holloway, L., Kneafsey, M.: Reading the space of the farmers' market: A preliminary investigation from the UK. Sociologia Ruralis 40(3), 285–299 (2000)
5. ISO(ed.) Information technology – Automatic identification and data capture techniques – QR Code 2005 bar code symbology specification. Number 18004 in IEC. ISO/IEC, 2 edn. (2006)
6. Kirwan, J.: The interpersonal world of direct marketing: Examining conventions of quality at uk farmers markets. Journal of Rural Studies 22(3), 301–312 (2006)
7. Harrison McKnight, D., Chervany, N.L.: The meanings of trust. Technical Report 94-04, Carlson School of Management, University of Minnesota (1996)
8. Harrison McKnight, D., Cummings, L.L., Chervany, N.L.: Initial trust formation in new organizational relationships. The Academy of Management Review 23(3), 473–490 (1998)
9. Robinson, J., Wakeman, I., Chalmers, D., Basu, A.: The North Laine shopping guide: A case study in modelling trust in applications. In: Proceedings of IFIP conference on Trust Management, May 2008, pp. 183–197. Springer, Boston (2008)

10. Robinson, J., Wakeman, I., Chalmers, D., Horsfall, B.: Augmented reality support for poster presentations (submitted for publication, 2010)
11. Underhill, P.: Why We Buy: The Science of Shopping. Simon and Schuster, New York (2008)
12. Wakeman, I., Chalmers, D., Fry, M.: Reconciling privacy and security in pervasive computing. In: 5th International Workshop on Middleware for Pervasive and Ad-Hoc Computing (MPAC 2007), Los Angeles, Ca (November 2007)

Incorporating Interdependency of Trust Values in Existing Trust Models for Trust Dynamics

Mark Hoogendoorn, S. Waqar Jaffry, and Jan Treur

Vrije Universiteit Amsterdam, Department of Artificial Intelligence,
De Boelelaan 1081a, 1081 HV Amsterdam, The Netherlands
{mhoogen,swjaffry,treur}@few.vu.nl

Abstract. Many models of trust consider the trust an agent has in another agent (the trustee) as the result of experiences with that specific agent in combination with certain personality attributes. For the case of multiple trustees, there might however be dependencies between the trust levels in different trustees. In this paper, two alternatives are described to model such dependencies: (1) development of a new trust model which incorporates dependencies explicitly, and (2) an extension of existing trust models that is able to express these interdependencies using a translation mechanism from objective experiences to subjective ones. For the latter, placing the interdependencies in the experiences enables the reuse of existing trust models that typically are based upon certain experiences over time as input. Simulation runs are performed using the two approaches, showing that both are able to generate realistic patterns of interdependent trust values.

Keywords: Trust modeling, interdependence, trust dynamics.

1 Introduction

Within multi-agent systems, the concept of trust is often a key element in the relationship between agents. For example, an agent's trust in other agents might influence the selection process for task delegation. As a result, a variety of models related to trust have been proposed, see e.g. [3],[4],[7]. In most of these trust models, the trust an agent has in another agent is seen as the result of experiences the agent has with that other agent, and certain personality attributes (see e.g. [4], [7]), and is independent of trust in other agents. More complex trust models also address a more advanced interpretation of the experiences, for example using a cognitive attribution process (see e.g. [3]).

Merely considering experiences the agent has with a single other agent is however not always sufficient nor realistic. Sometimes experiences with an agent or the trust value in an agent can influence the trust in another agent. Imagine the following scenario: somebody wants to buy a new television. He currently has experience with two websites that sell televisions (referred to as w_1 and w_2). Given these experiences, he has a high trust in w_1 and a low trust in w_2. As a result, he decides to buy the television at w_1. Unfortunately, he gets a negative experience as the television is delivered

M. Nishigaki et al. (Eds.): IFIPTM 2010, IFIP AICT 321, pp. 263–276, 2010.

with a broken screen and they do not accept the liability. Of course, this negative experience brings down the trust the person has in w_1, however it might also result in an update of the trust in w_2. Essentially, there are three options for this dependency: (1) a positive trust dependency, whereby negative experiences with one trustee have a negative influence upon the trust level of another trustee as well, and a negative experience has a negative influence upon the trust level of other trustee; (2) a negative trust dependency, whereby a negative experience with one trustee has a positive influence upon the trust of another trustee and a positive experience a negative influence, and (3) no trust dependency, meaning that there is no influence because the agent does not perceive a relationship. For the example, a negative trust dependency between w_1 and w_2 could be the case if the human perceives them as substitutable competitors (given the experience with w_1, w_2 was actually not that bad) and a positive trust dependency in case the human sees the trustees as representatives from the same group (all Internet stores cannot be trusted).

In order to address these dependencies, a possibility is to incorporate such relationships in the trust model explicitly. This approach is for instance taken in [4], and has been refined in this paper. A disadvantage of such an approach is however that this does not allow the reuse of the currently existing trust models, each having their own specific pros and cons. Another option which is therefore investigated in this paper is to model a process which transforms the objective experiences into subjective experiences for each of the agents, thereby considering the dependencies as expressed before. This does allow for the reuse of existing trust models. Hereby, first a model to translate objective into subjective experiences is created with a number of parameters that can be set to tune the precise relationship between the experiences with each of the trustees. Simulation runs have been performed using both approaches to investigate whether the models are able to generate the desired behavior.

This paper is organized as follows. First, a trust model which incorporates interdependency directly is presented in Section 2, followed by the model to translate objective into subjective experiences and feed this into an existing trust model in Section 3. Section 4 presents compatible existing trust models and simulations results using all variants are presented in Section 5. Section 6 presents related work, and finally, Section 7 concludes the paper and gives directions for future work.

2 Relative Trust Model

This section describes a dedicated trust model of human trust on interdependent trustees incorporating the interdependence in the trust model itself. Note that this model has been inspired on [4] but has been slightly simplified to obtain higher transparency. In this model trust values have some degree of interdependency (competition, neutral, cooperation) where the human trust on a trustee depends on the relative trust in the trustee in comparison to the trust on other trustees. This model includes human personality characteristics like trust decay, flexibility and the degree of interdependency among trustees. Figure 1 shows the dynamic relationships in the model. Here, the trust value of one trustee is directly dependent on the trust values on other trustees.

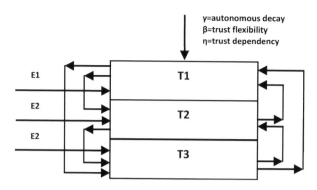

Fig. 1. Dynamic relationships in relative trust model

In the model described in Figure 1 it is assumed that trustees $\{S_1, S_2, \ldots S_n\}$ provide experiences ($E_i(t)$) to human at each time step continuously, these experiences have value from the continuous interval [-1, 1]. Here, -1 indicates the most negative experience whereas 1 is the most positive. The human updates the trust value on a trustee by keeping trust values on other trustees under consideration along with the interdependency relation of the trustees (η). Furthermore, human personality attributes like trust flexibility, expressing how much an experience counts (β) and autonomous trust decay (γ), indicating how fast trust goes back to a neutral value when there are no new experiences also play a role in this process. On receiving an experience $E_i(t)$ from a trustee S_i at time point t, the human trust on S_i at the next time point (t+1) is the sum of the human trust on S_i ($T_i(t)$) and the experience $E_i(t)$ minus the autonomous decay in trust, this is expressed as follows

$$T_i(t+1) = (1-\beta)*T_i(t) + \beta*E_i(t) - \gamma*T_i(t)$$

In differential form

$$dT_i/dt = \beta*\left(E_i(t) - T_i(t)\right) - \gamma*T_i(t)$$

To introduce the notion of trustees interdependence in this model, the relative trust of the human is defined. The relative trust of the human on S_i at time point t ($\tau_i(t)$) is the difference between the human's projected trust on S_i ($T'_i(t)$) and the average of the human's projected trust on all trustees times the degree of trustees interdependency η. The human projected trust on S_i at time point t is the human trust on S_i projected from the range [-1, 1] to [0, 1] as follows:

$$T'_i(t) = \left(T_i(t) + 1\right)/2$$

The human's relative trust on trustee S_i at time point t can be calculated as follows

$$\tau_i(t) = \eta*\left(T'_i(t) - \sum_{j=1}^{n} T'_j/n\right)$$

Where η is the degree of trustees interdependency in the range [-1, 1]. A negative value of η denotes cooperation while a positive value represents competition among the trustees and n is the number of trustees. The human relative trust is designed to fulfill the requirements for different interdependencies among trustees as shown in Table 1.

Table 1. Value of Relative Trust with different interdependencies

Trust Value	Interdependency	Relative Trust Value
Above average	Cooperation	Negative
Above average	Competition	Positive
Equal to average	Cooperation	Zero
Equal to average	Competition	Zero
Below average	Cooperation	Positive
Below average	Competition	Negative

This relative trust is introduced as a bias in the above trust equation with experience and trust values as follows

$$dT_i/dt = \beta * \left(E_i(t) - T_i(t) + \tau_i(t) \right) - \gamma * T_i(t) .$$

3   Subjective Experience Based Trust Model

This section describes a model of human trust on interdependent trust values using experience transformation, thereby allowing for the reuse of existing trust models. In this model the trust values for different trustees have some degree of interdependency among themselves (competition, neutral, cooperation), similar to the model presented in Section 2. In this case, the human trust on a trustee depends on the relative experiences with the trustee in comparison to the experiences it has obtained from the other trustees. This model includes human personality characteristics like trust decay, flexibility, trust bias on experience, and degree of interdependency among trustees. Figure 2 shows the dynamic relationships in the model used.

The model expressed in Figure 2 is composed of two models: one for transforming an objective experience with a trustee into a subjective experience (on the left), and another model for updating the human trust value based on this subjective experience (on the right). In this case, it is assumed that the trustee continuously provides the human with objective experiences ($E_i(t)$) which are transformed into subjective experiences ($E'_i(t)$) also on the interval [-1, 1]. This transformation depends on the human trust bias on experience (α) and the degree of interdependency among trustees (η). Thereafter this experience is passed on to the trust model (which can in principle be any compatible existing trust model). The computational models for Figure 2 are described in the following sections.

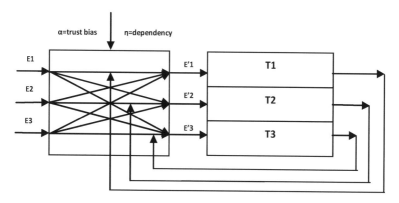

Fig. 2. Dynamic relationships in subjective experience based trust model

3.1 Transforming Objective into Subjective Experience Using Trust Interdependency

This section explains the design of the mathematical model for transforming an objective experience provided by the trustee into a subjective experience using trust interdependency. The human's subjective experience at any time point t is based on a combination of two parts: the trust biased part, and the trustee's interdependency part. For the latter part an important indicator is the human's relative experience of trustee S_i ($E_i(t)$) at time point t (denoted by $\tau_i(t)$): the difference of the human's experience of S_i to the average human's experience from all trustees at time point t times the degree of trustees interdependency η. This is calculated as follows:

$$\tau_i(t) = \eta * \left(E_i^{'}(t) - \sum_{j=1}^{n} E_j^{'}(t)/n \right)$$

Here it should be noted that $E_i^{'}(t)$ is the objective experience from trustee S_i at time point t projected from the interval [-1, 1] onto the interval [0, 1]. The trust interdependency parameter (η) can take values from the continuous interval [-1, 1], where negative and positive values of η denote cooperation and competition respectively similar to the model presented in Section 2. The human's relative experience is designed to fulfill the requirements as expressed in Table 2 for different interdependencies among trustees.

Table 2. Change in objective experience with interdependencies

Objective experience	Interdependency	Change in Objective Experience
Above average	Cooperation	Negative
Above average	Competition	Positive
Equal to average	Cooperation	Zero
Equal to average	Competition	Zero
Below average	Cooperation	Positive
Below average	Competition	Negative

To calculate the experience when taking the interdependency into account, the relative experience at time point t is added to the objective experience $E_i(t)$ from trustee S_i at time point t:

$$E_i(t) + \tau_i(t)$$

In addition, a trust bias is included when transforming the objective experience into a subjective experience at time point t. Hereby the factor α (trust bias on experiences) is used to take α percent of the value of the trust a human has in a trustee i at time point t $(T_i(t))$ and $(1 - α)$ percent of the trustees experience in combination with the interdependency relation:

$$V_i = \alpha * T_i(t) + (1 - \alpha) * (E_i(t) + \tau_i(t))$$

For further smoothing of this transformation (following approaches often found in neurological modeling), a threshold function $th(\beta_1, \beta_2, V_i)$ is used with threshold β_1 and steepness β_2, defined as follows:

$$th(\beta_1, \beta_2, V_i) = \frac{1}{\left(1 + e^{(-\beta_2(V_i - \beta_1))}\right)}$$

As the value of this threshold function resides on the interval [0, 1], this value is projected onto the interval [-1,1] according to the following formula:

$$E_{si}(t) = 2 * th(\beta_1, \beta_2, V_i) - 1$$

3.2   A Sample Trust Model

In order to illustrate how this experience can be used in a trust model, a very basic trust model is explained here. This model is an extension of a model present in the literature [7], which accumulates experiences over time and updates trust accordingly. Other trust models that are also suitable and have been found in existing literature are expressed in Section 4. In the trust model presented below, the trust is based on experiences in combination with two personality characteristics trust flexibility β and autonomous trust decay γ (defined similarly as in Section 2). In this model, it is assumed that the human trust on a trustee S_i at time point t is $T_i(t)$ (a value from the interval [-1,1]). On receiving a subjective experience $E_{si}(t)$ from trustee S_i trust of human on the trustee at time point $t + \Delta t$ adapts as follows:

$$T_i(t + \Delta t) = T_i(t) + (\beta * E_{si}(t) - \gamma * T_i(t)) * \Delta t$$

in differential form:

$$dT_i/dt = (\beta * E_{si}(t) - \gamma * T_i(t))$$

Here it could be noted that trust would be in equilibrium if

$$\frac{T_i(t)}{E_{si}(t)} = \frac{\beta}{\gamma}$$

4 Experience-Based Trust Models from Literature

This section describes two other experience based models taken from literature, and it will be shown that they also can be combined with the subjective experience model as proposed in Section 3. In [8] a simple trust model is proposed which accumulates experiences over time without temporal discounting of experiences. The model is defined by the following equation:

$$dT_i/dt = \beta * (E_i(t) - T_i(t))/t$$

In the equation, β is the trust flexibility (i.e., how much an experience counts) while $E_i(t)$ is the experience with trustee i (in this case, the subjective experience if it is integrated with the proposed model). Similarly, another trust model described in [8] also accommodates experiences from the environment (but this time in discounted form), and the trust values are then updated as follows (with the same parameters):

$$dT_i/dt = \beta * (E_i(t) - T_i(t)) * \left(e^{\beta * t}/\left(e^{\beta * t} - 1\right)\right)$$

Here it can be noted that the exponential part in this model supports temporal discounting of experiences over time. Other, more complex trust models that are based upon experiences exist as well, see Section 6 for more details.

5 Simulation Results

The models described in Section 2, 3 and 4 have been used to conduct a number of simulation experiments to see what patterns emerge using the different models, and how the different models compare. Here, first the experimental configurations of the simulations are described briefly followed by some of the simulation results.

Table 3. Model configurations used for simulation experiments

Parameters	Symbols	Values
Threshold	β_1	0
steepness	β_2	1
degree of trustees interdependency	η	[-1, 0, 1]
Trust bias on experience	α	0.25
autonomous trust decay	γ	0.10
trust flexibility	β	0.10
time step	Δt	0.10
initial trust on trustees	T(0)	0, 0, 0

The experimental configurations for the simulations are shown in Table 3. During the experiments, the initial trust value of the human on all trustees is considered neutral (zero) and the effect of the degree of trust interdependency has been observed using three different values [-1, 0, 1] of η for cooperation, neutral and competition. The models were analyzed against several experience sequences. An experience sequence is the series of experience values received by human from different trustees over time. The experience sequences used in the graphs presented in this section are shown in Figure 3. Here, three trustees are assumed namely S_1, S_2 and S_3, giving experiences E_1, E_2 and E_3 respectively, where S_2 and S_3 give positive (1) and negative (-1) experience values respectively for the whole experiment (2000 time steps) while S_1 gives negative (-1) and positive (1) alternating periodically in a period of 500 time steps each (see Figure 3a). Moreover, in Figure 3b, S_1 gives positive (1) and neutral (0) experiences and S_2 gives negative (-1) and positive (1) alternating periodically in a period of 500 time steps each, while S_3 gives neutral (0) experiences for the whole experiment. This approach of using a shift in experience after a certain number of positive and negatives experiences is inspired on different empirical validations techniques of experience based trust models presented in literature (see e.g. [6]). The presented experience sequences in this paper are selected to show adaptation of different trust models over sudden shifts in the behavior of the trustees.

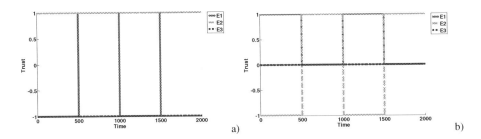

Fig. 3. Experience Sequence used for Simulations

5.1   Experiment 1: Relative Trust Model

In this experiment the experience sequence of Figure 3a is used for the relative trust model as explained in Section 2. The results are shown in Figure 4. In Figure 4a, 4b and 4c the trust values T_1, T_2 and T_3 of the trustee S_1, S_2 and S_3 are shown on the y-axis for competitive, neutral and cooperative trust interdependency, respectively, while time is on the x-axis. In Figure 4a the interdependency is competition, so it can be observed that when S_1 gives positive experiences, the trust values of the other two trustees become lower and vice-versa. In Figure 4b, η is set to zero that means the trust values of trustees are mutually independent which shows in the graphs as well. In Figure 4c cooperation is introduced by setting $\eta = -1$. Hence in Figure 4c it can be seen that when S_1 gives positive experiences it also effects the trust values of the other two trustees positively and vice-versa. Furthermore in the competitive case (Figure 4a) the maximum and minimum values of trust attained is higher than the neutral and cooperative cases. This is because competition gives an additional increase to the positive and negative trust values towards extremes while cooperation brings them closer to each other.

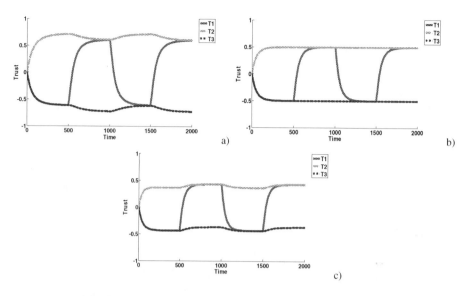

Fig. 4. Dynamics of relative trust model a) $\eta=1$, b) $\eta=0$ c) $\eta=-1$

5.2 Experiment 1: Subjective Experience Based in Combination with Simple Trust Model

In this experiment the experience sequence of Figure 3a was used for the subjective experience based model described in Section 3 in combination with the simple trust model shown in Section 3.2. In Figure 5a, 5c and 5e the values of the subjective experiences for trustee S_1, S_2 and S_3 are shown on the y-axis for competitive, neutral and cooperative trust interdependency respectively and in Figure 5b, 5d and 5f the respective trust values are shown. The patterns shown resemble the ones shown for the model presented in Section 2. In Figure 5b it can be noted that when trustee S_1 gives negative objective experiences, due to the competition values the subjective experiences of S_2 and S_3 become slightly higher and vice-versa. In Figure 5c as the interdependency value η is 0, no mutual effect of the subjective experiences on each other could be observed. The curves shown in Figure 5c also show the effect of the threshold function used in the model. In Figure 5e where $\eta = -1$, representing coopera-tion, it can be seen that an increase in objective experience of S_1 gives a positive boost to the subjective values of S_2 and S_3 and vice-versa. Furthermore, in the competitive case (Figure 5a) the maximum and minimum values of the subjective experiences are higher than for the neutral and cooperative cases. This is due to that fact that competi-tion gives an additional increase to the positive and negative subjective experience values towards extremes while cooperation brings them closer to each other. Similarly these subjective experiences have a direct effect on the trust values of the trustees in each case (see Figure 5b, 5d, 5e).

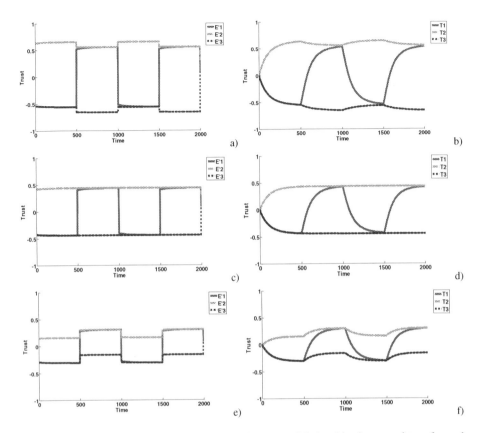

Fig. 5. Dynamics of subjective experience based trust model a) subjective experience for η=1 b) Trust for η=1, c) subjective experience for η=0, d) Trust for η=0 e) subjective experience for η=-1, f) Trust for η=-1

5.3 Experiment 1: Subjective Experience Based in Combination with Trust Model from Literature

In this experiment the experience sequence of Figure 3a was used for the subjective experience for trust model from literature described in Section 4. One of the two models described in this literature is not accounting temporal discounting of experiences while the second does. In Figure 5a, 5c and 5e simulation results for the model without temporal discounting of experience are shown. In this case it can be observed that this simple model does not show the type of results as expected and generated by the other models. In Figures 6b, 6d, and 6f the simulation results for model incorporating temporal discounting of experiences are shown. In Figure 6b it can be noted that when trustee S_1 gives negative objective experiences, due to the competition values the trust of S_2 and S_3 become slightly higher and vice-versa. In Figure 6d as the interdependency value η is 0, no mutual effect of the trust values on each other could be observed. In Figure 6f where η = -1, representing cooperation, it can be seen that an increase in objective experience of S_1 gives a positive boost to the subjective values of S_2 and S_3 and vice-versa. Furthermore, in the competitive case (Figure 6a, 6b) the maximum and minimum values of the trust are higher than for the neutral and cooperative cases. This is due to that fact that competition gives an additional increase to the positive and negative trust values towards extremes while cooperation brings them closer to each other (see Figure 6c, d, e, f).

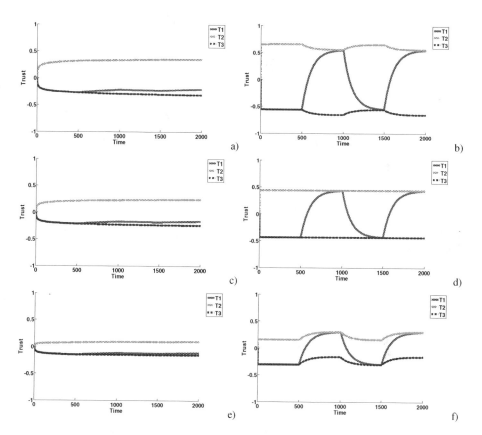

Fig. 6. Dynamics of subjective experience based on trust models from literature a) without temporal discounting and $\eta=1$ b) with temporal discounting and $\eta=1$, c) without temporal discounting and $\eta=0$, d) with temporal discounting and $\eta=0$ e) without temporal discounting and $\eta=-1$, f) with temporal discounting and $\eta=-1$

5.4   Experiment 2: Relative Trust and Subjective Experience Based Trust Models

In this experiment the second experience sequence was used where trustee S_1 gives positive (1) and neutral (0) and S_2 gives negative (-1) and positive (1) experience values alternating periodically every 500 time steps, while S_3 gives neutral (0) experiences for the whole experiment (see figure 3b).

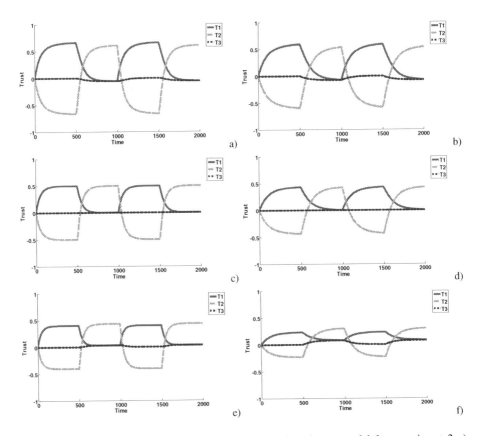

Fig. 7. Dynamics of relative and subjective experience based trust model for experiment 2 **a)** relative trust model for η=1, **b)** subjective experience based model for η=1, **c)** relative trust model for η=0, **d)** subjective experience based model for η=0 **e)** relative trust model for η=-1, **f)** subjective experience based model for η=-1

In Figure 7a (relative trust model) and 7b (subjective experience based trust model) it is shown that when trustee S_2 gives negative experiences, and there is a competitive interdependency the trust values of S_1 become slightly higher than the trust values of S_1 in Figure 7c and 7d (where there is a neutral interdependency). In Figure 7c and 7d as the interdependency value η is 0, no mutual effect of trust values on each other can be observed. In Figure 7e and 7f where η = -1 representing cooperation among trust values of trustees, it can be seen again that an increase in trust of S_2 due to positive experience gives a positive boost to S_1 and S_3 and vice-versa. Furthermore, in the competitive case (Figure 7a and 7b), the maximum and minimum values of trust attained for the trustees is higher than for the neutral and cooperative cases. This is due to that fact that competition gives an additional increase to the positive and negative trust values towards extremes while cooperation brings them closer to each other. Also here as S_3 is giving neutral experience in Figure 7c and 7d, there is no change in trust value of S_3 because initial value of the trust is neutral as well. But the effect of competition and cooperation on S_3 can clearly be seen in Figure 7a, 7b and 7e, 7f.

6 Related Work

A variety of computational models have been proposed for trust. Falcone and Castelfranchi [3] for example, present an approach which includes a cognitive attribution process to update the trust of an agent. This process has been incorporated into their trust model because they claim that the simple idea that positive experiences increase the trust is not always valid, and therefore a more complex process is needed. They do however not directly take interdependencies of trust levels into account. Although in this paper simpler trust models have been used, the model as proposed by Flacone and Castelfranchi is certainly compatible with the subjective experience model as presented in this paper. Jonker and Treur [7] present a formal framework for the analysis and specification of models for trust evolution and trust update. Here, both quantitative and qualitative examples are shown of trust functions. In this paper, the quantitative example model has been used to exemplify that the subjective experience approach is compatible with an existing trust function. The qualitative example could in principle also be used in combination with the proposed function for subjective experiences, however a mapping would be needed from the qualitative to the quantitative values and vice versa. [9] incorporates the notion of relativeness as an extension of the trust model presented by [5]. In [9] for determining trust, as a basis trust values determined by the model presented in [5] are taken and then these values are used in order to make statements about different trust values for different agents which does not incorporate the experiences with other agents that can perform similar tasks. In [4] a computational model of trust which does represent interdependencies between trust levels is presented. In the current paper refined version of this model has been used as a comparison with the presented alternative that allows the reuse of existing trust models, thereby showing that similar patterns can be generated. For a more extensive overview of existing computation trust models, see [12] and [11].

Besides formalised computational models for trust, also informal trust models have been proposed in other fields, for example, in the field of management sciences. An interesting example is the model proposed in [10] which specifically addresses trust in collaborative environments. However, the focus is not so much on how trust values are influenced due to interdependencies, but more on the requirements of trust values different agents have in each other in order to make cooperation successful.

Next to trust models, the notion of reputation is also frequently modeled. Hereby, reputation can be defined as the opinion or view of someone about something (cf. [12]) and according to [11] can mainly be derived from the aggregation of opinions of members of a community about one of them. In this paper, the main focus has been on the sole experiences of one agent, and the community view has not been addressed. Nevertheless, it would be an interesting part of future work to investigate how trust interdependencies affect the overall reputation of agents in a society. For an overview of computational models for reputation, see [12], and [11].

7 Conclusions and Future Work

In this paper, the notion of interdependent trust has been addressed. Hereby, two approaches have been taken: (1) to use a dedicated trust model which incorporates interdependent trust (which is a refinement of the model presented in [4]), and (2) to develop a model that transforms objective experiences into subjective experiences that can be fed into an existing trust model. In order to evaluate the two approaches, simulation runs have been performed to investigate to which extent comparable patterns come out of the approaches. In the simulations of the subjective experience variant three trust models have been used to generate such patterns (of which two were taken from literature). The patterns that appeared in accordance with the expectations.

For future work, a validation of the model based upon experiments with humans is planned. Furthermore, the integration of the subjective experiences with more complex models such as for instance the model of Falcone and Castelfranchi [3] is also planned.

References

1. Bosse, T., Jonker, C.M., Meij, L., van der Sharpanskykh, A., Treur, J.: Specification and Verification of Dynamics in Agent Models. International Journal of Cooperative Information Systems (in press, 2009)
2. Braynov, S., Sandholm, T.: Incentive compatible mechanism for trust revelation. In: Proceedings of the 1st International Joint Conference on Autonomous Agents and Multiagent Systems (AAMAS 2002), pp. 310–311 (2002)
3. Falcone, R., Castelfranchi, C.: Trust dynamics: How trust is influenced by direct experiences and by trust itself. In: 3rd International Joint Conference on Autonomous Agents and Multiagent Systems (AAMAS 2004), pp. 740–747 (2004)
4. Hoogendoorn, M., Jaffry, S.W., Treur, J.: Modeling Dynamics of Relative Trust of Competitive Information Agents. In: Klusch, M., Pechoucek, M., Polleres, A. (eds.) CIA 2008. LNCS (LNAI), vol. 5180, pp. 55–70. Springer, Heidelberg (2008)
5. Jones, A.: On the concept of trust. Decision Support Systems 33(3), 225–232 (2002)
6. Jonker, C.M., Schalken, J.J.P., Theeuwes, J., Treur, J.: Human Experiments in Trust Dynamics. In: Jensen, C., Poslad, S., Dimitrakos, T. (eds.) iTrust 2004. LNCS, vol. 2995, pp. 206–220. Springer, Heidelberg (2004)
7. Jonker, C.M., Treur, J.: Formal Analysis of Models for the Dynamics of Trust based on Experiences. In: Garijo, F.J., Boman, M. (eds.) MAAMAW 1999. LNCS, vol. 1647, pp. 221–232. Springer, Heidelberg (1999)
8. Jonker, C.M., Treur, J.: A temporal-interactivist perspective on the dynamics of mental states. Cognitive Systems Research 4, 137–155 (2003)
9. Kluwer, J., Waaler, A.: Relative Trustworthiness. In: Dimitrakos, T., Martinelli, F., Ryan, P.Y.A., Schneider, S. (eds.) FAST 2005. LNCS, vol. 3866, pp. 158–170. Springer, Heidelberg (2006)
10. Mokhtar, M.R., Wajid, U., Wang, W.: Collaborative Trust in Multi-agent System, Enabling Technologies. In: 16th IEEE International Workshops on Enabling Technologies: Infrastructure for Collaborative Enterprises (WETICE 2007), pp. 30–34 (2007)
11. Ramchurn, S.D., Huynh, D., Jennings, N.R.: Trust in Multi-Agent Systems. The Knowledge Engineering Review 19, 1–25 (2004)
12. Sabater, J., Sierra, C.: Review on Computational Trust and Reputation Models. Artificial Intelligence Review 24, 33–60 (2005)

Author Index

Aberer, Karl   108

Basu, Anirban   248

Chakraborty, Debasish   95
Chalmers, Dan   248
Chen, Ing-Ray   141
Chia, Pern Hui   232
Cho, Jin-Hee   141
Cohen, Robin   216
Crispo, Bruno   63

del Alamo, Jose M.   17
Dong, Changyu   125
Dulay, Naranker   125

Fernandez, Antonio M.   17
Fuchs, Andreas   200

Gal-Oz, Nurit   1
Gheorghe, Gabriela   63
Gilboa, Niv   1
Gudes, Ehud   1
Gürgens, Sigrid   200
Guttman, Joshua D.   79

Hashimoto, Kazuo   95
Hobbs, Tyler L.   184
Hoogendoorn, Mark   263

Jaffry, S. Waqar   263

Kitagata, Gen   95
Kubo, Akira   172

Lank, Edward   32
Larson, Kate   216
Light, Ann   248

Monjas, Miguel A.   17

Nakata, Keiko   48
Neuhaus, Stephan   63
Nordheimer, Khrystyna   157

Ogawa, Satoshi   95

Papaioannou, Thanasis G.   108
Pitsilis, Georgios   232

Robinson, Jon   248
Rudolph, Carsten   200

Sabelfeld, Andrei   48
San Miguel, Beatriz   17
Sato, Hiroyuki   172
Schulze, Thimo   157
Shiratori, Norio   95
Swami, Ananthram   141
Swanson, Colleen   32
Swarup, Vipin   79

Takeda, Atushi   95
Thayer, F. Javier   79
Trapero, Ruben   17
Treur, Jan   263

Urner, Ruth   32

Veit, Daniel   157
Vu, Le-Hung   108

Wakeman, Ian   248
Winsborough, William H.   184

Yelmo, Juan C.   17

Zhang, Jie   216